HOLLYWOOD CENSORED

Cambridge Studies in the History of Mass Communications

Series Editors

Kenneth Short, *University of Houston*
Garth Jowett, *University of Houston*

Other books in the series

Cinema and Soviet Society, 1917–1953, by Peter Kenez
Hollywood's Overseas Campaign: The North Atlantic Movie Trade, 1920–1950, by Ian Jarvie
Ronald Reagan in Hollywood: Movies and Politics, by Stephen Vaughan

Cambridge Studies in the History of Mass Communications includes books that examine the communications processes and communications systems within social, cultural, and political contexts. Inclusive of empirical, effects-based research, works in this series proceed from the basis that the histories of various media are an important means to understanding their role and function in society. The history of a medium – its pattern of introduction, diffusion, acceptance, and effects – varies in each society, interacting with and, in turn, shaping its culture. Moreover, each society reacts differently to the introduction of a medium, and regulatory policies are shaped by both political and cultural forces. The detailed study of various communications forms and their complex message systems is now understood to be the key to unraveling the evolution of modern society and its culture.

HOLLYWOOD CENSORED
Morality Codes, Catholics, and the Movies

Gregory D. Black
University of Missouri–Kansas City

CAMBRIDGE
UNIVERSITY PRESS

Published by the Press Syndicate of the University of Cambridge
The Pitt Building, Trumpington Street, Cambridge CB2 1RP
40 West 20th Street, New York, NY 10011-4211, USA
10 Stamford Road, Oakleigh, Melbourne 3166, Australia

First published 1994

First paperback edition 1996

Parts of this book have previously been published in the form of articles by the author; these are reproduced with the permission of the original publications:

"Censorship: An Historical Interpretation," *Journal of Dramatic Theory and Criticism* (Fall 1991), 167–85.

"Hollywood Censored: The Production Code Administration and the Hollywood Film Industry, 1930–1940," *Film History* 3 (1989), 167–89.

"Movies, Politics, and Censorship: The Production Code Administration and Political Censorship of Film Content," *Journal of Political History* 3 (Spring 1991), 95–129.

Printed in the United States of America

Library of Congress Cataloging-in-Publication Data
Black, Gregory D.
Hollywood censored : morality codes, Catholics, and the movies / Gregory D. Black
p.   cm. – (Cambridge studies in the history of mass communications)
Filmography: p.
Includes bibliographical references and index.
ISBN 0-521-45299-6 (hardback)   ISBN 0-521-56592-8 (paperback)
1. National Legion of Decency. 2. Motion pictures – Censorship – United States.
3. Motion pictures – Moral and ethical aspects.. I. Title. II. Series.
PN1995.5.B49   1994
323.44'5'0973 – dc20   93-48340
                                                                            CIP

A catalog record for this book is available from the British Library.

ISBN 0-521-45299-6 hardback
ISBN 0-521-56592-8 paperback

To
Gaylord Marr,
teacher

CONTENTS

ILLUSTRATIONS

ACKNOWLEDGMENTS

Few books are written in the solitary confines of the author's study; this one certainly was not, and I would like to thank those who played a part in its creation. First, I thank the University of Missouri Research Board for the support it gave me by providing research funds for travel to distant archives and allowing me the time to write this book.

Historians could not function without archivists who preserve the written records from which we interpret the past. I am especially indebted to the following people:

Sam Gill and the staff at the Margaret Herrick Library of the Academy of Motion Picture Arts and Sciences in Beverly Hills, California, for help with the Production Code Administration files;

Ned Constock at the Dohney Library of the University of Southern California for his help with MGM production files;

Jerry Gibson and his staff at the Library of Congress Motion Picture Division;

Msgr. Francis J. Weber of the Archives of the Archdiocese of Los Angeles;

the staff of the Jesuit Missouri Province Archives in St. Louis, Missouri;

Don Buske, Archivist of the Archives of the Archdiocese of Cincinnati;

H. Warren Willis, Archivist of the United Catholic Conference in Washington, D.C.;

Nicholas B. Scheetz, Manuscripts Librarian of Georgetown University; and

Mary Corliss and Terry Geesken of the Museum of Modern Art.

My research assistant, Siew Ang, spent countless hours in the library tracing obscure articles, reading microfilm, organizing data, and helping me think about this project. I thank her for all her help and support. Two friends, Chuck Bishop and Doug Schlosser, also contributed in important ways to the final product.

A number of people read the manuscript at various stages and saved me serious embarrassment. I thank Ted Wilson, Garth Jowett, Kenneth Short, Tom Poe, and Clayton Koppes for their encouragement and support. At Cambridge University Press my editor, Beatrice Rehl, and production editor, Michael Gnat, were a pleasure to work with.

My friend and colleague Richard McKinzie was especially supportive. We talked for hours about the book, and he forced me to consider areas that I often ignored. He read the manuscript at various stages and had a profound influence on my thinking. Tragically, Dick died during the last stages of the book. It is a great personal loss for me, for UMKC, for his wife Eileen and son Robbie, and for the historical profession as a whole.

A second colleague who played a major role in the construction of the book is Gaylord Marr, Curator of the Marr Sound Archives at the University of Missouri–Kansas City and a Professor of Communication Studies at UMKC. He is also one of the most knowledgeable persons I know on American popular culture. Dick McKinzie, Gaylord, and I spent many an afternoon hoisting a few and talking about movies and popular culture. Gaylord provided Dick and myself with countless recordings from his private collection for our research and our teaching. Dick encouraged me to dedicate this book to Gaylord for years of support and patience with us, and I do so with great pleasure.

Finally, I want to thank my wife Carol and son Jason. Carol has read more about and suffered through more old films than she ever wanted to. She is an excellent editor and critic, and I thank her for her understanding and patience.

INTRODUCTION

In February 1992, Roger Mahoney, Roman Catholic Cardinal of Los Angeles, told the Hollywood Anti-Pornography Coalition that the motion picture industry was an "assault against the values held by the vast majority of the people in American society." The movie industry, he maintained, could not continue to "hide behind a misplaced cry for 'freedom of expression.'" To curb the excessive sex and violence in current films, Mahoney called for the reinstitution of the Hollywood Production Code, which had ruled the American film industry from its adoption in 1930 until it was replaced in 1966 by the current ratings system. Industry officials expressed dismay at this plea to censor the movies.

Cardinal Mahoney's call for a modern crusade against the movies was no surprise to Hollywood. In 1930 another Catholic priest, Father Daniel Lord, S.J., believed that the movies were corrupting American moral values. To counter the influence of immoral movies he wrote a movie code that prohibited films from glorifying criminals, gangsters, adulterers, and prostitutes. Lord's code, which soon became the Bible of film production, banned nudity, excessive violence, white slavery, illegal drugs, miscegenation, lustful kissing, suggestive postures, and profanity from the screen. However, it went further than simply banning things from films; his code also held that films should promote the institutions of marriage and home, defend the fairness of government, and present religious institutions with reverence.

A basic premise of this code was that movies did not enjoy the same freedom of expression as the printed word or theatrical performances. This most democratic of art forms had to be regulated, Lord argued, because movies cut across all social, economic, political, and educational boundaries, attracting millions of people to its theaters every week. In order to protect the masses from the evil influence of the movies, they had to be censored.

Will Hays, president of the industry trade association, the Motion Picture Producers and Distributors of America (MPPDA) – popularly known as the Hays Office – agreed. He sponsored Lord's code, which was adopted by the motion picture industry in 1930. Yet the Catholic church and other religious organizations were not satisfied with the way the industry enforced the code. In 1934 Catholics launched a Legion of Decency (LOD) campaign. Millions signed pledges to boycott movies judged immoral by church authorities.

To pacify religious organizations, especially the Catholic church, Hays created a new MPPDA Hollywood censorship office in 1934 – the Production Code Administration (PCA) – and gave it total control over film content. He named a lay Catholic, Joseph I. Breen, director. Breen and his staff combed every script for improprieties, whether sexual or political, before issuing a PCA seal of approval. After 1934 no film could be exhibited in a major American theater without a PCA seal.

Pressuring Breen to remain ever vigilant was the National Catholic Legion of Decency, headquartered in New York City. The Legion reviewed and rated every film released by Hollywood and distributed its ratings to every Catholic church in the United States. The LOD stood ready to condemn any film it considered immoral or dangerous. Catholics were forbidden to attend any film condemned by the church.

This system of "self-regulation" dominated film production during Hollywood's golden era of studio production. The impact of this censorship on the content, flavor, feel, and image of Hollywood films has not been fully understood or appreciated. This book, using archival materials from the studios, the Hays Office, and the Catholic church, details how the dual forces of industry self-regulation – the Hays Office (and its censorship arm, the PCA) and the Catholic Legion of Decency – fought Hollywood studios for control of film content during the 1930s. By the end of the decade the war was over: The PCA stood supreme and the Catholic Legion of Decency struck fear in the hearts of every Hollywood producer. No film could be produced or exhibited without PCA approval, and Hollywood did not dare to challenge Catholic authorities.

Cardinal Mahoney's plea is for a return to those heady days when prelates and censors, who presumed they spoke for the American people, controlled what people saw and heard at the movies.

CHAPTER I

RESTRICTING ENTERTAINMENT:
THE MOVIES CENSORED

Movies are schools of vice and crime . . . offering trips to hell for [a] nickle.
— Rev. Wilbur Crafts

Hollywood. The name was magic, the lure overwhelming. Generations of Americans spent untold hours in darkened theaters captivated by a magical fantasy world. Young girls swooned over the latest Hollywood heartthrob while boys dreamed about a life of adventure and glory. As had their pioneer ancestors before them, thousands trekked westward; their goal was Hollywood. Most were rejected by the magical kingdom, but a lucky few were "discovered" and became "stars" — America's royalty of the twentieth century.

The lure of Hollywood reached far beyond the dreams of innocent youth. Artists of all varieties made pilgrimages to the world's film capital. From New York, London, Vienna, Rome, Moscow, and even Paris came the famous, the talented, the hopeful, the has-beens, and the desperate, hopeful that this mecca of worldwide entertainment would bestow massive blessings of fame, wealth, and power.

In the spring of 1925 a young writer was about to live that modern dream. Ben Hecht, journalist, novelist, and playwright, was down and out. Despite having published a well-received novel, *Erik Dorn* (1921), and editing and publishing the *Chicago Literary Times,* Hecht was broke. A recent migrant to New York, he was two months behind in his rent when a telegram arrived from Hollywood. "Will you accept three hundred per week to work for Paramount Pictures. All expenses paid. The three hundred is peanuts. Millions are to be grabbed out here and your only competition is idiots."[1] The telegram from his friend and fellow writer Herman Mankiewicz changed his life. Hecht dashed out to Hollywood, and within two weeks Paramount rewarded him with a $10,000 bonus for an eighteen-page outline of the 1927 gangster film *Underworld.*

Hecht was an enormously talented writer, one of that rare breed who could write quickly and effectively for the screen. He was said to

3

be "the fastest hack" in the West. His Hollywood career extended over four decades and included original screenplays, adaptations, and an enormous amount of work as an uncredited "script doctor."[2] By his own account he worked on over sixty scripts. For his forays into Hollywood he was lavishly paid – from $50,000 to $125,000 for two to eight weeks' work. He once demanded, and got, from Howard Hughes $1,000 per day paid sharply at 6:00 P.M. David O. Selznick hired him at a slightly reduced rate of $3,000 a week to dash off dialogue for *Gone with the Wind*. Despite his monetary success, Hecht always kept Hollywood at arm's length. Like many writers, he did not consider his work for the movies serious art; it was more a means of replenishing his bank account. When his work was finished, he retreated to New York.[3]

As much as anything it was the movies' lack of honesty that disenchanted Hecht. On his arrival in Hollywood in 1925, Mankiewicz gave him the formula for successful screenwriting:

I want to point out to you . . . that in a novel a hero can lay ten girls and marry a virgin for a finish. In a movie this is not allowed. The hero, as well as the heroine, has to be a virgin. The villain can lay anybody he wants, have as much fun as he wants cheating and stealing, getting rich and whipping the servants. But you have to shoot him in the end. When he falls with a bullet in his forehead, it is advisable that he clutch at the Gobelin tapestry on the library wall and bring it down over his head like a symbolic shroud.[4]

Hecht followed this sage advice and gave Paramount *Underworld*. It had no heroes, only villains.

In early 1951 Hecht was back in Hollywood. When Mankiewicz had summoned him westward two decades earlier, Hollywood had been a boom town; now it seemed more like a ghost town. Hollywood had changed. The golden age of studio production was over. The war, the federal government's breakup of the studios as a monopoly, and the challenge offered by a new technology, television, were changing the industry. At the end of a long night, Hecht and David O. Selznick, a producer and friend of more than twenty years, walked the deserted streets of the movie capital. Perhaps depressed by too much alcohol, Selznick looked back on the "golden age" of the movies. He saw nothing, he told Hecht, but a "flood of claptrap," not "ten out of ten thousand" films were worth remembering. What could have been an art form at "the center of a new human expression" turned out to be "a junk industry." When Hecht told Selznick he was having trouble determining what to say in his memoirs about his long career in Hollywood, the producer turned to him and said: "Write the truth."[5]

Hecht's book – among the most revealing portrayals of tinsel town – claimed that the movies "have slapped into the American mind more human misinformation in one evening than the Dark Ages could muster in a decade. One basic plot only has appeared daily in their fifteen thousand theaters – the triumph of virtue and the overthrow of wickedness." In the movies, wrote Hecht, "any man who broke the laws, man's or God's, must die, or go to jail, or become a monk, or restore the money he stole before wandering off into the desert." In the movies "anyone who didn't believe in God . . . was set right by seeing either an angel or witnessing some feat of levitation by one of the characters"; in the movies "the most potent and brilliant villains are powerless before little children, parish priests or young virgins with large boobies"; and in the movies there "are no problems of labor, politics, domestic life or sexual abnormality" that cannot "be solved happily by a simple Christian phrase or a fine American motto."[6]

Why did the movies fail to become a new center of human expression? Why did they lack honesty? Why was virtue ever triumphant over wickedness and social problems resolved by simplistic pieties? Part of the answer naturally rests within Hollywood's "studio system" of production. Movies were the product of a large corporate, collaborative enterprise. The cost of production and distribution was enormous. The goal of the studios, and of the corporations that controlled them, was profit, not art. Ever fearful of losing any segment of their audience, the studios either carefully avoided controversial topics or presented them within a tightly constructed framework that evaded larger issues.

However, as Mankiewicz, Selznick, and Hecht knew all too well, much of the blame for the failure of the movies to deal more frankly and honestly with life lay with a rigid censorship imposed on the industry. Cities, states, foreign governments, and, most important, the industry itself had prescribed rigid restrictions on the content of films during its golden era of studio production. This system of censorship, which the film industry not only accepted but embraced, encouraged, and enforced, was a major reason for the failure of Hollywood to develop film beyond the "harmless entertainment" label that has been firmly fixed on it.

Censorship is a key ingredient in understanding how films were made during the studio era, and is vital in any analysis of their content or structure. From the early 1930s to the mid-1960s, every story considered, script written, and film produced was subjected to a thorough cleansing by industry censors before reaching the screen. Preproduction censorship, administered by the Motion Picture Producers and Distributors of America (MPPDA) – commonly known as the Hays Office – was an integral part of the studio production system.

This was especially true during the 1930s, when this system of industry "self-regulation" was established. Determined to keep worldwide markets open to Hollywood films, and opposed to any type of viewer age restriction on their product, the Hays Office adopted a pre-production censorship system that attempted to prevent questionable material, both moral and political, from reaching the screen. The Hays Office movie code – written by a Catholic priest, Father Daniel Lord, S.J., and eventually enforced by a lay Catholic, Joseph Breen – maintained that movies did not have the same latitude as books, plays, magazines, and newspapers in presenting alternative views on controversial topics to a mass audience. No film, foreign or domestic, played in any major American theater without being submitted to industry censors who used Lord's code to determine acceptable screen material. Standing outside this system of industry censors were state and municipal censorship boards and, after 1934, the Catholic Legion of Decency, which were prepared to pounce on any film they deemed offensive.

The major Hollywood production studios – MGM, Warner Bros., Universal, United Artists, Paramount, RKO, Columbia, and Twentieth Century–Fox – bitterly fought this censorship system, which prevented them from making more realistic and honest films. While more committed to box-office profits than art, the studios did attempt to bring some realistic, hard-hitting drama to the screen, but were thwarted by industry censors. It became impossible after the mid-1930s and beyond, for example, to make a reasonably accurate film from Zola's *Nana,* Tolstoy's *Anna Karenina,* or Steinbeck's *The Grapes of Wrath.* These novels were too frank in their discussions of adultery, corruption, and injustice; their screen versions were altered to make them more in tune with the conservative moral, political, and economic value system that dominated the movie censorship code.

Born in American cities at the turn of the century, entertainment films quickly transcended ethnic, class, religious, and political lines to become the dominant institution of popular culture. By 1907 a revolution had taken place in the entertainment industry. Motion picture theaters in New York City recorded a daily attendance of over two hundred thousand a day – a figure that doubled on Sundays, when working-class families flocked to the movies in droves.[7] Nationally some three thousand nickelodeons lured more than two million customers daily. By 1910 there were ten thousand such movie theaters in the United States. The nation, wrote *Harper's Weekly,* had a case of "nickel delirium."[8]

Typically, these nickelodeons were storefront theaters – dimly lit, dingy, unventilated rooms – where audiences of adult men, young unchaperoned working girls, hordes of unsupervised children, and entire families were crammed together. The nickelodeons ran nonstop from early in the morning to late at night. With no set show time, people drifted in and out, after shopping, after work, on Sunday – whenever they had fifteen or twenty minutes and a nickel to spare. As one early report from the mill town of Homestead, Pennsylvania, noted: "Men on their way from work, stop for a few minutes to see something of life outside the mill and home; the shopper rests while she enjoys the music . . . and the children are always begging for five cents to go to the nickelodeon."[9]

The movies were popular because they were cheap and readily available; but most of all, they were enormously entertaining. According to widely held myth, the stuff of silent cinema was an endless chase scene of "Keystone Kops," leering villains, or a mindless parade of slapstick comedy. Early silent films, most people seem to believe, were crude entertainment for undiscriminating audiences who knew little or no English and were more fascinated by the novelty of the technology than by the quality of the art.

Like most general impressions, there is some truth in this view; but only some. Almost from the beginning, filmmakers turned to popular literature, drama, and contemporary issues for film plots. Historians Kay Solan and Kevin Brownlow have shown that the content of silent films was contemporary, wide-ranging, and frank. Brownlow chronicles a silent cinema that revealed "the corruption of city politics, the scandal of white slave rackets, the exploitation of immigrants," with gangsters, pimps, loan sharks, and drug addicts sharing the screen with Mary Pickford.[10] Solan noted that "the cinema championed the cause of labor, lobbied against political 'bosses,' and often gave dignity to the struggles of the urban poor."[11] These early flickers often poked fun at militant suffragettes, upheld or debunked Victorian moral standards, and "ridiculed labor unions and [well-known] business tycoons."[12]

Early films, such as *Capital versus Labor, The Molly Maguires, or The Labor Wars in the Coal Mines, The Cocaine Traffic, The Drug Traffic, Suffragettes' Revenge, The Candidate, The Governor's Boss, Votes for Women,* or *The Reform Candidate,* indicate that the people who flocked to the films got more than just comedic release for their nickel.[13] According to film historian Lary May, some of these first motion pictures delighted in ridiculing "Victorian values."[14]

These films, which brought delight to millions, deeply disturbed others. Movies were born during the height of the Progressive reform movement in the United States. Progressives exposed corruption in government, and shocked the American public with lurid exposés of child labor, urban living conditions, prostitution, and alcoholism. As remedies they sponsored legislation to regulate the use of child labor, used the licensing power of the state to enforce safety and sanitary

codes, passed compulsory education laws, regulated the production
of consumer products with "pure food and drug" acts, and reformed
the electoral process on the local, state, and federal level. The entire
reform movement was responsible for myriad changes that attempted
to make American cities more livable, educate immigrants as to American values, protect the general public from exploitation by big business, and make government responsible for the public's general welfare.

Progressives also worried about the impact of modernization and
urban living on the moral fiber of the nation. They argued that neighboring saloons, dance-halls, and houses of prostitution destroyed traditional family life. They looked to government to create a more livable environment and reinforce traditional Victorian moral standards
through "protective" legislation. They were well aware that, in advocating a ten- or eight-hour workday for adults and eliminating child
labor, they were creating "leisure" time; they hoped that this time
could be used to "restore American ideals in a pure form."[15] It was
essential, therefore, to protect the public from amusements that might
corrupt this "uplifting" process. With religious fervor, Progressives attacked saloons, dance-halls, houses of prostitution, and equally harmful "immoral" books, magazines, newspapers, plays – and, of course,
movies.

To counter these "immoral" amusements, Progressives advocated
creating "green space" within the concrete jungle of American cities.
As one leader of the playground movement said: "No one who has
observed children carefully in any city . . . between the close of school
and supper has found any considerable percentage of them were doing
anything that was worthwhile."[16] Cities had the responsibility, they argued, to build parks and playgrounds where adults and children could
spend their leisure time in a "moral" climate. Good playgrounds, said
one reformer, could instill "more ethics and good citizenship . . . in a
single week than can be inculcated by Sunday school teachers . . . in a
decade."[17] Notably in the first ten years of the century there was an
explosion of park building across the United States. In Chicago more
than $15 million was spent on parks and recreation centers in less
than a decade.

The movies were an especially troublesome form of recreation for
Progressive reformers. The environment was all wrong: Rather than
open space, with clean air and exercise, the theaters to which children
were flocking were dirty and dingy. Sitting passively in the dark, their
young minds were being polluted by vile movies just as their lungs
were being polluted by unclean air. "Free hours determine the morals
of the nation," intoned Joseph R. Fulk, Nebraska's superintendent of
schools.[18] With millions of urbanites pouring into the movie theaters

each day, Progressive reformers worried that a new generation of children would learn their moral lessons at the movies.

Jane Addams, the consummate reformer whose Hull House in Chicago brought her international recognition, wrote that the movies were a "veritable house of dreams" for the children of America. Addams was convinced, like so many of her day, that movies were a more powerful influence on the minds of children than any other form of communication or education. She believed that what they saw on the screen directly and immediately was transformed into action. If children saw crime movies, they would become criminals; if they saw movies with an "immoral" theme, they would adopt those values as their own and would reject the efforts of home, school, and church to instill traditional middle-class values of behavior. Addams wrote that it was "astounding that a city allows thousands of its youth to fill their impressionable minds with [movie] absurdities which certainly will become the foundation for their working moral codes."[19]

Yet Addams and the Progressives recognized that, conversely, if films could preach positive values, their potential to educate, to play a positive role in socializing the citizenry, was unlimited. Convinced that movies were "making over the minds of our urban population," Addams thought films ought to preach good citizenship, the superiority of Anglo-Saxon ideals, and the value of hard work. If movies could be turned into morality lessons for workers, they could become an ally in the Progressive's fight to protect the masses against the combined forces of poverty, corruption, and injustice.

Ministers, social workers, civic reformers, police, politicians, women's clubs, and civic organizations joined in, accusing the movies of inciting young boys to crime by glorifying criminals and of corrupting young women by romanticizing "illicit" love affairs. These "moral guardians" – a loose-knit confederation of reformers who ranged from thoughtful and perceptive critics like Jane Addams to religious reactionaries like Canon William Shaefe Chase, rector of Christ Church in Brooklyn – claimed that movies were changing traditional values, not reflecting them, and demanded that government use its licensing and regulatory powers to censor this new form of entertainment.

Film producers, however, were interested in profit, not preaching. Progressives and moral guardians, unable to control film content, increasingly became convinced that movies were the cause of many of society's ills, and came to see them as a major social evil. In the view of such reformers, regulating this new industry was akin to regulating manufacturers of tainted meat. As one YMCA official stated:

Unless the law steps in and does for moving-picture shows what it has done for meat inspection and pure food, the cinematograph will continue to inject into our social order an element of degrading principle. The only way that the people, and especially the children, can be safeguarded from the influence of evil pictures is by careful regulation of the places of exhibitions.[20]

At a conference on child welfare in 1909, Edward H. Chandler characterized motion pictures as "a new and curious disease [that] had made its appearance in our cities, selecting for its special victims only boys and girls from ten to fourteen."[21] The minister of the Calvary Evangelical Church in Philadelphia called movies "schools for degenerates and criminals."[22] Another minister, the Reverend Wilbur F. Crafts, said movies were "schools of vice and crime . . . offering trips to hell for [a] nickle."[23] A professor of philosophy at the University of Kansas warned the nation that

pictures are more degrading than the dime novel because they represent real flesh and blood characters and import moral lessons directly through the senses. The dime novel cannot lead the boy further than his limited imagination will allow, but the motion picture forces upon his view things that are new, they give firsthand experience.[24]

Canon Chase, who campaigned against the movies for three decades, called films "the greatest enemy of civilization."[25]

These self-designated "guardians of public morality" began to agitate for legislation to control this new "vice." Chicago's Vice Commission first recommended that the city "oversee dance halls, ice-cream parlors," and demanded that movies be shown only in "well-lighted halls."[26] When this impractical suggestion was rejected, commissioners countered with the demand that "indecent vaudeville, picture-slot machines, [and] nickelodeons" be banned entirely.[27] When that proposal failed, Chicago used its licensing power to establish America's first ordinance empowering censors to regulate the content of films. Enacted in November 1907, the ordinance required exhibitors to secure a permit from the Superintendent of Police before any film could be exhibited to the public. This "prior censorship" allowed a film to be banned if police censors judged it

immoral or obscene, or [if it] portrays depravity, criminality or lack of virtue of a class of citizens of any race, color, creed or religion and exposes them to contempt, derision or obloquy, or tends to produce a breach of the peace or riots, or purports to represent any hanging, lynching or burning of a human being.[28]

The job of censoring films was assigned to Chicago's police department. While their intent was presumably moral, the police almost immediately fell into the trap that would characterize movie censorship for decades to come. One of the first films censored was a version of Shakespeare's *Macbeth*. Lieutenant Joel A. Smith, who pruned the film, told reporters he had nothing against Shakespeare, but "[t]he moving picture people get a bunch of Broadway loafers in New York to go through the motions and interpret Shakespeare, and when it gets on the canvas it's worse than the bloodiest melodrama ever."[29] How much Smith knew about Shakespeare is unclear. What is clear is that he felt free to censor films that he did not like as well as those he considered immoral. His successor, Sergeant Charles O'Donnell, pledged to pass only those films he considered "proper for women and children to witness."[30] The attitudes and concerns expressed by Smith and O'Donnell would be reflected by film censors for the next fifty years.

When Chicago refused permits for two straightforward accounts of western outlaws, *The James Boys* and *Night Riders,* the film industry challenged in court the legality of censorship. In *Block v. Chicago* (1909), the industry argued that the law was discriminatory because it applied only to movies and not to other theatrical productions, and that because censorship was imposed prior to exhibition, the rulings to ban had deprived the exhibitor of his property without due process. As film historian Garth Jowett noted in his study of the legal effects of censorship, "all of these arguments were swept aside."[31] The court held that the state had the constitutional right to protect the public from "immoral" and "obscene" productions. Moreover, there had been no violation of the Constitution because no one had the right to profit from immoral and/or obscene materials.

While the court understood that the films were based on historical events, it held that when movies attempted to recreate the violent lives of the outlaws they "necessarily portray crime," and in so doing "represent nothing but malicious mischief." Exhibiting these movies, the court held, "would necessarily be attended with evil effects on youthful spectators"; therefore, the city of Chicago was within its legal rights in preventing these films from being shown even if they were based on historical characters or events. The films were immoral because the events and the people they depicted were immoral, and because children watching these films would be corrupted.[32] While this ruling might, at first glance, seem preposterous, state and federal courts would consistently rule in favor of censorship of the movies on similar grounds until midcentury.

The antimovie/procensorship campaign gained steam as films grew in popularity. The *Pittsburgh Post* declared many films were "not fit to be seen by self-respecting adults," and called for the city to pass "more stringent regulations."[33] In Cincinnati the *Times-Star* accused movies of "depicting situations which would never be accepted on the stage"; they were, the editorial claimed, a "perversion of . . . public morals."[34] The Chicago *News* regretted that an "invention which offers such possibilities in the way of wholesome amusement should ever be the means of exploiting crime, robberies and tragedies."[35] In Kansas City, after a local theater owner was arrested for exhibiting "immoral pictures," the Franklin Institute commissioned a study of the local cinema by Miss Beebe Thompson, a prominent settlement worker. Within a year Kansas City had created a municipal censorship board to protect children from the corrupting influence of movies.[36]

Naturally, the cinema had defenders. With millions of adults as well as children delighting in the movies, defenders countered it was implausible that they were as vile, immoral, offensive, and corruptive as moral guardians would have people believe. The St. Louis *Globe Democrat* told its readers that the argument that little boys would begin to steal and become criminals was downright silly: It was like suggesting that society ban ice cream because little boys love it and might steal a penny or nickel to get it. In Somerset, New Jersey, the *Record* assured readers that "children obtain nothing but amusement" from movies.[37] W. Stephen Bush, editor of the trade paper *Moving Picture World*, saw nothing "prurient, suggestive or demoralizing; on the contrary, each [film] pointed a strong moral in a forceful way." "I dare anybody," he challenged, "to show me a film that was objectionable because of its immorality or viciousness."[38] Even more bluntly, the Mayor of Topeka, Kansas, who opposed censorship, told movie critics "if you have a boy who can be corrupted by the ordinary run of moving picture films you might as well kill him now and save trouble."[39]

The issue of film censorship gained national attention when New York's Mayor George B. McClellan suddenly ordered all movie theaters in the city closed on December 24, 1908. More than a year earlier the New York fire commissioner had denounced movie theaters as a fire threat, "a menace to life," and the police commissioner had recommended that McClellan close all of them[40] – this in the film industry's headquarter city, where over 500 theaters operated, many of them on Sunday.

While New York's police and fire departments primarily concerned themselves with the physical conditions in which films were shown, a coalition of New York ministers, led by Canon William Sheafe Chase, demanded that the mayor safeguard audiences from movie content and prohibit their exhibition on Sunday. Chase, who lobbied against the movies and the evils of "horse racing, boxing, modern [popular] dance, gambling in any form, rackets of all sizes, shades and hues and even bobbed hair and short skirts," told the mayor it was "his duty" to restrict movies because theater producers and owners had "no scruples whatever."[41]

Under pressure to act, Mayor McClellan scheduled a public hearing for open debate on the movies in late December 1908. A boisterous crowd packed City Hall. Frank Moss, director of New York's Suppression of Vice Committee, condemned the movies for corrupting children. A score of ministers hurled similar charges. Reverend J. M. Foster bellowed: "Is a man at liberty to make money from the morals of people? Is he to profit from the corruption of the minds of children?"[42] Another minister asked why the city was spending millions of dollars for education and then allowing movies to "contaminate and corrupt the youth" of the city.[43]

When Charles Sprague Smith, founding director of the People's Institute, a New York reform organization, retorted that there were many things in the city far worse than the movies, the packed gallery hooted its support. The mayor issued "a stern rebuke" to them and threatened to clear the hearing.[44] J. Stuart Blackton of Vitagraph, representing the producers, opened the door for compromise. He cited the Chicago law and offered "to have films censored before they were displayed" by an independent group in exchange for continued Sunday showings.[45]

To the delight of the ministers and the dismay of millions of New Yorkers, McClellan simply revoked the licenses of every theater in the city. On Christmas Day 1908, the lights went out in movie theaters all over town. The reaction of the industry was swift: They appealed the decision in court and were immediately granted an injunction holding that McClellan's action was "arbitrary, tyrannical and unreasonable."[46] Most theaters were open for business within a few days, but the message to the industry was clear: Unless they took some action to clean up their image, improve the physical condition of the theaters, and, most important, address the concern of critics that movies were corrupting children and adults, they could expect continued attacks by moral guardians, who would continue to press for restrictive legislation. Neither was good for business – and business was booming.

Charles Sprague Smith and the People's Institute offered the film industry a solution. One of the few reform organizations that did not see movies as evil, the Institute had combined with the New York Women's Municipal League to study the movies in 1908. Their report decried the conditions under which movies were exhibited, but praised them for furnishing "healthy and even educational amusement."[47] After defending the industry at the mayor's public hearing, Smith and John Collier, executive secretary of the People's Institute, brought together ten blue-ribbon New York civic organizations, including the Federation of Churches, the Public Education Association, the Women's Municipal League, and the Society for the Prevention of Crime, to form a New York Board of Motion Picture Censorship, later called the National Board of Review (NBR).[48]

Collier proposed that this board of civic volunteers preview films before exhibition, identify offending material, and "suggest" cuts. If the industry would "voluntarily" submit films for "self-regulation" to this community board, Collier believed much of the criticism against movies would decrease, and the threat of formal government censorship would be eliminated.

The producers readily agreed. Like other businesses in the Progressive era, filmmakers were searching for a common national standard for their product that would allow movies free circulation across the United States. A proliferation of state censorship boards, each with different standards, would make it next to impossible for producers to make films accessible to the huge, diverse American audience. As *Moving Picture World* editorialized: "The duty of a Board of Censorship is to guide and stimulate the manufacturers so that the pictures they produce will appeal to the best intelligence of the widest possible public."[49] Self-censorship, in other words, was just good business.

The Motion Picture Patents Company, a confederation of the nine largest film-producing companies, spearheaded by Thomas Edison, agreed to submit their films to the new community censorship board, cut offending material, and exhibit only those films that carried a seal of approval from the board. The organization further offered to screen all the films for the volunteers and to pay a "censorship fee" to support the cost of the operation. Other companies quickly followed, and in March 1909 the National Board of Review began reviewing films.

Frederic C. Howe, a vice reformer in New York and Cleveland (and, as of 1914, the U.S. Commissioner of Immigration at Ellis Island), was appointed chairman of the censorship board. John Collier headed the subsidiary committee, made up of more than one hundred volunteers, that did the actual censoring. Both men opposed censorship in principle and believed that movies had the right to portray social issues honestly. Howe viewed the role of the new board as one of "moral coercion" rather than censorship.[50] He opposed government censorship because he thought it violated the First Amendment and would "stifle . . . the freedom of the industry as a mirror of the everyday life, hopes and aspirations of the people." Movies, as "democracy's theater," were an important part of the free exchange of ideas, Howe insisted.[51]

Collier agreed. He urged his volunteers not to be "too critical" of the movies.[52] The standards adopted by the National Board of Review reflected Howe's and Collier's views. The board would reject a film or request cuts if it contained obscenity, vulgarity, blasphemy, indecency (all undefined), morbid or brutal crime scenes, detailed crime scenes that might instruct audiences in how to commit a crime, any libelous material that might cause injury to living persons, or scenes that "have a deteriorating tendency on the basic moralities or necessary social standards."[53] It did not, however, reject a film or demand cuts simply because a film contained a crime scene or material that might be unsuitable for children.

The National Board of Review attempted to judge "the real effect of each film on the composite (American) audience."[54] So long as a film did not offend "fundamental morality," it would be approved. The board announced it would not censor films "for any particular audience," nor would it be placed in the role of arbiter of "good taste" or protector of "children, or delicate women."[55]

Within a year the board was reviewing more than 80 percent of the films exhibited in the United States. Every day, wrote Robert Sklar, "dignified women in broad-brimmed flowered hats and dour-faced men, sat down to watch seven or eight of the producers' latest offerings."[56] Although Sklar implies that the board was strict, its liberal views were attacked by moral guardians: By allowing films that dealt with prostitution, corruption, and other vices all too common in American society, the board was being too lenient; children were not being protected by the National Board, critics maintained.

Pennsylvania declared the National Board of Review ineffective, and in 1911 passed a law that created its own board to screen films before exhibition in the state. Kansas and Ohio followed suit in 1913. By 1915 a host of municipal and state censorship boards had been created to impose local community standards of morality on films. There was no real consistency: Pennsylvania was the most strict, refusing, for example, to show pregnant women or even scenes of mothers-to-be making baby clothes; Kansas was the most pristine, limiting screen kisses to a few seconds and banning scenes of smoking and drinking.

The common denominator for all these censorship boards was their commitment to eliminating depictions of changing moral standards, limiting scenes of crime (which they believed responsible for an increase in juvenile delinquency), and avoiding insofar as possible any filmed portrayal of civil strife, labor–management discord, or government corruption and injustice. The screen, these moral guardians held, was not a proper forum for discussing delicate sexual issues or for social or political commentary.[57]

The constitutional challenge to film censorship came in Ohio, where the state board was especially restrictive: It held that only "such films as are in the judgment and discretion of the board of censors of a moral, educational or amusing and harmless character" could obtain the necessary prior approval.[58] Ohio's censorship board, like most, charged a fee to film distributors to have their films licensed for exhibition.

Harry E. Aitken's Mutual Film Corporation, an interstate film exchange, perhaps overly confident that the courts would extend to movies the same free-speech rights enjoyed by the press, sought an injunction against the state. The Ohio law, Mutual claimed, restrained trade by forcing Mutual to pay a license fee for each film exhibited; moreover, the legislature improperly delegated their legislative powers because the standards for gaining approval were vague and unclear. Mutual further maintained the law was a clear violation of the free-speech provisions of the federal and Ohio constitutions. When the District Court denied the injunction, Mutual appealed to the U.S. Supreme Court. It would prove to be a calamitous decision.[59]

Before the Supreme Court, William B. Saunders, Mutual's lawyer, argued that the Ohio law was discriminatory against movies, was vague in its lack of specific definitions of what was acceptable, hindered interstate trade by requiring a license fee, and inflicted prior restraint on the movie industry by prohibiting exhibition until Ohio censors had approved the product. However, he spent most of his time before the Court justices attempting to envelop the movies in the protective confines of free speech.[60]

Movies were, he claimed, "dramatizations of standard novels," depictions of "subjects of scientific interest," re-creations of "historical and current events – the same events which are described in words and by photographs in newspapers, weekly periodicals, magazines and other publications." Saunders maintained that movies were no different from other forms of communication protected under the provisions of free speech; therefore, movies were "part of the press" and were "increasingly important . . . in the spreading of knowledge and the molding of public opinion upon every kind of political, educational, religious, economic and social question." Simply put, Saunders summarized, the movies are "publications" and should be seen as filmed books. The film exchanges, he asserted, provided theaters with films and should be seen as "circulating libraries"; therefore, the state had no right to assess fees or restrict content prior to exhibition.[61]

In a stunning decision, the Supreme Court – including Oliver Wendell Holmes, Jr., and Charles Evan Hughes – unanimously rejected Saunders's arguments. Justice Joseph McKenna wrote the opinion. It was a curious document. McKenna accepted without question that movies were instruments of opinion. He added, however, "We feel the argument is wrong or strained which extends the guaranties of free opinion and speech" to theater, the circus, or movies because "they may be used for evil." There are, he continued, "some things which should not have pictorial representation in public places." Local communities, which included states, have traditionally exercised police power "in granting or withholding licenses for theatrical performances as a means of their regulation."[62] The Court stated that movies were "a business pure and simple," and not "regarded by the Ohio constitution, we think, as part of the press . . . or as organs of public opinion."[63]

As Garth Jowett has written, even though the Court recognized that movies communicated ideas, it was unwilling "to leave the general public unprotected from what they saw as a powerful, unregulated social force."[64] In the 1907 Chicago case and in the Supreme Court in 1915, jurists described movies as "evil." This was music to the ears of moral guardians everywhere. In both cases the judges recognized that movies communicated more effectively and more seductively than any of the traditional forms of communication or education. Moreover, the ideas they disseminated – that a criminal could be a hero; adultery might not always be wrong; police, judges, politicians, and businessmen were sometimes corrupt; the free enterprise system could be brutal; labor unions were good; and women should have the vote – were potentially "evil."

This logic, strange as it may seem today, was not outside the American judicial mainstream. In upholding the Ohio law, the Court affirmed the power of local communities to protect themselves from outside "evil" through licensing powers. These powers could involve licensing the physical theater and/or the content of the product offered the public.

The industry was dumbfounded by the ruling. "Are We Outlaws?" asked *Moving Picture World*.[65] John Collier blasted the decision as founded in "blank ignorance."[66] Yet the film industry should not have been surprised. Still strongly competitive, the industry had no single spokesperson capable of marshaling forces for an all-out fight for public opinion that would demand freedom of expression for the movies, or for slowly building a legal foundation for a favorable decision before rushing to the Supreme Court. Having done little or nothing to ensure a more favorable ruling, the movies suffered a crushing legal defeat. Collier, however, struck at the real meaning of the ruling when he noted that the basis for the decision was not so much legal as it was social. According to him, "the court was swayed by what it believed about public opinion and public necessity; . . . its grounds for decision were psychological, not primarily legal, and were the consequences of its lack of first-hand experience with motion pictures."[67]

Frederick Howe was more direct. To Howe the real issue was the "question of the *ultimate* effect of the assumption by the State of the right of regulating this most important avenue of expression [the motion picture]. Should the State pass upon the desirability of the portrayal of labor questions of socialism, the Industrial Workers of the World, and the other insistent issues crowding to the fore?" Howe contended that legal censorship would subject filmmakers "to the fear of suppression, so that only the safe and sane, the purely conventional, the uncontroversial film will be produced."[68] Howe was directly on target.

No matter how ill-informed or unfair the Mutual decision was, the hard reality was that it was the rule of law for the next four decades. Government censorship of movies prior to their exhibition was legal. The very thing the industry feared most – an explosion of municipal and state censorship laws, each conflicting with one another – now seemed probable. Had filmmakers been willing to produce films for specialized audiences (adults only, family, children), the impact of the Supreme Court decision might have been lessened; but the movers and shakers of the movie industry wanted or needed the largest possible market. The likelihood of censorship boards strung across the United States became frightening. The only way industry leaders could fend off that eventuality was to censor their own products. As Howe predicted, movies would become safe, sane, and purely conventional.

Notes

1 Ben Hecht, *A Child of the Century* (New York: Simon & Schuster, 1954), p. 466.

2 For a complete listing of Hecht's credits see Jeffrey Brown Martin, *Ben Hecht: Hollywood Screen Writer* (Ann Arbor: University of Michigan Press, 1985), pp. 183–209.

3 Otto Friedrich, *City of Nets: A Portrait of Hollywood in the 1940s* (New York: Harper & Row, 1986), p. 358.

4 Hecht, *Child of the Century*, p. 479.

5 Ibid., p. 467.

6 Ibid., p. 469.

7 Robert C. Allen, "Motion Picture Exhibition in Manhattan, 1906–1912," in John Fell, *Film Before Griffith* (Berkeley: University of California Press, 1983), pp. 162–3.

8 Barton W. Currie, "The Nickel Madness," *Harper's Weekly* (Aug. 24, 1907), in Gerald Mast, *The Movies in Our Midst* (Chicago: University of Chicago Press, 1982), p. 45.

9 Garth Jowett, *Film: The Democratic Art*, p. 40.

10 Kevin Brownlow, *Behind the Mask of Innocence*, p. xv.

11 Kay Solan, *The Loud Silents*, p. 3.

12 Ibid.

13 Ibid. See also Brownlow, *Behind the Mask of Innocence*, p. xv.

14 Lary May, *Screening Out the Past*, p. 39.

15 Ibid., p. 52.

16 Paul Boyer, *Urban Masses and Moral Order in America, 1820–1920*, p. 244.

17 Ibid.

18 Ibid., p. 40.

19 Jane Addams, *The Spirit of Youth and the City Streets*, pp. 78–80.

20 Letter to the Editor, from Darrell O. Hibbard, Boys' Work Director, YMCA, Indianapolis, Indiana; in *The Outlook* 105 (July 13, 1912), p. 599.

21 Jowett, *Film: The Democratic Art*, p. 79.

22 *Moving Picture World* 4 (Aug. 8, 1908), p. 106.
23 Wilbur F. Crafts, *National Perils and Hopes, A Study Based on Current Statistics and the Observations of a Cheerful Reformer* (Cleveland: O. F. M. Barton, 1910), p. 39.
24 May, *Screening Out the Past*, p. 40.
25 Quoted in Brownlow, *Behind the Mask of Innocence*, p. i.
26 Boyer, *Urban Masses and Moral Order*, p. 217.
27 Ibid.
28 Garth Jowett, " 'A Capacity for Evil': The 1915 Supreme Court Mutual Decision," p. 63. See also Ira H. Carmen, *Movies, Censorship and the Law;* Richard S. Randall, *Censorship of the Movies;* Edward de Grazia and Roger Newman, *Banned Films.*
29 *Moving Picture World* 4 (June 13, 1908), p. 511.
30 "The Censorship in Chicago," *Moving Picture World* 5 (Oct. 9, 1909), p. 487.
31 Jowett, "'A Capacity for Evil'," p. 64.
32 Ibid.
33 *Moving Picture World* 5 (Jan. 9, 1909), p. 33.
34 Ibid.
35 Ibid.
36 *Moving Picture World* 3 (July 25, 1908), p. 63.
37 *Moving Picture World* 3 (June 13, 1908), p. 511.
38 *Moving Picture World* 6 (Mar. 26, 1910), p. 462.
39 *Moving Picture World* 11 (May 22, 1915), p. 1290.
40 Charles M. Feldman, *The National Board of Censorship of Motion Pictures, 1909–1922*, p. 4; see also Nancy J. Rosenbloom, "Between Reform and Regulation," pp. 307–8; Robert Fisher, "Film Censorship and Progressive Reform," pp. 143–56.
41 *New York Times,* Dec. 24, 1908, p. 4. Robert Francis Martin, III, "Celluloid Morality," p. 52. See also Eileen Bowser, *The Transformation of the Cinema, 1907–1915*, pp. 49–52, and Richard Koszarski, *An Evening's Entertainment*, pp. 198–201.
42 Ibid.
43 Ibid.
44 Ibid.
45 Ibid.
46 *New York Times* (Jan. 9, 1909), p. 32.
47 "A Tribute to Moving Picture Shows," *Moving Picture World* 3 (Mar. 7, 1908), p. 181.
48 The name change to the National Board of Review of Motion Pictures was made in 1915 to remove the stigma of censorship. For the sake of consistency, National Board of Review will be used in this volume.
49 *Moving Picture World* 4 (June 26, 1909), p. 867.
50 Frederic C. Howe, "What to Do With the Motion-Picture Show: Shall It Be Censored?," *Outlook* 107 (June 20, 1914), pp. 412–16.
51 W. P. Lawson, "The Standards of Censorship," *Harper's Weekly* 130 (Jan. 16, 1915), p. 63. See also Lawson, "How the Censor Works," *Harper's Weekly* 130 (Jan. 9, 1915), pp. 39–40; "National Board of Censor-

ship of Motion Pictures," *Moving Picture World* 5 (Oct. 16, 1909), pp. 524–5.

52 Feldman, *National Board of Censorship,* p. 31.

53 "Passed by the National Board of Review," *Review of Reviews* 50 (Dec. 1914), pp. 730–1. See also "Applying Standards to Motion Picture Films," *Survey* 32 (June 27, 1914), pp. 337–8.

54 Lawson, "Standards of Censorship," p. 63.

55 Ibid. See also Bowser, *Transformation of the Cinema,* pp. 37–52.

56 Robert Sklar, *Movie Made America,* p. 31.

57 Gregory D. Black, "Hollywood Censored," p. 169.

58 "Censorship of Motion Pictures," *Yale Law Journal* 49 (Nov. 1939), p. 88. See also "Film Censorship: An Administrative Analysis," *Columbia Law Review* 39 (1939), pp. 1383–1405; Douglas Ayer, Roy E. Bater, and Peter J. Herman, "Self-Censorship in the Movie Industry: An Historical Perspective on Law and Social Change," *Wisconsin Law Review* (1970), pp. 791–838; Felix Bilgrey and Ira Levenson, "Censorship of Motion Pictures – Recent Judicial Decisions and Legislative Action," *New York Law Review* 1 (1955), pp. 347–59.

59 Jowett, "'A Capacity for Evil'," p. 66.

60 *Mutual Film Corporation v. Ohio Industrial Commission,* 236 U.S. 230, U.S. Supreme Court (1915), p. 236. Also representing Mutual were Walter N. Seligsberg and Harold T. Clark.

61 Ibid., p. 238.

62 Ibid., p. 242.

63 Ibid., p. 230.

64 Jowett, "'A Capacity for Evil'," p. 68.

65 "Are We Outlaws?" *Moving Picture World* 11 (Mar. 6, 1915), p. 1417.

66 "Back of Our Footlights: The Half-Forgotten Social Functions of the Drama," *Survey* 34 (June 5, 1915), p. 214. Collier wrote an eight-part series on the Supreme Court ruling under the general heading of "The Lantern Bearers."

67 John Collier, "The Learned Judges and the Films," p. 516. The sarcastic title suggests what Collier thought of the opinion. See also Jowett, "A Capacity for Evil," p. 70.

68 W. P. Lawson, "Do You Believe in Censors?" *Harper's Weekly* 130 (Jan. 23, 1915), p. 88.

CHAPTER 2

THE HAYS OFFICE AND A MORAL
CODE FOR THE MOVIES

Will Hays is my shepard, I shall not want, He maketh me to lie down
in clean postures.   – Gene Fowler

"The United States in the twenties was dotted with a thousand Xana-
dus," wrote movie-theater historian Ben Hall.[1] The nickelodeon had
been replaced by massive picture palaces that seated thousands. Going
to the movies was much like going to the theater or the opera. Moviegoers were greeted with huge ornate lobbies, often decorated with im-
ported artwork and staffed by polite, efficient, uniformed ushers and
usherettes who guided patrons to their seats. Fresh, inexpensive snacks
were available, and many of these new movie theaters offered free,
professionally staffed nurseries so parents could enjoy an evening's entertainment without the added cost of a baby-sitter.

Samuel Lionel "Roxy" Rothapfel was primarily responsible for creating this theatrical atmosphere for the movies. Roxy, first at New
York's Regent Theatre and then on Broadway at architect Thomas
Lamb's dazzling 3,500-seat Strand, combined lush settings, full or-
chestral accompaniment, musical acts, and, almost as an afterthought,
a feature movie for fifteen cents in the balcony seats or fifty cents for
front orchestra. As Roxy told reporters: "I give them a fine picture,
and an hour and a quarter's entertainment, and a first-class orchestra
to boot for the same price."[2] Critics agreed. "Going to the new Strand
Theatre last night was very much like going to a Presidential reception,
a first night at the opera or the opening of the horse show," wrote Victor Watson, dramatic critic for the *New York Times*.[3] Watson admitted that "if anyone had told me two years ago that the time would
come when the finest-looking people in town would be going to the
biggest and newest theatre on Broadway for the purpose of seeing motion pictures I would have sent them to the mental ward at Bellevue
Hospital."[4]

By the early 1920s the Roxy formula had been duplicated all over
the nation with a frenzy of picture-palace construction. Movie-theater

21

architects such as Thomas Lamb, whose signature was classical, Chicago's Rapp and Rapp (renowned for their "Sun King style"), and John Eberson, whose "atmospheric" theaters featured ceilings of drifting clouds and stars, built fifty-five 1,000–5,000-seat theaters in less than a decade. Hundreds more were built by other architectural firms. Exotic theaters, such as Sidney Grauman's Egyptian and Chinese in Los Angeles, San Antonio's Aztec, and Detroit's Fisher, which resembled a Mayan temple, brought streams of movie fans into a fantasy world they otherwise could never experience. Loew's Midland Theatre in Kansas City, which seated 4,000, boasted a ladies' smoking lounge built from materials salvaged from the William Vanderbilt mansion in New York. For their fifteen cents the women of Kansas City got a movie and a smoke in Vanderbilt's Oriental Room![5]

The culmination of this orgy of theater construction was The Roxy, New York's 6,200-seat "cathedral" of movies. The theater featured a five-story rotunda large enough to hold 4,000 people, an architectural theme that grafted "Renaissance details on Gothic forms with fanciful Moorish overtones," ushers drilled by an ex-Marine, a music library, a set of twenty-one grand chimes weighing 10,000 pounds, fourteen Steinway pianos scattered throughout the theater, an electrical plant sufficient to serve a town of 25,000, and washroom facilities for 10,000.[6] And a movie.

By the early 1920s the industry had changed almost as dramatically as the theaters. The movies moved west. As early as 1910 films were being produced in California, but the center of movie production was New York. Once the early giant of the industry, Vitagraph, moved to Los Angeles in 1913 the rest of the industry soon followed. They sought, wrote Kevin Brownlow, "sun, space and somnolence." California's nonunion work climate, however, was as important as its sunshine.[7]

It was also during the decade of the 1920s that the modern film studios emerged. MGM, the crown jewel of Hollywood, began its corporate history in vaudeville. New York's Marcus Loew owned a small string of theaters that featured live variety shows and one-reelers. Frustrated over his inability to guarantee a steady supply of films for his theaters, in 1919 Loew bought Metro Pictures Corporation, a production and distribution company, which featured Mae Murray, John Gilbert, and Lon Chaney.

In 1924 Loew merged his Metro Pictures with independent producers Samuel Goldwyn and Louis B. Mayer to form Metro–Goldwyn–Mayer, a subsidiary of Loew's, Inc. Mayer, who made a fortune as a distributor and exhibitor in the Boston area, was appointed head of studio facilities at the MGM lot in Culver City (built by Thomas Ince), while Marcus Loew remained in New York to oversee the corporation's theater and distribution empire.

Under Mayer's direction MGM became synonymous with glamour and quality films. Mayer and his production chief, Irving Thalberg, brought an incredible array of talent to the MGM umbrella. In the 1930s the studio featured Wallace Berry, Clark Gable, Jean Harlow, Jeanette MacDonald, William Powell, Mickey Rooney, James Stewart, Spencer Tracey, and Judy Garland. It is important to remember, however, that the Hollywood studio was just one division of Loew's, Inc. in New York: Marcus Loew, not Louis B. Mayer, wielded the real corporate power. Mayer, who was to emerge all powerful in Hollywood by the early 1930s, took his orders from Marcus Loew and, after Loew's death in 1927, from Nicholas Schenck.

Paramount's history also began in the streets of New York. Adolph Zukor, a Hungarian immigrant, bought his first nickelodeon in 1904. By 1912 Zukor had a small chain of theaters and formed a production outfit, Famous Players Film Company, to provide a supply of quality pictures for his theaters. Four years later Zukor merged with Jesse Lasky and his partners, Samuel Goldwyn and Cecil B. DeMille, to form what eventually became Paramount.

Zukor was an organizational genius. He perfected the concept of vertical monopoly in the industry – production–distribution–exhibition – which allowed film companies to control their product from inception to final presentation. Zukor also understood, perhaps more so than any of the other original moguls, that stars sold films. He signed cowboy star William S. Hart, comedian Fatty Arbuckle, America's sweetheart Mary Pickford, and Douglas Fairbanks to contracts. When Pickford and Fairbanks left, Zukor introduced Gloria Swanson, Rudolph Valentino, Pola Negri, Clara Bow, W. C. Fields, Harold Lloyd, Claudette Colbert, Mae West, and Gary Cooper to American audiences.

Zukor used the tremendous drawing power of a Pickford or Fairbanks, and later a Valentino or Mae West, to force theater owners to buy in "block" all of Paramount's films in order to be guaranteed play dates for "star" films. "Block booking" became a staple of industry marketing practices. Zukor also is credited with forcing "blind booking" on exhibitors. This practice allowed films to be presold on little more than a promise that they would be made in the future. If exhibitors wanted Pickford, Fairbanks, Swanson, Valentino, or Mae West, they had to buy everything that Paramount produced.[8]

Block and blind booking became a major issue in the battle over film content. Film reform groups maintained that these wholesaling practices adopted by the film companies forced small-town exhibitors to play "immoral" films because they had to pay for them whether they wanted to show them or not. The federal government also attacked this process of selling films as an unfair trade practice. A cease-and-desist order was issued in 1927, but the industry was able to delay enforcement through a series of appeals; not until 1947 did the federal government finally divest the film companies of their vertical monopolies and stop block booking.

Controlling theaters was a key element at both MGM and Paramount. In 1919 Zukor raised $10 million and began to buy theaters. By the end of the decade Paramount owned over 900 of them, many of them first-run picture palaces. In 1926 the corporation opened a huge new studio on Marathon Street in Los Angeles and was producing over 100 films a year to feed its massive theater empire.

Twentieth Century–Fox traced its lineage to the nickelodeons of New York. William Fox, son of Jewish immigrants from Hungary, invested his life's savings in a penny arcade that included a small nickelodeon. From this modest beginning, Fox expanded to operating a small chain of theaters. In order to supply his theaters with films, he formed his own distributorship, and when Edison's Motion Picture Patents Company threatened to blackball him, he launched his own production studio. He was one of the first to understand the drawing power of "movie stars," and signed the legendary "vamp" Theda Bara and cowboy hero Tom Mix to contracts. In 1917 Fox moved from New York to Los Angeles, where he opened a new studio.

Fox, sole owner of the corporation, borrowed heavily to acquire a theater chain that would allow him to compete with MGM and Paramount. By 1929 he controlled more than 500 theaters, including the flagship San Francisco Fox, whose "foyers . . . lobbies and auditorium were an orgy of gilded French detail," and New York's Roxy.[9] An automobile accident in 1929 and the stock market crash devastated Fox's movie empire. He was forced out of the company in 1930, and five years later Fox Films merged with Darryl F. Zanuck's Twentieth Century Productions to become Twentieth Century–Fox.

The four Warner brothers began in the movie business in Youngstown, Ohio, when they bought a nickelodeon theater in 1904. The brothers, Albert, Harry, Jack, and Sam, struggled until they scraped together enough money to buy the movie rights to James W. Gerard's *My Four Years in Germany* in 1918, which they turned into a popular "hate-the-Hun" feature. They used their profits to move to California in 1919 and open their first studio on Sunset Boulevard.[10] Warner Bros.' first star was a dog, Rin-Tin-Tin, whose films were both popular and profitable.

In 1925 the brothers attained major status when they bought Vitagraph, and made their mark on film history with Al Jolson's part-talkie *The Jazz Singer* in 1927. Profits were poured into expansion. Acquisition of a theater chain and First National Pictures with its studio in Burbank converted this family firm into a motion-picture giant with a first-class studio and an empire of more than 500 theaters, 30 of which were first-run palaces. Following their first, canine star, the studio featured Joan Blondell, Edward G. Robinson, James Cagney, Barbara Stanwyck, Bette Davis, Paul Muni, Dick Powell, Humphrey Bogart, and, of course, Ronald Reagan.

Universal Pictures was founded by the diminutive Carl Laemmle, who opened a nickelodeon in Chicago in 1906. Frustrated by the lack of good films, he went into production as a way of supplying his theaters with quality product. His first production was a one-reel melodrama in 1909. In 1915 Laemmle bought a 250-acre ranch in the San Fernando Valley and built Universal City, a massive studio that contained multiple stages, a hospital, two restaurants, construction shops, and its own water reservoir. Laemmle maintained corporate offices in New York, and appointed his private secretary, Irving Thalberg, who later moved to MGM, as his first production chief. Like its competitors, Universal combined the essential elements of production–distribution–exhibition.

RKO, Radio–Keith–Orpheum, was created to market sound films. RCA's David Sarnoff joined forces with Joseph Kennedy, who owned a small production company, Film Booking Office of America (FBO), in 1928. They then merged with the theater chain Keith–Albee–Orpheum and emerged as RKO Radio Pictures with a studio on Gower Street in Hollywood. In 1931 David O. Selznick was hired as production boss, but corporate power rested in New York. The studio that brought *King Kong* (1933) and Orson Welles's *Citizen Kane* (1941) to the screen was eventually purchased by Howard Hughes.

Harry and Jack Cohn's Columbia Pictures was formed in 1924. A "Poverty Row" studio, Columbia's biggest star was director Frank Capra, whose productions kept the studio afloat during the 1930s. Brother Harry directed operations in Hollywood, signed Jean Arthur, Ralph Bellamy, and Glenn Ford, and lured Melvyn Douglas from RKO, Cary Grant from Paramount, Irene Dunne from Universal, and Rita Hayworth from Fox to round out his stable of stars. Jack Cohn ran the corporate offices, which included a major distribution outlet, from New York.

United Artists was slightly different. Formed in 1919 by Charles Chaplin, Mary Pickford, Douglas Fairbanks, and D. W. Griffith, UA was primarily a distribution company for their films. "The lunatics have taken charge of the institution," cracked Metro's Richard A. Rowland.[11] In 1926 UA's president, Joseph Schenck, acquired a theater circuit, which provided guaranteed screens for UA releases. In addition to the original stars, UA provided an outlet for such individual producers as Walt Disney, Darryl F. Zanuck, Alexander Korda, Walter Wanger, Hal Roach, and Sam Goldwyn.

These eight major studios were joined by Republic, Monogram, and PRC (Producer's Releasing Corporation), which specialized in low-budget westerns, serials, and "B" features. The minors either fully cooperated with and/or were totally dependent on the majors for access to the urban theaters controlled by the majors and their national distribution system.

By the late 1920s, MGM, Paramount, RKO, Universal, Fox, Columbia, and Warner Bros. were all mirror images of one another: large-scale, tightly controlled vertical monopolies that produced, distributed, and exhibited films. The films, produced in California, were shipped to corporate headquarters in New York for duplication and distribution. The corporations controlled huge theater chains and forced all other theater owners to buy their product in "block or blind" packages.

The explosion of movie popularity took place in a decade of stark contrasts in American society. The prewar idealism of Woodrow Wilson's "Crusade for Democracy" was replaced by postwar alienation. Warren Harding, an Ohio Republican, was elected President with a campaign promise to return America to "normalcy." Politically the nation turned conservative and inward. The United States rejected membership in the League of Nations, and the watchword of American diplomacy was isolationism. A hysterical fear of "radical" and foreign ideas, driven by the Bolshevik Revolution in Russia, resulted in a "Red Scare." Attorney General Mitchell Palmer rounded up foreign aliens, businessmen broke up labor unions, and liberals of all hues were purged under the guise of 100 percent Americanism.

Popularly identified as "The Jazz Age," the 1920s also witnessed the rebirth of the Ku Klux Klan and its short-lived but violent reign of hooded terror. A rise in religious fundamentalism blamed modern education, especially the teaching of Darwin's theory of evolution, for destroying traditional American beliefs. Americans raised their tariff barriers and passed restrictive immigration legislation. They toasted America with a last glass of champagne and voted in Prohibition, and in so doing created a new national folk hero – the American gangster.

The decade was also marked by the rise of the "new woman" and a "new morality." The ideal young woman of the 1920s was no longer the virginal "girl-next-door," but a "flapper." She wore her skirts short, taped her breasts flat, painted her face with rouge, danced the Charleston, and smoked cigarettes in public. Her music was hot, and her guru was Sigmund Freud or H. L. Mencken. Her taste in literature (if she chose to read at all) turned from William Dean Howells and Gene Stratton-Porter to scathing attacks on American culture and values by F. Scott Fitzgerald, Sherwood Anderson, Sinclair Lewis, Ernest Hemingway, William Faulkner, and Eugene O'Neill.

While not all women, or even young girls, were "flappers," the era proved a liberating experience for women. Technology freed millions from much of the drudgery of housework. The nation extended voting rights to women, Margaret Sanger campaigned tenaciously for legalized birth control, the National Women's Party demanded an Equal Rights Amendment to the Constitution, and women moved in large numbers out of the house and into the world of work. No longer was the ideal woman wife, mother, and keeper of the home.

It was Hollywood's fortune, or misfortune, to be a major interpreter of these events. Films advocating the values of Victorian morality were not going to fill up America's theaters. The "flapper," the gangster, the speakeasy, the new woman, liberal attitudes toward sex, marriage, and divorce were natural topics for the film industry. The new female stars of the decade were Gloria Swanson, Clara Bow, Greta Garbo, Pola Negri, and Norma Talmadge, all of whom conveyed an open, frank attitude toward sex that would have been unacceptable in the prewar era.

Male stars exuded the same sexual attraction. While Douglas Fairbanks was a romantic hero in *The Mark of Zorro, Robin Hood,* and the *The Thief of Baghdad,* the male star of the decade was Rudolph Valentino, a dark, handsome, former cabaret dancer, who was thrust into the role of an international sex symbol with a series of smash hits. In *The Four Horsemen of the Apocalypse, The Sheik, Blood and Sand, Monsieur Beaucaire,* and *Son of The Sheik,* Valentino literally swept women off their feet with grace, style, and exotic power. He represented "a symbol of mysterious, forbidden eroticism, a vicarious fulfillment of dreams of illicit love and uninhibited passions." Women swooned over his screen passion, and in so doing challenged the Victorian notion of women as passive, uninterested sexual partners. It was enough to make the blood of outraged moralists boil.[12]

Europeans brought exotic passion to the screen. Eric von Stroheim transformed his sadistic Hun role of World War I into a suave, dissolute, aristocratic European seducer of American women in *Blind Husbands* and *Foolish Wives.* Director Ernst Lubitsch left Germany for Hollywood in 1923 and began a long and successful career. With satirical wit he portrayed sex as a frivolous and sophisticated game of the idle rich in such hits as *The Marriage Circle, Forbidden Paradise,* and *Kiss Me Again.*[13]

However, it was the son of an Episcopalian clergyman who best epitomized the new Hollywood. Cecil B. DeMille had directed Mary Pickford in *The Little American* (1917), but was challenged by his studio to make films with "modern stuff with plenty of clothes, rich sets and action." DeMille responded with a series of enticing films, *Old Wives for New* (1918; adapted from David Graham Phillips's 1908 novel), *Don't Change Your Husband* (1919), *Male and Female* (1919), *Why Change Your Wife?* (1920), and *Manslaughter* (1922), all of which turned upside down the traditional view of marriage as a non-passionate relationship. Sexual pleasure, the films implied, was a necessary requirement for modern happiness; yet marriage often turned women into dour matrons and husbands into colossal bores. In *Why Change Your Wife?*, Gloria Swanson is such a nag that she drives her husband into the waiting arms of another woman. Swanson learns a lesson. She begins to dress in sexy clothes, becomes "modern," and seduces her husband back into her arms.[14]

In 1919 DeMille adapted James M. Barrie's stage play *The Admirable Crichton* to the screen with the luring title *Male and Female*. (DeMille claimed he changed the title because he feared audiences would expect to see a naval picture.) The play, first performed in London in 1902, was a popular vehicle that poked light-hearted fun at the rigidity of the English social class system. In his screen version DeMille's message was that sex could overcome class barriers. Gloria Swanson stars as the wealthy, stuffy, upper-crust Lady Mary, daughter of Lord Loam. Her arrogant butler, William Crichton (Thomas Meighan), runs the Loam mansion with rigorous efficiency and accepts his role as butler to the privileged class.

DeMille's camera lingers in Lady Mary's boudoir and bath. The likes of Lady Mary's bedchamber, wrote *Photoplay,* has "never been seen before" with "the glorious Gloria [Swanson] quite literally uncovered to view."[15] When Lady Mary moved from bed to bath DeMille followed every step. It was a typical DeMille bathtub scene, lavishly staged with "Swanson apparently nude."[16]

When Lady Mary, her beau, and the butler go on a romantic South Seas cruise aboard the family yacht, disaster strikes. A shipwreck forces the survivors onto a deserted island (filmed on California's Santa Cruz Island). The power roles are suddenly reversed: Crichton is the only one able to hunt, cook, and protect his blue-blooded employers. In emerging as the dominant male, the butler wins the love of Lady Mary. He says to her: "I was a King in Babylon and you were a Christian slave."

Quick as a flash DeMille turned the film into a lavish Babylonian fantasy. The butler is King, Lady Mary a young Christian slave "bedecked in headdress, pearls and little else."[17] The king demands that she give up her religion and become his mistress or be thrown to the lions. When she refuses, the King orders her thrown in the lion's cage. This fantasy scene suddenly ends, and the shipwrecked party is rescued, with Lady Mary and Crichton returning to their proper English roles. Film historian and critic Lewis Jacobs called the film "more daring in its subject matter than any other picture Hollywood had produced." Producer Adolph Zukor admitted the film "would probably not have been acceptable to prewar audiences."[18]

In *Manslaughter* DeMille used a contemporary setting from which to cut back to a more bacchanalian era. The film's slender plot centers around a modern young flapper who is charged with manslaughter after her "joy ride" ends in tragedy. During her trial the district attorney tells the judge that the current collapse in moral standards is the very thing that caused the collapse of ancient Rome. Before the audience could blink, the screen was filled with a writhing Roman orgy in full blast:

Steps lead up to the throne on which sits a Roman patrician . . . Lydia [Leatrice Joy] in magnificent Roman costume. Below, her guests are at a long table, feasting. Wine is being passed by black nude slaves. Bacchanalian dancers are circling in front of the table. Several young nobles [very drunk] grab pretty dancers, pulling them down into their laps, bend them back, giving them wine. The guests at the feast are leaning forward eagerly watching the Chief Dancer, whose long scarf had almost unwound. The last of it drops from her as she reaches the throne, entirely nude.[19]

It was classic DeMille. Spectacular costume epics filled the screen in the early 1920s, although the costumes were often as brief as possible. As Betty Blythe remarked of her leading role in *Queen of Sheba* (1921): "I wear twenty-eight costumes and if I put them on all at once, I couldn't keep warm."[20] The *New York Times* agreed: *Queen of Sheba* "looks as if the Ziegfeld Frolic had been borrowed for the production."[21]

While DeMille always ended his films with a strong defense of the Victorian moral code – husbands and wives were reunited, wild flappers chastened – the overall impression of these films was that they "attacked the genteel tradition, flaunted sex, advocated new morals, condoned illicit and illegal relationships, set up new ideals, established a new tempo in living, and broke down pre-war distinctions with the new emphasis on money, luxuries, [and] material success."[22]

Moral guardians were furious at this new drift in American films. Despite the fact that millions flocked to see DeMille's latest epic, criticism continued unabated that movies were directly responsible for America's changing moral values. The National Board of Review – blamed for failing to "censor" these new movies – received a devastating blow to its reputation when the General Federation of Women not only severed its relationship in 1918 but began a national campaign for increased state censorship.

The General Federation conducted surveys of the movies in various states and municipalities. In Michigan the women declared the National Board of Review "a sham" and condemned movies as "vile and atrocious."[23] The Chicago Federation of Women pronounced that their members found a mere 20 percent of the 1,700 films surveyed fit to be seen. At their national meeting in Hot Springs, Arkansas, Mrs. Guy Blanchard summarized the Federation's various surveys: 20 percent of the movies seen by the women were declared "immoral"; 40 percent "not worthwhile"; and a third "contained questionable behavior." In the early 1920s resolutions condemning the movies as evil were resoundingly approved by the Baptist, Episcopalian, Methodist, and Presbyterian conventions.[24]

By 1921 support for the National Board of Review had all but disappeared. The final blow to the prestige of the board came from a series of articles in the *Brooklyn Eagle,* which revealed the financial support the industry gave to the board and implied that, in return, commissioners steered "controversial" films to the more "lenient of the 'volunteer' reviewing committees."[25] This exposé created new interest in expanding federal and state censorship boards.

Industry problems intensified when over a hundred antimovie bills were introduced in state legislatures in 1921. The most important and potentially the most damaging was in New York. New York City, with its Broadway picture palaces, was America's cultural center. It was also the corporate center of the industry, and most films were opened with gala premieres on Broadway, then duplicated for national distribution. Producers thus feared a New York censorship board would set national standards. Determined to fight back, the industry marshaled its forces in Albany to contest the proposed bill.

William Brady was the industry spokesperson. A Broadway impresario and independent producer, Brady had been appointed in 1916 to head the newly organized National Association of the Motion Picture Industry (NAMPI), a loose confederation of producing companies.[26] He brought to Albany a parade of witnesses, including D. W. Griffith, to argue for movie freedom, and displayed the industry's new "Thirteen Points" – an agreement that asked producers not to stress sex, white slavery, illicit love, nudity, crime, gambling, or excessive drinking, or to ridicule clergy or public officials in films. Brady asked legislators for a year's grace period during which he pledged to "clean up the industry," but his pleas were ignored: The censorship bill swept through the legislature. Governor Nathan Miller signed it and told reporters "it was the only way to remedy what everyone conceded had grown to be a great evil."[27] Miller dismissed the industry pledge to censor itself: "The moving picture people say now that they will be good, but you have heard that old story before."[28] New York censors began work in April 1921.[29]

The demand for action against the movies accelerated when a series of sensational sex scandals about the private lives of the stars rocked the industry. The most famous centered around rotund comedian

Roscoe "Fatty" Arbuckle. Second only to Charlie Chaplin in popularity, Arbuckle was at the peak of his career when an actress, Virginia
Rappe, died after a wild Hollywood party hosted by Arbuckle at San
Francisco's St. Francis Hotel. The press had a field day with Arbuckle,
insinuating that the combination of his weight and perverse sexual ap-
petite had killed the woman. While three trials failed to prove Arbuckle guilty of anything, public opinion judged him guilty.

Nor did the scandals stop with Arbuckle. Director William Des-
mond Taylor was found murdered, and a series of front-page stories
revealed a life-style of drugs and sex. America was shocked when
matinee idol Wallace Reid died from drug complications. Even America's sweetheart, Mary Pickford, was caught in the web of sexual im-
propriety: Her quickie divorce from actor Owen Moore and marriage
to Douglas Fairbanks shocked the nation. The conduct of the stars and
the content of the movies confirmed for critics that Hollywood was
the modern Babylon.

The embattled moguls fired William Brady after his inept performance as spokesperson, dissolved NAMPI, and joined forces in January 1922 to create a trade association, the Motion Picture Producers
and Distributors of America (MPPDA). Movies, the moguls believed,
needed a squeaky clean image and an astute politician who could or-
ganize effective political campaigns to combat censorship bills at the
federal and state level. They chose as their new front man the Hoosier
William Harrison (Will) Hays, Postmaster General in President Warren Harding's cabinet and chairman of the Republican National Committee.

Hays was an inspired choice. His roots were solidly midwestern, his
politics conservatively Republican, and his religion mainstream Protestant. Teetotaler, elder in the Presbyterian church, Elk, Moose, Ro-
tarian, and Mason, Hays brought the respectability of mainstream
middle America to a Jewish-dominated film industry. He symbolized
the figurative Puritan in Babylon. As one wit put it, Hays was "the visi-
ble sign of invisible grace."[30]

Hays served as the lightning rod for public complaints. Promoted
by press agents as the movie "czar," Hays was in fact no more than an
employee of the moguls who quickly brought a sense of order to the
industry. With appropriate fanfare he established a "morals clause"
in Hollywood contracts, urged the companies to downplay the lavish
life-styles of the stars, set up a Central Casting Corporation to monitor
the use of Hollywood extras, and negotiated union contracts with theatrical craft unions.

As a public relations agent, he was an unqualified success; as a censor or regulator of movie content during the 1920s, he was a failure.
From his offices in New York, Hays had little contact with the Los An-

geles studios and even less control over the content of films. The moguls had hired a spokesperson and lobbyist; they were reluctant to allow Hays to interfere with their producers in Hollywood. Hays searched for a device that would give him control over film content, to undercut vocal opposition to the movies while wooing the largest possible audience.

Hays opened his office at the MPPDA in March 1922. That spring one hundred movie-censorship bills were introduced in thirty-seven states. A censorship bill had passed the Massachusetts legislature and awaited a required statewide referendum to become law. With censorship firmly established in Pennsylvania, Ohio, Florida, New York, Maryland, Kansas, and Virginia, Hays was determined to prevent any more states from establishing censorship boards. Massachusetts became a referendum on the movies.

Proponents for the bill used the familiar arguments that the movies were corrupting children, were generally immoral and vile, and that a bill to license films would give protection to the state from outside influences. Bishop William Lawrence of Boston favored the new law because the board would view "the films not after they are shown publicly and have done the damage to the children, but before." They would license those films that they believed were fit for public consumption. B. Preston Clark, a Bostonian who led the coalition in favor of film censorship, continued the argument that censorship was nothing more than protection from harmful influences. "When you eat your fish or your meat, or see your child drink her glass of milk, isn't it good to know they have been censored, so they will nourish and not poison?" he asked voters. There would be no loss of individual freedom by having "the dirty spots" removed from films: "This censorship Bogie is bunk," Preston claimed.[31]

Hays dispatched Charles C. Pettijohn, his expert on legislative affairs, to Boston, where he and Hays organized a political campaign against censorship. With a war chest of $300,000 they hammered away at the theme that censorship was un-American. "Censorship," Hays wrote in an article in the *Boston Globe,* drove the "pilgrims to Plymouth Rock . . . forced the Minute Men to Concord Bridge . . . and caused the Boston Tea Party." Americans, Hays continued, "were against censorship of press, against censorship of pulpit and against censorship of the movies." The movie industry was opposed to censorship not because they wanted to make "dirty movies" but because "the motion picture is an American business."[32]

Whether or not the voters of Massachusetts believed this tortured logic, they rejected the censorship bill by a three-to-one majority. It was a tremendous victory for Hays, who never tired of proclaiming that this was the only time the public was given the opportunity to vote for or against censorship. The Massachusetts vote stopped the momentum toward government censorship of the movies. Interestingly, no other state adopted a censorship bill after the Bay State's referendum, and despite innumerable bills introduced in Congress, none became law. If the movies were to be regulated by a single source, it seemed, it would be Will Hays.

Hays first attempted to achieve self-regulation for the MPPDA in 1924 when he presented the Board of Directors with "The Formula." This requested each studio to forward a synopsis of every play, novel, or story under consideration for a future film to the Hays Office, which would then judge the suitability of the material for the screen. In most ways, this voluntary scheme failed. During the next six years the Hays Office rejected 125 proposals. Presumably each one, had it been made, would have brought intensified howls from the antimovie lobby. Still, "The Formula" did little to quiet protests: Hays was more afraid that the federal government would take antimonopoly action against the industry than he was that it would impose federal censorship. To keep from drawing attention to the collusion of the producers, he refused to publicize the fact that a book, play, or story had been collectively rejected. In so doing, he lost an opportunity to counter the claims of the antifilm lobby that his office was ineffective.[33]

In an effort to gain some control over the studios and the content of films, Hays created a Studio Relations Department (SRD) and appointed Jason Joy, a former executive secretary of the American Red Cross, as its director. Headquartered in Los Angeles, Joy worked closely with the studios trying to delete material that would offend censors. The SRD drew up a code of the most common demands of municipal and state censorship boards. This working document became known as the "Don'ts and Be Carefuls" and prohibited, among other things, profanity, nudity, drug trafficking, and white slavery; it also urged producers to exercise good taste in presenting such adult themes as criminal behavior, sexual relations, and violence. Even so, each studio interpreted these guidelines according to its own inclination. Meanwhile the antimovie lobby fulminated and grew ever larger and more threatening.

The antimovie lobby consisted mainly of alienated Protestants. The Women's Christian Temperance Union (WCTU), the Reverend William H. Short's Motion Picture Research Council, and Canon William Shaefe Chase's Federal Motion Picture Council had long lobbied Congress for federal action. The culmination of these efforts to control the movies came in 1926 when Chase and Short led a delegation of more than 200 ministers and women's clubs representatives to Washington, D.C., to demand federal regulation of the movies.

Chase's 1921 book *Catechism on Motion Pictures* had advocated federal regulation, claiming that the industry's "Hebrew" owners and producers were vile corrupters of American morals.[34] Testifying before the House Committee on Education, Chase branded the movies a "threat to world civilization." He denounced the industry's practice of block booking, which forced theater owners to rent films not individually by title but in a block. This practice, Chase testified, forced local theater owners to play films unacceptable to their communities and made local control ineffective. Only the federal government, Chase asserted, was powerful enough to control Hollywood.

The House members pressed the lobbyists to name films that were corrupting or offensive. Few, it turned out, could cite specific titles. While the ministers and the women's organizations considered themselves "experts" on obscenity, they could not define it; but they knew it when they saw it. In this case, anything they saw on the screen that offended their sense of propriety, whether it was social, political, or moral in nature, was defined as obscene and had to be banned.

Although Chase and his supporters blamed the movies for America's social ills, they also demanded censorship of the press. One woman, striving for an image of quiet erudition, told the House Committee on Education that she would be fully satisfied if Congress would adopt for the movies the same type of copyright system the government had for books. In order to get a copyright, she said, authors had to submit their books to the government for approval; the federal government should do the same for movies. When committee members patiently explained that no censorship was involved in getting books copyrighted, the woman was appalled. She then lectured committee members on the necessity to control obscene literature. Her testimony and that of several others exposed the coalition as narrow bigots. They failed to stir Congress.[35]

If these moral guardians were upset by silent cinema, they were infuriated when films began to talk. The talkies opened up new dramatic possibilities, and the movies became more popular than ever. Now sexy starlets could rationalize their immoral behavior; criminals using hip slang could brag about flouting law and order; and politicians could talk about bribery and corruption. Film dialogue could and did challenge conventional norms. In 1928 the New York State censorship board cut over 4,000 scenes from the more than 600 films submitted, and Chicago censors sliced more than 600 scenes.

In 1929 a small group of Catholics, not Protestants, offered Hays and the movie industry a formula for control. The Catholic church had previously played no organized role in the controversy over film content. Throughout the 1920s, as the Protestant campaign against the industry intensified, Church leaders and lay activists had refused to support efforts to enact federal censorship or block-booking legislation.

This did not mean that Catholics were more liberal than Protestants or philosophically opposed to censorship; in fact, quite the opposite was true. The Catholic church had for centuries maintained a list of banned books. Catholics decried the modern trend in literature toward realism, and even a liberal journal like *Commonweal* refused to review or discuss James Joyce, D. H. Lawrence, F. Scott Fitzgerald, or Ernest Hemingway.[36] The purpose of literature, wrote Father Francis X. Talbot, S.J., in the Jesuit publication *America,* was to teach a moral lesson.[37] Robert Broderick, literary critic for *Ave Maria,* wrote that "a writer could . . . write about evil and failure as long as he showed that right must predominate over wrong."[38] Father Robert Parsons, S.J., who worked with Talbot at *America,* thought American Catholics "hopelessly Victorian" and noted that young Catholic students refused to read Catholic writers because of the "pious preachment" that dominated their fiction.[39] There was a strong movement in the church that held that the mere reading "of most modern literature . . . might result in eternal damnation."[40] In general, the Catholic hierarchy longed for a return to Victorian constraints.

The movies had not been a priority agenda item for the church during the 1920s. While individual priests might have protested the local screening of what they considered an "immoral" movie, the church had accepted entertainment as a feature of modern life. Catholics had neither banned members from attendance nor restricted Sunday viewing. By 1929, however, a small group of Catholic laymen and priests were becoming more and more uncomfortable with what they perceived as the declining moral quality of films.

Martin Quigley, a staunch lay Catholic and owner and publisher of the industry trade journal *Exhibitors Herald-World,* published in Chicago, took the first steps toward Catholic involvement. An advocate for theater owners, Quigley opposed government censorship as ineffective. He cited his own city of Chicago, whose censorship board had a national reputation for strictness toward sex and screen violence, as a prime example. In recent years Chicago censors had banned *The Red Kimono, Underworld, Camille, The Alibi,* and *The Trial of Mary Dugan;* yet every one of the films played in Chicago theaters because, Quigley charged, the industry "handled" local politicians who issued permits despite the censors' objections.[41]

To Quigley, the way to control what people saw in films was not political censorship or the elimination of block booking – which, he argued, was in the financial interests of small theater owners because it reduced the overall price they had to pay for individual films – but rather to devise a foolproof method to ensure that films were made without censurable material. If, Quigley argued, censurable material could be eliminated during production, censorship boards would be unnecessary. In turn, this would also undercut the demands of the Protestant lobby for an elimination of block booking. Quigley advocated stricter self-regulation by the industry as a means of reducing criticism and ensuring continued popularity of the movies.

While he opposed Protestant methods, Quigley shared their conviction that movies were increasingly immoral. He was further convinced that movies ought to avoid social, political, and economic subjects. Movies, in his view, should be entertainment, not social commentary. In the summer of 1929 he began to formulate a new code of behavior for the movie industry, one that would force moviemakers to consider the moral issues in their films as well as the entertainment values.

At the same time, Will Hays also was thinking of more intense self-regulation because of the frequent attacks by religious organizations and the increasing strictness of censorship boards across the country. In August 1929 Hays sent his chief legal council, Charles C. Pettijohn, to Chicago to try to "abrogate official censorship."[42] On Chicago's censorship board sat Father FitzGeorge Dinneen, S.J., pastor at St. Ignatius parish in Chicago, a close friend of Quigley and confidant to one of America's most powerful Catholics, Cardinal George W. Mundelein of Chicago. Dinneen was an activist priest who often condemned "immoral" films shown in his parish. His organization of local film boycotts had brought him to the attention of Mundelein, who had recommended Dinneen as his representative to the Chicago censorship board in 1918.

Dinneen vociferously objected to Pettijohn's assertion that the film industry did not need local censorship. When Pettijohn then suggested that censorship be shifted from the city to the church, Cardinal Mundelein objected. Quigley and Dinneen then offered a counterproposal: the movie industry, using a Catholic code, would ensure that movies were made correctly and thereby eliminate the need for censorship.[43] Pettijohn and Hays were interested.

Father Dinneen arranged for Martin Quigley to meet privately with Cardinal Mundelein to discuss his concept of a Catholic code for the movies. Mundelein had long favored police censorship of the new medium. Quigley argued that a new code of behavior written by Catholics and backed by the hierarchy of the church would eliminate the need for police or political censorship. Quigley told the Cardinal that a moral code strictly enforced during production could convert films into powerful lessons of morality for the masses. Rather than undermine the basic teachings of the church, this popular entertainment medium would become an ally.

Quigley also tried to explain to the Cardinal the industry's financial problems. Dependent upon a large and steady flow of box-office dollars to sustain the massive production studios, to buy and build theaters, to convert the industry to sound, and to sell their products to a worldwide audience, Hollywood was clearly vulnerable to economic boycotts. The industry could little afford any disruption of box-office revenues. While the studios had always borrowed to finance their operations, the recent conversion to sound had brought Wall Street into Hollywood boardrooms.

The Catholic church, twenty million strong, heavily concentrated in urban centers, and boasting its own national press with a circulation of more than six million readers a week, was in a unique position to exert influence on the industry. Being more centralized than the Protestant denominations, the mere threat of united Catholic action, Quigley argued, would force the industry to reform. He was also aware that Cardinal Mundelein's banker, Halsey Stuart and Company, was a heavy investor in the movie industry. Could the Cardinal convince Halsey Stuart and Company that improving the morals of the movies made good business sense?[44]

Cardinal Mundelein accepted Quigley's reasoning, although it is clear he had no intention in 1930 of leading a united Catholic protest against the film industry.[45] Determined to remain in the wings, Mundelein was not willing to stake his reputation or that of the church on any "reform the movies campaign." He did, however, like Quigley's idea that the church draft a moral code for the movies. When Father Dinneen suggested bringing in Father Daniel Lord, S.J., to write the document, the Cardinal gave his blessing.[46]

No reclusive cleric, Lord was professor of dramatics at St. Louis University and editor of the widely read *The Queen's Work,* which preached morality and ethics to Catholic youth. Lord, like so many Catholic intellectuals, deplored the modern trend in drama and literature that dealt in increasingly realistic terms with modern ideas and social issues; he warned his young readers to be wary of modern ideas and teachers who advocated them.[47] He had begun a prolific publishing career in 1915 with an attack on George Bernard Shaw in *Catholic World.* In editorials in *Queen's Work,* in pamphlets, and in Catholic newspapers and journals, Lord attacked the ultrasophistication of modern living as reflected in literature and drama. Other topics like evolution, birth control, abortion, secular education, and the growth of communism also drew his wrath. As Lord later recalled, he and Dinneen "often groaned together over the horrible stuff that came pouring out of Hollywood."[48]

As a boy Lord had often attended the movies with his mother; but they had been increasingly embarrassed by what they had seen:

The commonest thing was for the innocent heroine, thinking herself totally alone (except for the director, cameraman, stage crew, other actors standing by, and a potential audience of several million), to pause at the brink of the sylvan lake, drop off all her clothes, and dive naked into the water.[49]

He had been raised in an era, he wrote, when "virtue was virtue and vice was vice, and nobody in the audience had the slightest doubt when to applaud and when to hiss."[50]

As a young man he had been overwhelmed by D. W. Griffith's *The Birth of a Nation,* leaving the theater convinced that he had seen a new medium of communication powerful enough to "change our whole attitude toward life, civilization, and established customs."[51] He had maintained that view through maturity, and by the early 1920s had become convinced that the real problem with the movies was their spreading of the literature of the "ultra-sophisticates" to every small town in America. As a young priest, he had been selected to work as a technical adviser for Cecil B. DeMille's production of *The King of Kings* (1927). He and DeMille had struck up a lasting friendship, but Lord's first-hand experience in Hollywood had solidified his view that the movies needed spiritual guidance.[52]

His impressions were confirmed at a matinee performance of *The Very Idea,* which Lord saw at a local theater in St. Louis. The audience was packed with children. When a group near the priest whispered: "This is certainly dirty stuff," Lord was shocked. He told Quigley that the film was proof that "the sophisticated stuff which Broadway may enjoy simply comes as a shock, a surprise, and a source of discomfort to the less sophisticated audiences." He blamed the screenwriters, whom he said were "in the lower caste," more than the moguls, "pants pressers and glove merchants," for this decline.[53]

Joseph I. Breen was yet another key figure in this small group of aroused Catholics. An active Irish Catholic, he had graduated from St. Joseph's College in Philadelphia and begun a career in journalism as a reporter for the Philadelphia *North American.* After four years in the United States consular service, he had gone to Washington, D.C., as the Overseas Commissioner of the National Catholic Welfare Conference. He had continued his involvement in Catholic affairs when appointed press relations chief for the 1926 Eucharistic Congress in Chicago, where he had by then also become public relations director of the Peabody Coal Company.[54]

Breen combined political conservatism with deep religious conviction. He blamed "radical teaching in our great colleges and universities" for undermining American youth. He wrote, under the pseudonym "Eugene Ware," a series of articles for the Jesuit publication *America* on the threat of communism in the United States. In late 1929, when Peabody Coal was hit by a series of strikes, Breen branded the entire affair "a Communist undertaking."[55] He was strongly opposed to public discussion of such moral issues as divorce, birth control, and abortion. This was especially true in movies, because Breen believed that average moviegoers were "youngsters between 16 and 26," most of them "nit-wits, dolts and imbeciles."[56] An extreme anti-Semite, Breen held the Jewish moguls responsible for the decadence on the screen.

Breen and Quigley met through their Catholic connections. From the beginning Breen saw himself as a potential censor. His first suggestion was that he head a Chicago "Board of Examination" to censor film scripts before production. Although this proposal was rejected, Breen would eventually emerge in 1934 as the director of the Production Code Administration.[57]

For several months Quigley, Breen, Lord, Father Dinneen, and Father Wilfrid Parsons, editor of the Catholic publication *America,* discussed a new and more stringent code of behavior for the movies. They all agreed that government censorship would not assure "moral" films. They believed the only way to make morally and politically acceptable films was to exert influence during their production and thus – if films were made correctly – they would need no censorship. After studying various state and municipal censorship codes, the Hays Office's "Don'ts and Be Carefuls," and the objections of Protestant reformers, Daniel Lord drafted a Catholic movie code. What emerged was a fascinating combination of Catholic theology, conservative politics, and pop psychology – an amalgam that would control the content of Hollywood films for three decades.[58] (See Appendix A for a copy of this document.)

While this code is most often discussed as a document that prohibited nudity, required married couples to sleep in twin beds, and effectively ruined the movie career of that saucy favorite, Mae West, its authors intended it to control much more. Lord and his colleagues shared a common objective with Protestant film reformers: They all wanted entertainment films to emphasize that the church, the government, and the family were the cornerstones of an orderly society; that success and happiness resulted from respecting and working within this system. Entertainment films, they felt, should reinforce religious teachings that deviant behavior, whether criminal or sexual, cost violators the love and comforts of home, the intimacy of family, the solace of religion, and the protection of law. Films should be twentieth-century morality plays that illustrated proper behavior to the masses.

As Lord explained, Hollywood films were first and foremost "entertainment for the multitudes," and as such carried a "special *Moral Responsibility*" required of no other medium of entertainment or communication. Their universal popularity, cutting across social, political, and economic classes and penetrating local communities, from the most sophisticated to the most remote, meant that filmmakers could not be permitted the same freedom of expression allowed producers of legitimate theater, authors of books, or even editors of newspapers.[59]

Movies had to be more restricted, Lord believed, because they were persuasively and indiscriminately seductive. While audiences of books, plays, and newspapers were self-selective, the movies had universal appeal. Hollywood's films, its picture palaces, and its beautiful and glamorous stars combined to create an irresistible fantasy. In the late 1920s when sound was combined with striking visual images, a sensation was created that Lord believed would be irresistible to the impressionable minds of children, the uneducated, the immature, and the unsophisticated. These very groups, Lord believed, comprised a large majority of the national film audience. It was because this massive film audience was incapable of distinguishing between fantasy and reality – or so Lord and the film reformers believed – that self-regulation or control was necessary.

Therefore, the basic premise behind the code was that "no picture should lower the moral standards of those who see it." Recognizing that evil and sin were a legitimate part of drama, the code stressed that no film should create a feeling of "sympathy" for the criminal, the adulterer, the immoralist, or the corrupter. No film should be so constructed as to "leave the question of right or wrong in doubt." Films must uphold, not question or challenge, the basic values of society. The sanctity of the home and marriage must be upheld. The concept of basic law must not be "belittled or ridiculed." Courts must be shown as just and fair, police as honest and efficient, and government as protective of all people. If corruption was a necessary part of any plot, it had to be restricted: A judge could be corrupt but not the court system; a policeman could be brutal, but not the police force. Interestingly, Lord's code stated that "crime *need not always be punished, as long as the audience is made to know that it is wrong.*" What Lord wanted films to do was illustrate clearly to audiences that "evil is wrong" and that "good is right."[60]

"I received this morning your final draft of our code," Quigley wrote Lord in November 1929. Quigley was excited by Lord's blending of Catholic attitudes toward entertainment with traditional movie taboos. Quigley's strategy was to combine economic threat with moral pressure. Cardinal Mundelein was the key player in Quigley's plan: Quigley envisioned an industry pledge to the Cardinal to uphold the provisions of the code.[61] With the power of the church behind him, Quigley took Lord's draft to Hays and began agitating for industry adoption. According to Hays: "My eyes nearly popped out when I read it. This was the very thing I had been looking for."[62] Pettijohn agreed that Lord's document was a "fair, sincere and most constructive out-line of what motion pictures ought to be," but he warned Quigley, it was doubtful that movies could ever be as innocent as Lord intend-ed.[63]

With the dramatic stock market crash only a few weeks behind them, film corporation heads in New York were jittery, and Hays con-vinced them that the code would be good for business: It could quiet demands for federal censorship and undercut the campaign to elimi-nate block booking. Hays objected to any direct pledge to Mundelein and pointed out that the code would be worthless without the backing of the studios in Hollywood. It remained for Hays to convince Holly-wood producers that the code made good sense from an entertain-ment, as well as an economic, point of view. With the full support of the corporate offices in New York and the backing of Cardinal Mun-delein in Chicago, Hays and Quigley set off for Los Angeles to "peddle a script" for movie behavior.[64]

Not surprisingly, Hays found the producers less than enthusiastic over the tone and content of Lord's code. In fact, the code was, as one scholar of modern Catholicism has written, "hopelessly out of sympa-thy with the creative artistic mind of the twentieth century." Lord's document, which would have made perfect sense to such diverse nineteenth-century "literary minds as George Bancroft, James Lowell, Ralph Waldo Emerson and William Dean Howells," made little sense as a guide for the movies. Taken literally, it forbade movies from even questioning the veracity of contemporary moral and social stan-dards.[65]

A small group of producers – MGM's head of production Irving Thalberg, studio boss Jack Warner of Warner Bros., production head B. P. Schulberg of Paramount, and Sol Wurtzel of Fox – offered a counterproposal.[66] They rejected Lord's basic contention that the movies had to be more restricted in presenting material than did other art forms. They maintained that films were simply "one vast reflection of every image in the stream of contemporary life." In their view, audi-ences supported movies they liked and stayed away from those they did not. No other guidelines were needed, it seemed to them, to deter-mine what audiences would accept. They argued that the advent of sound brought a wider, not a more restrictive, latitude in subject mat-ter to the movies. With the addition of screen dialogue, they held, actors and actresses could "speak delicately and exactly" on sensitive subjects that could not be portrayed in silent films. Therefore, the pro-ducers countered, the talkies should be able to use "any book, play or title which had gained wide attention."[67]

The producers saw no reason to adopt Lord's code of ethics. In-stead they pledged to use "good taste" in all films and promised a special effort to include "compensating moral values" in all their films. They also offered to allow Hays's representative in Hollywood, Jason Joy, to be "empowered to stop the distribution of any picture which it is felt violates the letter or spirit" of his office.[68]

The two documents could not have been further apart. From the producers' perspective Lord's code, representing reformers of all ilk, asked them to present a utopian view of life that denied reality and, frankly, lacked box-office appeal as they understood it. But Daniel Lord, convinced that the screen was undermining church teachings and destroying family life, wanted a partnership among the movie industry, church, and state that would advocate a fair, moral, and orderly society.

Lord admitted that the world's imperfections were the stuff of good drama, but he saw no reason why films should not show simple and direct solutions to complex moral, political, economic, and philosophical issues. The producers countered that film was no different from any other medium of entertainment and required no special restrictions. The American people, they argued, were the real censors, and the box office was their ballot box.

Hays and Quigley, afraid the new code would be rejected by the producers, asked Lord to come to Los Angeles to explain it. On February 10, 1930, Lord, Quigley, Hays, and Jason Joy met with moguls Jesse Laskey, Irving Thalberg, and Jack Warner and studio representatives B. P. Schulberg of Paramount and Sol Wertzel of Fox to work out an agreement. Lord spent several hours explaining his code and enumerating the complaints of movie reformers in general. It was, he later told Mundelein, "an excellent opportunity for bringing moral and ethical reasons before the motion picture industry."[69] The next day the producers accepted Lord's code.

The fascinating aspect of this conflict was that Lord's position, backed by Hays and the Catholic church, was accepted almost without a whimper. Why the producers would adopt a code that, if interpreted literally, would eliminate important social, political, and economic themes from movies and turn the industry into a defender of the status quo remains a mystery. Why would the industry, enjoying an all-time high of ninety million paid admissions per week, agree to such severe restrictions on content and form?

There are several possibilities. One is that Will Hays wanted to extend his influence from New York to Hollywood. Since his appointment in 1922, Hays had very little actual control over the Hollywood studios. This lack of control kept him in continual hot water with the reformers. When Quigley first approached Hays with Lord's code, Hays was supportive. He recognized immediately that this Catholic plan did not ask for federal intervention, did not demand outside censorship, nor did it attack the financial cornerstone of the industry: block booking. It placed movie regulation squarely in the Hays Office, precisely where Will Hays believed it belonged. Furthermore, acceptance of the code by the industry might actually undercut the various religious reform groups. By accepting the Catholic code, Hays prevented – at least temporarily – a Catholic–Protestant antifilm coalition.

Adopting the code also made good economic sense. While the industry was booming at the box office, its financial structure was always fragile. Any major interruption in the cash flow from the box office or from the bankers could bring the movie house of cards tumbling down. The industry likewise needed a steady flow of loans to finance its 500-plus features a year. Catholic threats to pressure bankers, combined with their implied threat of box-office pressure, were not lost on Hays or those in the corporate headquarters in New York.

From the producer's point of view, filmmakers had lived and prospered with codes since 1911. The various municipal and state censorship boards had been irritating, but not destructive. Moreover, it should be noted that some producers, Louis B. Mayer for one, believed that Lord was basically right. Perhaps there was too much sex, too much crime, too much drinking, too much corruption, too much violence, and too little good taste in films. Furthermore, few people in Hollywood believed the code meant exactly what it said. Even if it did, the producers insisted on one concession that gave them, not Hays, the final say over film content. If any studio felt the Hays office interpreted the code improperly, a "jury" of producers, not MPPDA officials, would decide whether or not the offending scene should be cut. With that understanding, the code was accepted by the Hollywood producers. No formal acceptance was possible, however, until the next board of directors meeting in New York at the end of March 1930. All parties, therefore, agreed to keep the new code a secret until a formal announcement could be made. They also agreed to keep the Catholic connection secret.[70]

While a facade of harmony appeared on the surface, it is clear that from the very beginning there was fundamental misunderstanding over what had been agreed to in Los Angeles. Lord, for example, informed Mundelein that Jason Joy, who was to be the enforcer of the code for Hays, had the authority to reject scripts, which meant "that the picture will not be filmed"; further, that finished films rejected or questioned by Joy would be submitted to a committee or jury of producers who could prevent the film from being shown. Lord left Los Angeles with the impression that his code would be rigidly enforced by Joy and that the producers were in full agreement. Nothing could have been further from the truth. As it will soon be made clear, the producers fought Joy from the beginning and looked on the code at best as a general guideline for movie morality.

Quigley was pleased with what had been achieved in Hollywood, but remained suspicious of Hays and the producers. As publisher of a major industry trade magazine, he was anxious to "scoop" his rival *Variety* with the code story and to feature himself in the starring role. Lord, Breen, and Hays would have supporting roles. However, before he could announce his moral coup, *Variety* blared one of its irreverent headlines, "Warming Up Film Cinderellas." The bible of the entertainment industry printed the entire code on February 19 and forecast that censorship boards throughout the country would go out of business.[71]

"Hays is a worm," screamed Quigley. By his own account, he served Hays a "declaration of war" for double-crossing him and giving *Variety* a major story that put Hays "in a position to take all the credit" for the code. Hays, of course, denied that he had leaked the code and expressed some embarrassment over the entire affair.[72] Quigley was not easily appeased. "He will cover his tracks with a million words, gestures and references to what President Whoosis said in his father's house in Indiana," but in the long run it was "all the usual Hays bunkum," he told Lord.[73] Quigley spent the next thirty years trying to reclaim credit for the code; his relationship with Hays never fully recovered.[74] Cardinal Mundelein was also taken aback by the *Variety* story, which failed to mention his role. He sulked over this lack of publicity and withdrew from any further active role in the film censorship fight until the Legion of Decency crisis in 1934.

What this incident illustrated more than anything else was the deep resentment within the studios over the restrictions that the code placed on them. It is most likely that a producer, perhaps Thalberg, leaked the code to *Variety,* which was no accidental choice for the release: The paper was decidedly anticensorship and lost no opportunity to class film reformers as narrow-minded bigots. Clearly the studios did not intend to give in to moral reformers without a fight, public and private.

Hays tried desperately to regain control. Untypically effusive, he proclaimed that the code marked "the greatest step taken by the industry in the direction of self-government," and pledged that "good taste" and a proper regard for the sensibilities of the audience "would now be the guiding principle of the movies." In the movies crime would no longer be presented in a sympathetic manner, and the sanctity of marriage would be upheld.[75]

The nation's intellectual elite greeted the announcement of the code with derision if not outright contempt. "Virtue in Cans," sneered the *Nation*. Will Hays, the "Moses of the Movies," has just descended from 469 Fifth Avenue "with no less than twenty-one commandments intended for the guidance of the Children of Hollywood." Hays and the industry were so "transparently simple-minded" in their attempt to use "virtue for commercial purposes" that it hardly deserved comment, the magazine charged. How else could one explain such provisions as "crimes against law shall never be presented in such a way as to throw sympathy with the crime." Taken literally that meant that "law and justice" are assumed to be the same, which should rule out any future films about the "Boston Tea Party." If all ministers were to be portrayed as good, "hypocrisy" as a subject has been eliminated from the movies. While the code demanded that the history, institutions, prominent people, and citizenry of other nations were to be presented fairly on the screen, the *Nation* reminded its readers that American films did not go to Russia, so the "Bolsheviks need not be considered as 'people.'" And in case of future war, "all citizens of the enemy country automatically become villains and sadists." The industry had discovered some time ago, the *Nation* observed, that the public demanded films that were "as lurid, as salacious, and as tawdry" as possible. Accordingly, the Hollywood formula was to give the audience "five reels of transgression followed by one reel of retribution." A better prescription for the movies might be to produce an occasional film which "justified adultery" or otherwise admitted that children were sometimes born out of wedlock, and perhaps such an honesty would eliminate the seeming necessity of having almost every film "deal with seduction arrested at the bedside."[76]

The *Outlook and Independent* agreed. Noting the similarity between the 1927 "Don'ts and Be Carefuls" and the 1930 version, the editors believed the movie fan would either be "indignant or weak with laughter at the notion" that the new code will be effective. The solution was not in a "moral code hypocrisy," but the hope that talking films will begin to show profits without "resorting to sleazy suggestiveness."[77]

For three decades the movies had both entertained and infuriated Americans. They were often vulgar, rude, and crude; but vulgar, rude, and crude could be entertaining, and movies enjoyed unparalleled popularity. In less than three decades this new industry had become the entertainment outlet for millions of people all over the world, speaking to people in a way no other popular entertainment form had enjoyed, penetrating all cultural, economic, political, and social barriers.

This was precisely why so many people wanted them censored. The code adopted in 1930 by the industry was an attempt by conservative forces to define permissible limits. The next four years would see a battle between Hays and the studios over whether the code was a flexible, general guideline or a literal prescription.

Notes

1 Ben Hall, *Best Remaining Seats: The Story of the Golden Age of the Movie Palace* (New York: Bramhall, 1961), p. 93.
2 Ibid., p. 41.
3 Ibid., p. 39.
4 Ibid., p. 40.
5 David Naylor, *Great American Movie Theaters* (Washington, D.C.: Preservation Press, 1987), p. 156.
6 Hall, *Best Remaining Seats,* pp. 72–90; see also Koszarski, *An Evening's Entertainment,* pp. 7–61, for a wonderful account of "Going to the Movies" in the 1920s.
7 Kevin Brownlow and John Kobal, *Hollywood: The Pioneers* (New York: Knopf, 1979), p. 90.
8 Koszarski, *Evening's Entertainment,* p. 72.
9 Naylor, *Great American Movie Theaters,* p. 247.
10 For a history of the development of the studios, see Gene Fernett, *American Film Studios.* Joel Finler's *The Hollywood Story* is a colorful treasure trove of information.
11 Anthony Slide, *The American Film Industry: A Historical Dictionary* (New York: Limelight, 1986), p. 358.
12 Ephraim Katz, *The Film Encyclopedia* (New York: G. P. Putnam, 1979), p. 1182.
13 Robert Sklar, *Movie Made America,* p. 100.
14 Alexander Walker, *The Celluloid Sacrifice: Aspects of Sex in the Movies* (New York: Hawthorn, 1967), p. 29.
15 *Photoplay* (Dec. 1919), 72–3, in Anthony Slide, *Selected Film Criticism, 1912–1920,* p. 169.
16 "*Male and Female,*" in Frank N. Magill (ed.), *Magill's Survey of Cinema: Silent Cinema II* (Englewood, N.J.: Salem Press, 1982), p. 691.
17 Ibid.
18 Lewis Jacobs, *The Rise of the American Film,* p. 400; Adolph Zukor with Dale Kramer, *The Public Is Never Wrong* (New York: G. P. Putnam, 1953), pp. 202–3.
19 Phil Koury, *Yes, Mr. DeMille* (New York: G.P. Putnam, 1959), pp. 198–9.
20 Brownlow and Kobal, *Hollywood: The Pioneers,* p. 120.
21 *New York Times,* April 11, 1921, p. 9.
22 Jacobs, *Rise of the American Film,* p. 400.
23 Feldman, *The National Board of Censorship (Review) of Motion Pictures, 1909–1922,* p. 141.
24 Jowett, *Film: The Democratic Art,* pp. 215–16.
25 Koszarski, *An Evening's Entertainment,* p. 205.
26 Ibid., p. 157.

27 Charles Feldman, *The National Board of Censorship of Motion Pictures, 1909–22,* p. 191.
28 Jowett, *Film: The Democratic Art,* p. 159.
29 Ibid. See also Terry Ramsaye, *A Million and One Nights,* pp. 482–3; Benjamin B. Hampton, *History of the American Film Industry from Its Beginnings to 1931,* p. 293; Ruth Inglis, *Freedom of the Movies,* p. 86.
30 "The Hays Office," *Fortune* 18 (Dec. 1938), pp. 68–70. See also "Czar and Elder," *New Yorker* 9 (June 10, 1933), pp. 18–21; Albert Shaw, "Will Hays: A Ten Year Record," pp. 30–1. Despite the fact that Will Hays was head of the MPPDA from 1922 until his retirement in 1945, very little has been written about Hays or his tenure as industry czar. Raymond Moley's eulogy, *The Hays Office,* unfortunately remains the main source for this mysterious but tremendously important figure in the development of movies.
31 *Boston Globe,* Oct. 29, 1922, p. 1. See also *Variety,* Nov. 3, 1922, p. 47.
32 Ibid.
33 Moley, *Hays Office,* pp. 59–63. Will Hays, *The Memoirs of Will H. Hays,* p. 431.
34 Gregory D. Black, "Hollywood Censored," p. 170.
35 House Committee on Education, Hearings, Proposed Federal Motion Picture Commission, H. Rep. 4094 and H. Rep. 6233, 69th Congress, 1st Sess., Washington, D.C., 1926.
36 William M. Halsey, *The Survival of American Innocence,* p. 107.
37 Ibid., p. 108.
38 Ibid., p. 111.
39 Ibid.
40 Ibid.
41 Martin Quigley to Father FitzGeorge Dinneen, Nov. 26, 1929, Daniel Lord Papers, Province Archives, St. Louis, Mo. (hereafter LP).
42 Daniel Lord to Patrick Scanlan, Aug. 13, 1936, box 1, Martin Quigley Papers, Georgetown University (hereafter QP).
43 Quigley to Dinneen, Nov. 26, 1929, LP.
44 Ibid.; Daniel Lord, *Played By Ear,* p. 296.
45 Joseph Breen to Father Wilfrid Parsons, box C-8, Wilfrid Parsons Papers, Georgetown University (hereafter PP).
46 Lord, *Played By Ear,* p. 289.
47 In *Queen's Work,* for example, he continually wrote serial novels with strong moral lessons. See *Clouds Over the Campus* (1940) or *Murder in the Sacristy* (1940).
48 Lord, *Played By Ear,* p. 289.
49 Ibid., p. 275.
50 Ibid.
51 Ibid., pp. 273–6, 285–91.
52 Ibid., pp. 285–91. For Lord's views on various topics, see Daniel Lord, *Fashionable Sin: A Modern Discussion of an Unpopular Subject* (1929), *Speaking of Birth Control* (1930), and *Murder in the Classroom* (1931), all serialized in *Queen's Work.*
53 Lord to Quigley, Dec. 7, 1929, LP.

54 Daniel E. Doran, "Mr. Breen Confronts the Dragons"; Walter Davenport, "Pure as the Driven Snow," *Collier's* 94 (Nov. 24, 1934), pp. 10–11, 34–7; J. P. McEvoy, "The Back of Me Hand to You," *Saturday Evening Post* 211 (Dec. 24, 1938), pp. 8–9; Timothy Higgins, "No-Man in Yes-Land."

55 Breen to Father Wilfrid Parsons, Sept. 9, 1929, and Jan. 14, 1930, PP.

56 Breen to Father Corrigan, Oct. 17, 1930, box 42, Will Hays Papers, Indiana State Historical Society, Indianapolis, Indiana (hereafter HP).

57 McEvoy, "Back of Me Hand," pp. 8–9; Elizabeth Yeaman, "The Catholic Movie Censorship," p. 233.

58 The details of the controversy are beyond the scope of this chapter. Quigley campaigned for twenty years to have the credit for the code bestowed on him. At one point he softened his feud with Breen and asked for a formal letter from the PCA director crediting him with authorship (see Breen to Quigley, June 19, 1937, box C-81, PP). The debate, which really heated up when Lord's autobiography was published shortly after his death in 1955, simply represents the deep levels of disagreement over the direction of the entire movement. In 1929, when relations were friendly, and perhaps more accurate, Quigley wrote to Lord: "I have received this morning your final draft of our code." Only a few minor changes were made in the document approved by the industry. There is little doubt that Quigley contributed many ideas that were incorporated into the code, but Lord wrote it. See Quigley to Lord, Nov. 26, 1929, LP.

59 Several drafts of the code are in the Lord Papers. The code has been printed in a variety of film books. For an excellent discussion see Jowett, *Film: The Democratic Art,* pp. 240–3, 468–72.

60 "Suggested Code to Govern the Production of Motion Pictures," n.d., LP.

61 Stephen Vaughn, "Morality and Entertainment: The Origins of the Motion Picture Production Code," *Journal of American History* 77 (June 1990), pp. 39–65. Vaughn's article is by far the most complete analysis of the adoption of the code by the industry.

62 Hays, *Memoirs,* p. 439.

63 C. C. Pettijohn to Quigley, Nov. 28, 1929, LP.

64 Hays, *Memoirs,* p. 440.

65 Halsey, The Survival of American Innocence, pp. 107–111.

66 "General Principles to Govern the Preparation of a Revised Code of Ethics for Talking Pictures," n.d., LP. The copy of the document in Lord's papers has "Irving Thalberg" written on it. Whether this means that Thalberg wrote the document or merely presented it to the meeting is unclear. There are no known records of the meeting, but it is clear that the producers had a radically different view of the movies and their role in society than did Lord.

67 Ibid.

68 Ibid.

69 Lord to Mundelein, Feb. 14, 1930, LP.

70 For accounts of the various meetings see: Quigley to Lord, Jan. 3 and 10, Feb. 17, 24, and 28, and Mar. 1, 1930, LP; Lord to Mundelein, Feb. 14, 1930, LP; Lord, *Played By Ear,* pp. 298–304; Hays, *Memoirs,* pp. 439–43.

71 *Variety,* Feb. 19, 1930, p. 9.

72 Lord to Quigley, n.d., and Quigley to Lord, Feb. 28 and Mar. 1, 1930, LP.
73 Quigley to Lord, Mar. 1, 1930, LP.
74 Quigley also had a falling out with Lord, and after 1934 was increasingly bitter about any credit Lord was given for writing the code.
75 Press release, "Motion Picture Industry Formulates New Code Made Necessary by Sound," April 1, 1930, box 42, HP.
76 "Virtue in Cans," *Nation* 130 (April 16, 1930), p. 441.
77 Ibid.; *Outlook and Independent* 54 (April 16, 1930), p. 612.

CHAPTER 3

SEX, SEX, AND MORE SEX

Silent smut had been bad. Vocal smut cried to the censors for vengeance. — Daniel Lord, *Played by Ear*

Several months after the code was adopted, Will Hays appointed Jason Joy the guardian of filmdom's morality. One of his first assignments was to judge the compatibility of Lord's moral code with Josef von Sternberg's *The Blue Angel* (1930). The film introduced Marlene Dietrich to American audiences as a sultry, if somewhat tawdry, nightclub singer, Lola, who lures a shy, retiring, respectable high-school professor (Emil Jannings) to bed, to the altar, and eventually to humiliation and ruin. Dietrich's Lola exudes raw sexual prowess every moment she is on screen. The genteel intellect of Jannings's character is no match for her. The film certainly violated the code both in specific provisions and in spirit; yet when Joy was invited by Paramount to view the film, his reaction was that it "was superb."[1] He found nothing objectionable in this serious, intelligent film about an older man falling hopelessly in love with a beautiful young woman.

This was not the case, however, for C. V. Cowan, censor for Pasadena, California. Cowan was outraged by the blatant sexuality of the film and ordered it banned from the city. When the owner of the local theater begged him to allow it to play, the censor relented and went to work with his scissors. After trimming the offensive scenes, he issued a permit for *The Blue Angel* and proudly attached a seal attesting to his approval. When *The Blue Angel* opened at the Colorado Theater, the audience greeted the censor's seal "with such a terrific razzing" that the theater was forced to remove the statement that the film had been censored.[2]

Pasadena was hardly a hotbed of California liberalism. It was, and is, a conservative community. Certainly many people would have been offended by the original film; yet those who saw it deeply resented having had it slashed to pieces by the city's censor. This episode is symbolic of the lingering debate over film censorship. Where some saw art

50

and intelligence, others saw sexuality that needed repression. Pasadena audiences wanted to judge for themselves.

Although the industry adopted Lord's code, it was not clear how Joy was to enforce it, or precisely what the code meant. Joy had no problems with *The Blue Angel*. While there is no record of Lord's reaction, it would have been closer to Cowan's view than Joy's. Whether a movie was good or bad, art or exploitation, serious or titillating, intelligent or subversive was in the eye of the beholder. Joy, given the task of enforcement, had a very small staff and no authority to force producers to accept his views; yet his office was expected to ensure that the more than 500 feature films produced yearly by the studios obeyed the code. This might have been possible if everyone in the industry – Hays, the corporate heads, the studio heads, the producers, the directors, and the writers – had been in agreement on the necessity of the code and, more important, on the boundaries of expression for the movies.

There was no such agreement. The studios believed they had every right to make films that appealed to contemporary audiences. During the debate over the code, Irving Thalberg had argued for complete freedom of expression for the industry. He lost when the code was adopted, but it was clear from the very beginning that the philosophy behind the code – that movies had to be more restrictive than other forms of entertainment because they appealed to a wider audience – put the producers and the Hays Office on a collision course with the studios and the guardians of morality.

There was no way for the creative, artistic community in Hollywood to make movies without violating one or more provisions of the code. The studios, while they might agree with some of the provisions, would resist any literal interpretation or enforcement; Lord and other faultfinders would demand nothing less than a literal interpretation. The Hollywood studio heads and producers like Louis B. Mayer and Irving Thalberg at MGM, B. P. Shulberg at Paramount, and Darryl F. Zanuck at Warner Bros. challenged the assertion of censors that films caused crime or changed basic moral values. They believed American audiences were much more receptive to films that questioned traditional views of morality. The box office proved that a bit of sex and violence brought fans into theaters.

Joy and Dr. James Wingate, who succeeded him in 1932 as Director of the Studio Relations Department (SRD), were caught in the middle. If they applied the code loosely, using perhaps a dash of common sense – recognizing that the very popularity of Hollywood was built on popular culture that, like America itself, was often vulgar, crude, direct, and disrespectful of authority and tradition – they would inevitably provoke the wrath of the censors, who demanded that movies be inoffensive. If Joy or Wingate attempted to apply the labyrinthine restrictions demanded by Lord, the studios would revolt.

The relationship between Will Hays and the studios further complicated the picture. Hays worked out of New York and had been hired to clean up the industry's image, but not necessarily to interfere with the creative side of the industry located in Hollywood. Corporate executives in New York were reluctant to force their studio heads and producers to change basic formulas that had made films the most popular form of mass entertainment ever known. In 1930 Hays did not have the authority to order a studio to remove material from a movie: He could plead, beg, or reason with industry officials, but he could not ban specific films or demand that specific scenes be removed.

The conflict between the various parties was obvious from the start. Movies, from their inception, had challenged tradition and offended people like Daniel Lord. Suddenly, given the technical ability to speak, they were being asked to restrict themselves from commenting, either seriously or humorously, on issues of social and political significance. The question for Hays, Joy, Wingate, and finally Joe Breen, who took over as censor in 1934, was this: How should the code be interpreted and enforced? A central question was whether Lord really meant what he had written. In the area of morality, for example, the code clearly and unequivocally stated that adultery should never be presented as alluring or attractive; but how else could Hollywood present it? Movies are a visual medium. The beautiful seductress was part and staple of the Hollywood product. So were Hollywood actresses. Were dour, frumpy actresses to play the role of seductress under the code? Did Lord really mean that there were no circumstances under which audiences might be sympathetic, or at least understanding, of sin? What did Lord mean when he wrote that adultery was "*never* a fit subject for a comedy," nor should bedrooms be used by movies for comedic purposes. Did that eliminate all bedroom comedies from the Hollywood repertoire? Were sexual farces banned? Were Lord's fears of what went on in bedrooms shared by the public? What did the priest mean by "lustful kissing" or "suggestive postures and gestures"? Was Lord's definition of "lustful" universally accepted? How many people, for example, would agree with the priest when he wrote that sexual passion is "subversive to the interest of society, and a peril to the human race"? Did that mean that Hollywood had to ban love stories? Did Hollywood have to confine its presentation of American mores and morals to those acceptable to a Catholic priest?

These questions, which do not seem to have been considered during the briefing conducted by Lord, were troubling to the producers. On the other hand, they knew and trusted Jason Joy, and there was no reason to expect him suddenly to demand the sterile, purified cinema the code seemed to demand. Joy was no prude, and unlike many who were demanding change, he liked films and saw his role more as an advisor to producers than as a censor of films. He wanted to guide studios away from topics that would engulf the industry in controversy. His close working relationship with the various censorship boards nationwide sensitized him to certain community restrictions; yet he also strongly believed that Hollywood had every right to make films on controversial topics. The two positions were not necessarily contradictory: Joy wanted to steer producers from overt nudity or unnecessarily titillating scenes, but believed that the industry was entitled to deal intelligently with issues such as adultery, prostitution, divorce, crime, or political corruption. The question was how these topics were presented. Films that were considered immoral by religious clergy and other guardians of morality were often seen by Joy and Wingate as good entertainment, satire, comedy, or legitimate commentary on contemporary social, moral, or political issues. Always viewing the code as a general guideline, Joy tried to mesh its general spirit with the demands of popular entertainment. It was not an easy fit, and in the long run would satisfy neither side in the continuing battle over screen content.

These complex issues were intensified by a sudden and dramatic collapse at the box office caused by the Depression. The conversion from "silent cinema" to "sound movies" had brought an explosion of curious fans to theaters. In 1926, the last year of a totally silent cinema, the industry averaged fifty million paid admissions per week. In 1930, the first year that sound dominated the screen, there were an average of ninety million weekly paid admissions – an incredible figure in a nation of 120 million people. The movies, it seemed to Hollywood, were a national obsession, and the moguls confidently predicted that Hollywood would be the one industry that would prove to be "depression proof." Americans, they gloated, needed their weekly celluloid "fix." This was, of course, pure Hollywood hokum.

Beginning in mid-1930, shortly after the adoption of the code in March, the industry began to experience a serious drop-off at the box office, and by the end of 1931 weekly attendance had plunged to some sixty million. Sixty million paid admissions per week was still an amazing figure given the severity of the Depression, and had the industry not borrowed so heavily during the late 1920s to finance expansion and its conversion to sound, it might have ridden out the economic firestorm that hit it. But the studios had indeed borrowed heavily, and their repayment schedule, along with their huge weekly payrolls, put them in financial jeopardy. The industry experienced a classic cash-flow problem. Hollywood's entire production and financial structure was built on appealing to a worldwide mass audience. The studios, with their assembly-line production techniques, huge numbers of technical personnel, and creative staffs of producers, directors, writers, and actors and actresses who were under contract, could only profit by constantly churning out films that attracted a mass, not a specialized, audience. Cash from the box office fueled the studios; any interruption in the flow of dollars augured financial crisis. The theaters, in turn, demanded a constant influx of new movies to attract customers. The Depression put Hollywood in a difficult position: Studios could not shut down because so many employees were under contract and were paid whether or not they worked, and slowing production directly affected their box-office revenue.

In a desperate move to lure back customers, the industry slashed admission prices. MGM, for example, reduced prices at its first-run theaters to fifteen cents for matinees and twenty-five cents for seats at all other performances. By 1933 the average price of admission had fallen to just twenty-three cents. Despite reduced prices, and added gimmicks such as double features, cash and merchandise giveaways, and live entertainment, box-office revenue continued to drop. While Hollywood had enjoyed a box-office revenue of $730 million in 1930, by 1932 figures had dipped to a meager $527 million. Cinema box-office charts resembled Wall Street stocks – they went down, down, and down.

"The dream factory," wrote Andrew Bergman, "was stricken along with the steel factory."[3] Studios that once had gloated over record profits turned in staggering losses in 1931 and 1932. Warner Bros., which had led the charge into sound, was typical: The studio had borrowed heavily in the late 1920s from Wall Street investment firms not only to finance conversion to sound, but also to buy control of some 700 theaters (all of which needed such conversion) to exhibit its product. When the novelty of sound brought patrons streaming to the theaters, borrowing to expand seemed to be a wise financial decision on top of a brilliant technological coup. In 1929 the studio showed a huge profit of $17 million, and 1930 registered a respectable $7 million; but by 1931 the downturn in box office resulted in an $8 million loss, and a year later, when the full impact of the Depression hit, Warners stumbled into 1933 with a staggering $14 million deficit.[4]

The moguls, fiercely independent self-made men, suddenly faced bankruptcy. No studio was immune. The most famous example was William Fox. As was mentioned in Chapter 2, Fox, the son of immigrants, had entered the entertainment industry in 1904 by buying a penny arcade. Thence he expanded into a small chain of movie theaters, branched into film production, and by the early 1920s controlled his own studio, which produced fifty-plus films a year. Fox, however, was too ambitious to settle for being a mere equal among moguls: By the mid-1920s Fox controlled more than 500 theaters nationwide, and in 1929 he borrowed $36 million to finance construction of a larger studio and build even more theaters. That same year, Fox borrowed another $50 million from Halsey, Stuart and Company to buy a controlling interest in Loew's and to invest in a British theater chain. When the crash came in October 1929, no one fell farther or faster than William Fox. Bankers moved into Fox corporate headquarters.

Similar fates reverberated throughout the industry. Paramount lost $21 million and collapsed into financial reorganization. RKO fell into receivership before moving into bankruptcy. United Artists and Columbia barely kept above water. Only MGM, under the stewardship of Louis B. Mayer and Irving Thalberg, showed a profit.

Not until 1934 did the industry begin a slow but steady recovery at the box office. That year the industry recovered to seventy million customers per week, and leveled off to average around eighty-five million paid admissions weekly in the last half of the decade.

The point is that just when Hays convinced industry leaders that a new morals code would be good for the industry, the box office collapsed. Had the economic situation remained stable, Hays and his enforcer, Jason Joy, might have been able gradually to convince the studios that less sensational movies were in the long-term economic best interests of Hollywood. Whether or not a slow change away from the most sensational films would have satisfied the more strident industry critics is doubtful.

However, when box-office revenues first sagged and then simply collapsed, and studios were forced to sell off their assets, including their theaters, to meet payroll and interest payments, the moguls were in no mood to comply with a restrictive morals code that not only prevented them from dealing with controversial moral issues such as divorce, birth control, abortion, and premarital sex, but also seemed to demand that movies avoid depicting the harsh realities of the Depression. In 1930 the human drama of unemployment, breadlines, failed relief programs, "Hoovervilles," and unresponsive and seemingly uncaring federal, state, and municipal governments was not fiction; it was a reality that faced millions of Americans every day. Reformers, however, held that while these subjects were not "immoral," neither were they fit subjects for mass entertainment. Films that dealt with racial prejudice, lynching, and the myriad of social and political issues confronting America at the beginning of 1930 were labeled "propaganda." Whatever might be defined as sordid, vulgar, obscene, sensational, or otherwise unpleasant should not be screened. Movies, they maintained, should not broach any topic that could not be discussed in "polite company."

The debate that would follow for the next four years – indeed, the whole debate over film censorship that had been raging from the beginning of the century – centered over what subjects Hollywood could make into films. It is wrong, it seems to me, to think of the debate as "moral" vs. "immoral" or to see Hollywood as only wanting to produce lurid, "immoral" movies on the one hand, and the reformers, on the other, advocating clean "moral" movies. The debate, in a broader sense, was not over excessive nudity or seminudity on the screen, or whether or not too many screen characters drank alcohol or smoked cigarettes, or exhibited low morals; rather, it was over whether or not Hollywood could make films that challenged traditional moral and political views held by a vocal, powerful minority. More precisely, could Hollywood, which refused to limit certain films to adult audiences, and whose product penetrated into every neighborhood in America, make bedroom comedies? Could Hollywood film slapstick comedy that relied on bedroom and bathroom humor? Could it make a reasonably accurate film from a classic novel such as Tolstoy's *Anna Karenina,* which dealt with seduction, corruption, and illegitimate birth? Or were the classics too sordid for American youth? What about modern works, such as Theodore Dreiser's *An American Tragedy,* Noël Coward's *Design for Living,* Ernest Hemingway's *A Farewell to Arms,* Sinclair Lewis's *Ann Vickers,* William Faulkner's *Sanctuary,* and a host of other novels and short stories read by millions of Americans? Was some literature, classic or otherwise, simply too daring, too risqué, too blunt, too sordid, too vulgar for the screen without radical transformation?

On the political side, how far could Hollywood go in depicting the unsavory elements in American industry and the American government? Could the screen dramatize the incredible rise of the American gangster and the political corruption that accompanied it? Could the seedy underside of American life be portrayed? Could the movies explore in any meaningful way racial prejudice against blacks or Jews? Could the movies examine the distribution of wealth in America, or was this topic too explosive to be screened? Was Hollywood even interested in making movies on these subjects? In Chapters 4 and 5 – the first dealing with sexual and moral themes, the second with crime and political films – these issues will be discussed.

There is little doubt that early sound films were more frank, direct, hip, and open in dealing with sexual relationships than were their silent counterparts. It is not that silent movies ignored these themes; it is just that the addition of dialogue brought another dimension to the presentation. Characters could discuss their feelings and desires, they could express feeling trapped in an unfulfilling marriage, they could be serious about sex or joke about it. When Maude Aldrich, President of the Women's Christian Temperance Union, complained to delegates at a 1929 WCTU meeting in Philadelphia that the movies glorified "the Jazz age baby type" of girl, thus causing "good men and bad men alike" to ignore the "well-mannered, old fashioned girl," she was right.[5] The movies did not trumpet the straitlaced morality of old-fashioned girls to a mass audience. Hollywood was in the business of selling sex, glamour, and entertainment – and no one did it better than Cecil B. DeMille.

When DeMille sent his script for *Madame Satan* to Joy's office, there was some concern. DeMille was a Hollywood legend who specialized in biblical spectaculars and "socioromantic triangles spiced with a liberal sprinkling of sex and neutralized by nineteenth-century Victorian moralism."[6] *Madame Satan* was typical DeMille. Reverting to the theme he had popularized in the early 1920s with such films as *Don't Change Your Husband* and *Why Change Your Wife?*, DeMille's *Madame Satan* explored the familiar theme that men were forced to have affairs because, once married, women turned into sexless matrons and mothers. In this sound version of an old theme, Bob Brooks (Reginald Denny) is a very rich, often drunk, and very definitely spoiled playboy. Angela Brooks (Kay Johnson) is the suffering wife who suspects her husband is having an affair. Her suspicions are confirmed when she sees a headline in the gossip column of the morning paper: "Bob Brooks and 'his wife' were arrested for drunken driving." The distraught Angela tells her maid that "Mrs. Brooks was home alone in her bed last night!"

What little plot there is centers around the efforts of Angela to win back the affections of her husband. When she confronts him, he openly admits he is having an affair. The fault is hers, he claims, because she has turned into a "school teacher," not a lover. The mistress, Trixie, is unconcerned when Angela demands she leave her husband alone. She even models her secret weapon: a very brief nightgown. Angela is shocked: "Why you can see right through it." "Why not," counters Trixie, "I've nothing to hide." Angela is determined to beat Trixie at her own game. Her opportunity comes when she is invited to an exotic masquerade ball. Guests are invited to come in costume "or nothing at all." Angela decides to go as Madame Satan. The script called for her costume to cover her face to conceal her identity. The rest of her was "half-nude," as were the other women. Eve was "dressed" with only a small fig leaf, the Spider Girl wore a transparent web, while another guest wore only a few strategically placed diamonds. The ball was described as a wild orgy of drinking and dancing that ended predictably with Bob and Angela reunited in a happy marriage.

DeMille, with characteristic efficiency, had managed to put almost all of the objections of the reformers into one script. The script debunked virtue, justified adultery, made light comedy of drunken debauchery, and featured beautiful women who unashamedly exposed their bodies for the pleasure of men. Adultery was just a game sophisticated rich adults played. All this was justified, however, when the hero returns to his wife and a life of respectability.

When Joy read the script he recognized that the film was nothing more than a lighthearted bedroom comedy, but he feared *Madame Satan* would encounter censorship problems. In this early period of industry censorship, Joy had no authority to force DeMille to change anything in his script. Instead he suggested that the film would encounter stiff resistance from state censors who would want, he believed, "to protect the young women of the country from the idea that they must employ 'passion and deceit' in order to live successfully with their husbands."[7]

DeMille, who had encountered more than his share of censorship problems, was willing to cooperate with Joy. The two men worked out a compromise. They agreed to put less revealing costumes on the girls at the masquerade party. Body stockings, larger fig leaves, and translucent fishnets took care of most of the nudity. Madame Satan's dress exposed a bare back but nothing else. The drinking scenes were toned down and Trixie's "nightgown" disappeared entirely, along with her conversation with Angela. In the film Mrs. Brooks tells her maid that she is going to become "Madame Satan" to show her husband how foolish he had been acting.[8]

Joy was delighted with the result of his collaboration with DeMille. When he saw the finished movie in September 1930, he told the director that he liked the film and "admired the good taste" of the production. He admitted "a few censors and some public groups" will fail to find the "moral" of the story, but assured DeMille he was "not greatly concerned." When the Ohio board of censors approved *Madame Satan* without cuts, DeMille was astounded: "Hurrah for you and the Ohio censors. Let Joy be unconfined," he proclaimed.[9]

The first three years of the 1930s were marked by a proliferation of films dealing with divorce, adultery, prostitution, and promiscuous behavior. While *Madame Satan* laughed at the frivolity of the upper crust, other films looked at the dark reality of the Depression, which forced men and women into situations where moral and ethical decisions were not always crystal clear. Marlene Dietrich in Joseph von Sternberg's *Blonde Venus* openly beds a gambler in order to raise money for an operation for her dying husband, Herbert Marshall. When he condemns her act of love for him she begins an "epic journey into squalor."[10] Yet it is clear that the "sinner" is not Dietrich but Marshall, and few people left the theater without sympathy for the plight of a selfless woman who loved her husband enough to use des-

Figure 1. Kay Johnson and Reginald Denny in *Madame Satan*. Courtesy the Museum of Modern Art / Film Stills Archive.

perate means to save his life. In *Faithless,* Tallulah Bankhead also takes to the streets to save a dying husband. "There isn't anything I won't do," she says. Her understanding landlady sympathetically adds: "The things us women do for their husbands." A similar theme was used in Clara Bow's *Call Her Savage.* In this case Bow is a rich rancher's daughter who marries poorly. Deserted by her husband and rejected by her father, Bow finds herself penniless with a sick child. Reluctantly she takes to the streets to buy medicine for the child. Her tragedy continues when she returns home to find the child dead. There was little doubt as to where audience sympathy was directed.

If women were not prostitutes, then it seemed a large portion of them lived with boyfriends or were kept as mistresses. While Joy defended DeMille, and understood that contemporary economic conditions were causing people to make difficult moral decisions, he was increasingly concerned that studios were turning to more lurid themes to lure audiences to their theaters. He told Hays that "with box-office figures down, with high pressure methods being employed back home to spur the studios on to get in a little more cash, it was inevitable that sex . . . should be seized upon" as a general theme by the studios.[11]

In 1931, Joy found himself overwhelmed by scripts he found questionable. *Private Lives,* with Norma Shearer as the deceived wife, upset Joy. He wrote to Hays that he "disliked [it] from the first, argued against it, offered a counterplot, and fought inch by inch." Yet, as he told Hays, the studio released the film without incorporating any of his ideas. *Safe in Hell* was a similar story. The studio offered no script and simply refused to accept Joy's suggestions. The film was "sordid," he told Hays. Columbia's *Love Affair* and *Shopworn* were considerably altered by Joy during the production, but even then they "were badly censored" by state boards, he later admitted to Hays.[12]

As might be expected, Joy had trouble convincing MGM's Irving Thalberg that stricter adherence to the code was necessary. The two men clashed over the MGM project *Possessed,* which starred Clark Gable and Joan Crawford. The film, based on the stage production of *The Mirage* by Edgar Selwyn, was another "kept woman" drama. Concerned that the film violated the code by showing adultery in a positive way, Joy asked Irving Thalberg to drop the project. Thalberg refused. He told the censor that in his opinion adultery, as a subject, was not a violation of the code. There would be no nudity in the film, and he reassured Joy that the relationship between the two lovers would be handled with "good taste." The only concession Thalberg was willing to grant was to insert a few lines of dialogue for Crawford indicating how important marriage was to her.[13] Clearly, Thalberg refused to accept Lord's contention that adultery should never be shown as "alluring" or given "sympathetic" treatment.

Frustrated over this lack of cooperation, Joy asked Hays to intervene in New York. While Joy could insist that the film be submitted to a jury of Hollywood producers, he and his assistant, Lamar Trotti, concluded there "was not a chance in hell" they could win. Concerned that an increase in "kept women" films would bring additional protests from the movie reformers, Hays went directly to MGM boss Nicholas Schenck in New York. He told Schenck that in his opinion there was "possible danger in the theme" of *Possessed,* and asked that Schenck discuss it with Thalberg in California. Schenck politely but firmly refused to get involved in the dispute.[14]

The film was produced as Thalberg wanted it. Crawford played a beautiful girl who is bored by her small town and depressing job in a local factory. She leaves for the excitement of New York, where she meets a dashing, successful, and unhappily married attorney played by Gable. They fall madly in love, and Gable sets Crawford up in a private love nest. All goes well until Gable is bitten by politics. He runs for governor, and when it appears that he will win, his opponent exposes his affair with Crawford. In the final scene Gable is giving an important political speech when hecklers planted in the crowd begin to ask him about his relationship with Crawford. He is clearly uncomfortable, but Crawford, who is in the audience, leaps to her feet and defends her lover. His only crime is that we fell in love. Is that such a horrible thing? she asks. She then renounces her affair. The audience turns, not on Gable to demand answers, but on the hecklers who are humiliated into silence.

Where did audience sympathy lie? In Atlanta, Georgia, it clearly fell on Crawford and Gable. Mrs. Alonzo Richardson, a member of the Atlanta Board of Review, which had passed the film over her protest, saw the film in a downtown Atlanta theater that was crawling with teenage girls. Mrs. Richardson overheard one young girl, who was one of the first but by no means the last Atlanta female to be infatuated with Clark Gable, whisper to her friend: "I would live with him too, under any conditions." Mrs. Richardson was appalled, and told Will Hays that in her view the film was a total attack on the "sanctity of marriage." Is this what Hollywood has to offer young people as a model for "standards of right living?" she demanded.[15]

Creighton Peet, film critic for the *Outlook and Independent,* shared at least some of Richardson's concerns. He noted that Joan Crawford and Norma Shearer, playing a series of "kept women," were among the "slickest, the handsomest, the best-dressed and the most scintillating" products Hollywood had to offer. To a great many of the nation's youth they "represent the apex of all modern thought in matters of morals and marriage." While Peet had no moral objection to films showing unmarried men and women living together, he did object to the "cheap, false, sleazy emotions which motivate the characters, their snide sophistication, and the shoddy, trashy story in which they are involved." He predicted that "school girls and serving maids will pay Metro hundreds of thousands of dollars to watch this film, and dream about it for days afterward." They did. That reality horrified Mrs. Richardson, shocked Father Lord, and gave Will Hays many a sleepless night.[16]

Still, *Possessed* played throughout the country without significant protest. Although Mrs. Richardson was appalled, her local censorship board approved the film, as did those in most other areas. However, it should be pointed out that this type of film caused the industry considerable trouble. Mrs. Alice Winter, who represented the Federation of Women's Clubs in Hollywood, was also troubled by films that featured beautiful women whose morals seemed questionable. She sent Hays the following assessment of 1931 films: *Men Call It Love* was "demoralizing in its treatment of marriage"; *Born to Love* and *Un-*

faithful were "unwholesome"; *Three Girls Lost* had confusing moral values, Mrs. Winter told Hays, because the "gold digger" won and the nice girl lost. Jean Harlow's *Iron Man* drew Winter's wrath because of Harlow's lack of "costumes" and "unnecessary drinking"; *Bachelor Apartments* was simply "vulgar." While all the films were produced under the code, and most conformed to its strict details, the films were objectionable to Mrs. Winter and the women's groups she represented because, as she told Hays, they "leave a bad taste in the mouth and suggest coarse and low standards of social life."[17] To put it mildly, she disapproved of the films.

Given the rising level of protests flowing into his office, in the spring of 1931 Will Hays invited Father Daniel Lord to judge the effectiveness of Joy's enforcement of his code during its first year of operation and to evaluate projects that the studios had in production for the coming year. Lord, who had been regularly receiving script evaluations from Joy and had been keeping a keen eye on the industry from St. Louis, was shocked by the changes he saw in Hollywood.[18]

In a long report to Hays, Lord assessed Joy's attempts to censor the movies. "The public has," he told Hays, "no conception of the criticism to which scripts have been subjected, the number of plays and books banned, the thousands of feet actually cut from finished film, and the hundreds of thousands of dollars which the companies willingly have expended in making changes to conform to the Code." Despite some films of which he did not approve, Lord was impressed with Joy's work and urged Hays to publicize his successes.[19] Hays, however, chose not to publicize industry self-censorship.

It was the 1932 schedule, not the 1931 products, that alarmed Lord. He was deeply disturbed, he told Hays, to find the industry so deeply concerned with social problems. A year earlier Lord believed most films could be cleaned up by removing a scene or two. Now the problems involved the whole idea behind the film. Upcoming movies expressed a "philosophy of life." In script after script he found frank discussions of "morals, divorce, free love, unborn children, relationships outside of marriage, double standards, the relationship of sex to religion, and marriage and its effects upon the freedom of women." Equally dangerous were films that featured "defiance of the laws" and youthful rebellion against authority. Lord again blamed Broadway plays and modern literature for corrupting the screen. Although at a certain level his complaints were predictable, insiders were shocked when Lord declared: "no matter how delicate or clean the treatment, these *subjects are fundamentally dangerous*" and unfit subjects for film.[20] To Lord, Mrs. Winter, Mrs. Richardson, Canon Chase, Dr. Eastman from the *Christian Century,* and other self-appointed guardians of morality, it did not matter how carefully Hollywood presented certain subjects: In their view, changing moral values simply had no place in mass entertainment.[21]

Lord's solution was for the industry to disallow all plots that involved gangsters, "degenerates, libertines, prostitutes and unfaithful wives and husbands." He wanted *"wholesome and clean"* films about American national heroes like "Lindbergh, Bobby Jones, Knute Rockne, Babe Ruth and even Al Smith." He urged Hays to lead the studios away from screenplays based on "sophisticated best-sellers" and Broadway plays – none of which he thought were "written for America." He urged Hays to press producers for more films about American heroes – business and industry leaders, sports figures – and western dramas and religious films that would promote American values. Lord went so far as to write a film script about a hockey player, which he tried, unsuccessfully, to sell to a studio. Lord blamed the downturn at the box office in 1931 on "too much sex."[22] Hollywood's producers drew exactly the opposite interpretation.

It was increasingly clear that if the movie industry was to satisfy the reformers it had to give up – not simply clean up – films that dealt with social and moral issues. This position, repeated again and again by Daniel Lord and others, is rarely understood in any analyses of the debate over movie censorship. Will Hays and Irving Thalberg understood it only too well. When pressed, the reformers would have to admit they were not asking for "good taste," but were demanding a ban of all discussion of changing moral values. For people who blamed the movies for creating social problems, no amount of self-cleansing would be satisfactory. Hays knew that but hoped, by steadily increasing the strictness of his code, to identify the antifilm lobby as a "lunatic fringe."

Lord's prescription offers a useful insight into the collective mind of movie reformers. Most reformers were inarticulate, but knew what they did not like when they saw it; Lord articulated what they only felt. While no one had any indisputable evidence that films were harmful, many people believed that films could change behavior.

Joy's was a larger view of the world. He recognized a complexity that Lord and the others did not want to see illustrated on the screen. Joy did not defend cheap exploitation films, and was willing to censor a film containing material that offended unnecessarily; but he did not reject out of hand, as Lord would have him do, films that broached controversial subjects intelligently. As we shall see in Chapter 4, Joy defended gangster films: They were moral dramas, and to ban them would be "small, narrow [and] picayunish."[23]

Nor was Joy overly concerned with the comedies like *No Man of Her Own* (1932), starring Clark Gable and Carole Lombard. The film featured Gable as a big-city gambler who runs a crooked card game and fleeces rich businessmen. When the police put pressure on him he leaves town until the heat cools off. He goes to a small town where he becomes infatuated with the local librarian (Lombard), whom he pursues relentlessly. In order to impress Lombard, Gable passes himself off as a successful big-city businessman. Lombard, desperate to escape the drudgery of small-town life, is receptive to Gable's advances – but not *that* receptive. Gable is frustrated, and when Lombard suggests a flip of the coin – heads to bed, tails to the altar – he accepts. They, of course, are married and go off to the city. Lombard, thinking her husband a businessman, insists that he get up early in the morning to go to work and be in bed at an early hour. Naturally, she soon discovers his real profession and demands that he turn to honest employment. By the final reel Gable has turned himself into the police, gone to jail to pay his debt to society, and is reunited with his wife.

All this is a setting for a lighthearted comedy based on the age-old theme of a woman regenerating a good man gone bad. Yet when Father Lord saw the film in a local St. Louis theater, he "writhed" throughout the entire performance. This film, Lord believed, contained "fundamentally bad" themes. "I stormed to my office . . . and burned up the typewriter," he later wrote. *No Man of Her Own,* he told Hays, was "filthy" and "violated every possible article" of the code by glorifying a man who was "a crook, gambler, and thoroughgoing rogue," who lives off women, throws them aside ruthlessly, and "hunts down innocence." It featured seduction and bedroom scenes "with every possible detail." The women in the film were "required to undress" and shower "evidently for the men in the audience." From the costuming in the film, Lord added sarcastically, he was beginning to believe that all the producers owned large amounts of stock in "lingerie companies." In his view, the film actively promoted sin and degraded the "routine of a small town" and the normal life of a young working woman "as tiresome, ugly, and boring." The entire picture "was a sin." Lord's reaction was made the worse because he saw the movie on a Sunday afternoon, and the audience, by his own admission, "seemed to thoroughly enjoy themselves."[24]

Hays and Joy were shocked at the vehemence of Lord's attack on the film. Yes, Gable was the hero and a cad. He used women and intended to use Lombard. But the real message was that Lombard won; she did not give in to his advances. Purity won over lust. There were a few scenes with Lombard and Dorothy Mackaill, who was part of Gable's team, dressed in lingerie. While these may have embarrassed Lord, it is doubtful if many people were offended. In the film both Lombard and Gable shower, separately, not together. The camera shows Gable to the waist, Lombard only to the shoulder – with a shower cap! Perhaps it was the portrait of small-town America – dead-end jobs, no place to go, and nothing to do – in contrast to big-city life – top hats and tails, nightclubs, champagne, and money – that upset Lord.

Few found it "filthy." *Variety* called the film "entertaining." *Film Daily* said it had everything "the ordinary picture fan looks for: drama, romance, comedy and . . . human interest." From the big city the *New York Times* called the film a view of "the lighter side of the gambling profession."[25] No one commented on showers, seductions, or silk underwear. Even *Harrison's Reports,* always quick to condemn "immoral movies," told exhibitors the movie was "fairly entertaining" with "many laughs."[26] Despite Lord's claim that films of this sort were unacceptable outside of New York and Los Angeles, trade sources reported the film "ran along nicely" in Lincoln, Nebraska; did well in St. Louis, where it was reported that "Gable's getting them as usual"; and brought in over $38,000 in one week in Chicago, where seats ranged from thirty-five to seventy-five cents.[27] The film brought much-needed cash into the Hollywood coffers, and few reasonable people would expect the industry to abandon this type of film.

Joy, who tried to balance what he believed was the spirit of the code with the practical needs of the producers, often found he could please neither side. Fans expected Gable and Lombard to be lovers: That's why they went to the movies. They also went to see spectacle, at which no one was better than Lord's old friend Cecil B. DeMille. In 1923 he had released *The Ten Commandments* and followed with *The King of Kings* (1927), on which Lord had served as a technical advisor. Both were huge hits. After a period of producing as an independent, DeMille returned to Paramount. He selected a topic he knew would be a box-office smash: the pagans versus the Christians, in which he could combine "sex, nudity, arson, homosexuality, lesbianism, mass murder, and orgies."[28] DeMille's spectacular production of *Sign of the Cross* (1932) set off another debate over what was "moral" or "immoral" entertainment.

Sign of the Cross was based on a play by Wilson Barrett and adapted for the screen by Waldemar Young and Sidney Buchanan. The cast featured Claudette Colbert as the sexy, sultry Empress Poppaea, wife of Nero, who wanted to bed Marcus Superbus, prefect of Rome; Charles Laughton as Nero, who is more excited by burning Rome and murdering Christians than with his wife's casual affairs; Fredric March as Marcus Superbus, who refuses to bed the Empress, not out of loyalty to his Emperor, but because he is infatuated with a pious Christian virgin, Mercia, played by Elissa Landi. The film featured a wild Roman orgy highlighted by a lesbian dance of "temptation," plus the slaughter of hundreds of gladiators and helpless Christians for the entertainment of blood-thirsty Romans. The film was so violent that women fainted at its New York premiere. This combination of spectacle, sex, and sadism, however, was a box-office bonanza for De-Mille and Paramount. Predictably, it brought screams of wrath and outrage from pulpits nationwide.

DeMille was at his very best in graphically illustrating the splendor and decadence of Rome. With a budget of $650,000 he hired four thousand extras and built a huge miniature set of Rome, which he burned to the ground. He constructed a massive amphitheater for the gladiators, emptied local zoos of wild animals including lions, tigers, and elephants to devour and trample Christians, and scoured Hollywood for giants, dwarfs, and every kind of strange-looking "human freak" he could find. Happily, Los Angeles had a ready supply.

No DeMille film was ever complete without a beautiful woman taking a bath. *Sign of the Cross* did not disappoint. DeMille spent considerable time and energy in constructing a huge bath based on Roman models. He filled it with real milk and for four days shot scenes of Colbert, surrounded by a bevy of beautiful handmaids, drifting about in this luxurious setting. Unfortunately for Colbert and the crew, the heat from the lights turned the milk into cheese; but Colbert was a trouper and made her smelly, gooey bath seem "eye-openingly erotic."[29]

The costuming, designed by Mitchell Leisen, was both beautiful and erotic, plain and modest. DeMille and Leisen used fashion to illustrate the difference between pagan and Christian values. Father Lord, who worked with DeMille on *The King of Kings,* feared as much. When he got word of the project, he wrote to DeMille to beg him not to "make your pagans attractive warm-blooded, alive human beings and your Christians plaster saints."[30] DeMille ignored him. Claudette Colbert and the Imperial women of Rome were strikingly beautiful. They were not shy about wearing flimsy gowns, backless and cut to the waist in the front, slit to the thigh on each leg. Whenever they moved the dresses gaped openly, the camera lingering lovingly over their exposed flesh. In contrast, Christian women wore plain homespun that covered them from neck to toe. As DeMille explained it, this costuming symbolized "good vs. evil." His critics charged that it was pure hypocrisy designed to show as much female flesh as possible.

Good sex and killing Christians seemed to drive daily life in Rome. The plot, such as it was, went something like this: Claudette Colbert wants to seduce Marcus. She flirts and throws herself at him at every opportunity. Marcus, a brave warrior and an even better lover, rejects her advances and lusts instead after a beautiful young Christian virgin, Mercia. He is distraught when she refuses him. Growing up in pagan

Figure 2. Fredric March and Claudette Colbert in Cecil B. DeMille's *The Sign of the Cross*. Courtesy the Museum of Modern Art / Film Stills Archive.

Rome he has never before been rejected by any woman. His male ego is crushed until he discovers that it is her religion that gives Mercia the strength to resist him. To tempt her to reject her beliefs and to lure her to his bed, Marcus hosts an orgy; but even this setting of wild debauchery (which DeMille constructed with loving detail) with a host of half-dressed drunken men and women falling all over each other, fails to tempt Mercia. In a final desperate attempt to break her will, Marcus recruits Ancaria, the most beautiful lesbian in Rome, played by Joyzelle Joyner, to seduce her by dancing her infamous dance of the "naked moon." Mercia is unmoved by the wild gyrations of the beautiful seductress. Her faith allows her to remain pure.

Marcus now recognizes the tremendous strength of this new religion. His original lust for Mercia's body is now transformed into respect and love. When he discovers that hundreds of Christians, including Mercia, are to be used as bait for a massive gladiator battle, he begs Nero to spare her. Nero is about to grant his wish, when Poppaea, see-

Hollywood Censored **68**

ing one last chance at Marcus, convinces her husband to deny the request. Off to the arena where the slaughter has begun: In a frenzy of blood the crowd cheers madly as lions devour and elephants trample Christians. Beautiful Amazon women butcher pygmies. A nearly naked Christian girl is chained to a post – a toy for a huge gorilla.

The Empress Poppaea is delighted by this entertainment. She is wildly excited because she has plotted to have Mercia brought into an empty arena to be the last Christian sacrificed. This, she believes, will snap Marcus out of his love for the girl and throw him into her arms. But Marcus, unknown to Poppaea, has decided to join his love in death. The final scene has the young girl and the prefect of Rome walk hand in hand into the arena. Poppaea is crushed. Christianity, virtue, morality, and humility have again triumphed over the temptations of the flesh. So argued DeMille.

Variety told readers that the film contained some of the "boldest censor-bait ever attempted" and correctly predicted that it would "make the church element dizzy trying to figure which way to turn."[31] "Nauseating," screamed *Commonweal*. "Intolerable," said Father Lord.[32] "Highly offensive," said a representative of B'nai B'rith, and a prominent Protestant minister in New York found the film "repellent and nauseating" as well as "cheap ... disgusting, suggestive and unclean." Protests from the Knights of St. John of Lorain, Ohio, the Daughters of Isabella from Owensboro, Kentucky, and other religious and women's organizations poured into Paramount.[33] Martin Quigley condemned the film in his *Motion Picture Herald*.[34] The Jesuit *America* labeled the dance of the "naked moon" the "most unpleasant bit of footage ever passed by the Hollywood censors."[35] The *Southern Messenger* called on Catholics to boycott the film, which it said was nothing more than "downright filth."[36] Many Catholic clerics around the country agreed with Cleveland Bishop Joseph Schrembs, who chose a New Year's Eve mass to attack the film as a "damnable hypocrisy."[37]

Surprisingly, given the level of reaction, the script caused no such outrage when it was sent to Joy for his inspection. The Hollywood censor made no objections to the bathing scenes, the orgy, the lesbian dance, or the wholesale slaughter of Christians. He did, however, express some concern about the shot "of the naked girl" tied to the pedestal about to be ravished by a gorilla.[38] In applying the code, Joy believed that the overall message of the film was moral; he therefore allowed DeMille some leeway in illustrating the temptations that were used to lure Christians away from their faith. For example, he told Paramount that he did not object to the "kootch" dance at the orgy because he interpreted it as an attempt to "tempt" the Christian girl and it failed; however, he warned the studio that state censor boards might not agree with him.[39] Hays was informed that although the film was bound to be controversial, DeMille "has refrained . . . from running wild with Roman orgies."[40]

DeMille wrote in his autobiography that Will Hays called him during the controversy over the dance of the "naked moon." Hays said, according to DeMille, that he was with Martin Quigley and they wanted to know what he was going to do about the scene. "Will," DeMille said, "listen carefully to my words because you may want to quote them. Not a damn thing."[41]

Perhaps he said it, perhaps he didn't. With Paramount officials DeMille was more circumspect. He told George J. Schaefer he was opposed to any cuts. The people who wanted cuts were the same people, he reminded Schaeffer, who had opposed *The Ten Commandments* and *The King of Kings*. "Are there many people," he asked, "who will stay away from a theater today because of a sensational dance?" Yet DeMille was a practical businessman above all else. He gave Schaeffer permission to make any cuts he wanted to if, in his opinion, the original footage would "hurt box-office value."[42]

Nor was opinion universally against DeMille and Paramount. Just as the public debated the celluloid gangsters, so too did they hold differing views on the moral lessons to be learned from seeing the vivid debauchery of screen pagans. Concerned about Catholic opinion, Paramount actively sought religious reaction to *Sign of the Cross*. Father Louis Emmerth of Marist College in upstate New York endorsed the film, which he saw four times! Father Joseph Dufort of Ironwood, Michigan, took his altar boys to see the film because he found it "full of religious instruction." Father McGabe in Portland, Oregon, urged all his parishioners to see the film. The film was also endorsed for Catholics by the archdiocese of New Orleans.[43]

State censorship boards found little to protest. Kansas and Pennsylvania passed the film with no cuts, and it suffered only minor changes (the milk-bath scene and the gorilla's girl snipped) in the other states. Mordaunt Hall of the *New York Times* praised the film as a "striking pictorial spectacle."[44] *Harrison's Reports,* which usually lashed out at "immoral" films, told exhibitors that no one "could afford to overlook" *Sign of the Cross:* The orgies were handled "delicately," and *HR* believed that few in the audience would understand the "lesbian dance." The violence, the review continued, "like the violence in *I Am a Fugitive from a Chain Gang, Frankenstein* and *Dracula,*" should "not prove detrimental to the box-office."[45] Nor did it. Despite being released during the depths of the Depression in 1932, fans paid a "road show" price of $1.50 to see *Sign of the Cross*. During its general release the film played to capacity houses over a bank holiday, and theaters were forced to accept IOUs from customers who could not get money from their bank accounts. According to reports every one was redeemed at full value. *Sign of the Cross* put millions of dollars into Paramount coffers at a time when the studio was facing bankruptcy. DeMille reestablished his box-office pull with his biblical spectacle.

By the summer of 1932 Joy had worked for five years with producers and state censorship boards. Frustrated over his no-win position, he told Hays he was resigning to accept an executive position with Fox but would remain in office until Hays could name a successor.[46]

Joy's resignation opened Hays to increased criticism that the industry was not enforcing its own code. Quigley warned Hays, in a stinging editorial in the *Motion Picture Herald,* that the current situation was a "Portent of Danger." The industry would lose its position of purveyor of mass entertainment if it continued to offer a product "that is repugnant to American ideals."[47] When Hays responded by asking Quigley for his recommendations for a replacement, the publisher blasted him again for refusing to enforce the code. "It is my belief," Quigley wrote, "that the whole Code scheme has become a wash-out" and the "responsibility . . . may be laid directly at your door." The publisher threatened Hays that if he did not force producers to take the code seriously, he would be held "accountable by millions of the public and by thousands of persons important in various religious, social and educational activities."[48]

Joe Breen, who was doing public relations work for Hays in Los Angeles and occasionally helping Joy, agreed. He complained to Father Wilfrid Parsons that "nobody out here cares a damn for the Code or any of its provisions." Venting his frustration, Breen claimed Hays sold them all "a first class bill of goods when he put the Code over on us." But Breen also blamed the Jews in Hollywood for the problem. He conceded that Hays sincerely believed "these lousy Jews out here will abide by the Code's provisions but if he did he should be censured for his lack of proper knowledge of the breed." Breen charged that Jews don't even know what the word morality means:

They are simply a rotten bunch of vile people with no respect for anything beyond the making of money. . . . Here [in Hollywood] we have Paganism rampant and in its most virulent form. Drunkenness and debauchery are commonplace. Sexual perversion is rampant . . . any number of our directors and stars are perverts. . . . These Jews seem to think of nothing but money making and sexual indulgence. The vilest kind of sin is a common indulgence hereabouts and the men and women who engage in this sort of business are the men and women who decide what the film fare of the nation is to be. They and they alone make the decision. Ninety-five per cent of these folks are Jews of an Eastern European lineage. They are, probably, the scum of the earth.[49]

The vehemence of these comments to a Catholic priest is shocking; yet the undercurrent of anti-Semitism and the charge that Jews were responsible for "immoral" movies was a prominent feature of the antimovie campaign. Canon Chase belabored the "Jewish issue" in attacks on the industry. Breen sprinkled his letters with anti-Semitic comments, and available records show no rebuke from any of his correspondents. This is not to say they shared his views; it simply confirms that they did not feel strongly enough to protest. (Anti-Semitism as a factor in the demand for movie censorship is developed more fully in Chapter 6.)

Hays's first choice for a replacement for Joy was Carl Milliken, his executive assistant. Milliken begged off, telling Hays his temperament "would be toward too great a combativeness and not enough yielding in questions of interpretation . . . which might be especially serious in the next few months when economic necessity is inevitably going to tempt producers towards sensational easy money pictures." More likely, Milliken realized the no-win nature of the position. He suggested that Hays allow Joy's assistants, Lamar Trotti and Joe Breen, to run the office, and that Hays become more involved in day-to-day operations.[50]

Hays finally solved the problem when he announced that Dr. James Wingate, chief censor for the State Education Department in New York, had accepted the post. A graduate of Union College, Wingate had been involved with movie censorship in New York since 1927. He was a strong opponent of gangster films, but had worked effectively with the MPPDA in getting films approved for the lucrative New York market. Hays was confident that Wingate's experience as a state censor would enable him to work effectively with the studios.

In an ominous sign for Hays and the movie industry, Catholic discontent with Hollywood began to surface across the country. While individual Catholics like Lord and Quigley had tried to work with Hays, the hierarchy of the church had remained aloof; this situation began to change during 1932–3. The national Knights of Columbus publication *Columbia* asked: "Does anyone know what became of the code?"[51] *Catholic Action* told readers the movies continued to be as "subversive of morals and destructive of Christian principles" as they had ever been.[52] The National Council of Catholic Men protested Hollywood's "open appeal to sexual lust" and its ridicule of "all the sanctities that have made father and mother, home and children, modesty, personal integrity, discipline, and probity, words of highest honor among us."[53] The Catholic Daughters of America condemned movies as evil.[54] *Ave Maria* asked Catholics to voice disapproval by boycotting immoral films.[55]

Wingate's appointment brought a direct response from *America,* the influential Jesuit publication edited by Father Wilfrid Parsons. In

"An Open Letter to Dr. Wingate," *America* demanded Wingate improve the morals of the movies. "Four or five years ago the films exalted the virgin; today they glorify the wanton." *Possessed* was cited as an example of the kind of film *America* believed corrupted American morals. While there was not one objectionable line or scene in the movie, the entire plot was condemned because the "guilty union" between Gable and Crawford was presented as something "tender, deep, beautiful, magnificently loyal" and filled with "complete happiness." The result was that the audience "was led to sympathize with the sinners and to approve their love completely." *America* concluded their plea to Wingate by hoping that 1933 would bring about a marked change in the content of films. Within less than a year the Jesuit magazine would call for Wingate's removal and the Catholic church would be headlong into its Legion of Decency campaign, which would force Hollywood to accept strict censorship of its product.[56] (This campaign is the subject of Chapter 6.)

Wingate, who took over responsibility for interpreting the code in late October 1932, could not have assumed his duties at a more difficult time. He had no more than settled into his office when Paramount Studios inquired about the possibility of making a film based on Mae West's stage play *Diamond Lil.*

In 1933 Mae West emerged in Hollywood as the woman who best personified the sexual revolution of the past decade. West was kept by no man, needed no nudity to suggest sexuality, and both delighted and infuriated moviegoers with the way she flouted tradition. If any single performer in the United States embodied what film reformers and the code did not want in the movies, it was Mae West. Queen of the double entendre, West had been delighting and shocking theater audiences for years with her ribald humor. After a long career in vaudeville, West wrote and starred in *Sex,* which opened on Broadway in 1926. Even though local newspapers refused to take advertising for the production, it ran for 375 performances before New York officials suddenly concluded the play was "corrupting the morals of youths." West was arrested, fined $500, and sentenced to ten days in prison. Undeterred by what she considered unhealthy attitudes toward sex, she wrote *The Drag,* a serious look at homosexuality, which enjoyed a successful run in New Jersey but was banned from Broadway.[57]

While *Sex* and *The Drag* brought West notoriety, it was her 1928 rendition of a turn-of-the-century bawdy-house entertainer in *Diamond Lil* that brought her the respect and admiration of New York audiences and critics alike. Starring as a Bowery Jezebel, West is the mistress of a New York hoodlum whose nightclub is a front for a lucrative "white slavery" racket. In the play she accidently kills a female member of the gang, happily seduces a Salvation Army captain who turns out to be an "undercover" policeman, and lives happily ever after with him! West delighted audiences with her aggressively sexual musical numbers, "Frankie and Johnny," "Easy Rider," and "A Guy What Takes His Time." One critic judged the play itself as "largely bosh," yet sensed that West was as "alive on stage as nobody is in life, she shines, she astonishes – shocks, if you like – engages and puzzles you." *Diamond Lil,* wrote the *New Republic,* was "popular theater's joke on our theater of culture."[58]

This was both West's strength and her downfall. She poked fun at society, especially at those people who wanted to repress all discussion of sexuality. By becoming the aggressor, the female who initiated seductions, she challenged the traditional view of women as passive, uninterested sex partners. The role West carved out for herself was that of a woman who enjoys sex, who controls men not by her body but by her brain: She simply outsmarts them. Women loved it, and they loved her. Her biting humor made relationships between men and women appear fun and funny, with the men seeming foolish and weak. In a culture that developed and perfected the image of the "dizzy blonde," Mae West was a popular culture counterforce who delighted most of the public and enraged reformers. She was not responsible, as some historians have suggested, for the creation of the Production Code Administration of Joseph Breen or the Catholic Legion of Decency; but she did, like DeMille, help define the limits of cinematic expression.

An entertainer as popular and as controversial as West had a natural attraction for the movie industry. Her talents, however, had not easily transferred to the screen in the era of silent films. It was the introduction of sound that made Mae West attractive to Hollywood. In 1930 Paramount asked the Hays Office for permission to bring West and her production of *Diamond Lil* to the screen. The studio was informed the Hays Office had banned the play because "of the vulgar dramatic situations and the highly censurable dialogue," which would result in an "unacceptable" film.[59]

With the box office booming in 1930, the studio had accepted Hays's ruling; but by 1932 the situation had changed radically.[60] Given the economic emergency, a potential box-office personality like Mae West could not be ignored. Paramount faced payments on a debt in excess of $100 million, and for 1932 reported a loss of $21 million. The studio was desperate for more hits like DeMille's *Sign of the Cross.* Despite its stable of stars, which included Marlene Dietrich, Carole Lombard, Claudette Colbert, Kay Francis, George Raft, Gary Cooper, Fredric March, and Cary Grant, Paramount films lagged at the box office. The financial crisis also brought internal reorganization: Production head B. P. Schulberg was fired; Jesse Lasky, one of the industry founders, was eased into retirement; and Emanuel Cohen was brought in to spice up Paramount's product.[61]

Neither Cohen nor West had much respect for Haysian formulas. One of Cohen's first decisions as production head was to bring Mae West to Hollywood. When she got off the train in Los Angeles she told somewhat startled reporters: "I'm not a little girl from a little town makin' good in a big town. I'm a big girl from a big town makin' good in a little town." Her screen debut was in a George Raft vehicle, *Night After Night* (1932). Mae was originally set for a small part and fourth billing, but no one could upstage her. She slithered through the film in her unforgettable style of hip-swinging, wisecracking humor and, as Raft admitted, "She stole everything but the camera." Encouraged by the enthusiastic reception of West and even more by the box-office returns, Cohen offered her $100,000 to make another film. She accepted, but insisted that the vehicle be *Diamond Lil*. West had battled censorship in New York and was not afraid of Hollywood. She had done something for theater that had never crossed the minds of even the most liberal of the Hollywood moguls – she had gone to jail.[62]

Technically, Paramount could not produce a film version of *Diamond Lil* as long as the property remained on the MPPDA forbidden list; but 1932 was a desperate time for millions of people, among them Paramount executives, who proceeded with production plans without clearance from Hays or his Los Angeles censors. Even as Hays reminded Adolph Zukor that the studio was in violation of MPPDA guidelines, Paramount began production of the script written by West and John Bright on November 21, 1932. Wingate refused to read scripts submitted by Paramount until the studio had MPPDA clearance; Paramount refused to request any and went forward with the production. This logjam was finally broken when at a special board meeting the Hays Office formally approved of *Diamond Lil* as long as that title was not used, West not depicted as a "kept woman," the young missionary not identified as a member of the Salvation Army, and the "white slavery" angle avoided.[63] Wingate worked with the studio during production to soften the film by eliminating references to Lady Lou's (Mae West) past, substituting counterfeiting for white slavery and advising that the film be played as a "comedy" rather than a serious drama. Paramount and West certainly had no problem with the last request.

She Done Him Wrong was finished in only eighteen shooting days at a cost of $200,000 – over half of which went to West. The film was made so quickly that Wingate had little opportunity to react to the script or to the lyrics of the various songs that West would use to highlight her performance. He did insist that a few lines be snipped from

"A Guy What Takes His Time."[64] However, as *Variety* noted, specific lyrics made little difference to West because she could not sing a "lullaby without making it sexy."[65]

Wingate discovered this when he attended the premiere in February 1933. The setting was the "bawdy Bowery of the Gay Nineties." West is the beautiful Lady Lou, a singer at Gus Jordan's (Noah Berry, Sr.) saloon. Lou is technically Jordan's girl, but everyone who comes into contact with her instantly falls in love with her. Jordan, unbeknownst to Lou, is running an illegal racket out of his saloon. While it is never stated, it is obvious that Jordan and the Russian Rita (Rafaella Ottiano) and her lover Serge Stanieff (Gilbert Roland) are into white slavery in addition to the more acceptable cinema crime of counterfeiting. When a young girl tries to commit suicide on the premises, Lou innocently helps her and turns her over to Rita, who leeringly asks the poor girl if she has ever heard of "the Barbary Coast." While Rita's intent is clear to the audience, the scene also establishes that Lou has no knowledge of the criminal activities taking place in the saloon. She is just a torch singer who packs the bar every night.

And her songs are red hot: To an audience of men she grinds out "A Guy What Takes His Time," whose lyrics, like those of the Pointer Sisters' hit "Slow Hands," were clear, with West's rendition making the obvious more so. Mae, as always, plays the male libido and ego for a sucker: While she sings, a group of beautiful young women work the room as pickpockets. The men suspect nothing as Mae groans:

A guy what takes his time
I'll go for any time.
A hasty job really spoils the master's touch
I don't like a big commotion.
I'm a demon for slow motion or such
Why should I deny
That I would die
To know a guy what takes his time?
There isn't any fun
In gettin' somethin' done
If you're rushed when you have to make the grade.
I can spot an amateur
Appreciate a connoisseur at his trade
Who would qualify
No alibi
To be a guy what takes his time.

While Mae is busy singing, the rumor on the street is that a new supercop is in town: "The Hawk," who is after Jordan and his gang. The Hawk is disguised as a young missionary, Captain Cummings (Cary Grant), who runs a city (*not* a Salvation Army) mission next door to Jordan's saloon. Grant is the perfect straight man for the aggressive West. When she meets him she coos: "Why don't ya come up and see me sometime. I'm home every evening." When he feigns disinterest, West counters, "You can be had." Later, Cummings sets her up for another zinger: When he asks her if she's ever met a man who could make her happy, West retorts, "Sure, lots of times." This is no shy, innocent coquette.

The thin plot advances quickly. Captain Cummings is clearly smitten by Lou. When she visits her old boyfriend in jail, it is like old home week: Every bird in the joint knows Lou. She is the type of woman who gets around. Another love angle develops when Serge Stanieff, Rita's lover, announces his love for Lou by giving her some of Rita's jewelry. Rita is furious when she finds out, and pulls a knife on Lou. The two women fight, and Rita is killed. When Lou and her bodyguard dispose of the corpse, she says (presumably to the audience): "I'm doing a job that I never did before." This establishes the killing as accidental, not cold-blooded murder.

The grand finale comes when the police take testimony from some of the girls who have been victims of Jordan and the now "late" Russian Rita. The Hawk sweeps down on the bar, rounds up the gang, and approaches Lou with handcuffs. "Are those absolutely necessary?" she asks. "You know, I wasn't born with them." Shaking his head Cummings replies, "No. A lot of men would have been safer if you had." Smiling Lady Lou, ever with the upper hand, retorts: "I don't know. Hands ain't everything." As the two ride off in a carriage, perhaps to jail, perhaps to a local hotel, the Hawk presents Lou with a diamond ring. She accepts, and he says, "You're going to be my prisoner and I'm going to be your jailer for a long, long, time. You bad girl." Naturally, the last line belongs to Lou. She smiles archly and adds: "You'll find out."

"Nothing much changed except the title, but don't tell that to Will Hays," snickered *Variety*.[66] Censor Wingate was troubled. He knew, of course, the pressure Paramount had put on Hays, and he was well aware of Paramount's financial problems. Still, he warned the studio that the film "is liable to be displeasing to . . . censor boards and others in public positions." The heroine "is portrayed as committing, first homicide, and then conniving to conceal the body." Both crimes go unpunished, which violated the code. He also warned the studio that they should be prepared to remove the song "A Guy What Takes His Time."[67] He wired Hays that he was not convinced "this type of picture will do the industry any good," but he also admitted that when he saw the film at a Los Angeles theater the audience howled with delight throughout the film and seemed thoroughly to enjoy Mae West.[68]

Figure 3. Cary Grant and Mae West in *She Done Him Wrong.* Courtesy the Museum of Modern Art / Film Stills Archive.

Wingate was right on both counts: Censorship boards struck with enraged fury, and fans besieged box offices around the world. When his ex-colleagues at the New York censorship board heard West sing "A Guy What Takes His Time," they shot a telegram to their old friend: "Have you analyzed the words of the song?" Wingate sheepishly replied that he had warned Paramount.[69] When New York, Ohio, Maryland, Massachusetts, and Pennsylvania removed the song from prints playing in those states, Hays leaped into the fray. He worked privately with Paramount's Adoph Zukor in New York to trim the song "to an entrance by Mae West, one opening and closing verse," which Hays hoped would take out most of the sting.[70] Despite that cleansing, fans in Ohio and Pennsylvania also missed most of the one-liners dished out by West: The censors had cut them all. The film was banned in Atlanta and rejected by Australia, Austria, and Finland.[71]

The real story of West and *She Done Him Wrong* lies not in its having a few lines snipped here and there, nor its being banned in some areas, but in its astonishing popularity. West instantly became a cult figure on an international scale. While ministers, women's clubs, and state and local censors condemned her as immoral, New York City policemen, who had arrested West for her theater performances, were called out to control crowds trying to buy tickets for the film. The film earned more than $2 million in less than three months; within six it had chalked up over 6,000 showings and broken box-office records everywhere. So desperate were people to see West that *Night After Night* enjoyed over 5,000 rebookings after its original run. Her appeal was not just national, but international, universal. Moviegoers in London and Paris mobbed the theaters for tickets, and she was as popular in the small towns of America as she was in the international centers of Europe. From Kasson, Minnesota, a theater owner reported the film "pleased most everyone," calling it his best box-office draw in a year. From Adair, Iowa, the theater owner noted that when West deadpanned "come up and see me sometime" and "you can be had," she "brought the house down." It makes one "purr," wrote *Rob Wagner's Scripts*.[72] Although it had been banned in Atlanta, Frank Daniel, film critic of the *Atlanta Journal,* "highly recommended" the film and wrote a scathing comment on the censorship board, which he said had "abandoned dignity to become interfering, vindictive, and a petty nuisance."[73] Most Atlantans agreed: A small theater just outside the city limits did a land-office business with *She Done Him Wrong.* By the summer of 1933 West had broken all the box-office records set by Garbo and Dietrich. Both stars, vacationing in Europe, scurried back to Hollywood.[74]

Predictably, after seeing *She Done Him Wrong,* Father Lord penned another protest to Hays complaining that the film was a total violation of his code. Hays was sympathetic and admitted that the film "illustrates virtually every one of our problems." He recounted his unsuccessful attempts to keep *Diamond Lil* off the screen, but asked Lord to understand that Paramount's economic problems were so severe that the studio was allowed to gamble on West. Hays also reminded Lord that reviewers had almost "unanimously hailed" the film as "a splendid comedy" and, more important, it was "breaking box-office records."[75]

West was too hot to be roped in by any code in 1933. The studio rushed another West vehicle, *I'm No Angel,* into production to satisfy her millions of fans. Wingate hurried through the script, pronounced that it "contained no particularly objectionable sex scenes," and asked for no changes. He had little contact with the studio during production and, except for a few modifications in song lyrics, the film was not altered. When Wingate was invited to see the completed product, he informed Paramount officials that he "enjoyed the picture as a piece of entertainment" and believed that it was within the code. He told

Hays the studio should "be congratulated" because there was nothing "questionable" in the entire film.[76] Playing on her bad-girl image, *I'm No Angel* – which everyone already knew about West – hit American screens in the fall of 1933.

The setting this time was the big top. West is a carnival performer, Tira, a midway dancer/entertainer in Big Bill Barton's sleazy little traveling sideshow. As a sideline she and her john set up and rob male suckers who cannot resist Tira's charms; but her luck runs out when one of the suckers, after being bashed on the head, recovers and runs to the police. Now at the mercy of her boss (Edward Arnold), who helps her escape the police, Tira agrees to become a lion tamer for the circus. They open in New York, and when Tira steps into the cage and cracks her whip, all of New York goes wild. As usual, men battle for her favors, and even the lions are no match for her. When she steps into the cage the wild beasts act just like the human ones: They jump through hoops upon command.

The romantic angle is provided by Jack Clayton (Cary Grant), a young, debonair millionaire who falls in love with Tira. The double entendres fly hot and heavy: "When I'm good, I'm very good. But, when I'm bad, I'm better," she brags. When Tira is accused of "knowing" lots of men, she does not protest the implication, but rather retorts, "It's not the men in my life, but the life in my men." And so on. It was pure West, uncensored, raw by the standards of the times, but always good, if not totally clean, fun. Audiences loved it. Some critics praised it, others panned it. Mordaunt Hall, writing in the *New York Times,* praised West as a "remarkable wit" and the film as "rapid fire entertainment, with shameless but thoroughly contagious humor." Martin Quigley must have blanched when writers for his *Motion Picture Herald* advised theater owners to "blaze the star's name all over the marquee." *Variety* panned the plot but advised theater owners to get ready for the onslaught of devoted fans. The New Orleans *Tribune* saw West as a performer who "has caught the trick of satirizing the flamboyant creatures she impersonates. That imperils the morals of nobody but the humorless." The *New Republic* gushed that West was the best performer in Hollywood next to Charlie Chaplin. "Her time sense is unequaled," wrote Stark Young. Was she obscene, he asked? No, he concluded, because her power was her wit, not the "filthy egotism" that marked too many American films. He noted that audiences began to laugh in expectation of West's one-liners. Fans saw her films time and time again, and you could see the delight in filmgoers' faces as they anticipated a wisecrack from West. In the final analysis, Young wrote, "to think of *I'm No Angel* makes you smile."[77]

It did not bring smiles to the lips of the clergy in Haverhill, Massachusetts. They condemned the film as "demoralizing, disgusting, suggestive and indecent." Hogwash, countered the Haverhill mayor and city council when they killed a motion from the ministers to have the movie banned. The municipal officials agreed with Wingate, and found *I'm No Angel* contained nothing "harmful or objectionable." In nearby Plymouth, the Reverend Paul G. Macy branded the film the lowest he had ever seen. The *Christian of Kansas City,* however, proved that not all Christians were without a sense of humor, nor all midwesterners Bible-thumping fundamentalists. An article by Jack Moffitt commented on the West phenomenon:

Women are more tickled at Mae West than men are, because it is the picture of woman triumphant, ruthlessly and unscrupulously triumphant, over poor, blundering simple-minded men. . . . And perfectly respectable matrons, who would rebel at any other kind of vampire, accept the vulgar, funny, and happy type represented by Mae West, are all of them delighted by her. Very few of these respectable matrons would pursue her tactics, but they like to see it done.[78]

By the end of 1933 more than forty-six million movie fans – including, no doubt, a great many of the matrons Jack Moffitt described, had seen the two films, and West was ranked eighth in 1933 as a Hollywood box-office attraction. Her massive popularity brought millions of needed dollars into Paramount coffers. No one was more appreciative than Paramount President Adolph Zukor: "I must pay tribute to another durable trouper, Mae West, for the powerful lift she gave us out of the depression mire."

Yet within seven months, both *She Done Him Wrong* and *I'm No Angel* would be removed from circulation. Despite her tremendous popularity, or perhaps because of it, West became one of the central casualties in the effort to force the studios to a strict adherence to the code.[79]

Paramount's success with West could not be ignored by the other studios. When Harry Warner heard that West had been cleared by Hays and that MGM was bringing *The Painted Veil* to the screen, he told Hays, "I want to know how to run our business in the future" and threatened to bring more daring topics to the screen.[80] Within a few weeks Warner Bros. began *Baby Face.* MGM studio executive Sidney Kent was more direct: He told Hays that *She Done Him Wrong* was the "worst picture I have seen" and he could not "understand how your people on the Coast could let this get by." He predicted it would open up the floodgates in Hollywood.[81] Paramount, which needed no encouragement, bought the screen rights to William Faulkner's *Sanctuary,* a story of rape, murder, and perversion, and Ernest Hemingway's *A Farewell to Arms,* a World War I love story that featured a "guilty union." RKO announced its intention to film *Ann Vickers,* a novel by Sinclair Lewis, whose heroine is a successful social worker who has an abortion, several lovers, and an illegitimate child yet lives happily ever after.

Hollywood's attempts to screen these controversial novels enraged moral guardians even more than did Mae West.

Notes

1 Joy to McKenzie, July 23, 1930, *The Blue Angel*, PCA.
2 Internal memo, Dec. 13, 1930, *The Blue Angel*, PCA.
3 Andrew Bergman, *We're in the Moneys*, p. xxi.
4 Janet Wasko, *Movies and Money: Financing the American Film Industry* (Norwood, N.J.: Ablex Publishing, 1982), pp. 47–90.
5 Robert Francis Martin, III, "Celluloid Morality," p. 121.
6 Ephraim Katz, *The Film Encyclopedia* (New York: G. P. Putnam, 1979), p. 326.
7 Joy to Cecil B. DeMille, Jan. 14, 1930, *Madame Satan*, PCA.
8 Joy to DeMille, Sept. 19, 1930, *Madame Satan*, PCA.
9 Joy to DeMille, ibid; DeMille to Joy, Oct. 1, 1930, *Madame Satan*, PCA.
10 Molly Haskell, *From Reverence to Rape*, p. 111.
11 Joy to Hays, Dec. 15, 1931, *Possessed*, PCA.
12 Ibid.
13 'Notes Joy–Thalberg Conference,' Oct. 21, 1931, *Possessed*, PCA.
14 Hays to Schenck, Oct. 24, 1931, *Possessed*, PCA.
15 Mrs. Alonzo Richardson, Atlanta Board of Review, to Hays, Dec. 8, 1931, *Possessed*, PCA.
16 Creighton Peet, "*Possessed*," *Outlook and Independent* 159 (Dec. 2, 1931), 439.
17 Memo to Files from Alice Winter, May 1931, box 42, HP.
18 Daniel Lord, "The Code – One Year Later," April 23, 1931, box 42, LP.
19 Ibid.
20 Ibid.
21 Ibid.
22 Ibid.
23 Joy to Wingate, Feb. 5, 1931, *Little Caesar*, PCA.
24 Lord to Hays, Feb. 20, 1933, LP.
25 *New York Times*, Dec. 31, 1932, p. 10.
26 *Harrison's Reports* (Jan. 7, 1933).
27 *Variety*, Jan. 10, 1933, p. 8.
28 Jay R. Nash and Stanley R. Ross, *The Motion Picture Guide*, p. 2914.
29 Haskell, *From Reverence to Rape*, p. 324.
30 Lord to Quigley, Jan. 30, 1933, LP.
31 *Variety*, Dec. 6, 1932, p. 14.
32 *Commonweal* 18 (Dec. 21, 1932), p. 215; Lord, *Played by Ear*, p. 310.
33 Alfred Cohen to Milliken and Christian F. Reiser to A. L. Selig, Oct. 5, 1932, *Sign of the Cross*, PCA.
34 Quigley to Lord, Jan. 30, 1933, LP.

35 Gerald B. Donnelly, S.J., "DeMille's Roman Holiday," *America* 48 (Dec. 17, 1932), pp. 257–9.

36 *Harrison's Reports*, Feb. 18, 1933.

37 Ibid.

38 Joy to Harold Hurley, July 5, 1932, *Sign of the Cross*, PCA.

39 Joy to Hurley, Nov. 16, 1932, ibid.

40 Wingate to Hays, Dec. 18, 1932, ibid.

41 Cecil B. DeMille [ed. Donald Hayne], *The Autobiography of Cecil B. De-Mille* (Englewood Cliffs, N.J.: Prentice Hall, 1959), p. 324.

42 DeMille to George Schaeffer, Jan. 24, 1933, box 143, Cecil B. DeMille Collection, Harold B. Lee Library, Brigham Young University, Provo, Utah (hereafter DM).

43 For letters of endorsement see George Schaeffer to Mr. E. J. Sage, Mar. 14, 1933, box 143, DM.

44 *New York Times*, Dec. 1, 1932, p. 25.

45 *Harrison's Reports*, Dec. 17, 1932. It might be added that when the film was reissued after Breen took over as head of the PCA, he demanded that the dance scene be eliminated, and the Legion of Decency demanded that Colbert's bath scene be struck. See *Sign of the Cross*, PCA.

46 Quigley to Hays, Aug. 4, 1932, box 44, HP.

47 Martin Quigley, "Portents of Danger," *Motion Picture Herald* (May 14, 1932), p. 3.

48 Quigley to Hays, Aug. 4, 1932, box 44, HP.

49 Breen to Parsons, Oct. 10, 1932, box 1, PP.

50 Carl Milliken to Hays, June 25, 1932, box 44, HP.

51 *Columbia* 10 (Feb. 1931), p. 19.

52 *Catholic Action* 14 (Dec. 1932), p. 20.

53 *Catholic Action* 15 (Sept. 1933), p. 22.

54 Leo Litzky, "Censorship of Motion Pictures in the United States," p. 65.

55 *Ave Maria* 35 (Mar. 5, 1932), p. 307.

56 Gerald B. Donnelly, S.J., "An Open Letter to Dr. Wingate," *America* 48 (Oct. 29, 1932), pp. 84–6.

57 Robert James Parish, *The Paramount Pretties* (New Rochelle, N.Y.: Arlington House, 1972), pp. 298–300. June Sochen, *Mae West: She Who Laughs, Lasts* (Chicago: Arlan Davidson, 1992).

58 *"Diamond Lil," New Republic* 55 (June 27, 1928), p. 145.

59 Joy to Files, Jan. 11, 1930, and Hays to Joy, April 22, 1930, S*he Done Him Wrong*, PCA.

60 Joy to Files, Jan. 11, 1930, *She Done Him Wrong*, PCA.

61 "Paramount," *Fortune* 15 (March 15, 1937), pp. 194–6.

62 Parish, *Paramount Pretties*, p. 302.

63 McKenzie to Files, Nov. 28, 1932, and Wingate to Harold Hurley, Nov. 29, 1932, *She Done Him Wrong*, PCA.

64 Wingate to Hurley, Dec. 6, 1932, *She Done Him Wrong*, PCA.

65 Wingate to Hays, Dec. 2, 1932, and Wingate to Hurley, Dec. 6, 1932, *She Done Him Wrong*, PCA.

66 *Variety*, Feb. 14, 1933, p. 12.

67 Wingate to Hurley, Jan. 11 and Feb. 13, 1933, *She Done Him Wrong,* PCA.

68 Wingate to Hays, Feb. 13, 1933, *She Done Him Wrong,* PCA.

69 Hart to Wingate and Wingate to Hart, Feb. 3, 1933, *She Done Him Wrong,* PCA.

70 Hays to Wingate, Feb. 27, 1933, *She Done Him Wrong,* PCA.

71 Hart (New York Motion Picture Commission) to Wingate, Feb. 3, 1933; Wingate to Hart, Feb. 3, 1933; Hays to Wingate, Feb. 27, 1933, *She Done Him Wrong,* PCA. Zukor agreed to cut most of the song from the prints being shipped to the various film exchanges.

72 Reprinted in Anthony Slide, *Selected Film Criticism, 1931–1940,* p. 227.

73 K. L. Russell to Hays, April 20, 1933, box 45, HP.

74 New York *Daily News,* Feb. 11, 1933 (in box 45, HP); Julia Shawell, "Mae West Curves Herself a Career," *Pictorial Review* (Feb. 1934), p. 7; "Confounding Censors," *Motion Picture Herald* (May 19, 1934), p. 46.

75 Lord to Hays, Feb. 20, 1933, and Hays to Lord, Feb. 28, 1933, LP.

76 Wingate to Hays, Sept. 20, 1933, *She Done Him Wrong,* PCA.

77 *New York Times,* Oct. 14, 1933, p. 18; *Motion Picture Herald,* Oct. 7, 1933, p. 38; *Variety,* Oct. 17, 1933, p. 19; Stark Young, "Angels and Ministers of Grace," *New Republic* 76 (Nov. 29, 1933), 73–5.

78 All quoted in K. L. Russell to Hays, Nov. 17, 1933, box 46, HP.

79 Adolph Zukor with Dale Kramer, *The Public Is Never Wrong* (New York: G. P. Putnam, 1953), p. 267.

80 Harry Warner to Hays, Oct. 19, 1932, *She Done Him Wrong,* PCA.

81 Sidney Kent to Hays, Feb. 27, 1932, *She Done Him Wrong,* PCA.

CHAPTER 4

MOVIES AND MODERN LITERATURE

In this group [objectionable books] would be placed *Ann Vickers* of Sinclair Lewis and those of Hemingway, Faulkner and their ilk. These novels are vicious in their depths . . . .
— Father Francis Talbot, *America*

Complaints against the sexual content of films encompassed not only sultry "soap operas" like *No Man of Her Own* and the ribald comedies of a Mae West, but also works of recognized literary merit. A basic premise of the code was that Hollywood did not have the same freedom accorded book authors and Broadway playwrights to produce artistic works. Reformers feared that screening the "modernism" that pervaded contemporary literature would be far more corruptive on the mass audience of moviegoers than it was on "readers." As Lord urged Hays, movies should abandon the so-called sophisticated best-sellers in favor of uplifting religious dramas and patriotic salutes to business leaders and sports heroes.

The trend of twentieth-century American writers critically to examine American morals and manners outraged the defenders of traditional cultural values. The dean of American literature in the late nineteenth century, William Dean Howells, believed that American writers should "concern themselves with the more smiling aspects of life, which are the more American"; and, for the most part, American writers had done just that. However, in the first two decades of the twentieth century, a new generation of writers had emerged. Dubbed "naturalists," they were more likely to be midwestern instead of eastern, and working or middle class rather than upper class. They challenged the literary establishment by writing about people whose lives were often filled with base emotions, poverty, tragedy, passion, and despair.

This new breed of writers (and artists and intellectuals) saw a different America than did their nineteenth-century counterparts. Rejecting American Puritanism and Victorian morality, and attacking capitalism as an enemy of the people, they questioned accepted values and assumptions in all areas of American life. Theodore Dreiser's *Sister Carrie* (1900), the story of a young girl who openly and willingly cohabits with men in her search for a better life, shocked a generation raised on genteel literature. The poverty and oppression of industrialized America was vividly described in Upton Sinclair's *The Jungle* (1906), Frank Norris wrote of victimized farmers in *The Octopus* (1901), and muckrakers like Lincoln Steffens and Ida Tarbell scrutinized a nation driven by political corruption and industrial greed.

The experience of World War I, with its senseless destruction of human life and crushing of Wilsonian idealism, intensified the sense of disillusionment artists of all varieties felt toward modern civilization. John Dos Passos, in his USA trilogy (*The 42nd Parallel* [1930], *1919* [1932], and *The Big Money* [1936]), presented a theme heard throughout the 1920s and 1930s: American culture – indeed, America itself – was shallow and hypocritical. Writers like F. Scott Fitzgerald, Ezra Pound, Ernest Hemingway, Eugene O'Neill, and William Faulkner painted unflattering portraits of the United States.

No one represented this trend more or better than Sinclair Lewis, born and raised in Sauk Center, Minnesota. Lewis's portrayal of the petty and dreary nature of life in small-town America, beginning in 1920 with *Main Street* and continuing in his scathing debunking of boosterism in the American classic *Babbitt* (1922), established Lewis as an important American observer. He followed quickly with *Arrowsmith* (1924), *Elmer Gantry* (1927), and *Dodsworth* (1929). Recognition came with a Pulitzer Prize for *Arrowsmith,* which he refused, and a Nobel Prize for Literature in 1930, which he agreed to accept.

When in December 1930 Lewis stood on the platform on a cold, dark evening in Stockholm, Sweden, to address the distinguished audience, no one knew what he would say. His tongue was reputed to be as sharp as his pen. Lewis did not disappoint: Although the occasion might have called for diplomacy, Lewis chose to attack the ultraconservative American Academy, still steeped in the Howells tradition, for its refusal to recognize a new generation of writers. He also chastised American readers and writers for refusing to support and create a truly great literature:

In America most of us . . . are still afraid of any literature which is not a glorification . . . of our faults as well as our virtues. We still most revere the writer for the popular magazine who [offers] a hearty and edifying chorus chant that the America of a hundred and twenty million population is still as simple, as pastoral, as it was when it had but forty million; . . . that . . . America had gone through the revolutionary change from rustic colony to world-empire without having in the least altered the bucolic and Puritanic simplicity of Uncle Sam.[1]

In his remarks about prevailing opinions of modern literature, Lewis also excoriated the attitudes of the procensorship lobby toward films and their role in society. He mocked the idea of literature as a culture's cheerleader – exactly the role Lord and the moral guardians demanded for film.

The Catholic church, which saw books, especially literature, as potential threats to its teachings, had for centuries published "Index Librorum Prohibitorum," a list of banned publications (popularly known as the Catholic Index). Catholics, at one time or another, had been forbidden to read (for example) Dante's *The Divine Comedy,* Fielding's *Tom Jones,* Flaubert's *Madame Bovary,* Hawthorne's *The Scarlet Letter,* Hugo's *Les Misérables,* and Molière's *Don Juan.* The list was wide-ranging, and brought together one under heading a mixture of political philosophers all deemed dangerous to Catholic minds: Confucius, Lenin, John Locke, John Stuart Mill, Thomas Paine, Jean-Jacques Rousseau, Trotsky, and Voltaire. The list of forbidden volumes represented the world's great seminal ideals in philosophy, economics, and social theory. Contemporary novelists on the list included John Dos Passos, Theodore Dreiser, William Faulkner, Ernest Hemingway, and Sinclair Lewis.[2]

In the early 1930s the church began to intensify its attack on "obscene" and dangerous literature. At the annual meeting of Catholic bishops in Washington in 1932, just one year before the Legion of Decency campaign against the movies was launched, the hierarchy adopted a resolution that deplored the lack of "uplifting" literature and called on Catholics to avoid "immoral" books.[3] Father Lord joined the battle. In a speech to the New York chapter of the International Federation of Catholic Alumnae, he complained of too few Catholics among distinguished authors, dramatists, and poets. He condemned the writings of such authors as Theodore Dreiser, James Joyce, and Eugene O'Neill because they were fraught with the "sordid things of life."[4] It is doubtful whether Lord or anyone in his audience saw any connection between the Catholic attitude toward literature and the paucity of distinguished writers who promoted church policy. More typical was Rev. Francis X. Talbot, S.J., who on radio and in the pages of *America* demanded federal censorship of novels with "literary pretensions" that, he said, were hiding behind the protection of the First Amendment. Talbot called Sinclair Lewis, William Faulkner, and Ernest Hemingway "crawling vermin."[5] Talbot would later become a major force in the Legion of Decency.

It was only natural that Hollywood would attempt to bring the works of popular American authors to the screen. Best-sellers brought name recognition and proven public appeal, yet filming them induced a clash of cultures. Moral guardians believed the books were either obscene or, at best, vulgar, and were determined to keep them off the screen. Hollywood was equally determined to bring filmed versions of Faulkner, Hemingway, and Lewis to the public.

The process of adapting novels to the screen and retrofitting them to the strictures of the code further illustrates the problems Hollywood faced in the early 1930s. Will Hays, who did not favor filming modern works that challenged traditional views, declared in 1931 that the greatest of all censors, the people, had voted "thumbs down on the 'hard-boiled' realism in literature." Postwar America, he claimed, was through with its "preoccupation with morbidity" and the "orgy of self-revelation" that marked a "large portion of modern authorship."[6] It was wishful thinking on his part. Hollywood and the public wanted screen versions of the works of modern writers. As the *Washington Post* noted, it was absurd to think that a movie version of a book would somehow be more corrupting than the book itself.[7] Just how far Hollywood would be allowed to go in adapting these works was yet another front in the battle to control the screen.

The adaptation problem was illustrated by Paramount's attempt to bring Ernest Hemingway's powerful antiwar novel *A Farewell to Arms* to the screen. Hemingway, who had served on the Italian front as a Red Cross ambulance driver during World War I, had been deeply disillusioned, as were millions of Americans in the decade, by America's participation in the war. In 1929 he published the simple but tragic story of an English nurse and a young American ambulance driver during the war. Hemingway conveyed the horror, the brutality, and the utter stupidity of war through the lives of these two.

The story is set in northern Italy. Catherine Barkley, a nurse whose fiancé was killed in France, and Frederic Henry, an American volunteer in the Italian medical corps, fall in love. They are lovers for only a short time before Frederic is injured in an artillery attack and is sent to Milan to recuperate. Miss Barkley is also transferred to the same hospital.

The lovers are happy in Milan. Barkley volunteers for night duty so they can make love. When she discovers she is pregnant, neither she nor Frederic is distraught about this fact. Confident of their love for each other, they simply go about their lives and look for whatever happiness they can find. When Frederic is returned to the front, each deals with that fact of war without hysterics.

With the return to the war, however, their lives begin to unravel. In place of the joyful camaraderie that existed before his injury, Frederic discovers his unit is overcome with cynicism and depression. His best friend, Dr. Rinaldi, is no longer a skilled surgeon by day and happy-go-lucky officer by night: The endless slaughter of the war has turned him into a depressed alcoholic suffering from syphilis. When Austrian armies break through the Italian lines at Caporetto, the hospital unit is caught in a massive retreat that collapses into total chaos. In a desperate attempt to regain control, the Italian military police arrest and execute not only officers but anyone suspected of being a German spy.

Frederic is arrested but miraculously escapes before his execution. His only thought now is to find Catherine and, with no real intention to do so, he deserts the Italian army. He and Catherine are reunited and escape to Switzerland, where they find happiness and plan their marriage while they await the birth of their child.

Their happiness, however, is an illusion. The two lovers can no more escape the tragedy of war than can the millions of other innocent victims. Escape to idyllic Switzerland represents only a temporary haven. When the baby comes, Catherine has a long and painful delivery, and the child is stillborn. Frederic, who serves as narrator for much of the novel, realizes that:

Now Catherine would die. That was what you did. You died. You did not know what it was about. You never had time to learn. They threw you in and told you the rules and the first time they caught you off base they killed you. . . . Or they gave you syphilis like Rinaldi. But they killed you in the end. You could count on that. Stay around and they will kill you.[8]

In America the novel sold extremely well and was even adapted as a stage play, which enjoyed a successful run on Broadway; but despite the popularity of the book, bringing a faithful version of the novel to the screen would provoke serious censorship problems. On the moral side, *A Farewell to Arms* contained happy and unashamed "illicit love" with a resulting pregnancy. A hospital nurse openly slept with a patient, and their relationship was condoned by most of their friends. Frederic's desertion was portrayed as a justified act. Even more sensitive, in the movie industry's view, was the portrayal of the Italian army as ineffective, inhumane, and corrupt. Would the Italian government allow such a film to be shown in Italy? Could a faithful version of *A Farewell to Arms* be made under the restrictive provisions of the code given Hollywood's demand for a worldwide market?

Even before any studio expressed an interest in the book, SRD's Lamar Trotti read it and warned Joy that it contained "profanity, illicit love, illegitimate birth, desertion from the army and a not very flattering picture of Italy during the war." When Warner Bros. expressed an interest in the novel, the Hays Office warned that the book was "anti-Italian" and that Nobile Giacomo de Martino, the Italian Ambassador in Washington, had "already complained" to Hays, hinting that any movie version would be banned from the Italian market. The prospect of losing that lucrative market, and perhaps other countries as well, forced Warner Bros. to drop the project.[9]

Paramount was not as easily discouraged. In the summer of 1932 DeMille's *Sign of the Cross* and Mae West's *She Done Him Wrong* were both in production on the Paramount lot. The studio, determined to fight its way out of the Depression, bought the film rights to Hemingway's novel and rushed into production. Paramount assigned director Frank Borzage to the project and cast Helen Hayes as Catherine, Gary Cooper as Frederic, and Adolphe Menjou as the sophisticated, if not dissipated, Major Rinaldi. Paramount wanted the Italian market and informed Joy that screenwriters Benjamin Glazer and Oliver H. P. Garrett would work directly with the Italian consul in Los Angeles to resolve any censorship problems the film might have.

Borzage and the writers recognized that religious organizations and censors were likely to protest that Catherine and Frederic's romance was much too explicit for a mass audience. They were also aware that the antiwar theme of the novel might have to be toned down, both for potential censorship reasons and because that theme did not have a good record for creating huge box office. The story also ended tragically with Catherine's death; American audiences preferred "happy endings." Paramount was certainly more interested in marketing the film as a love story between Helen Hayes and Gary Cooper than they were in screening an antiwar novel.

The studio proposed a number of compromises. To resolve, or at least undercut, moral objections, they attempted to create the impression that Catherine and Frederic were married. In a scene designed to placate religious protest, a priest, played by Jack LaRue, seems to perform an "unofficial" marriage ceremony for Catherine and Frederic in the hospital. While the two lovers hold hands, the priest turns his back and mumbles a prayer. Were they married? Paramount hoped audiences would accept this scene as indicating that Catherine and Frederic had the blessing of a priest if not the church.

The script also modified the character of Catherine's best friend, Nurse Ferguson. In the movie, "Fergie," played by Mary Philips, consistently condemns the affair. She represents "a voice for morality," a defender of traditional values who was presumably speaking to the members of the movie audience as well as to the screen characters. To modify the tragedy of Catherine's death, Borzage shot two different endings: one with Catherine surviving, the other with her death. Theaters were given their choice of the "happy ending" (which *Variety* recommended) or the "sad ending."[10] With these modifications of Hemingway's story, the studio believed it could show the rest of their developing relationship more frankly.

The major political problems revolved around Frederic's desertion from the army and the visualization of the Italian retreat at Caporetto. The Italian embassy had warned the studio that "if the scenes in the picture were filmed as described in the book they would probably" ban the film.[11] Hemingway had set in great detail the conditions that caused the collapse at Caporetto and the subsequent chaos: Frederic does not so much desert in the face of the enemy as run from stupidity, brutality, and senselessness. In the film, all this is changed: Frederic leaves his post not because the Italian front has collapsed and he is ordered to retreat, but rather because his letters to Catherine have gone unanswered. He is so desperate to see Catherine that he runs away to find her. His decision is strictly personal.

In his quest for Catherine, Frederic is caught up in one of the most memorable scenes in American cinema history. Shot as a surrealistic montage by cinematographer Charles Lang (who won an Academy Award for his work on the film), Frederic's search for Catherine is intercut with shots of troop movements, airplane strafing, artillery fire, escaping civilians, and numerous images of crosses and crucifixions. The scene, which depicts the horror of war, does so without a clear-cut condemnation of the Italian army. The film ends, unlike the book, by announcing a great Italian victory. The studio submitted the script and the film to the consul for his approval, and also gave a private screening to Dr. A. H. Giannini, president of the Bank of America and a prominent Italian-American. When everyone endorsed the film, Paramount assumed they had avoided all censorship problems.[12]

However, Joy and Trotti worried that a screen version of *A Farewell to Arms* was potential dynamite. In their view, the film was littered with moral problems. The romance between Catherine and Frederic was much too explicit, as were the childbirth scenes – which, moreover, were specifically prohibited by the code. The censors also doubted the wisdom of the marriage scene. "What do you think," asked Trotti, "of the business of the priest seeming to marry the couple? Does this constitute a real marriage or is it a man of the Church condoning an affair?"[13]

Through the summer and fall of 1932, the studio proceeded with the film. By the time of its completion, Joy was working at Fox and Dr. James Wingate had taken his place as chief industry censor. When Wingate saw the film in November, he refused to approve it because it presented an "illicit" affair in a favorable light and contained scenes of a childbirth. Paramount was understandably furious: They flatly refused to consider additional cuts in the film, telling Hays they had made every political change the Italian consul had demanded and, in order to make the film a morality tale, had turned Ferguson into a character who clearly disapproved of Catherine's actions.[14]

Yet Wingate remained firm in his conviction that the film justified an unmarried couple openly having a sexual relationship, the woman becoming pregnant, and the couple then living together with no one objecting to their actions. The fact that Catherine dies in childbirth was irrelevant to Wingate: In his view the scene could not be in the movie anyway. He demanded that Hays appoint a jury of Hollywood producers to rule on whether or not *A Farewell to Arms* was a moral film.

When the jury, comprising Joe Schenck representing United Artists, Universal's Carl Laemmle, Jr., who produced *All Quiet on the Western Front,* and Fox's Sol Wurtzel, sat down in Paramount's screening room, they knew that Paramount was in dire financial straits. They also knew that *A Farewell to Arms* was a major financial investment for the studio. Helen Hayes, fresh from her Oscar-winning performance in *The Sin of Madelon Claudet* (1931) was one of America's finest actresses and would certainly prove a strong box-office attraction. Adolphe Menjou was a major Hollywood star, and Gary Cooper soon would be. Not surprisingly, they ruled for Paramount. While they admitted that childbirth scenes were prohibited by the code and that the affair was attractively presented, the intent of the studio was not, they ruled, to make a cheap, lurid love story, but to dramatize a novel.[15]

Ernest Hemingway was not so sure. When Paramount offered to arrange a private screening of the film in an exchange for an endorsement, the author refused. He found the premise for Frederic's desertion "preposterous," deeply resented the other changes the studio had made to satisfy Italy and the censors, and was "outraged" by the two-ending gimmick that Borzage had devised. In Chicago, Father Fitz-George Dinneen was also furious. If no one else knew how to interpret the scene of the priest in the hospital room, he did. He told Father Wilfrid Parsons that Paramount had made every change demanded by the Italian government because of box-office considerations; yet compare their concern with a "secular power" to that of the church, he told Parsons. "When it came to religion they dragged in a chaplain to gloss over the rotten moral condition and perform a fake marriage. Here in Chicago we got this passage cut out. But the picture went over the country with it in." The message to Dinneen was clear – if you wanted influence over the content of movies, you needed leverage at the box office. It was a lesson the Catholics were beginning to learn and would soon apply with a vengeance.[16]

The difficult production history of *A Farewell to Arms* offers a lucid example of the difficulty Hollywood producers faced in translating popular novels to the screen. Most critics agreed with the *Nation,* which called the novel "a remarkably beautiful book."[17] Yet it made little difference to the censors and moral guardians whether the subject was a mindless piece of nonsense like *Madame Satan,* a rowdy comedy like *She Done Him Wrong,* or a serious literary work like *A Farewell to Arms.* Movies, they insisted, could not portray moral, social, or political issues unless they were framed to reinforce traditional moral values for viewers.

From Wingate's appointment in October 1932 through the first six months of 1933, the future of the industry looked bleak. The only barometer used by the industry – the box office – continued to decline. Criticism that increasingly frank films caused this collapse continued unabated. The political atmosphere was as uncertain as the economic climate: Will Hays had confidently predicted that Herbert Hoover would easily defeat Franklin D. Roosevelt; but the nation soundly rejected continued Republican leadership. Industry officials worried that Hays might be ineffective in a new Democratic Washington.

By March 1933 the country seemed on the verge of economic collapse. FDR's declaration of a bank holiday on March 5 brought further panic. Box-office figures for early March were reported to have dropped to a mere twenty-eight million weekly admissions, less than a quarter of the revenue needed to keep the industry afloat.[18]

Hays's back was against the wall. In early March he received a confidential report from Joe Breen in Los Angeles: Martin Quigley had been making the rounds in Hollywood and came away convinced that the code "has completely broken down . . . because of a disposition on the part of the producers to ignore it."[19] Quigley, it seemed, was preparing another broadside against the industry. *Harrison's Reports,* on March 4, had already declared war with its lead editorial, "Is Sex the Only Theme for Suitable Entertainment?"[20]

On March 6, 1933 – just two days after Roosevelt's inauguration, and during a national banking crisis – Hays summoned the MPPDA Board of Directors for an emergency meeting. The session, which included MGM President Nicholas Schenck, Carl Laemmle and R. H. Cochrane from Universal, Columbia's Jack Cohen, Albert and Harry Warner, Paramount's Adolph Zukor, RKO Chairman M. H. Aylesworth, and S. R. Kent, President of Fox Film Corporation, lasted the entire night and was, according to Raymond Moley, "one of the most intense meetings in the history of the Hays Office."[21]

As bleak as the financial situation was, Hays concentrated on what he believed was the real crisis facing the industry: the refusal of the studios to adhere to the code. This was exacerbated, he added, by the board's refusal to support either him or Wingate. Hays demanded such support, and specifically named films then in production in Hollywood that he predicted would hurt the industry unless toned down. *Baby Face* was "demoralizing," he told Warners. MGM's *Red Dust* was "sordid"; Paramount's *The Story of Temple Drake,* just completed but not yet released, was "vile."[22] MGM's *Gabriel Over the White House* (discussed in Chapter 5) he blasted as dangerous.

The board gave Hays its support. In a formal statement released on March 7, the industry reaffirmed its pledge to uphold the code and promised to "raise the moral, artistic and educational values of motion picture production, while at the same time preserving the American principle of individual initiative, creation and achievement."[23]

Hays followed his board's endorsement with a letter to every studio in Hollywood in an attempt to coerce them into cooperation. Studio heads were informed that Hays and Wingate would insist that "objectionable pictures" be revised. If the studios refused to cooperate, Hays informed them, he would go directly to "company heads in New York." If the studios still failed to cooperate, Hays informed them, he would appeal directly to the industry bankers who financed films "on the grounds that dirty pictures imperil their investments." If all three failed, Hays threatened to appeal directly to the public not to support the film in question.[24]

In April 1933, Hays went to Los Angeles, where he delivered the message in person. "Hays Lays Down the Law," said the *Motion Picture Herald,* but the reporter noted that Hays's message was met with "silence and some surprise" by producers at MGM: Only after a forceful intervention by New York's Nicholas Schenck did MGM's producers agree to cooperate. Hays received similar reception at the other studios.

In Hollywood, producers refused to blame declining attendance on "immoral" movies. While Hays was urging the producers to take sex out of films, *Sign of the Cross* was packing theaters. Even Hays contributed effective evidence to counter the accusation that Hollywood's films were offending the majority of Americans. On a national level, of the 438 feature films released in 1931, a whopping 77 percent were given a "recommended" rating by one or more of the following organizations: the General Federation of Women's Clubs, the International Federation of Catholic Alumnae, the Daughters of the American Revolution, the Los Angeles Women's University Club, and the Young Men's Christian Association. This was a tough audience, and one that was certainly less tolerant of sexual content than the American public as a whole. Locally, the industry also fared well: A survey of twenty-one cities showed a significant approval rating for the movies. In Beloit, Wisconsin, local community groups approved of 98 percent of the films exhibited in 1931; Memphis, Tennessee, gave an approval rating of 85 percent; Wichita, Kansas, a 77 percent approval rating; Lansing, Michigan, 76 percent; and Richmond, Indiana, 74 percent. Only St. Louis, Missouri, home of Father Lord, found a majority of the movies unacceptable: St. Louis groups approved of only 40 percent of the films shown in 1931.

In Hackensack, New Jersey, the local paper praised the Hays Office for "immeasurably" improved pictures during 1932, and scoffed at "the self-appointed guardians" who condemned the movies. "The chief difficulty with the critics of the screen," the paper wrote, "is that they insist upon viewing motion pictures as a great social force, and nothing else. The truth of the matter is that the films are entertainment" and "the public is getting the kind of motion pictures it wants."[25] The *Philadelphia Inquirer* agreed when it told readers that in 1932 various critics had named 150 different Hollywood productions to "ten best" lists across the country.[26]

Producers were well aware of the level of support for movies throughout the country. It was the Depression, not movie content, that kept people at home, they argued.

Nor was it clear that Hays could or would actually do what he had threatened. While he might demand that some of the more daring films be returned to the studios, nothing in Hays's past performances indicated that he would be willing to go outside the industry to demand changes.

While Hays searched for a formula that would give him increased control over the studios, Hollywood continued to produce films that provoked both him and moral guardians. Two films cited by Hays as dangerous – those of William Faulkner's *Sanctuary* and Sinclair Lewis's *Ann Vickers* – challenged his ability to control the production wing of the industry. Despite the Board of Director's pledge of support for Hays and Wingate, New York officials did not interfere with creative decisions made in Los Angeles. Nor did Hays follow through with his threats to recruit bankers and public opinion to his side.

In 1929 William Faulkner, broke as usual, had decided to write "the most horrific tale" he could imagine to make some money. In three weeks he had cranked out *Sanctuary,* a morbid tale of rape, murder, sexual impotence, and perversion that ends with two men found guilty of murders they did not commit. The book was a best-seller in 1931. The Boy Scouts of America considered the novel so sordid they removed Faulkner as a local leader. Paramount saw the novel in a different light: They paid Faulkner $6,000 for the screen rights.[27]

Set in the 1920s, the novel traces the moral collapse of Temple Drake, the beautiful daughter of a local judge. It begins with Temple and her boyfriend, Gowan Stevens, a drunken no-good despite his high-society standing, on their way to a college football game. Gowan is determined to get some moonshine, and detours with Temple into the backwoods toward a still. On the way he wrecks his car, and he and Temple have to walk to the farmhouse where the still is hidden. The moonshiner is Lee Goodwin, who lives with his common-law wife Ruby and their infant son. Goodwin is distrustful, but not dangerous. Unfortunately for Temple, a local Memphis hoodlum, Popeye, is also at the farmhouse.

Gowan, after he sobers up, leaves without Temple, who is now stranded for the night. Ruby, fearing that one of the men might try to rape Temple, hides her in the barn for the evening and arranges for Tommy, a feeble-minded helper, to guard her; but Popeye discovers where Temple is hiding, kills Tommy when he tries to interfere, and then rapes Temple with a corncob because he is impotent.

Temple is transfixed by all this. Rather than resist Popeye, she is fascinated by this evil character and willingly accompanies him to Memphis, where they take residence in a local brothel. The perversion continues when Temple agrees to make love to "Red," another local hood, while Popeye watches. This ménage à trois falls apart when Popeye discovers that Red and Temple are seeing each other privately. He is so enraged by this act of disloyalty that he murders Red.

While all this is going on in Memphis, the police arrest Lee Goodwin for the murder of Tommy. Goodwin's lawyer, Horace Benbow, tracks Temple down and tries to convince her to tell the truth and free Goodwin. Temple refuses and testifies instead that it was Goodwin who murdered Tommy and raped her. In stereotypical Southern fashion, an enraged mob, determined to protect the honor of women, storms the jail and kills the innocent Goodwin. Temple's father sends her off to Europe so she can forget all this. Meanwhile Popeye, who has gotten away with murder, decides to drive to Florida. On his way he is mistakenly arrested, convicted, and executed for a crime he did not commit.

The idea of bringing William Faulkner's *Sanctuary* to the screen was horrifying to a wide range of opinion. *Harrison's Reports* called Paramount's decision to film the novel further evidence that federal control of the industry was required. Owner and editor P. S. Harrison told Adolph Zukor that the book was "filthy and vile," and that if Paramount proceeded, "you will do the greatest harm to the motion picture industry that has ever been done in its entire history."[28] Maurice Kann, writing in the *Motion Picture Daily,* labeled the novel "one of the most revolting tales in modern literature." Lamar Trotti agreed, telling MPPDA officials that *Sanctuary* was the most "sickening novel ever written in this country. . . . [I]t is utterly unthinkable as a motion picture." Hays ordered it banned from the screen.

In the fall of 1932, while Paramount executives were negotiating with Hays to bring Mae West's *Diamond Lil* to the screen, they quietly purchased the rights to *Sanctuary* and announced it would be produced under the title *The Story of Temple Drake.* Hays was furious. He ordered Wingate to keep him fully informed on the progress of script development, which he demanded occur under "the strictest supervision." Normally, Hays did not intervene directly in censorship activities; but he was so concerned about this project that he ordered Wingate not to allow anything in the film that even hinted at a code violation. "We simply must not allow the production of a picture which will offend every right-thinking person who sees it." Hays wanted Joe Breen, who oversaw studio publicity for Hays, to work closely with Wingate on this project and to key a sharp eye on the publicity campaign for the film. Hays worried Paramount would attempt to promote the film on a rape and perversion theme. He urged Wingate to demand a jury ruling if the studio was uncooperative. If they ruled against him, Hays pledged to have the MPPDA Board of Directors in New York overrule them.[29]

"Make a Sunday school story" out of *Temple Drake*, Wingate pleaded with Paramount. He was relieved by the script that came to his office, and told Hays that most of the offending material had been written out.[30] The Hollywood version of the film would center on Temple and the lawyer, Benbow. When Benbow, handsome but rather dull, asks the young, beautiful Temple to marry him, she goes on a little "wild streak." She is still raped in the corncrib, but by Popeye (Trigger in the movie), who needs no external ornaments to consummate his evil deed. After the rape, Temple happily follows Trigger, and together they set up a love nest in the Memphis whorehouse; but impotence, Red, and the ménage à trois are written out. Instead, the movie develops the regeneration of Temple, avoiding the more sordid aspects of her continual fall into degradation.[31] In the film, Benbow finds his fiancée living with Trigger in the whorehouse. When he asks Temple to testify to free an innocent man, she refuses because testifying will ruin her reputation and because she really does love Benbow and fears that Trigger will kill him if she takes the stand. After the lawyer leaves, Temple and Trigger quarrel, and she kills him.

The scene is now set for the trial. On the stand, Temple's dramatic and emotional testimony establishes the innocence of Goodwin (and clearly establishes her compliance with Trigger and her murder of him). After this emotional outpouring, she faints; her fiancé swoops her up in his arms while telling everyone how proud he is of her courage. This was one understanding guy, willing to take back a girl who had run away with a criminal, set up housekeeping with him, and witnessed one murder and committed one of her own. Presumably the reunited couple will pick up their lives as if nothing had ever happened.

In March 1933, Joseph Breen and James Wingate were invited to the Paramount lot to view the completed film. When the rather straitlaced Irish Catholic Breen saw what Wingate had more or less approved, he was horrified. His comments are especially interesting because, within less than a year, he would replace Wingate as Hollywood censor. The film was, he admitted, a "Sunday school story" compared to the novel; nonetheless, in his view it was "sordid, base and thoroughly unpleasant." Breen told Wingate that it was bad enough to witness Temple's "reckless conduct," which leads to her

Figure 4. Jack La Rue, William Gargan, and Miriam Hopkins in *The Story of Temple Drake*. Courtesy the Museum of Modern Art / Film Stills Archive.

rape; but then to see "the contentment with which she lives with Trigger – and later murders him . . . is highly offensive." Especially troubling to Breen was the lack of "any promptings of conscience" on the part of Temple. Breen would later insist that movies develop a moral conscience, but he was powerless to impose this demand at this juncture. He judged the entire movie as "highly invidious" and warned Hays that *The Story of Temple Drake* was exactly the type of film that brought down on the industry the "wrathful condemnation of decent people everywhere." Hays understood Breen's close connections with Martin Quigley and the Catholic church. He was determined to challenge Paramount.[32]

In Los Angeles, Wingate, under orders from Hays, refused to approve the film. He told the studio the rape scene was too explicit, and the corncobs scattered about must be removed because the audience would know the context from the novel; also, it was the opinion of the Hays Office that the film would be improved considerably if Trigger would drag Temple off to Memphis against her will. In New York, Hays pounded away at Adolph Zukor, asking him to pressure the studio to revise the film. The combination worked when studio boss Emanuel Cohen assured Hays that Paramount would make any cuts deemed necessary for approval, but requested that Temple not be required to state that she was a "prisoner" of Trigger. Cohen argued that Temple going willingly with Trigger "did not violate the code," and to change this aspect of the film would "destroy the dramatic value of her confession and . . . cause the picture to lose all of the moral force of the girl's redemption."[33]

Despite Cohen's assurances, nothing was done to incorporate the changes Wingate suggested. The studio proceeded with plans to open the film in New York, and submitted it to New York censors. Irwin Esmond, head of New York's censorship board, astounded the studio when he rejected the film out of hand.[34] Paramount and Hays now had a real problem: The studio had invested heavily in the project, and in the spring of 1933 was by no means out of financial difficulty. Although Hays did not like the film, he did not want to see Paramount sink into further financial difficulty by having *Temple Drake* banned from the lucrative New York audience. It was also possible, considering the sensational aspects of the novel, that a ban in New York would snowball into similar rulings from the other state censorship boards. To avoid that potential disaster Paramount, Hays and the New York board huddled to agree on cuts that would sanitize the morals of *Temple Drake*. In this instance, Hays was no longer a censor, but an advocate for the film. His job, after all, as trade association president, was to open markets for films even if he didn't like them. It was a role he would play increasingly in the next few years.

Faced with losing the most important domestic market, Cohen agreed to make whatever changes were necessary for New York approval. Hays pleaded with Esmond to understand the financial problems the industry faced, pointing out that Paramount could not afford at this late date to lose the New York market. Esmond finally agreed that *Temple Drake* could play in the state if all scenes dealing with sex and violence were reduced to the absolute minimum. When New York was satisfied, another ban was threatened by Ohio. Hays intervened to calm Ohio's censors, but was told in return that the board was "sick and tired" of having to demand massive cuts from films that should not have been made in the first place. Ohio insisted that the scene showing a "negro laundress ironing Temple's underwear" – and saying that were Temple's father to wash her underwear, he would know a lot more about his daughter's sex life – be struck from the Ohio version.[35]

Critics both blasted the film as "immoral" and praised Hollywood for bringing adult drama to the screen. Miriam Hopkins gave "a brilliant performance as Temple," according to *Time,* which judged the film as "dingy and violent" and "more explicit about the macabre aspect of sex than any previous" Hollywood product.[36] George Raft, originally penciled in as Trigger, refused to play the role because he felt it would have a negative impact on his career. It went instead to Jack La Rue, "a heavy-lidded young Italian" who was "effectively sinister."[37] Director Steven Roberts was praised for "exacting the last ounce of horror" out of a superb script written by Oliver H. P. Garrett. [38]

The Washington *Times* called it "rash." The reviewer in the Chicago *Tribune* told her readers she felt she had been "investigating a sewer" while watching the movie. The New York *American* branded it a "shoddy, obnoxiously disagreeable . . . trashy, sex-plugged piece."[39] In Syracuse the film critic retitled the film "The Shame of Temple Drake."[40] *Harrison's Reports* warned theater owners that "never before have sex situations been so boldly and luridly pictured. No exhibitor can show this picture to decent people."[41]

Yet, like so many other films, opinion was divided. William Troy, reviewing the film for the *Nation,* called it "truly extraordinary" in capturing the "essential quality" of Faulkner's novel, which was the "destructive power of evil." He warned his readers that they might not "like that quality," but that no one could deny its presence. Yet that was precisely what the censors and moral reformers wanted to do.[42] Richard Watts, Jr., of the *New York Herald Tribune* found the film "fascinating" and declared that, despite the controversy, "I'm a defender of the film." In Philadelphia readers of the *Inquirer* were urged "not to miss it." From the Midwest the Kansas City *Star* said *Temple Drake* was "better than average."[43] Yet there is little doubt that the overall impact of the film was negative for the industry: Those who saw the film and found nothing much wrong with it said little; those who found it "vile," like P. S. Harrison, stepped up the intensity of their demands that movies reform.

The reaction to the film version of Sinclair Lewis's novel *Ann Vickers* was much the same. When Daniel Lord urged Will Hays to make films about American heroes, neither Lord nor any of the other censors and/or reformers had in mind films about a modern heroine like Lewis's Vickers. Published in 1933, *Ann Vickers* was an enormously popular novel, zooming to the top of the best-seller lists and selling over a hundred thousand copies.

Ann Vickers is the story of a young woman of solid middle-class credentials. Her intellectual growth begins when she is educated at an outstanding liberal arts college; afterward, she drifts into the suffragette movement. Her real education, however, starts when she discovers that the movement is stifled by incompetence and prejudice. She leaves, but is determined to continue to fight for just causes. Moving to New York City, she becomes a social worker. On the eve of American entry into World War I, she meets a handsome young army officer with whom she has an affair. Pregnant, she discovers he does not love her, and she has an abortion.

On the rebound from a broken heart and the abortion, Ann marries a nice but very dull man. Their marriage is torn apart by Ann's rising fame as a reformer and by her attraction to a distinguished New York judge. As a social worker she is an advocate for birth control, better housing, and improved welfare; but her reputation soars when she writes a best-selling exposé of American prisons that depicts the corruption of America's criminal justice system. The prisons are brutal and the jailers inhuman thugs; drugs and sex are rampant, correction nonexistent. Ann corrects this situation when she becomes warden of a model prison.

On a public level, Ann is a paradigm of virtue and respectability; privately, she continues to challenge the accepted norms of behavior. She falls in love with Barney Dolphin, a Tammany judge, and carries on a torrid love affair with him while living with her husband. When word of this affair reaches the prison board, there is an unsuccessful attempt to oust her. Ann fights for her rights as a professional, and wins; but tragedy strikes when Dolphin is sent to prison for corruption, and Ann is again pregnant. She decides to leave her husband and have Dolphin's baby. When he is freed from prison, the lovers are reunited and, with outraged moral condemnation from society, carry on their lives. The point of the novel was, said Lewis, that "women have almost caught up with men" as complete human beings with "ideas, reasons, ambitions . . . with virtues and faults."[44]

Reviews of the book were mixed. "Beautiful . . . compassionate and true," wrote *Books*.[45] The *Boston Transcript* hailed it as "woman's triumph over the customs of an older world."[46] "Delightful," said the *Saturday Review of Literature*.[47] "Brilliantly done," agreed the *Spectator* from London.[48] William Soskin, writing in the *New York Evening Post*, labeled the book "an excellent indictment of the American prison system and a cutting satire on the various reform movements" of the past decade.[49] The *New York Times* found it dull.[50] The *Catholic World* charged that Lewis delighted in drawing attention "to the refuse, the garbage, the dumps, the cesspools" of life, and warned readers to "stay at a safe distance from this book."[51] The Jesuit publication *America* called *Ann Vickers* obscene.[52] A Michigan reader agreed, calling Lewis a "disgusting, obscene, maggot" and *Ann Vickers* a "stinking and filthy" story.[53] Not surprisingly, *Ann Vickers* was forbidden reading for American Catholics.

The story had tremendous potential as a movie, despite its obvious conflicts with the code. It featured a strong heroine and was, at heart, a love story. Given the tremendous success of the novel, there was little doubt that Hollywood would bring Miss Vickers to the screen. In May 1933, RKO bought the screen rights and began production. The production history of *Ann Vickers* provides another illustration of the huge gulf between the production studios and the Hays Office over what was, and was not, permissible under the code.

After battling producers over *A Farewell to Arms* and *Temple Drake,* Wingate and his assistant Joe Breen were in no mood to compromise. In Hollywood, Breen was taking an increasing role in the evaluation of scripts. When RKO submitted *Ann Vickers* to the Studio Relations Committee in May 1933, Wingate asked Breen for his opinion. "This script simply *will not do,*" screamed Breen. He told Wingate that he had not "read anything quite so vulgarly offensive" in years. Despite the immoral behavior of Vickers, the script was a "patent attempt to build up sympathy for the leading character" and violated the "sanctity of marriage" clause, which Breen considered the "very foundation of society." While he recognized that the book was a best-seller, Breen repeated prevailing Catholic views when he told Wingate that it was "known to be vile and offensive." If the script was not rejected at once, Breen predicted, the industry was in for "great trouble."[54]

Wingate agreed totally with Breen, and informed RKO that the script was unacceptable because the heroine was allowed to demonstrate "utter disregard for the conventions of society." The code administrator maintained that the script violated the code by presenting Ann Vickers as an intelligent, attractive, well-educated social worker who shows no remorse for her actions; nor "does a major character call it to her attention." Where is the "moral lesson"? Wingate asked. Why doesn't she go through a "moral struggle"? Without a "condemnation of this flaunting of the laws of convention," the sympathy of the audience could not help but be with Vickers; therefore, it was the "unanimous opinion of our staff that the present treatment violates the spirit and the letter of the code."[55]

RKO was furious at Wingate's assessment of their script. Merian Cooper, vice-president in charge of production, who coproduced and codirected *King Kong,* fired back a stinging reply: The script was based on a best-selling novel by a Nobel Prize–winning author. In Cooper's view, RKO had developed a straightforward, honest, dignified, and distinguished story of a young woman who wants more from life than simply to be married and have children. While he admitted that the story included some material that was controversial, "it does not pander to cheap sex, nor to cheap and vulgar emotions."[56] The studio planned for the film to be a major production, and Cooper assured Wingate that the story of Ann Vickers would bring acclaim to the motion picture industry.[57]

Wingate refused to budge, and RKO flatly refused to consider most of his demands, although they did agree to try to soften the "approval of adultery." With the dispute unresolved, the studio went forward with the production. Irene Dunne was scheduled to play Vickers and Walter Huston set as Judge Barney Dolphin, with Bruce Cabot and Conrad Nagel playing supporting roles. The offending screenplay was adapted by Jane Murfin and directed by John Cromwell.

Behind the scenes the battle continued. Wingate complained that the studios refused to take him seriously. Studio boss B. B. Kahane protested directly to Hays that he found Wingate's attitude toward the project "quite discouraging and disturbing." RKO realized, Kahane wrote, that adultery should not be attractive; the studio had, in fact, changed the basic story a great deal in recognition that an accurate screen version of the novel might be offensive to a good many people. Vickers, he told Hays, would not be married when she had her affair, and she would suffer because of it by being forced from her job by the scandal it caused. To emphasize that point, Vickers would fall into a life of poverty and be shunned by her friends as a result of her actions. That seemed punishment enough to Kahane, but now Wingate was insisting that in every picture where adultery was shown there had to be "a definite affirmative denouncement" of it by a "spokesman for accepted morality." (More than likely it was Breen who was asserting this change: A "voice for morality" became a key element during his administration.) That is not, Kahane told Hays, our understanding of the code.[58]

Moreover, RKO repeated a familiar story: The studio had already invested over $300,000 in the project and cast such major players as Dunne, Huston, Nagel, and Cabot. The studio expected the movie to be a money-maker, and with "business conditions the way they are we cannot afford to risk this amount of money with a chance that after we finish the production Dr. Wingate will renew his objections or make new ones." Kahane wanted to cooperate, and claimed his studio had spent over three weeks trying to rewrite the script to satisfy Wingate, but was "frankly doubtful that he [Wingate] had a broad enough viewpoint regarding the Production Code." In a total reversal of procedure, Kahane demanded that Hays assemble a jury to judge the merits of the script.[59]

Hays was stunned by Kahane's letter, which challenged his authority. Although Hays had threatened the studios in March and had ordered Wingate to demand a jury, in May he had backed away from an open confrontation with RKO. He now told Kahane that he saw no reason to invoke a jury if the studio were to alter the basic story as they implied. The most important issue was that the film must be careful not to create any feeling of sympathy for Vickers. The code was very clear, Hays wrote: "It is necessary . . . to establish in the minds of the audience that adultery is *wrong, unjustified* and *indefensible.*"[60]

If Hays thought a calming letter would pacify RKO, he was wrong. Kahane fired back an angry reply, telling Hays that he was going beyond the code in requiring films to "affirmatively establish . . . that adultery is wrong and unjustified" and in implying that the studio had to make all the changes "suggested" by Dr. Wingate. RKO, he said, had no such understanding of the code or of the authority of the Studio Relations Committee. The studio was willing to take Hays's views and Wingate's under advisement, but Kahane did not believe the studio was compelled to make changes with which it did not agree. RKO was in open revolt.[61]

Hays was cornered. All he could do was write another letter to all the studios. He repeated the charges he leveled earlier: Films dealing with "illicit sex relationships" are "never justified" no matter how well they are treated. He told RKO that he considered *Of Human Bondage* and *Ann Vickers* a "very grave danger" to the industry. MGM was scolded for Jean Harlow's *Bombshell* and Joan Crawford's *Dancing Lady.* Paramount was warned about Noël Coward's *Design for Living* and the Marx Bros.' political satire *Duck Soup.* Hays again threatened that if these films did not confirm to the code, he would personally intervene.[62]

RKO agreed to make a few additional cuts in *Ann Vickers;* this pacified Wingate, who told Hays that the "subject has been handled as well as it could be."[63] RKO's investment had been protected, and the film was released in the fall just as the Catholics began the Legion of Decency crusade. Despite howls from film reformers, the sanitized version of *Ann Vickers* suffered only a few cuts from state and municipal censorship boards; yet it would be placed on the Catholic Legion of Decency's condemned list along with *She Done Him Wrong, I'm No Angel, A Farewell to Arms, Of Human Bondage,* and *The Story of Temple Drake.* By July 1934, Breen would demand that each of these films be removed from circulation.

It is clear that during 1930–3, Joy, Wingate, and Hays worked very hard to try to fit films within the general guidelines of the code. It is also clear there was genuine disagreement about what the code really meant. During his tenure as industry censor, Jason Joy tried to apply the code in a constructive manner and avoid the pitfalls of "narrow" censorship. (This will become even clearer in Chapter 5, which discusses Joy's refusal to censor gangster movies.) When Wingate moved from New York to Hollywood, he attempted to enforce the code in a similar manner. His first test case was with Mae West, and although he, like censorship groups, saw some problems, he understood that

West represented comedy and satire. It is no accident that West's best films, *She Done Him Wrong* and *I'm No Angel,* were produced during this period. As the pressure to tighten restrictions grew in the first half of 1933, Wingate was caught between the studios, who demanded more freedom, and a rising chorus of complaint from religious groups, women's organizations, and trade papers such as *Harrison's Reports* and Quigley's *Motion Picture Herald.* In New York, corporate officers were reluctant to interfere, and while they gave pledges of support to Hays, they did not force Hollywood producers to accept the advice of Wingate or Hays. It was at this time that rumblings of discontent began to emerge from the Catholic church: Articles, editorials, and sermons began to denounce the movies.

In Los Angeles the studios continued to refuse to recognize a major premise of the code: that movies had a special responsibility to uphold traditional morality. They did not believe they were producing immoral films when they filmed versions of popular novels by America's foremost authors. When the code had been adopted in 1930, producers had challenged that premise, maintaining that sound gave them the opportunity to bring new subject areas to the screen; they had then proceeded to do just that. The producers viewed the entire procensorship movement as a minority effort, not one of the majority of movie fans. The studios viewed the SRD as advisory, and saw state censorship boards and other would-be censors as unrepresentative of mainstream America. From their perspective, producing films that would please Canon Chase, the WCTU, or Father Lord would ruin the industry.

In many ways, they were correct. Movie fans were not shocked by *A Farewell to Arms* and were entertained by *Ann Vickers.* By June 1933, the battle lines were clear: The studios were determined to forge ahead, and Hays was searching for a formula that would allow him to retain control of the industry through "self-regulation." Quigley and Lord, no longer interested in cooperating with Hays, were seeking their own formula.

Movie sexuality, however, was only one part of the complaint that films were changing American behavior. Civic leaders, judges and law enforcement officials, moral guardians, and film censors accused film gangsters of creating a new class of American criminals. Movies had to be purified, this coalition of concerned citizens argued, not only of prostitutes and illicit sex, but also of criminals and corrupt politicians.

Notes

1 Speech quoted in Carl Van Doren, *Sinclair Lewis* (Port Washington, N.Y.: Kennikat Press, 1933), p. 8.

2 Johnathon Green, *The Encyclopaedia of Censorship* (New York: Facts on File, 1990), pp. 137–9. The church also published a "white list," official-

ly known as the Catholic Book Survey, of books that Catholics could safely read. To qualify, the book "must be worthy of mature intelligence," must not "offend the Christian sense of truth and decency," and must "bear the marks of good literary craftsmanship." The list was published quarterly. For a sample, see *New York Times*, Sept. 20, 1932, p. 20.

3 Raphael M. Huber, *Our Bishops Speak* (Milwaukee: Bruce, 1952), p. 199.

4 *New York Times*, Nov. 20, 1932, p. 30.

5 Francis X. Talbot, S.J., "Smut," *America* 48 (Feb. 11, 1933), pp. 460–1, and "More on Smut," ibid. (Feb. 25, 1933), pp. 500–1. See also *New York Times*, Feb. 23, 1933, p. 15. Within the year, Father Talbot would emerge as one of the leaders of the Legion of Decency movement.

6 *Literary Digest* 109 (April 25, 1931), p. 23.

7 *Washington Post*, Sept. 3, 1933, p. 20.

8 Ernest Hemingway, *A Farewell to Arms*, p. 327.

9 Fred Herron to H. A. Banday, Sept. 2, 1930, *A Farewell to Arms*, PCA; *All Quiet on the Western Front*, PCA.

10 Frank M. Laurence, *Hemingway and the Movies*, p. 48.

11 *New York Times*, Oct. 12, 1932, p. 25.

12 Trotti to Files, July 19, 1932, *A Farewell to Arms*, PCA.

13 Ibid.

14 Memo to Files, Nov. 25, 1932, *A Farewell to Arms*, PCA.

15 Memo to Files, Dec. 7, 1932, *A Farewell to Arms*, PCA.

16 Dinneen to Parsons, Jan. 2, 1932 [1933], box 202/203, PP. Dinneen made the mistake common at the start of a new year and dated the letter 1932 when it should have been 1933.

17 *Nation* 129 (Oct. 12, 1929), p. 231.

18 Richard Maltby, "*Baby Face* or How Joe Breen Made Barbara Stanwyck Atone for Causing the Wall Street Crash," *Screen* 27 (1986), pp. 38–9.

19 Breen to Hays, Mar. 2, 1933, box 45, HP.

20 *Harrison's Reports*, Mar. 4, 1933.

21 Raymond Moley, *The Hays Office*, p. 78.

22 Hays to Mr. Blank, Mar. 7, 1933, LP.

23 Moley, *Hays Office*, p. 253.

24 Ibid. Hays went to Hollywood to deliver the message personally in April 1933.

25 *Hackensack Recorder*, Feb. 24, 1933 (in box 46, HP).

26 *Philadelphia Inquirer*, Jan. 29, 1933 (in box 46, HP).

27 Gene D. Phillips, *Fiction, Film, and Faulkner*, p. 69. See also E. Pauline Degenfelder, "The Four Faces of Temple Drake."

28 *Harrison's Reports*, Mar. 18, 1933. Harrison published his correspondence with Paramount; the studio countered by stating that the project had been approved by Wingate.

29 Hays to Wingate, Feb. 9, 1933, *The Story of Temple Drake*, PCA.

30 Wingate to Hays, Feb. 3, 1933, *The Story of Temple Drake*, PCA.

31 Phillips, *Fiction, Film, and Faulkner*, pp. 69–74.

32 Breen to Wingate, Mar. 17, 1933, *The Story of Temple Drake*, PCA.

33 Cohen to Hays, Mar. 24, 1933, *The Story of Temple Drake*, PCA.

34 Irwin Esmond to Wingate, April 14, 1933, *The Story of Temple Drake,* PCA.

35 Ibid. See also Hays to Zukor, Mar. 28, 1933, and Wingate to Botsford, Mar. 27, 1933, *The Story of Temple Drake,* PCA.

36 *Time* 21 (May 15, 1933), p. 36.

37 Ibid.

38 *Nation* 136 (May 2, 1933), pp. 594–5.

39 Quoted in K. L. Russell to Hays, May 23, 1933, *The Story of Temple Drake,* PCA.

40 *Syracuse Herald*, May 21, 1933 (in box 46, HP).

41 *Harrison's Reports*, May 13, 1933.

42 *Nation* 136 (May 24, 1933), pp. 594–5.

43 Quoted in K. L. Russell to Hays, May 23, 1933, *The Story of Temple Drake,* PCA.

44 *New York Times*, Mar. 7, 1933, p. 18.

45 M. C. Dawson, "Sanctuary," *Books* (Jan. 29, 1933), p. 1.

46 *Boston Transcript*, Jan. 28, 1933, p. 1.

47 *Saturday Review of Literature* 7 (Feb. 11, 1933), p. 143.

48 *Spectator* 147 (Feb. 3, 1933), p. 160.

49 *New York Evening Post*, Jan. 28, 1933, p. 7.

50 *New York Times*, Feb. 17, 1933, p. 18.

51 *Catholic World* 36 (Feb. 1933), p. 622.

52 Talbot, "More on Smut," pp. 500–1.

53 Mark Schorer, *Sinclair Lewis: An American Life* (New York: McGraw-Hill, 1961), p. 578.

54 Breen to Wingate, May 5, 1933, *Ann Vickers,* PCA.

55 Ibid.; Wingate to Meriam C. Cooper (RKO), May 8, 1933, *Ann Vickers,* PCA.

56 Cooper to Wingate, May 11, 1933, *Ann Vickers,* PCA.

57 Ibid.

58 B. B. Kahane to Hays, June 27, 1933, *Ann Vickers,* PCA.

59 Ibid.

60 Hays to Kahane, July 5, 1933, *Ann Vickers,* PCA.

61 Kahane to Hays, July 10, 1933, *Ann Vickers,* PCA.

62 Hays to Kahane, July 31, 1933, LP. The letter was sent to all studio heads; a copy was sent to Daniel Lord.

63 Wingate to Hays, Aug. 26, 1933, *Ann Vickers,* PCA.

CHAPTER 5

BEER, BLOOD, AND POLITICS

Many prisoners have told me that crime pictures started them on their
course.   – Lewis E. Lawes, Warden, Sing Sing Prison

When MGM announced plans for making a movie about Billy the Kid,
a psychotic teenage gunslinger who had achieved something of folk-
lore status in popular westerns, reformers protested. Elmer T. Peterson, editor of *Better Homes and Gardens,* told Will Hays that a film of
young Billy's violent life would be a mistake if it transformed the killer
into a "hero." It would promote disrespect for the law among children, and lead to an increase in juvenile delinquency, Peterson alleged.
Hays forwarded Peterson's letter to Joy, who immediately began
working with MGM writers to reform the gunslinger into a "religious
Scotchman" who is being "persecuted and harassed by a ruffian." Joy
assured Peterson that in the movie young Billy "is inspired by the love
of a fine girl" and is "on the side of law and order fighting to clean up
the territory." According to Joy, the only thing left of the "real story
of Billy the Kid is the name itself."[1]

While Joy succeeded in taming the teenage psychotic of western
lore, he would experience considerably more controversy over movie
versions of modern psychotic killers who prowled the wild West fron-
tier town of South Chicago circa 1925. Prohibition, the "noble experi-
ment," generated an unpleasant side effect few people had predicted.
With millions of dollars to be made from illegal alcohol, urban gangs
emerged as the primary suppliers of bootleg beer and whiskey. Gang
wars erupted on city streets, and in one five-year period in Chicago
480 gangsters were killed by either colleagues or the police. As the
bullets flew and beer flowed, the gangsters were sensationalized in the
press, either as brutal killers or modern-day Robin Hoods. Colorful
characters like "Scarface" Al Capone, his Chicago rivals Dion O'Bannion, Bugs Moran, and a host of other criminals were constant front-
page news. Their bloody gang wars, their dangerous and flashy life-
style, both shocked and fascinated the nation. Yet despite the fact that

107

almost everyone in America was familiar with gangsters' exploits, moral guardians held that movies dealing with their lives would harm American children. Gangsters, they contended, should be banned from the screen.

The motion picture code specified: "Law, natural or human, shall not be ridiculed, nor shall sympathy be created for its violation." It further demanded that no film create a feeling of audience "sympathy for criminals." Did these provisions prohibit filmmakers from building stories around a corrupt judge or an inefficient judicial system? Was the industry prohibited from any drama that dealt with injustice in society? Were comedies and political satires proscribed because they might poke fun at cops or politicians? Did the code mean that all crime films must show criminals as social deviants, people devoid of human qualities? Could there be no modern Robin Hoods on the screen? No kind-hearted criminals? Could Hollywood, for example, make a film that would show criminals benefiting by police incompetence and getting away with crime because of a corrupt judge?

Did the code, with its provisions that government be presented in a favorable manner, really mean that Hollywood could not make a film dealing with political corruption? Did the code prohibit the industry from interpreting modern social, political, and economic issues in entertainment films? Would Lord, Quigley, and the film-reform movement oppose films that were not "immoral" in any traditional sense, but did treat serious political and social issues in such a way that they might be thought controversial? Would these films violate the code?

No one in Hollywood believed the 1930 code was intended to prevent Hollywood from making films that touched on contemporary issues. While the industry had never been known for its commitment to realism, there were some producers who wanted to make films that combined good entertainment with social and political commentary. Gangster movies, realistic portrayals of life in America's prisons, and films dealing with the harsh realities of the Depression were viewed by Hays as dangerous. Self-censorship would force Hollywood producers away from this type of film.

It was only natural that the film industry would want to bring gangsters – colorful, violent men, whose daily activities were followed by millions of Americans – to the screen. Yet more than any other genre, the gangster film created problems for Hays, Joy, and Wingate in reconciling the code with drama. Gangster films cut to the very center of what was acceptable on the screen.

Contending that films based on the activities of criminals led to an increase in crime and juvenile delinquency, the movie reformers accused the industry of leading impressionable youth into a life of crime.

Canon William Chase, with typical hyperbole, claimed that "the motion picture screen for the past twenty-five years has been a school for
crime."[2] Dr. Fred Eastman, another long-time critic, wrote in the
Christian Century that "the movies were so occupied with crime and
sex stuff and are so saturating the minds of children the world over
with social sewage that they have become a menace to the mental and
moral life of the coming generation."[3] As a modern Huck Finn told
Alice Miller Mitchell in her 1929 survey of the effect of movies on
Chicago school children:

Movies sorter coax a feller. You know, you see them in the movies doing
things, looks so easy. They get money easy in the movies, holdups, rob, if
they make a mistake they get caught. A feller thinks he won't make a mistake if he tries it. I thought I could get the money, put it in a bank a long time
and then use it later.[4]

This budding investment banker seemingly confirmed what many people were convinced was true: Crime movies caused crime.

In the case of crime movies, traditional denouncers of film were
joined by police, judges, lawyers, mayors, newspapers, and civic organizations in condemning the harmful effects of the genre. Even the
Hays Office admitted that protests over gangster movies came from a
"growing body of public opinion" that was not normally associated
with the antimovie lobby. The highly respected reform warden of Sing
Sing Prison, Lewis E. Lawes, alarmed the nation when he claimed that
"many prisoners have told me that crime pictures started them on
their course." The public safety director of Philadelphia blamed a contemporary crime wave in his city on "the meticulous care which the
moving picture people take in instructing the youth of our nation exactly how to commit crime." His counterpart in Newark agreed: "Juvenile delinquency is directly caused by motion pictures."[5]

Many of the leading newspapers and magazines joined in the chorus
of complaints. The usually conservative *Christian Science Monitor* deplored the determination of Hollywood to create "an admiration of
the criminal as a dramatic figure." In Houston the *Chronicle* blasted
the industry for infecting the public with a plague of "bedroom, liquor, gangster and criminal themes." Newark, New Jersey, agreed
when the *Ledger* claimed gangster movies were "poisoning the minds
of the youth of this country"; in neighboring Summit, the *Herald* was
nauseated by movie "crooks and soiled women who strut their stuff."
Commonweal branded the movies as a "social milieu that serves as a
very fair kindergarten of crime." The *Kansas City Times* less hysteri-
cally observed that, although such films were not harmful to adults,
"they are misleading, contaminating and often demoralizing to children and youth."[6]

As crime films multiplied, state and local censorship boards began to snip furiously away, trying to curb the violence and disrespect for law and order on the screen. In Chicago, a city admittedly sensitive to screen criminals, nearly half of the cuts made in films during 1930–1 were for glorifying the criminal or showing the police as ineffective: As *Variety* so aptly put it, "Chi Censors Rank Gun Play Ahead of Sex in Their Taboos."[7] In New York, censors slashed over 2,200 crime scenes during 1930–2. The State of Virginia sent an official letter of protest to Hays over the rise of screen violence. The *Christian Century* lamented sarcastically that in 1931, another year of "Hays-Cleaned" movies, there were 260 film murders.[8] While this figure is tame by modern media standards of violence, it was considered excessive by film denouncers and many law enforcement personnel.

This avalanche of protest in the early 1930s was prompted by an explosion of flashy movie gangsters. The dangerous but fascinating urban underworld epitomized life in the fast lane: Movie gangsters spoke a colorful argot, their guns barked out their own form of law, and their cars squealed around corners at breathtaking speed. In an era of Depression, their reward was money, fast cars, admiring friends, fancy clothes, and even fancier women. These gangland hoods flouted the traditions of hard work, sacrifice, and respect for institutions of authority; that they lost all they had gained, either by death or arrest in the last reel of the film, did not undo the harm they caused to impressionable moviegoers, claimed critics.

Screens were flooded with gangster films in the early 1930s. *Doorway to Hell* (1930) was a "swell . . . trigger opera," said *Variety,* that "bumps off plenty of the boys" and introduced James Cagney as a tough guy.[9] Within months *The Finger Points, City Streets, The Secret Six, The Vice Squad, Quick Millions,* and *Star Witness* were released (all 1931). They featured tough, exciting guys willing to kill, boring, incompetent cops, and beautiful, sexy women. *Star Witness* was based on a real gang killing in Harlem in which several children were killed. *Variety* admitted the theme was "ghastly," but labeled the film "anti-gang propaganda."[10] *The Secret Six* was based on a vigilante committee in Chicago and featured crime violence and political corruption. One variation on the theme was *Blondie Johnson* (1933), in which Joan Blondell traded in her moll's negligee for more conservative dress as the head of the Mob. Driven to a life of crime by a failed economy, "Blondie" showed the men how to make big money in the rackets. In 1930 nine gangster films were released; 1931 saw twenty-six, 1932 twenty-eight, and 1933 fifteen.[11]

These latter films followed the overwhelming success of three released in 1931–2 that captivated the American movie public and infuriated law enforcement officials, reformers, and censors – Edward G.

Robinson as Rico Bandello in *Little Caesar,* James Cagney as Tom Powers in *The Public Enemy,* and Paul Muni in *Scarface: Shame of the Nation.* Robinson, Cagney, and Muni dominated their respective films, and, despite the fact that each was killed in the final reel, reformers believed each movie violated the code by creating "sympathy" for the criminal and/or taught the methods of successful crime to impressionable youth.

When *Little Caesar* opened in January 1931, at the Warner Bros.' Strand Theater at Broadway and 47th Street, New York City, police were summoned. There was no protest, just an estimated crowd of some 3,000 persons who "stormed the two box offices" and shattered two glass doors trying to crowd into the theater to see Edward G. Robinson's incredible portrayal of Al Capone as a sadistic, amoral, cold-blooded killer. *Little Caesar* focused the nation's attention on the gangster movie and on the question of what constituted proper entertainment.

In June 1929, Dial Press had published a sensational novel, *Little Caesar,* written by W. R. Burnett. In the mid-1920s Burnett had moved from Columbus, Ohio, to Chicago, where he was befriended by some local hoods. Burnett, who held all the middle-class values of small-town America, had been appalled by Chicago and the hoodlums who controlled the city.[12] He soon discovered that his values were seen as "utter nonsense" by his criminal friends, who killed without remorse. After viewing the aftermath of the St. Valentine's Day Massacre – "It was a slaughterhouse – blood all over the wall and guys lying around on the floor" – he had written *Little Caesar.* Burnett, who had had no literary training, shunned literary style for the street slang of the gangster, which shocked the critics and delighted readers; but perhaps more than style it was the novel's point of view that made *Little Caesar* stand out. Burnett had written from the perspective of the gangster: "I treated 'em as human beings."[13]

Little Caesar was tailor-made for Warner Bros. The studio had made its mark with low-budget, fast-paced features that had as heroes the victims and losers in contemporary American society. Warners' production head, Darryl F. Zanuck, had first come to the studio in 1924 as a writer and was promoted to chief of production in 1929. Under Zanuck the studio "emphasized male action films" and stark, hard-bitten reality.[14] The gangster genre was a perfect fit, and Burnett's story of a pathological killer fascinated studio boss Jack Warner, who paid $15,000 for the screen rights and rushed the film into production. Directed by Mervyn Le Roy, the film starred Robinson as Caesar Enrico Bandello, "Little Caesar," and featured Douglas Fairbanks, Jr., as Joe Massara, Rico's sidekick, and Thomas Jackson as

Sergeant Flaherty, the determined "copper" who beats Rico at his own game.

The film opens with a close-up of the front cover of Burnett's novel and then fades to a biblical quotation: "For all those that take the sword shall perish with the sword." From the quotation the film cross-fades to a car driving into a gas station late at night. A darkened figure emerges from the car and moves silently toward the station. The lights go out. Two shots shatter the silence. A man walks slowly toward the car, climbs in, and the car roars down the road. Caesar Enrico Bandello has struck.

Later, in a cheap roadside diner, Rico and his pal Joe muse over their latest crime. Rico picks up a discarded newspaper that headlines: "Underworld Pay Respects to Diamond Pete Montana." He is distressed that he is a small-time hood; he longs for the big time and the respect and admiration it obviously brings. Rico shuns the trappings of power – he neither drinks nor has his own moll – but lusts for power itself, and realizes that his gun is his ticket to respect. Like Burnett's gangster friends, Rico feels no remorse over killing: "When I get in a tight spot, I shoot my way out of it. Like tonight . . . sure, shoot first – argue afterwards. If you don't the other feller gets you. This game ain't for guys that's soft." Rico is headed for the big time.[15]

In the big city Rico is taken in by gang leader Sam Vettori (Stanley Fields), who warns him that gunplay is out. The city has a new crime commissioner, McClure, who the gang members are warned is incorruptible: Even the "Big Boy," a respected member of society who secretly bosses all the gangs, cannot bribe McClure. This comment demonstrates that the gangs operate at will because "respected" members of society protect them. Rico takes this warning from Sam with a measure of disgust. He now realizes that the gang and the bosses have become soft. They are ripe for the taking.

While Rico is climbing the ladder of success in the underworld, his buddy Joe has turned away from crime and taken a job as a dancer at the Bronze Peacock, headquarters of a rival gang leader, Little Arnie Lorch (Stanley Black). He has fallen in love with his beautiful dancing partner, Olga (Glenda Farrell), and longs to escape the clutches of Rico and his past life of crime.

Meanwhile Rico, without his boss's knowledge, has laid plans for a daring New Year's Eve robbery of the Bronze Peacock, forcing Joe to participate in the heist. Rico's plans are perfect, except for one unforeseen detail: Commissioner McClure is celebrating New Year's Eve at the nightclub. When he discovers that the Bronze Peacock is owned by a gangster, McClure storms out in protest and right into the middle of the robbery. Foolishly he reaches for his gun, and Rico guns him down in a hail of bullets. The city is outraged by this flagrant display of gang violence.

Figure 5. Edward G. Robinson in *Little Caesar*. Courtesy the Museum of Modern Art / Film Stills Archive.

The heat is on. The gangs are told to lay low. While Sergeant Flaherty knows that Rico killed the commissioner, he has no evidence, and watches helplessly as Rico continues his rise to fame. Rico easily pushes the weak-kneed Sam aside and now runs the local gang. When one of the Mob suffers from guilt over his role in a murder and rushes to confess his sins to his priest, Rico guns him down on the church steps. As Rico explains to his Mob: "I'm as religious as you are any day. But a guy who'll talk to the priest will talk to other people, too." When gang rival Arnie Lorch tries unsuccessfully to have Rico killed, Rico runs him out of town.

Rico is now the boss of the gangs, his ascendency confirmed when the "Big Boy" summons him to dinner and asks if Rico would like to take over the entire operation. Would he ever! Rico, now in charge, realizes that he needs someone he can trust. He has stabbed so many people in the back climbing to the top he turns to the only person on whom he can rely: his old friend Joe Massara. But Joe is terrified of Rico and tries to beg off. Rico is enraged and threatens to kill Joe's girlfriend Olga if he will not return to the gang. Joe begs Olga to run away with him, but she refuses. She explains to Joe – and presumably to all the kids in the audience – that if they are ever to be safe from people like Rico they must go to Detective Flaherty. The protection offered by the police is our only answer, she tells her cowering lover. She phones the police and tells Flaherty that Joe is willing to testify.

Suddenly Rico and another gunman burst into the room. He has come to kill Olga and Joe, yet even Rico has a fatal flaw: His love for Joe overcomes his desire for power. He cannot pull the trigger on his best friend. When the other gunman tries, Rico hits his arm, and Joe is wounded. With police sirens wailing in the background, Rico escapes: "This is what I get for liking a guy too much," he mutters. When Joe and Olga spill the beans on the gang, the police – totally helpless up to this point in the movie – suddenly spring into action. Rico's gang is rounded up and tossed in jail; only Rico has managed to escape.

The scene shifts to a dingy flophouse several months later. Three bums are reading a newspaper story, planted by Flaherty, that describes Rico as a yellow coward. "Meteoric as his rise from the gutter has been, it was inevitable that he should return there." The camera pans to another bed. Rico is, indeed, in the gutter. He is unshaven and dirty and guzzles cheap booze from a brown paper bag. As he listens to the men reading the newspaper account of his rise and fall, his prideful arrogance surfaces – just as Flaherty had hoped. Enraged at his description as a coward, he storms out of the flophouse and challenges Flaherty to come gunning for him. In the last scene Rico is machine-gunned down by the police and mutters, "Mother of Mercy – is this the end of Rico?" Little Caesar is dead. The crime wave is over.

Depending on how one looked at the film, it was either a sensational condemnation of the criminal or a dangerously inviting illustration of how successful a life of crime could be. Those who saw the film as the former pointed to the determination of the police to break up the gang, the lessons of Joe Massara, and the willingness of Olga to help society by giving evidence to the police. Although it is clear that Rico benefited in the short run, supporters of the film pointed to his rapid fall and inglorious death. The *New York Times* described Rico as a "cold, ignorant, merciless killer" that no one would want to emulate.[16]

Film reformers were not so sure: They believed audiences, especially young males, saw Rico as the hero. He was brash, clever, and daring whereas the police were dull, witless, and plodding. Edward G. Robinson completely dominated the film, and all action centered on him, not the police. In the end his downfall was caused by his own weakness, not by any cleverness on the part of the police. The reformers' view seemed confirmed when film critic Creighton Peet wrote:

"And let me tell you that when Sergeant Flaherty's machine gun cuts him down at the end, the audience goes home mighty quiet and depressed." To reformers, the appointment of the unbribable new crime commissioner implied that the gangs succeeded because the system was corrupt. While audiences across the nation flocked to see *Little Caesar*, protests poured into the Hays Office. New York Congressman Fiorello La Guardia saw the film and "raised hell" with Hays, threatening to introduce federal censorship legislation. Maurice McKenzie, Hays's executive assistant, calmly dismissed La Guardia's complaint: "My guess is that La Guardia is sore because *Little Caesar* [Edward G. Robinson] looks like him."[17]

Jason Joy was perplexed by the criticism. The submission of scripts was voluntary, and he had seen neither the script nor the film. To satisfy his own curiosity, Joy went to a local Los Angeles theater and watched *Little Caesar*. He reported back to the New York office that the "audience loved" the film and so did he. How anybody can object to any part of the film "is beyond me," he told McKenzie.[18]

In New York, however, the censorship board was embarrassed by the film's success and complaints from police, women's clubs, church organizations, and parents. Dr. James Wingate, director of the Empire State's censorship board and the person who would soon replace Joy, told Hays that his office had been flooded with complaints about *Little Caesar* from people who were appalled when children in the theater "applaud the gang leader as a hero." Wingate objected, in general, to films that showed criminals "riding around in a Rolls-Royce and living in luxury," and having enough money to buy the best lawyers who kept them out of jail. In his opinion, these films "lessen respect for law." Even if the gangster is killed in the last reel, Wingate was convinced that "the child unconsciously forms the idea that he will be smarter and will get away with it."[19] Wingate wanted *Little Caesar* censored.

In Los Angeles, Joy was totally befuddled by such logic. Defending *Little Caesar* as a stern "moral lesson" that crime does not pay, Joy argued that censorship did not entail, in his opinion, removing all reality from the screen. There were criminals and there were corrupt officials, and no moral lessons could be taught if the screen did not use real life to illustrate morality. "Always drama has been permitted to paint the unconventional, the unlawful, the immoral side of life in order to bring out in immediate contrast . . . benefits derived from wholesome, clean and law-abiding conduct." Joy believed *Little Caesar* was an excellent example of this contrast at work. Chiding Wingate, he added that in his view censors should not be "small, narrow, picayunish" individuals who only remove little details from films and fail to see the overall message. "We are sure," he wrote, "that it was never intended that censorship should be destructive . . . but rather that its duty should be a constructive one of influencing the final quality of the final impression left on the minds of the audience." If this were done, the code would work; if not, if censorship turned "narrow and picayunish," the producers would destroy the code because there would be no room to create serious drama.[20] Joy's comment went to the heart of the argument over the role of censorship: Should censors strike all things unpleasant from the screen or simply try to keep filmmakers from excessive or exploitative sex and violence? This question would dominate the debate over film censorship and self-regulation for the next three years. Its final outcome would rest with the "narrow and picayunish" constraints imposed by Joe Breen and the Catholic Legion of Decency.

Despite Joy's plea, New York's censors slashed the film, as did Pennsylvania's. *Little Caesar* was banned in the Canadian provinces of British Columbia, Alberta, and Nova Scotia and in Australia. *Parent's Magazine* declared the film unfit for children. Yet *Little Caesar* played without cuts, and seemingly without unleashing new crime waves, in the rest of the nation. In Joy's opinion, the censors only succeeded in making a meaningless gangster film out of a film "which would harm no one, be enjoyed by all, and really contains moral and ethical values which command it beyond most stories."[21]

While Hays and Joy were accused by movie reformers of not enforcing the code, Joy's views illustrate a clear difference of opinion over what was and was not censorable. Although he had not seen the script for *Little Caesar*, he would not have censored it if he had. In his view the film was good entertainment fused with a strong dose of "crime does not pay." His reaction was similar when Warner Bros. released another hard-hitting gangster drama just three months later.

The Public Enemy (1931) brought to the screen another fast-talking, trigger-happy hood who captivated movie audiences. With real events drawn from Chicago's Charles Dion "Deanie" O'Bannion, arch-rival of Al Capone, *The Public Enemy* did for Irish hoods what *Little Caesar* did for Italians. Based on an original short story by Kubec Glasman and John Bright, adapted for the screen by Harry Thew, and starring James Cagney, the film was directed by William Wellman, who promised producer Darryl Zanuck "the toughest, the most violent, most realistic picture" ever made. Wellman shot the film in a record twenty-six days and for a modest $150,000. This proved to be one of the best investments Warner Bros. ever made.

Broadway song-and-dance man James Cagney had come to Hollywood in 1930. After making *Sinner's Holiday* with Joan Blondell, he had landed a supporting role in the gangster film *Doorway to Hell,* which starred the boyish Lew Ayres as the gang boss. Cagney's brash "tough guy" had dominated the film and caught the attention of Wellman, who cast him in the lead role of *The Public Enemy:* Tom Powers, a cold-blooded killer who strikes whenever he wishes and totally without remorse. Cagney, like Robinson, fascinated audiences, who found themselves "rooting" for a killer. Unlike Rico, Powers spurns neither alcohol nor women: He is surrounded by a trio of sexy, lingerie-clad molls, played by Mae Clarke, Joan Blondell, and Jean Harlow. The role made a movie star of Cagney and forever typecast him as a "tough guy."

The film opens with a quick montage that establishes Tom Powers as a typical urban slum kid. While his family appears stable, his father, a policeman, is uncaring and brutal: His view of discipline is a good whipping with his belt. Tom's mother, played by Beryl Mercer, is loving but totally blind to her son's juvenile delinquency and graduation into a full-blown criminal. Tom's big brother Mike (Donald Cook) emerges from this same environment as a stable, hard-working war veteran who epitomizes the "raise-yourself-up-by-the-bootstraps" philosophy of life. Mike tries to persuade his young brother to lead an honest life, but Tom refuses.

The neighborhood where they live provides ample temptation to lead an easier life. Despite his father's occupation, or perhaps because of it, Tom aimlessly drifts into crime. He mocks his brother who is, in his view, "learning how to be poor." From occasional youthful petty theft, Tom meets a sleazy two-bit hood, Putty Nose (Murray Kinnell), who runs his own version of a boys' club, recruiting slum urchins to steal for him and then fencing the hot goods. Tom and his friend Matt (Edward Woods) are taught the tricks of criminal life, given guns, and sent off on their first big heist: a fur-storage warehouse. During the robbery Tom pulls back a rack of furs and is so frightened by a huge stuffed bear that he fires several shots. The noise brings the police, one of whom is killed by Tom as he and Matt escape. When Putty Nose refuses to hide them, Tom swears revenge. The scene establishes Tom as a criminal who is willing to kill and feels no guilt. For those critical of Hollywood, the killing of a policeman was reason enough to censor the film.

After being abandoned by Putty Nose, Tom and Matt turn to another local crook, saloon owner Paddy Ryan (Robert E. O'Conner), who brings the boys into the bootlegging business. During the day they double as honest deliverymen for a local trucking company; by night they rob. Prohibition has made alcohol illegal, and when Tom's company gets a contract to deliver alcohol to government facilities, he seizes a golden opportunity: The boys pull off a daring theft of government alcohol. The profits are enormous, and Tom's early lesson is that crime certainly does pay.

The easy money immediately bestows all the trappings of success: a fancy car, nice clothes, and lots and lots of money. Maître d's at Chicago's finest restaurants and nightclubs fawn over Tom whenever he appears. One evening he and Matt go into a local nightclub and spot two good-looking women, Kitty (Mae Marsh) and Mamie (Joan Blondell), sitting at a table with inebriated men. The girls are bored with their "dates," and Tom orders the waiter to "get rid of them two stiffs." Kitty and Mamie squeal with delight, and within a few minutes' screen time the foursome – Tom with Kitty and Matt with Mamie – have set up housekeeping in a large apartment. Matt and Mamie are in love and plan to be married, but the relationship between Tom and Kitty quickly turns sour. One morning Tom stumbles to the breakfast table, apparently hung over from an evening of hard drinking. Offscreen the audience hears the playful giggling of Matt and Mamie from their bedroom. Tom is in no such mood, and barks at Kitty:

TOM: Ain't you got a drink in the house?

KITTY: Not before breakfast, Tom.

TOM: I didn't ask you for any lip – I asked you for a drink.

KITTY: Gee, I wish . . .

TOM: *(explodes)* There you go with that wishing business. I wish you was a wishing well cause I could tie a bucket to ya and sink ya.

KITTY: *(head down and speaking softly)* Maybe ya found somebody ya like better.

Tom says nothing. He looks at Kitty with complete disgust, then picks up the grapefruit she has prepared for breakfast and smashes it in her face. Although it is a violent scene, with the sound track recording the impact of the fruit on Kitty's face, audience sympathy is not drawn toward Mae Clarke: She is a whining nag who has upset her man. Contemporary audiences laughed and cheered this scene – to the consternation of film reformers, who pounced on this as yet another example of making a hero out of a social deviant.

In the very next scene, Tom finds a woman who can excite him. He and Matt are driving downtown when they spot a voluptuous blonde bouncing down the street. Gwen Allen (Jean Harlow) simply oozes sex. They offer her a ride, which she accepts, and before she leaves she asks Tom for his phone number! Modern women were not bound by tradition. In a later scene that caused ministers and women's clubs to shudder, Tom and Gwen are talking in her hotel room. Dressed in a slinky negligee, she lounges on a settee; he sits on a chair, playing with his hat. They discuss their sexual relationship. Tom complains to Gwen that "all my friends think things are different." He feels frustrated that she is keeping him on a "merry-go-round." While "I Surrender, Dear" plays softly in the background, Gwen moves in for the kill. She sits on Tom's lap, pulls his head to her chest, and coos: "You're a spoiled boy, Tommy." Gwen confesses that she has been somewhat confused by her attraction to a gangster:

Men that I know, and I've known dozens of them – they're so nice, so polished, so considerate. Most women like that type. I guess they're afraid of the other type. . . . I thought I was, too, but you're so STRONG. You don't give . . . you take! Oh Tommy! I could love you to death.

It is readily apparent that Gwen was seeking neither middle-class respectability nor marriage: She wanted Tom because he was violent, powerful, and, above all, exciting. No longer interested in security, she realized that she wanted a man who would take what he wanted, including her, when he wanted it. She was more than willing to toss societal approval to the wind and live with a "common criminal." Moreover, Harlow was clearly the aggressor; even Cagney looked a bit uncomfortable. This was not the type of message the reformers wanted the movies to give to the young men and women of America.

While Cagney and Harlow are sorting out their feelings for each other, the gang war goes on over the "beer" territory. Tom is now working for Nails Nathan (Leslie Fenton), who is killed riding a horse. Tom does the only thing he can think of: He buys the horse and kills it to avenge the death of his boss.[22] The death of Nails brings another outburst of violence as the rival gangs slug it out for control of the territory. Paddy Ryan orders his boys to hide in an apartment that he has stocked with girls, booze, and cards until the heat cools off. One evening, after several days of hiding, Tom gets stinking drunk; the next morning he discovers, much to his disgust, that one of the girls seduced him. After slapping her around, Tom and Matt storm out of the hideout and into a hail of bullets from their rivals. Matt is killed, Tom is injured.

Like a raging bull, Tom sets out to avenge the death of his boyhood buddy. He single-handedly attacks the headquarters of the rival gang, and with two guns blazing kills several of its members. This is no sterile movie kill: The sound track is filled with cries of pain, groans of agony, and shrieks of fear as Tom blazes away at his enemies. People are dying. In the battle, Tom is wounded. He stumbles out into the street, blood pouring from his face, and mutters: "I ain't so tough." But everyone in the audience knows he is.

The next scene takes place in Tom's hospital room, where he is recovering from his wounds. His family is gathered around him. Tom's brother is now inexplicably willing to forgive him, and it has never occurred to his mother not to. Touched by this show of family love, Tom decides to give up his life of crime and return to the family hearth.

Back home everyone is excited about the return of the prodigal son. It is late at night. There is a knock at the door; it is Paddy Ryan, who tells Mike that the rival gang has kidnapped Tom. Ryan, out of love for his pal, has offered to leave the city and give up his gang if Tom's life will be spared. Then a phone call. Mike tells the family that Tom is coming home immediately. His mother rushes to prepare his room – her baby is finally returning to her nest. Another knock on the door. Mike opens it. It is Tom. His heavily bandaged and bullet-ridden body collapses into the living room. Tommy has finally come home. The criminals have served justice with their own code.

The Public Enemy was, true to Wellman's pledge, a violent and bloody portrayal of contemporary America. It was a Hollywood attempt, however feeble, to identify America's festering urban slums as a societal problem that created a criminal class, and a condemnation of Prohibition for providing criminals with the opportunity to gain semirespectability. Unlike *Little Caesar,* the film was loaded with sexual tension. Cagney openly lived with Kitty and was pursued by Gwen. He slapped his women around, and they either liked it or moved out. There was no doubt that this was a violent man.

Yet Cagney, like Robinson, was the "hero" of the film. His brother, who fought for his country and went to night school in an effort to "make good," came off as a goody-goody sap; there was no audience sympathy for him. His parents were no better: His father was an uncaring "brute" and his mother so dense that she failed to understand her son was a brutal killer.[23]

Rather than being shocked by this story of mayhem and sex, Joy found *The Public Enemy* "entirely satisfactory" and praised the studio for its "marvelous job" of depicting the "moral lesson" that crime did not pay. Joy found it hard to believe that anyone could desire a life as a criminal after watching the film. Lamar Trotti agreed: He told Hays that while the film was "potentially dangerous," it was generally defensible as "a piece of realism of current conditions."[24]

Variety, to Wellman's delight, called the film the "roughest, most powerful and best gang film to date."[25] The *National Board of Review Magazine* praised it not only for its realism of gangsters, but also for its treatment of women: "No girl, no matter how waywardly romantic, is likely to get any illusions about the thrill of being a gangster's moll from seeing how the ladies fare in this film." The *Review* was a bit troubled by the inescapable fact that the "strongest impression" in the film was that there "was something likable and courageous about the little rat [Cagney] after all." But even so, the review doubted that any young man was likely to get the idea that a career as a gangster "is any fun."[26]

Time reported that the audience was "spellbound" throughout the film.[27] When Cagney hit Clarke with the grapefruit, the audience howled with delight. It was rumored in Hollywood that Clarke's ex-husband, Monte Brice, saw the film repeatedly, and laughed with hysterical delight when that grapefruit smashed into his ex-wife's face. The point was that audiences everywhere loved Cagney's portrayal of a swaggering, cocky, little braggart turned killer. They mourned his death, just as they had Rico's. Because of this reaction, *Parent's Magazine*, long critical of gang films, warned parents that the film was "too violent" and "too exciting" for children.[28] The magazine advised concerned parents that *City Streets* was "a vivid and thrilling glorification of gangsterism," *Quick Millions* was "stupid," and *The Secret Six,* although one of the best of the genre, offered children "a liberal education in gang manners and methods."

State censors and women's groups agreed. The film, even after being slashed by the censors, caused a flood of protest to pour into the Hays office. New York censors eliminated the scene in which Putty Nose hands Tom and Matt a gun, removed all scenes of the warehouse robbery, cut the scenes showing the boys getting their payoff from the government liquor heist, edited out most of the scene of Tom killing Putty Nose, and dropped the seduction of Tom by one of Paddy's "girls" and Tom's slapping her around. New York similarly cut the other gangster movies, removing all scenes of gangsters with guns, thereby making these films senseless.[29]

By mid-1931 pressure from ministers, women's clubs, and civic organizations resulted in gangster films being banned in Worcester, Massachusetts; Syracuse, New York; Evanston, Illinois; and West Orange, New Jersey. Chicago's Mayor Anton Cermak threatened to ban all crime movies if Hollywood did not stop using the Windy City as its favorite backdrop for machine guns, murder, graft, and immorality.

Despite these protests film audiences were fascinated with this new breed of flashy movie gangster. They flocked to the theaters because the films were exciting, entertaining, and loud, challenged traditional values, and, above all, because they were so real. The *National Board of Review Magazine* told readers that gangster films had "more vitality" than any other type of film being made. Another commentator noted "the gang wars belong to here and now, with the vital reality of something that might be happening at the present moment in the next street. No wonder the pictures about them fascinate us, sometimes to the verge of terror and anger."[30] Creighton Peet summarized Hollywood's position when he wrote that "no matter how many women's clubs, clergymen, and judges wag their head over these terrible 'crime' films," they "are too alive, too exciting and too important a part of the economic and political life of the American community to be suppressed."[31]

A debate in White Plains, New York, seemed to confirm Peet's view. Clarence Darrow, America's greatest defender of civil liberties debated John Summer, director of the New York Society for the Suppression of Vice, on the issue of crime films. In those days before television, public debates over contemporary issues were popular forms of entertainment and information. Before a packed house, Summer repeated the familiar arguments of the suppressors. Moving pictures, he claimed, "glorify and make heroes of crooks and incite young folks to crime." He demanded government censorship to combat this modern evil and implored the audience to support his position. "Silly piffle," thundered Darrow. "I have never," he argued, "seen a picture in my life, and I do not believe one has ever been made, in which the crook or the wrong-doer is not both caught and adequately punished. Right always triumphs over wrong in the movies and that is more than we can say about real life."[32] In one of the few examples of true public expression, other than the box office, on this emotional issue the audience voted overwhelmingly for Darrow. They did not want their movies censored.

Despite Darrow's victory and the steady box-office support of the genre, Hays fretted when protests over gangster movies continued to pour into his office from such powerful groups as the Daughters of the American Revolution, the Veterans of Foreign Wars, the United Presbyterian Church, the Catholic Knights of Columbus, the National Federation of Men's Bible Classes, and a host of local organizations. Reacting to this pressure, Hays announced in his annual report to the MPPDA in late March 1931 that the gangster film was dead. "In recent months the motion picture screen," Hays declared, "has done much to debunk the American gangster. . . . You can't get away with it" has been the insistent theme of the gang movie:

But the fact remains that too many such films, however well treated the theme may be, tend to over-emphasize the subject matter. Furthermore, the fact is becoming evident that the American public is growing tired not only of gangster rule, but of gangster themes in literature, on the stage, and on the screen.

Hays told industry leaders that "hard-boiled realism" and the "postwar preoccupation with morbidity and crime in literature and drama" were out: The public, "the greatest of all censors," was demanding "clean, high-purposed entertainment." This was pure wishful thinking on the part of Hays, and there was little support for his views among Hollywood producers.

A few weeks after this speech, perhaps to counter the continuing criticism that would follow crime films released in the last half of 1931 and in 1932, Hays hired August Vollmer, one of the most respected law enforcement officials in the nation, to examine gangster films. Vollmer, considered by many "the father of modern police work," was a reform police chief in Berkeley, California, before moving to the University of Chicago as a professor of Police Administration. In 1931 he had headed a federal commission to study the effectiveness of American police departments. Vollmer's opinions were highly respected throughout the nation; he was an expert on urban crime, graft, and corruption and a strong voice for more highly educated and less violent police forces. Hays asked Chief Vollmer to analyze six 1931 films for their impact on children: *City Streets, The Finger Points, The Last Parade, The Public Enemy, Quick Millions,* and *The Secret Six.* Did these films incite crime, ridicule law, create sympathy for the criminal, or violate the Production Code? Hays asked Vollmer to examine them in light of the criticism they were receiving from law enforcement groups and film reformers. Should they, asked Hays, be banned?[33]

Over a four-day period Vollmer carefully studied the movie gangster through the eyes of a trained criminologist. He saw the films on the studio lots, where he discussed them with studio officials. Hays provided the chief with materials on the films from Joy's office, the reactions of state censorship boards, and protest letters from his office. Vollmer's reaction was much like those of Jason Joy and Clarence Darrow. He reported that he found nothing wrong with *The Public Enemy,* which he termed "more or less a correct depiction of events which transpired in Chicago recently." The film would, he believed, "make the potential gangster hesitate" because the moral of the movie was that in the end either the police or other gangsters will get you. He specifically praised the film's conclusion, which he believed clearly emphasized that the "gangster problem cannot be solved entirely until the factors that produced the gangster are eliminated." *Quick Millions,* a film based on the life of Chicago's Bugs Moran, was "a good picture." Would it cause children to long for a life of crime? Vollmer doubted it. He told Hays "only a weak-minded suggestible moron" would want to enter a life of crime after watching this movie. *The Finger Points,* based on the true story of a crooked Chicago journalist, was "not harmful" in any way; in fact, Vollmer maintained that although the film presented unpleasant aspects of American life, "it is just as well that the naked truth be revealed." In his view the arguments against these movies were the same as those continually raised against the dime novel. While adults might prefer that kids read "serious literature," no one has been able "to point [out] unerringly and with certainty that harm has resulted from the reading of such literary trash." Gang movies, Vollmer assured Hays, fell in the same category: They might be trashy and vulgar, but there was no proof they created criminals.[34]

Father Daniel Lord completely disagreed. In his view gangster films were sordid and should be suppressed. Lord cited a specific example: *Vice Squad.* While he admitted that the basic plot of the movie was based on fact, Lord strenuously objected to movies showing "constituted officers of the law, framing, railroading," and shaking down innocent citizens. Taken as a whole, the film appeared to Lord to be "a catechism of blackmail, framing, seduction, hotel prostitution, houses of ill-fame, evil police, etc." *Vice Squad* was, Lord maintained, a direct and clear violation of his code because it would teach youth how to commit crimes.[35]

The two men represented opposite sides of the debate over the influence of crime films. Vollmer, from his perspective as a police officer, knew full well that many of the events fictionalized on film had in fact taken place. Criminals were protected by corrupt politicians and romanticized in the press. He was unconvinced that well-adjusted children would suddenly sink into a life of crime after watching the rise of Tom Powers, especially after seeing his bullet-riddled body dumped into his living room. The message Vollmer heard, and that dominated these films, was that crime did not pay: If anything, he thought Hollywood guilty of overemphasizing the effectiveness of law enforcement in corralling the criminals. Yet for Lord, and for all those who protested that the movies were corrupting youth, the mere fact that these criminals were being visualized on the screen was a violation of "good taste." It did not matter whether or not the criminals were shot or arrested: The films were a violation of the code because the heroes were gangsters, not the police.

The continuing debate erupted anew in 1932 when the most outrageous of all gangster films, Howard Hughes's production of *Scarface,* finally hit the screen. Hughes, director Howard Hawks, and writer Ben Hecht combined to bring screen violence to a new level. Machine guns spat bullets at a frightening level. The movie was, said *Harrison's Reports,* "the most vicious and demoralizing gangster picture" ever produced.[36] To the *New York Times, Scarface* made "all the other gangster pictures appear almost effeminate."[37]

Hughes had bought the movie rights to Armitage Trail's *Scarface,* a rather conventional account of Chicago gang wars, in 1930. He originally signed W. R. Burnett, who wrote *Little Caesar,* to adapt the book into a screenplay, but Burnett produced a script that Hughes found too bland. Hughes then turned to the talented but slightly eccentric

Ben Hecht. Hecht was a natural for the project: He had made *The Front Page* with Hughes, and his reputation as a Chicago reporter who hung around with many of the town's leading hoods had grown tremendously in Hollywood after he won an Academy Award for *Underworld*. Hecht, however, was leery of working for Hughes again and demanded a salary of $1,000 per day to be paid promptly at 6:00 P.M. in cash. "In this way," Hecht wrote, "I stood to waste only a day's labor if Mr. Hughes turned out to be insolvent."[38] Even Hughes must have considered this a bit odd, but he complied.

As director, Hughes signed Howard Hawks. Hecht and Hawks got on famously: Working and drinking day and night, they produced a shooting script in eleven days. Hawks later wrote that "Ben's work was brilliant. . . . Of course, he knew a lot about Chicago so he didn't do any research."[39] Based on real events and real people in Chicago, *Scarface* brought Al Capone, Deanie O'Bannion, Johnny Torrio, and "Big Jim" Colosimo to the screen. As in real life they attacked each other, and anyone who got in their way, with deadly effectiveness. Hecht promised Hughes twenty-five killings; some reviewers reported they lost count at forty. In the last half of the film the killings happen so fast it is almost impossible to keep an accurate count: With the exception of Police Inspector Guarino, every major male character in the film is dead by the final reel.

The cast assembled by Hawks was superb. Playing Tony "Scarface" Camonte was Paul Muni in his first major screen role. George Raft, a would-be hood turned actor, was his faithful sidekick, Guido Rinaldo; Cesca Camonte, Tony's beautiful and flirtatious teenage sister over whom he is insanely jealous, was portrayed by Ann Dvorak. Poppy, the icy-cool blonde gun moll who sleeps with the head of the Mob, was played to perfection by Karen Morley. Boris Karloff, his British accent intact, was a rival gang leader, Gaffney.

If the film shocked people – and it did – the original script was even stronger than the censored version that finally hit American screens in 1932. Hecht's original version condemned American society not for creating the criminal class through poverty, but for tolerating the existence of gangsters. Respected citizens party with mobsters, and the state attorney general, Benson – a character cut from the film – hobnobs with the gangsters in private while denouncing them to the gullible public; he is on the take.[40] Also, Hecht's take on Mrs. Calamonte, Tony's mother, was unique and quite different from that in the film: Originally, she was fully aware that her son was a criminal and was not in the least bit bothered by it; indeed, she was more than happy to accept his money and gifts. She fretted and fawned over him as any mother would over a loving son. Finally, the film's conclusion had given viewers a totally unrepentant "Scarface": Trapped in his apartment, Tony is bombarded with police tear gas and bullets to no effect; not until the entire building is set on fire does he come out, but with his guns blazing, not crawling and begging for mercy. Despite being hit by several police bullets, he manages to come face to face with the copper who has dogged him through the entire film. Tony raises his gun and pulls the trigger. Only a "click" is heard: His gun is empty. The policeman raises his gun and fires a fatal volley into Tony. As he goes down for the last time, the script called for the audience to hear "click, click, click" as Tony attempts to fire his gun.[41] In the original, Tony dies, if not in a blaze of glory, at least fighting by his own standards.

The Hughes–Hecht–Hawks version of *Scarface* was too brutal, too truthful, too unrepentant a portrait of American gang life for the Hays Office.[42] "Under no circumstances is this film to be made," Hays told Hughes. "If you should be foolhardy enough to make *Scarface,* this office will make certain it is never released." Hughes was unfazed: "Screw the Hays Office." He instructed Hawks to "make it as realistic, as exciting, as grisly as possible."[43] Yet Hays was determined, given the protests against this type of movie, to modify this view of gangsterism in America, and despite the bombast from Hughes, concessions were made by the producer. Hays's first demand involved the title itself: He wanted to add the tag line "The Shame of the Nation," which he hoped would indicate that the industry was not glorifying another gangster. The addendum stuck, although most people simply referred to the film as *Scarface.*

Although graft and corruption in America were as commonplace as machine guns, the role of the corrupt politician was struck from the film as too sensitive. Also taboo was a mother who accepted her son's underworld life: In the revised version, Tony's mother clearly disapproves of him and warns her daughter that Tony "hurts" everyone. He is no good, she says time and time again. Finally, the gangster's heroic death was eliminated: In the revision, a single tear-gas bomb tossed into his hideout forces Tony out. He comes down the stairs begging for his life, and when he tries to run from the police he is shot down. This ending, Hays felt, would correct the tone and prove to audiences that, at heart, criminals were cowards.[44] As film historian Gerald Mast has written, *Scarface* "is a shadow of what it might have been."[45]

An opening prologue warns the audience that the film they are about to see is an "indictment of gang rule and the callous indifference of government" to put a stop to it. "What are you going to do about it?" The film is barely out of the credits before the first killing takes place. It is late at night and a waiter is beginning to clear the remains of what appears to have been a huge party. The tables and floor are littered with confetti, the waiter stoops and picks up a discarded bra.

The boys have had quite a time. The party has been given by "Big Louie" (Harry J. Vejar), boss of the South side. After everyone leaves, Big Louie remains to make a phone call. The camera moves away from him to the approaching shadow of a man, who begins to whistle. Big Louie greets him – clearly, they know each other. Suddenly, the shadow on the screen has a gun. It fires. Big Louie is dead, and the gang war is on.

The police know immediately who killed the gangster: Tony "Scar-face" Camonte, Big Louie's former bodyguard who has now thrown his lot in with his rival Johnny Lovo (Osgood Perkins). They arrest him immediately, but a lawyer springs Tony with a writ of habeas corpus. This sets the tone for the rest of the movie: The police know what is going on but are unable to prove guilt. Tony, who speaks with a heavy Italian accent, refers to the legal maneuver as "hocus pocus." He is ignorant, but protected by a legal system that allows him to kill.

After being set free by the police, Tony goes to Johnny Lovo's apartment, where he receives his payoff for the murder. Lovo warns Tony to stay away from the North side: He does not want to set off a gang war and is content to be the boss of the South side. Tony is not so sure. There is lots of money up North, he tells Johnny. Despite this rather frank discussion of murder and territorial expansion, it is soon clear that the two men are not alone. Johnny's moll, Poppy (Karen Morley), is getting dressed in the next room. Poppy, who is plucking her eyebrows, is dressed, like all molls, in a very short and revealing slip. Through an open door Tony leers at her, and Poppy, quite aware of being watched, enjoys it. She makes no effort to cover up. As Tony leaves the apartment he nods toward Poppy and whispers approvingly to Johnny, "Expensive." Tony is no Rico: He likes his women and sets out to capture Poppy from the weakling Johnny.

This type of scene – Tony being paid for murder, the open discussion of more violence, and a woman living with one man and openly flirting with another while dressed in flimsy underwear – simply drove moral guardians up the wall. They were to be even more outraged as the film continued to unfold its story of sex, perversion, and violence.

The other women in Tony's life are his sister Cesca (Ann Dvorak) and his mother (Inez Palange). Tony is obsessively protective of his young and beautiful sister, who longs to live the exciting life that the city offers. The movie hints, but never quite states, that Tony is more than protective – that perhaps the relationship is incestuous. Whenever he discovers his sister around any man, he explodes with anger. When she brings home a young fellow, he chases him out of the house and demands that Cesca stop seeing men; then, overcome with guilt, he offers his sister a large amount of money. She is willing to take it, but her mother calls it "blood money": Tony "is a no good," she warns her daughter. It is now the mother who is trying to protect her daughter from becoming the kind of person her son is – a view totally different from the original. This small concession was lost on those who saw the film in a negative light.

With these various relationships established, Tony and his buddy Rinaldo (Raft) start the gang war. They beat up and intimidate saloon owners, forcing them to buy their beer. In no time Tony, like Rico and Tom Powers, is rolling in money. He buys new clothes and moves into a huge apartment that he has outfitted with steel doors, steel shutters, and a secret escape. It is a modern version of an armed fortress.

With the South side in their hands, Tony decides to move north. He orders Rinaldo to assassinate O'Hara. Now the city is up in flames. The North side gang, led by Gaffney (Karloff), imports machine guns to kill Tony and his Mob. In broad daylight they machine-gun a restaurant where Tony and Poppy are eating. Thousands of bullets shred the place to pieces. Tony is thrilled by this demonstration of killing power: He recognizes immediately that with a few of these modern killing machines he can eliminate his enemies. When Rinaldo dashes out to retrieve one from a fallen thug, Tony is like a child at Christmas – he can hardly control his glee.

An orgy of killing follows. Cars squeal around corners dumping bodies and machine-gunning rivals. Everyone but Gaffney has been killed, and he has been forced into hiding. When Tony gets word that he has been spotted at a North-side bowling alley, he and his gang kill him in front of hundreds of horrified spectators. All this killing is too much for Johnny Lovo: Scared of Tony, and furious that Poppy is attracted to this rival, he orders an assassination; but Tony escapes, and revenge is quick when he and Rinaldo immediately kill Lovo.

Tony is now the undisputed leader of the gang. In a scene that made moral guardians fidget even more than the killing, he goes to Poppy's apartment after having Johnny killed. It is very late at night, and she is asleep. Tony wakes her to say that Johnny, her lover, is dead. Poppy gets out of bed. She is dressed in a very frilly nightdress (molls don't wear flannel) and is delighted by the news. Tony tells her to pack, and she greets him with a huge smile. Off she goes with her new lover, who has just killed her old paramour.

This outburst of mayhem forces Tony to lay low until the heat is off. He goes to Florida for a vacation. With Tony out of the way, Cesca, who has been flirting with Rinaldo throughout the movie, finally seizes her opportunity. They are secretly married. When Tony returns home, his mother frantically tells him only that Cesca has left home and is living in an apartment. She gives him the address, and Tony, suspecting the worst, goes off in a rage. He knocks at the door. Rinaldo opens it. Tony sees him in a silk bathrobe, his sister behind him. In uncontrollable fury, he guns his longtime friend to death. Cesca screams at him that they are married. Tony mutters as he stumbles away: "I didn't know, I didn't know."

This murder, unlike all the others that have taken place, causes the police to spring suddenly into action; why it does so is unexplained. They prepare for an attack on Tony's fortress. Cesca, meanwhile, is preparing her own revenge. Gun in hand, she sneaks into Tony's apartment through the secret entrance, determined to kill her brother; but when she faces him, she can't pull the trigger. Instead, she joins Tony in his last battle with the police. As Cesca loads guns for her brother, she is killed by a stray bullet. When police toss a tear gas bomb into the apartment, Tony decides to give up. Whining, almost crawling down the steps, Tony begs for his life; then he makes a break for it, and is gunned down. Another criminal's bullet-ridden body ends up in the gutter.

Was the moral lesson of *Scarface* that crime doesn't pay, or that police were helpless boobs? Did *Scarface* glorify the criminal by showing him with lots of money, dressed in the latest fashion, always seated at the best tables in nightclubs and restaurants, driving new cars and always, but always, surrounded by beautiful women? Did these images exert stronger appeal for the young boys in the audience than the grim fact that Tony, like Rico and Tom, ends up in the gutter?

The film was completed in 1931, but Hays was reluctant to approve it, insisting that new scenes be inserted to make clear that the public, not law enforcement officials, was to blame for the existence of gangs. Hays also demanded scenes that would show the effectiveness of the justice system in combating criminals. As Hays and Hughes bickered over changes in *Scarface,* an unfortunate incident took place in New Jersey. Two young boys, after watching a gang film, were playing "cops and robbers," and one of the boys killed the other with a gun he thought was empty. The outcry was immediate. *Parent's Magazine* demanded a national boycott of gang films. The *New York Times* editorialized about the evil effects of screen violence and reminded Hays and readers that the code specifically limited the use of guns in films and prohibited "brutal killings."[46] The New York Knights of Columbus charged that gang films "created a criminal instinct," and demanded that Hays stop their production.[47] Only a few pointed the blame toward the parents who kept a loaded gun in the house. It was the movies – specifically, *The Secret Six* – that had killed the young man, critics charged.

Perhaps this background caused Hughes to soften his original position. While neither Hawks nor Muni was available for retakes, the producer agreed to film two new scenes to win MPPDA approval for his gang epic. The first, inserted midway through the film, takes place in a newspaper office, where a group of concerned citizens have come to ask the editor to stop glorifying and publicizing the exploits of the criminals. After the citizens express their displeasure at the ineffectiveness of his paper and the police, the editor explodes:

You expect me to keep gangsters off the front page – that's ridiculous. We need to show him up and run him out of the country. . . . Don't blame the police. They can't stop machine guns from being run back and forth across state lines. They can't enforce laws that don't exist. You're the government. Make laws and see that they're obeyed, if we have to have martial law to do it. . . . Put some teeth in the deportation laws. Most of these criminals aren't even citizens. The army will help, so will the American Legion. We're fighting organized murder.

This scene, it was hoped, would soften the criticism that gang films always showed the police as hopelessly inefficient. The criminal was not a force in society because newspapers (read "movies") publicized their activities, but because the police were given insufficient tools with which to work. If people would provide law enforcement with new tools, then the criminal class would disappear, said the revised *Scarface*.

The new ending of the film called for Muni to be arrested rather than killed. Using a double, because Muni was doing a Broadway play, the revised ending showed Camonte brought to trial and sentenced to hang for his crimes against society. (This ending has disappeared from most prints now in circulation.) Sporting the new subtitle "Shame of the Nation," the Hays Office approved *Scarface* for public exhibition in the spring of 1932.[48]

State and municipal censors, however, refused to accept *Scarface* even with the Haysian homilies inserted. New York, where Hughes planned a grand premiere, flatly rejected the film. State censorship boards in Ohio, Virginia, Maryland, and Kansas, and municipal boards in Detroit, Seattle, Portland, Boston, and (of course) Chicago followed suit. Hughes was furious and threatened to sue everyone from Hays to local censors for preventing the public from watching *Scarface*. He issued a public statement condemning censorship:

It has become a serious threat to the freedom of honest expression in America when self-styled guardians of the public welfare, as personified by our censor boards, lend their aid and their influence to the abortive efforts of selfish and vicious interests to suppress a motion picture simply because it depicts the truth about conditions in the United States which have been front page news since the advent of Prohibition. *Scarface* is an honest and powerful indictment of gang rule in America and, as such, will be a tremendous factor in compelling our State and Federal governments to take more drastic action to rid the country of gangsterism.

The *New York Herald Tribune* praised him "as the only producer who has the courage to come out and fight this censorship menace in the open. We wish him a smashing success."[49] Hughes threatened to force an original uncut version before the public, and indeed he did release that version in areas that did not have censorship.

Yet it wasn't Hughes who got *Scarface* past the state censors, but Will Hays and Jason Joy. Their role illustrates the role of the MPPDA in protecting the financial investments of film producers. Although Hughes was a maverick and would cause Hays continual trouble with his productions over the next two decades, in this case he had already made some concessions. At the request of Hays, Joy visited each of the censorship boards that had rejected *Scarface*. He explained to them that the Hays Office was against glorifying criminals, argued that the gang films were documents against crime, and most likely cited Vollmer's report that crime films were not responsible for recent increases in the crime rate. Joy assured state censors that *Scarface* was the end, not the beginning, of a cycle. His mission was a tremendous success. One by one the censorship boards in New York, Pennsylvania, Ohio, Maryland, and Virginia, and the municipal boards, including Chicago, accepted *Scarface*. As Joy told Hays, they accepted "not the original, uncut, uncensored version sent out in defiance of the industry" by Hughes, "but the third version of this remarkable film."[50]

Joy's ability to convince censorship boards that the revised version of *Scarface* was a moral film only added fire to the determination of the moral guardians to continue their fight against the Hays Office. The *Christian Century* wrote that Joy's trip and his "spectacular" success demonstrated "the grim determination of the industry to defeat agencies which the public has set up to defend its children from vicious pictures."[51] Cooperation with the Hays Office was impossible. *Harrison's Reports* drew a similar conclusion: The example of *Scarface* proved that "censorship . . . is impotent to cure the evils of the motion picture industry."[52]

Despite the fulminations of religious journals and *Harrison's*, it must be remembered that millions of people saw and enjoyed *Scarface*. Rational voices noted that "the evil influence of motion pictures, even on youth, can be greatly exaggerated." Even Martin Quigley, who was no friend of Hughes, wrote that "there is no conclusive proof that a gangster picture is capable of doing any harm to the public, young or old."[53] And millions of other Americans wanted to see cinema free of the hypocrisy of censorship. In Pennsylvania the *Philadelphia Public Ledger* cheered Hughes's battle against the state censor as a victory "for freedom of the screen." "Banning *Scarface*," the paper wrote, "while showing apathy to the phase of life it depicts, is about as decent as pulling down the blinds to cover up dirty windows. Sure enough we wouldn't see them, but they'd still be there – dirty as ever."[54]

The film was good box office, and the reviews were favorable. The *National Board of Review Magazine* called it "as good as any gangster film that has been made. It is more brutal, more cruel and . . . much nearer to the truth."[55] *Time* told readers it was a "grisly, exciting picture."[56] The film came in tenth in the *Film Daily* top ten of 1932. Surprisingly, Quigley's *Motion Picture Herald* urged exhibitors to book *Scarface:* It may be cruel and depressing, "but it still has the box office 'it.'"[57]

A variation of the gangster theme was reflected in another spate of films that hit American screens in the early 1930s. Prison films like *The Big House, Ladies of the Big House, The Criminal Code,* and *The Last Mile* explored a familiar theme: a criminal justice system that was inequitable and incompetent. While gangster films showed police as incapable of arresting real criminals, prison films implied that American prisons contained too many innocent victims. Audiences were bombarded with portraits of prisons controlled by corrupt officials and sadistic guards, and exploited for profit by greedy businessmen. The criminal justice system was presented as so corrupt and so brutal that prisoners, guilty and innocent alike, were justified in taking violent action to regain some measure of human dignity. It was hardly the view of American society that Lord's code envisioned for the screen.

This theme of corruption and justified rebellion against authority permeated two prominent films about chain gangs produced in 1932: RKO's *Hell's Highway* and Warner Bros.' *I Am a Fugitive from a Chain Gang.* The real-life horrors of Southern chain gangs had become a national scandal when escapee Robert Elliot Burns was seized by Chicago police in 1929. His true story was indeed stranger than fiction.[58] As a young man in 1917, Burns had answered Woodrow Wilson's call to "make the world safe for democracy." Returning from the war in 1919, Burns had faced readjustment and unemployment. Along with thousands of others, he drifted around the country looking for work. The end of the road for Burns had come in Atlanta, Georgia, in 1922. Penniless, he had been tricked into taking part in the robbery of a small grocery store. The heist had netted $5.80; he was captured and sentenced to six to ten years of hard labor on a chain gang.

The prospect had been too much for Burns. With the help of fellow prisoners he escaped and made his way to Chicago. There, living under an assumed name, he had quickly gone from "rags to riches," and by 1929 was a prominent magazine publisher. His past, however, was to haunt him: He confided to the woman who ran his boardinghouse that he had escaped from a chain gang, and she in turn forced him into an unwanted marriage. When Burns had attempted to divorce her, she turned him in to the police.

His story had been a national sensation in 1929. Lurid details of abuse on chain gangs had shocked the nation and greatly embarrassed the state of Georgia. While Illinois and Chicago officials rallied around Burns and advised him to stay in the state, Burns accepted an offer from Georgia to serve a reduced sentence in return for a full pardon. When he returned, however, state officials reneged, slapped him back on a chain gang and ignored all pleas for clemency.

Incredibly, Burns escaped again, this time to New Jersey. In February 1932 he published a sensational exposé of life on the gangs, *I Am a Fugitive from a Georgia Chain Gang!*, and sold the movie rights to Warner Bros. for $12,500. The studio rushed into production while Burns remained in hiding, surfacing only for publicity interviews with the press.[59] Yet translating reality into a screenplay posed serious problems for the film industry: Chain gangs, while viewed with horror by most of the nation, were legal in Southern states; the code demanded that movies uphold, not ridicule, the law. Did that apply to chain gangs?

In 1932 two studios, hopeful of cashing in on the publicity created by the Burns case, worked furiously on chain-gang scripts. At RKO David O. Selznick was producing Rowland Brown's *Hell's Highway,* and on the Warner lot Darryl Zanuck and director Mervyn Le Roy were collaborating on *I Am a Fugitive from a Chain Gang.* Joy realized that both films could cause the industry trouble. How could Hollywood make a film that dealt realistically with chain gangs and not be critical of a legal form of punishment? As he told Hays, he realized that the "systems are wrong," but he doubted "if it is our business as an entertainment force to clear it up." Hays concurred.[60]

Determined to take full advantage of the national publicity created by the Burns case, RKO rushed to finish *Hell's Highway* before Warners could open with *Fugitive.* When Joy and his assistant, Lamar Trotti, read RKO's script, they discovered to their consternation that the American South was to be presented as a backward region where corruption and injustice reigned supreme. The script was littered with prison floggings, lynchings, shootings, stabbings, and barbaric punishment in sweatboxes – almost all done by prison guards with the consent of prison officials. Prisoners wore uniforms with a huge bull's-eye on the back – presumably to help prison guards take aim at escaping convicts. The hero of the film was another innocent man kept in prison by a corrupt prison board. When he and several fellow prisoners escape, the locals eagerly join in a manhunt for the "sport of killing prisoners." Joy urged RKO to drop the entire project, and warned Selznick that "you are in for more grief than you have ever had before" if you produce this film as represented in the original script. "Right now," Joy wrote, "the story is still an indictment of the system, and therefore of the state or section where the system prevails." This was not acceptable under the code, and Selznick was urged to "give . . . earnest thought to whether you ought to risk an investment at all in this story."[61]

When the studio refused to drop the project, the goal of the Hays Office was to ensure that the film did not give "offense to the South." Joy and Trotti held a series of meetings on the RKO lot "to get the politics right" for *Hell's Highway*. From the point of view of the Hays Office, it was essential that the film be an "individual story" of corruption "rather than an indictment of the whole penal system." If this were done, much of the sting would be removed from the film. Joy and Trotti "suggested" several changes to accomplish this: They asked that the hero not be arrested on "trumped up" charges, but rather for a "justifiable cause" based on strong circumstantial evidence; this would remove the implication that the judicial system was corrupt, and imply instead that an honest mistake had been made. The censors also urged that the prison board be presented to the audience as "upright men" trying to do the best job they could.[62]

With the implications of judicial corruption removed, the censors now pressed the studio to soften the image of chain gangs. Why not, Joy suggested, show that "orderly prisoners receive better treatment." If some chain gangs were presented as "happy, well-ordered and properly cared for groups," then the particular unit in the film could be presented as "the exception rather than the rule." In this way, the warden would be transformed from a "bad guy" to a "good guy," and Joy promised that the film would receive approval from the censorship office.[63]

Selznick and RKO agreed to take the film out of production until changes that would satisfy Joy could be incorporated into the script. Film audiences saw a different *Hell's Highway* than had originally been planned. Richard Dix, the star of the film, was a habitual criminal – a bank robber – not an innocent man. He was sentenced to hard labor on the Liberty Road chain gang, which was building a state highway – the titular hell's highway. Conditions were brutal: Men were whipped, beaten, and driven to violence against their guards. The villain of the film, however, was a private contractor who, through bribery, made the guards resort to inhuman tactics to work the men for his own profit. When one of the convicts dies in a sweatbox, the governor of the state sends an investigator to find out "all the facts" about the prison. Getting the politics right included several short scenes clearly indicating that the state had passed laws prohibiting brutal treatment of prisoners. In the grand finale the governor marches into the prison and orders the arrest of the contractor for murder. The film was an exposé not of a brutal, corrupt, sadistic system but of individual greed. In its review of the film for theater owners, *Harrison's Reports* noted, with some satisfaction, that "guilt is put on the private contractor," not the state. Jason Joy was relieved; yet he was also concerned, and assured Hays he was keeping a close eye on the studios "because none of these chain gang stories will ever be" completely safe for the industry.[64]

Certainly, *I Am a Fugitive from a Chain Gang* was far from safe. MGM had been the first to express an interest in filming the tragedy of Robert Burns. When producer Irving Thalberg had inquired as to the suitability of the project, Joy had tried to discourage him. The most important parts of the story, he told Thalberg – the "cruelty of the chain gang and detailed escape methods" – could not be shown on the screen. Nor could the film carry an anti-Southern slant if the studio expected to do business in the South. He reminded the producer that southerners still maintained that chain gangs were necessary to "control the large Negro" population. He admitted that "to us these methods may seem barbarous relics of the Middle Ages, still from a business standpoint we ought to consider carefully whether we are willing to incur the anger of any large section." MGM quietly dropped the project.[65]

Although MGM had been easily discouraged, Jack Warner was determined to film *Fugitive* despite a warning by his story department that it would cause hostility in the South: *Fugitive* might make a good picture, Warner was told, "if we had no censorship, but all the strong and vivid points in the story are certain to be eliminated by the present censorship system." When Joy was informed that Warners intended to bring *Fugitive* to the screen, he asked production boss Darryl Zanuck to consider carefully the Southern reaction to the film, and urged him to be very cautious in presenting a state that "has broken its word" and resorted to "petty vengeance."[66]

Despite these warnings Zanuck pushed forward. He cast Paul Muni, who had just finished *Scarface,* to play Burns, and signed Mervyn Le Roy to direct. In April 1932 he assigned staff writer Brown Holmes to adapt the book for the screen, and even brought Robert Burns to Hollywood. Known as "Mr. Cane" on the set, Burns floated around the studio for several weeks before going underground once again. The script went through several drafts, and Zanuck brought in Howard J. Green for a final polish. As Green recalled, Zanuck insisted – most likely because of the pressure from Joy – that Georgia not be identified and the script "minimize the polemics against chain gangs." Had he had his own way, Green wrote, "the script would have been a blasting tirade against the entire system. Mr. Zanuck sensed this and . . . insisted that I incorporate into my script sincere arguments in favor of chain-gang systems."[67]

Once production began on *Fugitive* there was very little contact between the studio and the censorship office: Until the creation of the Production Code Administration in July 1934, the system was still voluntary. The censor first saw *Fugitive* in October 1932, at a studio screening. Although apprehensive when the movie began, by the time the final credits rolled up on the screen Joy was delighted. While there were no "sincere arguments in favor" of chain gangs in the film, to Joy

[*Fugitive* is] not a preachment against the chain gang system in general, but a strongly individualized story of one man's personal experiences arising from one particular miscarriage of justice, and attended by later circumstances so unusual that in no sense can it be considered a general indictment of this form of legal punishment.[68]

Fugitive premiered at Warners' 3,500-seat Strand Theater on Broadway in November 1932. The injustice, the sweat, the dirt, the sadistic brutality, the dramatic escapes, and the double-crossing by the state were all there. In the final scene Robert Allen has been turned into a criminal – an animal lurking in an alley. Frightened, beaten by the system, he risks capture to see his fiancée. "How do you live?" she asks him. "I steal," he replies as he sneaks into the protective darkness.

"*Fugitive* BIGGEST BROADWAY SENSATION IN LAST THREE YEARS," cabled New York executives after the film opened. Thousands of curious movie fans were turned away, and one Warners executive gushed "WARNER PROSPERITY TURNS THE CORNER," with *Fugitive* opening in over 200 theaters nationwide. Film critics were as enthusiastic as Joy in their praise of the film. The National Board of Review called it "not only the best feature film of the year, but one of the best films ever made in this country."[69] Even the conservative Louella Parsons, film critic for the *Los Angeles Examiner,* praised the film: "If this motion picture," she wrote, "can do anything to correct an evil that is a blot on civilization, it will not have been made in vain." Martin Quigley's *Motion Picture Herald* issued a favorable review, as did *Harrison's Reports,* which approved the film as "a powerful drama for adult audiences."[70] Even Paul Muni got into the spirit. In an interview, the actor called on Hollywood to use its popularity to "arouse the world against all sorts of evils."[71] His plea would go unheeded in the film capital.

Joy was quite correct in his assessment that *Fugitive* was presented as one man's experience, not as a larger and more troubling social problem. Pare Lorentz, who would later gain fame for his haunting documentaries *The River* and *The Plow That Broke the Plains,* noted with some disappointment in his review in *Vanity Fair* that *Fugitive* might have been more effective had it used the story of Robert Burns to examine the social setting of the prison, rather than concentrate on a single individual. To Lorentz the real issue was why the prisons were so brutal. What drove the guards to be so sadistic? Why did such a form of legal punishment exist in twentieth-century America? Had the film approached these issues, Lorentz believed it could have been a powerful social instrument for reform; as it turned out, it was only another Hollywood melodrama with an unusually powerful ending.

Joy, for one, was delighted that the film did not move into the realm of social criticism suggested by Lorentz. It was brutal enough, he thought, in its vivid depiction of life on a chain gang: Audiences would have no difficulty in understanding that this particular system of justice was wrong. He told Warners that the film, in his opinion, was "one of the most important pictures of the year."[72] For Joy and Hays the issue was that, by dealing only with the central character and ignoring the plight of the rest of the prisoners, the industry was "thoroughly justified" in making pictures like this, so long as they were "free of sectional bias, presented dispassionately and free of propaganda, and recognized as entertainment." While Lorentz had hoped that film, especially this film, could be used to probe social injustice, Joy and the Hays Office were dedicated to keeping social criticism within the boundaries of dispassionate entertainment. Just how difficult that would be was illustrated in the first few months of 1933, when politics, profits, propaganda, and entertainment became intertwined in one of the most bizarre films ever made in Hollywood.

If politics makes strange bedfellows, consider the cast of characters who played major roles in the production of *Gabriel Over the White House:* Walter Wanger, a liberal Democrat whose politics tended to spill over into his films and who was often in trouble with the Hays Office because of it, produced the film for Cosmopolitan Studios owned by newspaper magnate William Randolph Hearst. Hearst, who was temporarily fascinated by FDR, intended the film as a tribute to the newly elected president and an attack on previous Republican administrations. *Gabriel* was produced on the MGM lot headed by Louis B. Mayer, a Republican stalwart and frequent guest at the Hoover White House, and distributed by Loew's, Inc. It was censored by Will Hays, ex–cabinet member in Warren Harding's scandal-ridden administration, and by Dr. Wingate.

Based on an obscure novel by Thomas F. Tweed, a major figure in the English Liberal Party, *Gabriel Over the White House* was a fictional plea for the establishment of a temporary dictatorship in the United States to solve the Depression. The book portrayed American democracy as hopelessly inefficient and unresponsive to the needs of the people. Political parties were controlled by "hacks" who looked on government as a means of increasing their own wealth. Congress was nothing more than a "debating society" of stuffy old men who argued endlessly and accomplished nothing. Prohibition had created an army of armed gangsters, who were the real rulers of American cities. In short, American democracy had collapsed.[73]

The problems of the nation are solved when a newly elected president, Jud Hammond – a true party "hack" whose only concerns were poker and his secretary-mistress – is injured in an automobile accident. With Hammond close to death, the angel Gabriel descends from heaven with a new political agenda. After this spiritual encounter, Hammond makes a dramatic recovery and astounds everyone by his sudden conversion to good government. He fires corrupt cabinet members, suspends Congress, eliminates unemployment by creating an army of the unemployed, rids the nation of gangsters, and forces the nations of the world to disarm and to repay their World War I debts. His mission on earth completed, Hammond dies a world hero.

Wanger, screenwriter Carey Wilson, and Hearst collaborated on the script during the autumn of 1932 and forwarded it to Hays Office censor James Wingate in late January 1933. This was America's "winter of despair": The policies of Herbert Hoover had been soundly rejected by the American people in the November 1932 election of Franklin D. Roosevelt, yet the new President would not take office until March 1933. During that long, cold, bleak winter unemployment rose to unprecedented heights, banks closed at a terrifying rate, relief aid dried up and the nation's economy ground to a halt. The government seemed completely and utterly paralyzed; and yet no one knew exactly what Franklin Roosevelt would or could do. As the nation anxiously awaited FDR's assumption of power, the script offering a cinematic solution for the nation's ills arrived on Wingate's desk.

An internal MGM synopsis labeled the script "wildly reactionary and radical to the nth degree."[74] Wingate agreed. He was completely stunned. While he admitted to MGM's production boss Irving Thalberg that *Gabriel* was "undeniably a powerful story," Wingate believed the film would project a negative image of the American government. The novel, which originally set the story in 1950, had been changed to the present. Wingate worried that this change would reflect directly on recent Republic administrations.

In the script, President Hammond kept a mistress in the White House and took little notice of the Depression. He mouthed simplistic pieties and urged the people to recovery by recapturing the pioneer spirit of America (as President Herbert Hoover had often done). One scene described an army of unemployed marching on Washington demanding a "revolution" and branding the government as "rotten" and run by "saps and suckers." Wingate told Thalberg that he doubted "whether any censor board would permit such outspoken vilification of existing governments."[75]

Hammond's conversion was equally troubling. An automobile accident leaves the president in a coma and his doctors helpless. As Hammond is about to die he is visited by the angel Gabriel, who gives him a new political agenda. Hammond suddenly recovers. He spurns his mistress, Pendie, fires his cabinet, dismisses Congress, and declares martial law. He ends Prohibition and, when the gangsters resist, orders the United States Army to arrest and execute the gangsters.

With domestic violence eliminated, Hammond turns to international politics. Disarmament and the European repayment of war debts was an emotional issue for Americans in 1933. *Gabriel* offered a quick and simple solution: President Hammond invites Washington diplomats to witness a display of American air power. American planes destroy several World War I battleships, and Hammond asserts that with "10,000 of those bombers" the United States can win any war.[76] When the diplomats claim that their nations are too poor to repay their debts, Hammond threatens war. Everyone thinks he is completely crazy. A journalist remarks that "the U.S. won't stand for war even from Jud Hammond." Meanwhile, the cabinet members fired by Hammond are plotting to take over the government. "You realize what this maniac's going to do? Put us against the world – when our navy isn't as big as England's alone! He's crazy!"[77] But Hammond wins when the foreign countries bow to the forceful America and not only sign a world disarmament treaty but also pledge to repay their war debts.

In a grand finale Hammond enters his White House office to sign the historic document. After he does so, he collapses and is taken by his mistress to his office. His doctor tells Pendie that the stress of the last year has been too much for the President, but that he will recover. When Hammond comes to, he insists that the doctor leave. The doctor reluctantly agrees, leaving Pendie some medicine and instructions to give Hammond a small dose should he have a relapse.

It is soon clear why Hammond wanted his doctor out of the room: The old Jud Hammond has finally come out of his year-long coma. He treats Pendie as his mistress, and she is horrified. Hammond wants to know how long he has been out. A year, she tells him. He is shocked. Then Pendie tells him that in that year he has become a great man. He fired his cabinet, declared martial law, ended Prohibition and gang rule, took the nation off the gold standard, created a civilian army of the unemployed, and ended a world arms race. Hammond is furious. Why hadn't somebody stopped him? "I am listening to a terrible indictment. . . . I have betrayed my party – my friends. . . . A mad dog has been loose in the White House. I owe those who elected me, who entrusted me with high responsibility, a humble apology."[78] Hammond is referring to his political cronies, not the people of the United States. He demands that his cabinet be reassembled immediately.

Boys, he tells his cabinet, "everything the President of the United States has done in the past year meets with my unqualified disapproval." He assures them his goal is "to get the old steam-roller going again." He will start by telling the gathering of world leaders, "the biggest conference of political bosses in the history of the world," that the United States is going to repudiate the treaty and "we're going to get all the gold – all the business – and have the biggest battleships – and they can all pack up their clean collars and go right back home and worry about their own problems." When his secretary, Beekman, objects that this will bring war, Hammond shrugs "what of it." Hammond then marches to the microphone to begin his speech, but collapses again before he can reveal his change of heart. This time the president is dead. He dies a public hero; only those behind the scene knew the real story of Jud Hammond.

While all this made perfect sense to William Randolph Hearst, Wingate worried that the film would prove offensive to Republicans. He cautioned Thalberg that the dismissal of Congress, the president as a dictator, the peacetime court martial, and the threat of war would weaken the American people's respect for government in this period of crisis. Was it wise, he asked, for a movie to portray an inept Congress? This sort of movie might lead to the enactment of adverse legislation against the industry. *Gabriel Over the White House* was, Wingate warned MGM, a "dangerous subject."[79]

Wingate brought Hays into the discussion when he informed his boss about the general nature of the script. "In these trying times," Wingate asked Hays, "should the industry allow studios to make films which show large groups of distressed, dissatisfied or unemployed people going in mass in an anti-government frame of mind to Washington to demand justice?" It was not beyond the realm of possibility, Wingate feared, that such a movie would encourage "radicals and the communists" and would "lessen the confidence of people in their government."[80]

Hays recognized that the film might embarrass the industry. As an ex-member of the Harding cabinet, he must have been sensitive to scenes that showed a president being dominated by a gang of card-playing cronies and maintaining a mistress in the White House. The scenes calling for the army's violent dismissal of a group of the unemployed could only evoke images of President Hoover's use of the U.S. Army to remove the Bonus Army of war veterans who thronged to the capital in 1932. The references to solving the Depression via uplifting rhetoric alone also struck too close to home for the Republican Hays.

Hays also worried that the dialogue of the war-debt issue would undoubtedly hurt the film in the lucrative foreign market. When Fred Herron, who was in charge of foreign trade in the Hays Office, read the script, he exploded: "We have a hell of a nerve to put anything like this in one of our pictures, and at the same time beg our various Embassies to constantly help us out with foreign governments." He found the entire debt treatment "absolutely absurd" and predicted it would create "tremendous anti-American feeling" everywhere American pictures were distributed. Clearly, *Gabriel* had to have a political reeducation before being viewed by the American or world public.[81]

Will Hays was so concerned that he cabled Louis B. Mayer to consider "earnestly" the "potential worry" that *Gabriel* would cause the industry. He asked Mayer to give his personal attention to the film. It was now "industry policy," declared Hays, that the film would show the president being given the authority by Congress "to crush gangsterism" and that the entire film would have a "decided spiritual angle to it." Mayer, who was only vaguely aware of this Cosmopolitan Studio production, assured Hays that he would watch the production of *Gabriel* very carefully. Walter Wanger was called in for consultation and agreed to make whatever changes were deemed necessary.[82]

When Mayer settled into his seat to preview *Gabriel* on March 1, 1933, in Glendale, California, he should have been prepared; but although forewarned, he had not taken the active role Hays had wanted. The film had been changed: Several of the "prosperity is just around the corner" speeches had been removed, the relationship between Hammond and Pendie softened by having her marry Beekman during the year that Hammond was "under," and the threat of war eliminated. The ending also was changed: In this version Hammond, after signing the treaty and collapsing, eventually recovers. It is the old Jud, and he is outraged when Pendie tells him what he has done to solve the Depression. "I've been disloyal to my party," he screams. "I hope I can undo what I've done in the last year." He is so upset that he collapses again, and this time Pendie, who no longer loves Hammond, recognizes that this "party hack" is about to do great damage to the United States and the world. She gives him a glass of water but does not put in the medicine the doctor gave her. Hammond dies before he can act.

By the time the last reel had spun through the projector, Mayer was seething with rage. Interpreting the film as an attack on presidents Harding and Hoover and the Republican Party in general, Mayer bolted "from the theater like an onrushing thundercloud," grabbed hold of Eddie Mannix, and shouted loud enough for people to hear, "Put that picture in its can, take it back to the studio, and lock it up."[83]

However, Hollywood was ruled by economics, not hysterics, and *Gabriel* was Hearst's film, not Mayer's. Rather than being buried in MGM's vaults, *Gabriel* was shipped to New York for political evaluation.

Hays thought political films as dangerous to the industry as sex films. He was furious that, in March 1933, with the Republican Party humiliated in a national election, with Wall Street in shambles and the film industry rapidly sinking in a sea of red ink, Hearst intended to release *Gabriel* – a film that openly advocated the establishment of an American dictator.[84]

Hays arranged a special screening of *Gabriel* for the MPPDA Board of Directors, who were outraged by what they saw. Only a few of the changes urged by Wingate and Hays had been incorporated into the film. Hays was especially furious that the time frame of the film had been shifted to the present, which he believed made the attack on Republicans all too clear. The ending of the film was also troubling.

The next morning Hays again screened *Gabriel*. After several viewings he became convinced that it could be salvaged. Hays, with the approval of Loew's President Nicholas Schenck, called Louis B. Mayer. We have an "unprecedented situation in this country," Hays told Mayer, and the people are looking at FDR "as a drowning man looks at a life saver . . . one eye on him and one eye on God." In Hays's view the country was expecting and deserved an "inspirational picture." Instead, *Gabriel* was a "direct indictment of the puerility and fallibility of today's government." The whole theme of the film was that only by a blow in the head could "righteousness and wisdom" be put in the head of the executive branch.[85]

It was essential, said Hays, that the film show a president with "at least a small amount of sense of duty," one who took positive action as a result of a "spiritual inspiration," not just a blow to the head. After all, Hays added, when a man does become President of the United States "a spiritual change actually occurs [so] that they kill themselves" trying to better the nation. Perhaps it could be implied that this is what happens to Hammond when the angel Gabriel touches him after his accident. If this could be accomplished – if Hammond could be seen to be acting on inspiration – then the propaganda in the film, Hays thought, would be less of a problem.[86]

Hays also demanded deletion of the scene showing the president and the cabinet playing poker. "We are in a war [against the Depression] and yet we go out and make a picture that shows the president as a cheap politician or worse, who opens his Cabinet meeting with 'Who's deal is it?'" The relationship between the president and the secretary had to be toned down to remove any implication that they were lovers. If these changes were made, Hays was confident *Gabriel* could be released.[87] A humbled Mayer assured Hays and Schenck that they had only seen a "working print."[88]

Wanger spent almost a month trying to reshape the general image of *Gabriel*. The original film had been shot in eighteen days with a working budget of $180,000. The editing and reshoots cost an additional $30,000. The alterations pleased Wingate, who told Thalberg

Figure 6. Walter Huston and Karen Morley in *Gabriel Over the White House.*
Courtesy the Museum of Modern Art / Film Stills Archive.

that he was "delighted" with the revised *Gabriel,* which has "freed the
picture from censurable and code" problems. In fact, the revised film
passed the various state and local censorship boards without tamper-
ing.[89]

The most dramatic change was the movie's ending: Now Hammond
collapses after signing the treaty and dies in his office without recant-
ing any of his actions. This change took much of the curse off the film
for Hays. Also, the removal of the threat of war over the war-debt issue made the film more agreeable for European audiences, and the
romantic role of Pendie was muted. Still, the experience with *Gabriel*
proved that no amount of reshooting or postproduction editing could
change the basic flavor of a film: Walter Huston, playing President Jud
Hammond, comes across as a real "party hack" who knows little and
cares less about the nation's problems. He is such a dolt that he insists
on driving at reckless speeds. After a serious accident, he is visited by
the angel, who inspires him to a new political agenda. While this little

scene may have taken much of the curse off the film for Will Hays, the almost inescapable conclusion is that the accident was the main factor in Hammond's new policies.

It is clear, even if it is less obvious than originally intended, that the relationship between the secretary and the president is more than platonic and professional. Only after the accident does the president reject the attentions of Pendie. Congress is still presented as ineffective, though in the revised edition it is the legislative body that allows Hammond to assume power. To make this clear to audiences, a newspaper headline was inserted: "CONGRESS ACCEDES TO PRESIDENT'S REQUEST: Adjourns by Overwhelming Vote – Hammond Dictator." This gave legal status to Hammond's actions, in Hays's view, and brought the picture in line with the code.

Despite these alterations, the overall impression given by the film was changed so little that the *Nation* entitled its review "Fascism Over Hollywood." Hays must have shuddered when he read this piece, which lambasted William Randolph Hearst's movie as a blatant attempt to "convert innocent American movie audiences to a policy of fascist dictatorship in this country." *Gabriel* even turned political commentator Walter Lippmann into a movie critic: After watching the film, he deadpanned that "the body politic is one kind of body that Hollywood had not yet learned about. Indeed, I never dreamed that such virginal innocence could come out of the moving-pictures." *Harrison's Reports,* on the other hand, told exhibitors that the movie dealt with "what the majority of the people of the United States have in their minds in reference to political, social and economic problems." Hays breathed a huge sigh of relief when box-office figures showed *Gabriel* failed to capture the nation's attention.[90]

Gangsters, chain gangs, and politics illustrated that the debate over film content was far more complex than an ecclesiastical ukase demanding that films be "morally pure." Daniel Lord told Hays in 1931 that it really did not matter how well the movies treated certain themes, like gangsters; there was simply no place for them on the screen. Lord was advocating not reform, but a total ban on subjects that dealt with things of which he did not approve. While he had no evidence that crime films caused an increase in crime, he believed they did. Those who demanded strict censorship agreed with Lord: Hollywood was presenting a side of American life of which they disapproved. Gangsters, prisons, and corrupt politicians did not represent their view of what America represented.

Although Hays and his censors were accused of not making a sincere effort to enforce the code, the fact is that there were legitimate differences of opinion over what was permissible on the screen. This was especially true for the gangster film. Jason Joy, August Vollmer, and a host of newspapers, magazines, film reviewers, and law enforcement personnel saw the clear moral lesson that "crime didn't pay" in the films. Even a critic as severe as Martin Quigley admitted there was no clear evidence that gangster films did anyone any real harm.

Hays's role was pivotal. Although loudly accused by his detractors of not enforcing the code, he was in fact constantly searching for ways to bring Hollywood producers more firmly under his control. While Hays preached "freedom for the movies" to the public, in private he worked to control their content. It was Hays, and his Hollywood censorship office, not religious reformers, that objected to the content of *I Am a Fugitive from a Chain Gang* and *Gabriel Over the White House*. More than anything, Hays feared controversy: Films that questioned basic values, as did the gangster genre, illustrated corruption and unfairness, as did prison dramas, or challenged the view that government was dedicated to the general welfare of the public, as did *Gabriel,* were worrisome to Hays.

It was not that the studios were determined to flood the screen with "hard-boiled" drama: They were not. Nevertheless, some studios – in particular, Warner Bros. – and some producers and directors were interested in expanding the perimeters of cinema, and objected to Hays's attempts to restrict their films.

The lesson Hays learned from the gangster films, especially *Scarface,* and from movies like *Gabriel* was that no amount of postproduction cutting and reediting could change a film's basic flavor. Controlling film content would require strong, firm, preproduction control at the studio level. Martin Quigley agreed. While Hays searched for a method to exert his influence over the producers, Quigley envisioned mustering Catholic legions to march against Hollywood.

Notes

1 Joy to Elmer T. Peterson, Sept. 26, 1930, LP.
2 *New York Times,* Jan. 2, 1928, p. 10.
3 Fred Eastman, "Our Children and the Movies," *Christian Century* 47 (Jan. 22, 1930), p. 110.
4 Alice Miller Mitchell, *Children and the Movies* (Chicago: University of Chicago Press, 1929).
5 "Protests Against Gangster Films," 1931, box 43, HP.
6 Ibid.
7 *Variety,* Jan. 21, 1931, p. 5.
8 John A. Sargent, "Self-Regulation," p. 50.
9 *Variety,* Nov. 5, 1930, p. 23.
10 Ibid., Aug. 4, 1931, pp. 7, 21.

11 John Baxter, *The Gangster Film* (New York: A. S. Barnes, 1970), pp. 119–60.
12 Pat McGilligan, ed., *Backstory I*, pp. 56–9.
13 Ibid.
14 Thomas Schatz, *The Genius of the System*, p. 137.
15 Gerald Peary, ed., *Little Caesar*, pp. 45–9.
16 *New York Times*, January 10, 1931, p. 19.
17 Creighton Peet, "Little Caesar," *Outlook and Independent* 157 (Jan. 21, 1931), 113; Maurice McKenzie to Joy, Jan. 27, 1931, *Little Caesar*, PCA.
18 Joy to McKenzie, Jan. 30, 1930, *Little Caesar*, PCA.
19 Lamar Trotti interview with James Wingate; Trotti to Hays, April 14, 1931, box 42, HP.
20 Joy to Wingate, Feb. 5, 1931, box 42, HP.
21 Joy to John Cooper, Toronto Censorship Board, Feb. 21, 1931, box 42, HP; "Good and Bad Movies," *Parent's Magazine* 6 (April 1931), p. 48.
22 This incident was based on a true story: When Chicago gangster Samuel J. "Nails" Morton was kicked to death by a horse, his henchmen stormed into the stable and paid the horse back in kind.
23 Ethan Mordden, *The Hollywood Studios*, p. 233.
24 Joy to Darryl Zanuck, Jan. 26, 1931, *The Public Enemy*, PCA.
25 *Variety*, April 29, 1931, p. 12.
26 *National Board of Review Magazine* 6 (May 1931), pp. 9–10.
27 *Time* 17 (May 4, 1931), p. 44.
28 "Good and Bad Movies," p. 48.
29 Trotti to Hays, April 13, 1931, box 42, HP.
30 Ibid.
31 Creighton Peet, "The New Movies," *Outlook and Independent* 158 (May 20, 1931), p. 90.
32 *Variety*, Jan. 28, 1931, p. 16.
33 August Vollmer to Hays, April 20, 1931, box 42, HP.
34 Ibid.
35 Daniel Lord, "The Code – One Year Later," April 23, 1931, LP.
36 *Harrison's Reports*, April 23, 1932.
37 *New York Times*, Mar. 13, 1932, viii, p. 4.
38 Ben Hecht, *A Child of the Century* (New York: Simon & Schuster, 1954), p. 486.
39 William MacAdams, *Ben Hecht: The Man Behind the Legend* (New York: Scribner's, 1988), p. 125.
40 Gerald Mast, *Howard Hawks, Storyteller* (New York: Oxford University Press, 1982), p. 74.
41 Ibid.
42 Unfortunately, the file for *Scarface* is missing from the PCA files at the Academy Library. For an excellent account of the production history of the film, see Jay R. Nash and Stanley R. Ross, *The Motion Picture Guide*, pp. 2759–63, and Mast, *Howard Hawks*, pp. 71–106.
43 Joseph McBride, *Hawks on Hawks* (Berkeley: University of California Press, 1982), pp. 43–52.
44 Mast, *Howard Hawks*, p. 75.

45 Ibid., p. 73.
46 *New York Times*, June 27, 1931, p. 16.
47 *Commonweal* 14 (June 10, 1931), p. 143.
48 MacAdams, *Ben Hecht*, pp. 131–2.
49 Tony Thomas, *Howard Hughes in Hollywood*, p. 75.
50 "Ten Years of Will Hays," *Harrison's Reports* (June 18, 1932).
51 *Christian Century* 49 (July 13, 1932), p. 877.
52 Ibid.
53 Martin Quigley, "Hughes and Censorship," *Motion Picture Herald* (May 28, 1932), p. 17.
54 *Philadelphia Public Ledger*, July 13, 1932 (in box 44, HP).
55 *National Board of Review Magazine* 7 (March 1932), 10–11.
56 *Time* 19 (April 18, 1932), 17.
57 *Motion Picture Herald*, May 28, 1932, p. 87.
58 Robert E. Burns, *I Am a Fugitive from a Georgia Chain Gang!* (Cutchogue, N. Y.: Buccaneer Books, 1990).
59 Howard J. Green, *I Am a Fugitive from a Chain Gang*, pp. 13–19. For other discussions of the film see Andrew Bergman, *We're In the Money*, pp. 93–6; Nick Roddick, *A New Deal in Entertainment*, pp. 123–6; Russell Campbell, "*I Am a Fugitive from a Chain Gang*"; Peter Roffman and Jim Purdy, *The Hollywood Social Problem Film*, pp. 25–9; John Raeburn, "History and Fate in *I Am a Fugitive from a Chain Gang*."
60 Joy to Hays, April 1, 1931, *I Am a Fugitive from a Chain Gang*, PCA.
61 Joy to Selznick, May 31, 1932, *Hell's Highway*, PCA.
62 Ibid.
63 Trotti to Files, June 2, 1932, *Hell's Highway*, PCA.
64 Joy to Hays, June 4, 1932, *Hell's Highway*, PCA.
65 Joy to Thalberg, Feb. 26, 1932, *I Am a Fugitive from a Chain Gang*, PCA.
66 Joy to Zanuck, July 27, 1932, *I Am a Fugitive from a Chain Gang*, PCA.
67 Schatz, *Genius of the System*, p. 145.
68 Joy to Albert Howson (Warners), Oct. 17, 1932, *I Am a Fugitive from a Chain Gang*, PCA.
69 Schatz, *Genius of the System*, p. 148.
70 *Harrison's Reports*, Nov. 19, 1932.
71 Ibid.; Green, *I Am a Fugitive*, p. 41.
72 Joy to Albert Howson (Warners), Oct. 17, 1932, *I Am a Fugitive from a Chain Gang*, PCA File.
73 The most complete account of the film is Robert L. McConnell, "The Genesis and Ideology of *Gabriel Over the White House*"; unfortunately, McConnell did not have access to the PCA files. See also Bosley Crowther, *Hollywood Rajah: The Life and Times of Louis B. Mayer* (New York: Holt, 1960), pp. 178–80; Roffman and Purdy, *The Hollywood Social Problem Film*, pp. 68–73; Bergman, *We're in the Money*, pp. 115–20.
74 A. Cunningham, "Synopsis," Dec. 29, 1932, *Gabriel Over the White House*, MGM Script Files, USC.
75 Wingate to Thalberg, Feb. 8, 1933, *Gabriel Over the White House*, PCA.
76 *Gabriel Over the White House*, Feb. 4, 1933, MGM Script Files, USC.
77 Ibid.

78 Ibid.

79 Wingate to Thalberg, Feb. 15, 1933, and Wingate to Louis B. Mayer, Feb. 16, 1933, MGM Script Files, USC.

80 Wingate to Hays, Jan. 30, 1933, MGM Script Files, USC.

81 Fred L. Herron to McKenzie, Feb. 27, 1933, MGM Script Files, USC.

82 Hays to Mayer, Feb. 16, 1933; Hays to Wingate, Feb. 16, 1933; Fred W. Beetson to Wingate, Feb. 17, 1933; McKenzie to Wingate, Feb 20, 1933; Wingate to Hays, Feb. 23, 1933, MGM Script Files, USC.

83 Quoted in McConnell, "Genesis and Ideology of *Gabriel*," p. 9.

84 Breen to Lord, Mar. 18, 1933, LP; Raymond Moley, *The Hays Office*, p. 78.

85 Hays to Wingate, Mar. 11, 1933, *Gabriel Over the White House*, PCA.

86 Ibid.

87 Ibid.

88 Copies of the telephone conversation and details of the cuts demanded are also in Hays to Wingate, Mar. 11, 1933, MGM Script Files, USC.

89 Wingate to Thalberg, Mar. 30, 1933, and Wingate to Hays, Mar. 31, 1933, *Gabriel Over the White House*, PCA.

90 "Fascism Over Hollywood," *Nation* 136 (April 26, 1933), pp. 482–3; Lippmann quoted in "A President After Hollywood's Heart," *Literary Digest* 115 (April 22, 1933), p. 13.

CHAPTER 6

LEGIONS MARCH ON HOLLYWOOD

The pest hole that infests the entire country with its obscene and lascivious motion pictures must be cleaned and disinfected.
— *Commonweal* (May 18, 1934)

In 1943 Jack Warner and his production boss, Hal Wallis, were discussing problems with Irving Berlin's patriotic salute to the soldiers in
World War II, *This Is the Army*. Hollywood was a boom town during
the war: The studios were grinding out some 500 pictures a year, and
weekly attendance soared to 85 million per week. As Warner and
Wallis talked, they began to reminisce about the problems the industry
faced a decade earlier. In 1933 economic conditions forced the studios
to lay off workers and slash salaries. The conversation then turned to
the influence of religious organizations on films. Warner told Wallis
"when mass church organizations start after you, you haven't a leg to
stand on."[1]

Even a decade later Warner vividly recalled 1933. It was in that
year that the Catholic church launched a national crusade, the Legion
of Decency, which signed millions of Catholic faithful to a pledge to
boycott movies judged by Catholic officials to be immoral. The Legion
established its own rating organization and applied pressure on the
studios to produce films that reflected Catholic theology. In response,
the industry installed a Catholic censor, Joseph Breen, to interpret and
enforce the 1930 Production Code.

But more than economics and irate Catholics were troubling the
moguls and their studios. In the spring of 1933 it appeared that the
slumbering federal government was finally awakening to the cry of
moral guardians for regulation of the movies. The presidential election
in 1932 was a rejection of the Republican Party and its symbol, Herbert Hoover. A New York Democrat, Franklin D. Roosevelt, was
elected in a landslide victory. FDR took office in March 1933 and
announced his New Deal for economic recovery. One plank of that
broad-based program was his National Industrial Recovery Act, estab-

149

lishing the National Recovery Administration, or NRA as it was popularly known, which called for government–business cooperation to spur economic recovery. At first blush it appeared to both film-industry officials and moral reformers that the NRA would bring the movies under the scrutiny of Washington's bureaucrats.

Much more damaging to the public image of the industry was the publication of nine books by respected American academics on the impact of movies on children. These books, known as the Payne Studies, appeared to prove what moral guardians had been saying about the movies for three decades – that films were harmful to children. The books, the NRA, and the Catholic Legion movement all occurred during 1933 and intensified the national debate about the movies. With Catholic Legions marching on Hollywood, armed with moral and academic arguments, the moguls were indeed besieged. Jack Warner was right: Hollywood didn't have a chance.

For ten years Hays had fought advocates of government censorship of the movies by working with community "Better Film" organizations and civic groups that reviewed and recommended good films. Using his political clout to work against antimovie legislation at the federal and state level, he argued that "censorship" was un-American, and continued to try to regulate film content through "self-regulation" of the Code, consistently maintaining that the movies, while sometimes in bad taste, were not, as critics charged, harmful to children or "immoral." For the most part, Hays had been successful. The movies remained America's most popular form of entertainment, and its most vocal critics were seen as antimovie fanatics who wanted to censor not only movies, but also the theater and books.

Hays's use of Father Lord was a perfect example. After his Code was adopted, Lord was retained as a "consultant" to the MPPDA. Hays sponsored several trips by Lord to Hollywood to work with Joy, Wingate, and the studios. He paid his expenses and corresponded regularly with the priest asking for opinions on scripts. Hays also sent Lord MPPDA conference minutes and correspondence to keep him up to date on the efforts of Joy and Wingate.[2]

By May 1933, however, Lord was convinced he had been used. He was extremely critical of Wingate, whom he characterized as "a complete washout."[3] Hays was desperate to keep Lord in the fold. It was the Depression, Hays told the priest, not a lack of commitment to the code, that had induced studios to make questionable films. While Hays thought the overall trend improving, collapsing box-office revenues put "tremendous commercial pressure" on the studios. The crisis was so severe, Hays told Lord, he had been "having daily . . . meetings . . . of purely economic" nature with industry leaders.[4]

In a rare show of support for Hays, Breen confirmed the impact that economics was having on the screen; he told Lord that the Depression had the industry "in a panic," convinced that "quick money" could be made with "over-sexy stuff." While Breen admitted that Wingate had been a disappointment, he assured Lord that Hays "is doing his darndest."[5] Even Quigley tried to convince Lord to continue working for stricter enforcement of the Code. He wrote to the priest that he was "convinced that Hays is now striving very hard to make" the Code work and had come to view his appointment of Wingate a mistake. It was especially encouraging, Quigley added, that Hays was "now looking for more help from Breen" for Code enforcement.[6]

Lord remained skeptical. The Hollywood producers were, in his view, "muddle-headed sheep" who would never change unless drastic action were taken.[7] When Hays asked him to go Los Angeles to work with Wingate and the producers, Lord seriously considered the offer. He wondered if he should refuse "the opportunity to uplift the morality of the industry" simply because he was frustrated, or was the film industry so "utterly hopeless" that it could go "merrily to hell."[8]

Lord decided the movies could go "merrily to hell." He wrote to Hays in late May that he "felt completely let down on the Code" and could see no point in trying to work with Wingate or the studios. In the last eight months, Lord claimed, the pictures "have grown worse and worse." Not "one man in twenty" in Hollywood had, in his view, the "slightest consideration for morality or decency." Lord then added an ominous warning: In addition to his own personal disappointment, he told Hays "powerful groups" were planning "aggressive action" against the industry. Lord felt that if he went to Hollywood at this particular time his presence would be seen as a signal that he believed further cooperation with the industry would produce results. "Frankly," he concluded, "I do not."[9]

Lord's defection was a major blow to Hays. The priest's reference to "powerful forces" was certainly threatening. It could only mean that the Catholic church, with some 20 million members, most of whom lived in large urban areas, was preparing to join the antimovie lobby. Almost simultaneous with Lord's withdrawal was the public release of the findings of four years of research conducted by the Motion Picture Research Council on the effects of movies on children.

In 1928 few people noticed when the Payne Fund, a philanthropic organization in Cleveland, granted $200,000 to the Reverend William H. Short and his Motion Picture Research Council to study the influence of movies on children. Short, who had been fighting the industry for more than two decades, understood that without direct evidence that movies harmed children his goal of a federally regulated movie industry would never be realized. He used the grant to hire academic social scientists from seven universities to gather information, conduct original research, and interpret data on the impact movies had on America's children. According to Robert Sklar, Short's goal was "to get the goods on the movies, to nail them to the wall."[10]

Under the direction of Professor W. W. Charters, director of the Bureau of Educational Research at Ohio State University, researchers attempted to measure scientifically the questions people had been asking about the movies for three decades:

Were children's attitudes toward violence and sex changed by the movies they saw?

What, if any, emotional impact did films have on children?

Were children able to distinguish "fantasy" from reality?

Did they retain "messages" from films with greater accuracy than they recalled information from books?

Did films cause children to lose sleep?

What types of films did children see?

How often did they attend the movies?

The studies took four years to complete and were released to the public in the spring of 1933, published in nine separate volumes. The researchers avoided sweeping conclusions. Crime movies had a greater influence on children who came from dysfunctional homes, said one. Another concluded that the influence of movies on children was strong, but it was essential to note that this influence was "specific for a given child and given movie." In other words, movies were in and by themselves no more harmful than other cultural influences on children.

These cautious academic findings were forgotten when Henry James Forman published a one-volume summary entitled *Our Movie Made Children*. Forman openly accused the movies of "helping shape a race of criminals."[11] The claim, in and by itself, was nothing new – critics, as we have seen, had been making outrageous statements about the effects of movies for years. It was the source for Forman's book that delighted the antimovie lobby, horrified millions of concerned parents, and rendered Hays speechless. Scientific research conducted by reputable academics, it seemed, had verified the impressionistic evidence that film reformers had cited for years.

Our Movie Made Children was a sensational indictment of Hollywood and quickly became a best-seller. Forman toured the country denouncing the movies. From editorial pages came a torrent of concern based not on the nine volumes written by the academics, which were less sensational, but on Forman's summary. *Survey Graphic,* a respected journal read by the nation's social workers, was typical.

"Here at last," the journal wrote, "we have the facts." Children made up 36 percent of the audience, and the average child went to the movies once a week. What they saw was startling: In an analysis of 115 films, readers of *Survey Graphic* were told, 66 percent showed drinking and 43 percent pictured intoxication, along with a plethora of violence that included 71 murders, 59 assaults, 17 holdups – in short, a total of some 449 assorted movie crimes.

Did children remember what they saw? Indeed they did, "with the indiscriminate fidelity of little cameras." Within a twenty-four-hour period children could recall 60 percent of what an average adult could remember from a film. Also, they retained it: Tested six weeks later, children could recall 91 percent of their earlier impressions. The study concluded that "pictures play a considerably larger part in the child's imagination than do books."[12]

This ability to recall vividly what they saw also caused children to lose sleep after seeing a movie. At Ohio State University, researchers hooked measuring devices to kids' bedsprings and measured how much they tossed and turned on a normal basis and how often they did so after seeing a movie. They found that movies increased restlessness by 26 percent for boys and 14 percent for girls, and concluded that "for highly sensitive or weak and unstable children the best hygienic policy would be to recommend very infrequent attendance" at carefully selected films.[13]

The kids lost sleep because the movies were exciting. Researchers measured the increase in pulse rates during movies like *The Mysterious Dr. Fu Manchu,* and were alarmed that children whose pulse rate was a normal 75–80 had it shoot up to 180 during the film. Their conclusion:

Such a situation is bad for health, represents a deplorable mental hygiene and might easily contribute to the habits which are popularly called "nervousness" in children. Where the boy or girl has a chance to work off emotions in the open, in exercise or play, it is splendid. Such excitement in a darkened theater is by no means splendid.

Children told researchers that they were scared and often had nightmares after seeing films like *Phantom of the Opera, The Dawn Patrol, Dr. Jekyll and Mr. Hyde,* and even *Tarzan, the Ape Man.* Dr. Frederick Peterson, a neurologist from New York, warned parents that the effect of watching such films could create "an effect very similar to shellshock."[14]

In one case a researcher took a young boy to see Warner Bros.' *Union Depot.* After a robbery scene the bad guys opened a violin case that was filled with money. The sociologist noted that although adults in the audience gasped with dismay, the young urchin was unmoved.

After the film he asked the boy why. "I expected a machine-gun," he replied. "Tell me any picture that ain't got a machine-gun in it. They all got typewriters [machine guns] in them." When asked who his favorite actor was, the boy shot back James Cagney. "You get some ideas from his actin'. You learn how to pull off a job, how he bumps off a guy, an' a lotta t'ings."[15] In a study of 110 young men in prison, the movies were blamed by 49 percent of them for instructing them on how to pull off a successful caper. "Movies have shown me the way of stealing automobiles, the charge for which I am now serving sentence," said one young felon. "I learned from the movies the scientific way of pulling jobs – leave no fingerprints or telltale marks," reported another.[16]

The facts, as *Survey Graphic* reported, were conclusive – movies harmed children. They not only showed them how to commit crimes and presented false values, but also damaged them physically and mentally. Dr. Fred Eastman, a longtime movie critic, wrote an eight-part series in the *Christian Century* that demanded federal regulation; but Eastman's readers were already convinced that the movies were evil. Far more damaging to the industry were summaries printed in the *New York Times*, the *Nation, Parent's Magazine,* the *Elementary School Journal,* and *School and Society,* which accepted without comment the conclusions of the Payne Studies as reported by Forman.[17]

Despite the hoopla, not everyone was convinced. Kaspar Monahan of the *Pittsburgh Press* thought the Payne Studies had about "as much scientific value as a recipe for noodle soup." The *Chicago Daily News* commented that the alarms expressed in *Our Movie Made Children* were "torn from the same cloth as prohibition. It is the voice of fear" trying to keep "youth insulated from life." The *Atlanta Journal* pointed out that the research was clearly "prejudiced against the movies" and offered "absurd" conclusions. In Minnesota, the *St. Paul Dispatch* wrote:

It is just a little amusing to see the investigators earnestly trotting up and dumping at the studio door all the ills of society from crime to vanity that have at other times been blamed upon co-education, the bunny-hug, jazz music, French novels, high heels, the split skirt, one-piece bathing suits and so many other things. The book is distinctly biased.

The Cleveland *Plain Dealer,* the New Orleans *Times-Picayune*, the Kansas City *Journal-Post*, the Philadelphia *Record* and *Public Ledger,* the Boston *American,* and New York's *Evening Post, Daily News,* and *Daily Mirror* all offered similar reactions and lampooned the conclusions of the Payne Studies.[18]

Despite this divided reaction, Hays remained silent. In so doing he missed an opportunity to thwart the forces of censorship that were gathering strength for a renewed assault on the industry.[19]

Figure 7. Will Hays, President of the Motion Picture Producers and Distributors of America, and Paramount's Jesse Lasky. Courtesy the Museum of Modern Art / Film Stills Archive.

In retrospect it is not surprising that Hays chose not to react publicly. He rarely went public with any debate, and gambled that calmer judgments would soon undercut the emotional reaction to the Payne findings. It was also a particularly difficult time for Hays, who was uneasy about the prospects of working with a new Democratic administration in Washington. "The General," as he liked to be called, had been hired by the industry primarily for his chummy connections with the Republican Party. From 1922 to 1932 this relationship paid big dividends for the industry as Hays worked quietly behind the scenes with his fellow Republicans to foil attempts at antimovie legislation. Hays had confidently predicted a victory for Hoover in 1932; he was embarrassed by the overwhelming rejection of Republicanism by the electorate. FDR's landslide victory led industry insiders and analysts to speculate on Hays's future. Would he be effective with the Roosevelt administration? Would government policy toward the industry change? Would the demands of Protestant reformers for a federal film commission, which would eliminate block booking, suddenly find a receptive ear in Washington? Would the moguls fire Hays and replace him with a prominent Democrat?

The answers to these questions came quickly when President Franklin D. Roosevelt signed into law the National Industrial Recovery Act in June 1933. The concept behind the legislation was to increase the profits of businessmen who, in turn, would pay workers a fair wage. To that end, the law incorporated the suspension of business competition and instituted collaboration. Businessmen, working in cooperation with labor and NRA bureaucrats, would write "codes of business practice." The goal was to bring economic stabilization by eliminating cut-throat competition, and to ensure a fair wage for a day's work for all American workers. Each industry was to have its own code – steel, coal, automobiles, and, of course, the movies. FDR appointed Hugh S. Johnson, a retired general and businessman, to head the agency, and Johnson in turn appointed Sol E. Rosenblat to produce a movie code.

The NRA movie code was the longest and in many ways the most complicated of all the NRA codes. Its authors accepted the business practice of vertical monopoly and block booking, which reformers and small exhibitors found so odious.[20] After a short but turbulent history, the NRA was declared unconstitutional by the Supreme Court in 1935.

The provisions of the NRA code, with one exception, are not especially important to this study. The exception is that the NRA movie code was the only government code to include a morals clause. The announcement that the federal government intended to write a "code" to define "rules of conduct" for the movies immediately attracted the attention of reformers. It appeared that the federal government had finally heard their plea to bring "moral" reform to Hollywood.

Even Martin Quigley, who had long opposed government censorship and regulation of the industry, was at first convinced that the NRA offered a unique opportunity to force the industry to produce moral films. Frustrated by what he perceived to be a lack of enforcement of Lord's code by the Hays Office, Quigley hoped to incorporate Lord's document, or a summary of it, into the NRA movie code. While the Hays Office would still be responsible for enforcement through "self-regulation," Quigley hoped that a strong morality clause in a government-sanctioned code would put the industry, specifically the producers, "on record in a formal contract with the president of the United States."[21] If the studios ignored attempts from the Hays Office to censor an immoral film, in his view they would be in violation of federal law. The full force of the federal government would then be directed at the offending studio. This, Quigley believed, would force even the most recalcitrant producers and studios to make moral movies.

During the summer of 1933, the possible inclusion of a morality clause in the NRA code arose at the same time as plans for a Catholic attack on "immoral" movies. Far from being surprised by either development, Hays and his staff participated in discussions with representatives from the church and the government.

On the West Coast Bishop John Cantwell was in a potentially embarrassing position: He was bishop of Los Angeles, a city many considered to be the "sin capital" of America. Over the years he had become increasingly concerned that the movie industry was causing a moral decline among Catholic youth, but he was perplexed about what he could do to change Hollywood. He favored neither a California state censorship law nor boycotts that might bring economic hardship to an industry that employed so many of his flock.

Cantwell's concern had been heightened with the arrival of Joseph Breen in Los Angeles in 1932. Breen, introduced to the bishop by Father Dinneen, became Cantwell's confidant, and the two men often discussed strategies for making the movies moral. Breen kept Cantwell abreast of the activities of other priests, told him of the internal problems facing Hays, and constantly pressed the bishop to intensify Catholic pressure on the industry. While working for Hays in the public relations department, Breen was a Catholic "mole" in Hollywood.

By that summer of 1933, Cantwell was convinced that something had to be done about the movies, but remained skeptical that his fellow bishops would agree on a unified program. Within church organization each bishop was a prince unto himself; few had shown as much interest as he or Cardinal Mundelein in Chicago. Cantwell also worried about the ability of the hierarchy to persuade large numbers of lay Catholics to give up movies. It would be embarrassing to launch a great public campaign only to have it fail from lack of support by the bishops and the laity.

Given these fears of failure, Cantwell and Breen planned a two-pronged attack. First, convince all the bishops at their annual meeting in Washington, D.C., that the content of motion pictures was a moral issue worthy of the hierarchy. Second, begin to use influential lay Catholics and private channels to communicate Catholic concern to Hays and industry officials. Cantwell first turned to a fellow bishop, John T. McNicholas, O.P., of Cincinnati. "I think the Bishops," he wrote McNicholas, "should, at their meeting in the fall, take action" against the moving pictures, which "are undoing much of the work of the Church in this country." Cantwell told McNicholas that threats against their income would get the attention of "the Jews who control" the industry. As a first step Cantwell suggested the hierarchy pressure "bankers who are loaning money to the picture people" and urge the laity to boycott films judged to be immoral.[22] McNicholas agreed to raise the issue.

With the agenda item set for November, Cantwell pressured the studios.[23] He personally visited MGM, Paramount, and several key producers at other studios to urge them to produce "clean" movies. He was graciously received and, despite verbal assurances of cooperation, Cantwell remained unconvinced: "promises . . . made to us by the Jews . . . will amount to very little" unless economic pressure was brought against the industry, he told Bishop McNicholas.[24]

Cantwell's trump card was his relationship with Dr. A. H. Giannini, president of the Bank of America in Los Angeles. Giannini, a prominent and active lay Catholic, was a prime lender to Hollywood studios and therefore a key player in the production of movies. Cantwell summoned the banker to his Santa Monica residence. The Catholic church, Giannini was told, was going to condemn the movies and everyone associated with their production. The Bank of America was included, Cantwell said, because it was corrupting Catholic youth by financing immoral movies. The meeting, according to Breen, "threw Giannini into a panic."[25] He immediately served notice on his Hollywood clients that the Bank of America would no longer "finance their products if . . . the Catholic church were to come out in opposition to their business."[26] Cantwell wrote to Cardinal Patrick Hayes in New York and asked him to deliver a similar message to Wall Street bankers.

Cantwell then brought in a prominent Los Angeles attorney, Joseph Scott, to carry his message to Hollywood producers. Cantwell told Scott that the bishops were planning action against the industry because it was "vile," doing "untold harm" to our children. He asked him to warn the studio heads and producers that, unless they reformed, the bishops would launch an all-out campaign in the fall.[27] Cantwell later admitted that bringing Giannini and Scott into the fold "initiated our endeavor."[28]

The next step was to confront the Hollywood establishment. This was Breen's job. He arranged for Giannini and Scott, both representing Cantwell, to meet with Hays and studio personnel at the Academy of Motion Picture Arts and Sciences offices. Summoned were Jack Warner; MGM's Louis B. Mayer; Paramount's Adolph Zukor, visiting from New York, and his studio head Emanuel Cohen; RKO's production head, R. Keith Kahane; Wilfred Sheehan and Jason Joy from Fox; UA's Joe Schenck; Universal's Junior Laemmle; and Hays and his staff members, Breen, Wingate, and Geoffrey Shurlock. It was a long and acrimonious meeting, made all the more so by recent disputes between Hays and the studios: Paramount's Cohen and Zukor had been battling Hays over Mae West, RKO's Kahane was in the midst of his disagreements with Hays over *Ann Vickers,* Warner was fresh from his fight over *Baby Face,* and Columbia was in the throes of a bitter strike.

Hays again repeated what he had told industry leaders in March: that certain movies were creating an increasingly hostile atmosphere against the industry. Conditions in August, however, were even more threatening than they had been just a few months earlier. The Payne Studies had galvanized a large segment of public opinion against the industry; the government was intervening via the NRA, and no one could predict how the new agency might affect business; and now the Catholic church was threatening a national boycott. This, Hays believed, was because the studios had been ignoring the code and were not cooperating with Wingate.

Hays then turned the meeting over to Giannini and Scott. Giannini told the group that the Catholic church was going to launch an anti-movie campaign in the fall unless the bishops were convinced that the industry was serious about adherence to the 1930 code. The Bank of America, Giannini continued, could not and would not finance films that were "prostituting the youth of America." The banker "pleaded" with the studio heads to stop producing the type of pictures that Hays had just mentioned.[29]

Scott then, according to Breen, "lashed into the Jews furiously." They were "disloyal" Americans, he charged, engaged in "a conspiracy to debauch the . . . youth of the land." Scott warned that a recent trial in California had exposed "communistic" radicals as "100 per cent Jews" and that the combination of "dirty motion pictures" and communist radicals "were serving to build up an enormous case against the Jews in the eyes of the American people." He reminded the producers that there were groups in America that were "sympathetic" with the Nazi assaults on Jews in Germany and were "even now organizing further to attack the Jew in America."[30]

Given this climate of opinion, Scott continued, Hollywood could not continue making "dirty" movies that could open not only the floodgates of censorship but racial hatred as well. The possibility of a united Catholic–Protestant front, which was certain to have a devastating impact on the box office, could likewise bring anti-Semitic groups into the open. Scott demanded that the industry stop this "damnable business," which he said brought "disgrace upon the Jews and upon America." The attorney's presentation, said Breen, was "positively brilliant."[31]

An uproar followed, with moguls, producers, and censors screaming at one another. Adolph Zukor leapt to his feet, gave an emotional apology for the "dirt and filth" that had invaded Paramount, and promised to do all in his power to clean up his films. Winfield Sheenan of Fox pledged that his company would "no longer tolerate any dirty pictures" and ordered Jason Joy to "lay down the law" to studio writers.

Only Joe Schenck from UA balked, saying what Thalberg had said in 1930: that Hollywood had the right to make serious movies. Schenck strongly objected to the thesis that movies were "immoral" or "dirty" simply because they portrayed serious issues. The vast majority of the American people did not agree, Schenck continued, that films like *A Farewell to Arms,* or the proposed *Of Human Bondage,* were immoral. The public demanded movie versions of these literary works. He added that it would be impossible to produce films that would satisfy both Catholic bishops and Protestant reformers and yet entertain millions of movie fans worldwide. He characterized reformers as "narrow-minded and bigoted" and belittled Scott, whom he labeled the "best actor" in Hollywood. He accused his fellow producers of being cowards for submitting to the anti-Semitic tirade to which they had just been subjected. Schenck told Hays and his fellow producers that he intended to run his business as he saw fit, and urged the others to have the courage to stand up and do the same.[32]

Breen scurried off to report the details of the meeting to Bishop Cantwell, telling him that there was "almost unanimous" agreement among producers to make clean movies; he did not report Schenck's opposition. Cantwell was unmoved and expressed "no faith" in industry promises: He demanded "evidence, concrete and specific" before he would do anything to stop the upcoming Catholic campaign.[33] In Chicago Cardinal Mundelein agreed. Catholic strategy would be to press ahead and "await developments in Washington."[34] Will Hays, hopeful that he had, at the very least, impressed on the studios the need for caution, headed back to New York to work on a morals clause for the NRA code.

During the three-day train ride back to New York, Hays had time to formulate strategy. He was in basic agreement with Quigley that a morals provision in the NRA code might strengthen his position vis-à-vis the studios. It was obvious, after this last go-round, that the studios were not fully convinced that radical change was necessary. Although Hays in the past had had oral commitments to support strict enforcement, the studios had responded by fighting every attempt to restrict content. Hays, who had been trying to extend his influence in Hollywood since 1922, feared both NRA and Catholic interference. He did not want to turn power over to the federal government or give in completely to religious forces. His goal was to minimize outside influence while maximizing his own.

By the time he reached New York, Hays had prepared a draft for a morals clause for the NRA. He rejected incorporating Lord's code in favor of a brief statement that pledged the industry to "maintain right moral standards" through self-regulation. Hays felt compelled to consult with Quigley and church representatives before the formal NRA hearing opened in Washington, D.C., in September. In mid-August Hays, Quigley, and Father Wilfrid Parsons spent a Sunday afternoon discussing morality and the NRA.

After Hays showed the two men his draft, Quigley "let him have it with both barrels."[35] Only a show of power, Quigley stressed, could force the studios to comply, and the NRA offered that opportunity. He gave Hays a longer, more detailed morals statement that bound the producers to "abide by the decisions of the industry" and specifically gave the government "full force and authority to punish violations" of the NRA morality code.[36] Hays agreed to back Quigley's plan.

The NRA hearings, held during a sweltering September heat wave, brought a gaggle of movie people to Washington: moguls hopeful that the NRA would allow them to reduce wages and would grant legal status to block booking; unions arguing for recognition and improved working conditions; and independent theater owners demanding an end to block booking. Added to this throng of movie people came the old-guard ministers and women's club representatives, determined to force the NRA to "regulate" industry morality.

Sol Rosenblatt, the NRA movie code administrator, "looking dark, pale and eagle-faced," listened patiently as a parade of witnesses testified. After a day of industrial testimony, the hearings turned to screen morality. Canon William Sheafe Chase, who had been testifying in Washington for over a decade, took the stand. In a long, emotional appeal to Rosenblatt, the minister repeated his demands for a regulated industry. The moral issues, he asserted, were as vital to the well-being of the youth of America as the economic issues were to economy. Chase was convinced that the NRA hearings were "historic," because the government was finally going to take over Hollywood. After him came the familiar parade of women's club representatives, typified by Mrs. Richard M. McClure of the General Federation of Women's Clubs, who denounced "crime and sex" films and spoke of the need for the government to set national moral standards and deliver a final blow against block booking.[37]

The silent presence of Will Hays once again frustrated the hopes of the reformers. General Hugh Johnson went on record during the hearings that the NRA would not "be placed in the position of having to regulate, govern or control motion picture morals."[38] Rosenblatt confirmed that view when he told reporters that "the Federal Government, in its NRA program, is not interested in censorship." Sounding for all the world like Will Hays, the NRA director said "the problem of the better screen is one of better public taste."[39]

The final code that emerged from months of bickering contained little about movie morals. Article VII of the NRA code, the so-called morals clause, stated that movies should be moral and that the industry would pledge to regulate itself; in other words, the Hays Office, not the government, would continue to preside over movie morality. The NRA code made no mention of block booking, thereby tacitly accepting it as a valid business practice. Exhibitors were given one concession: They could, under the NRA, cancel 10 percent of the films for which they contracted. Thus, in theory, no exhibitor had to play an "immoral" film; but this compromise did nothing to slow the production of films that Quigley and others considered immoral.

To Quigley and the entire reform lobby, the NRA experience was one more example of Haysian chicanery. Quigley maintained that Hays had left their August meeting committed to having a strong morals statement in the NRA code; yet it was Hays's original statement, not Quigley's, that was finally incorporated into the code. Quigley was furious. He told Lord that, in his view, the NRA was "a mess," and that the "time for action there [in the government] has passed." Father Parsons, who had attended the meeting with Hays and Quigley, told his readers in *America* that "the mounting tide of Catholic opposition to the movies will not be dammed by Article VII" of the NRA.[40]

Quigley was now determined to exploit the growing wrath of the Catholic hierarchy against the industry. Convinced that neither Hays nor the producers would cooperate unless forced to do so, Quigley, Parsons, Lord, Cantwell, and Breen began plotting for Catholic action against Hollywood. The most important step now was to convince the bishops that forceful action was needed. Quigley saw an opportunity when he learned that the newly appointed apostolic delegate to the United States, Monsignor Amleto Giovanni Cicognani, would deliver a speech to the Catholic charities meeting in New York. Archbishop McNicholas of Cincinnati arranged for Quigley and Breen to meet with Cicognani. After listening to their presentation, Cicognani agreed to incorporate into his speech a draft statement prepared by Quigley calling for Catholic action against the movies. "What a massacre of innocence of youth is taking place hour by hour," Cicognani told the assembly. "Catholics are called by God, the Pope, the Bishops, and the priests to a united and vigorous campaign for the purification of the cinema, which has become a deadly menace to morals."[41]

The strategy was clever and pointed. Cicognani was the Pope's representative in America. His speech was a papal directive. The question was no longer whether or not the bishops would take up the cause of "immoral" movies, but when and how. When the bishops gathered in Washington several weeks later, the film industry was an important item on the agenda.

At this conclave, held in November at Catholic University in Washington, D.C., Cantwell spoke at length about Hollywood.[42] The movies had always been vulgar, he began; but now with the addition of sound they were no longer just entertainment but had become an educational system that preached a "sinister and insidious" philosophy of life. A strong faithful marriage, purity, and the sanctity of home were "out-moded sentimentalities" in movies. Cantwell bemoaned the presentation of "social problems," such as divorce, race suicide, and "free love," on the contemporary screen, which "condoned" sin and "lowered the public and private standards of conduct of all who see them." Cantwell cited *Sign of the Cross* and *Ann Vickers* as specific examples of "vile and nauseating" films.[43]

Cantwell then reviewed Catholic attempts to improve movie morality. He told the bishops about Father Lord's code and how it had been evaded by the studios. He described his meeting with Dr. Giannini and Scott's confrontation with Hollywood producers. Who was responsible, he asked: "the Jews?" Yes and no. It was true, he continued, that Jews owned all but one studio and could, if they wished, keep the screen clean; but it was the "artists," especially modern writers, who were to blame for creating "all the filth." He blasted Broadway playwrights and "literary" successes of the "pornographic school" whose books were being adapted by the cinema. "*Seventy-five percent of these writers are pagans,*" he told fellow bishops.[44]

Cantwell ended with a plea for forceful action. It would not be enough for the bishops simply to issue a statement condemning the industry. The church had to wound Hollywood at the box office to stop the production of offensive films. Cardinal Mundelein suggested that Catholics back a law creating national censorship. Archbishop Michael J. Curley of Baltimore thought not; his state, he told the bishops, had a censorship board, but it "had proven a failure." After a lengthy discussion the bishops appointed an Episcopal Committee on Motion Pictures. McNicholas, who had placed the movie question on the agenda, was elected chairman, and Cantwell and Bishops John Noll of Fort Wayne and Hugh Boyle of Pittsburgh were asked to coordinate a Catholic Legion of Decency.[45]

This Legion of Decency, which would soon capture the attention of millions of Americans, was to spearhead a national Catholic attack on the movie industry. The bishops agreed to call for boycotts against films they judged to be immoral, to use the Catholic media as a weapon in the campaign, and to lash out from the pulpit against the evil of the movies.

"The pest hole that infects the entire country with its obscene and lascivious moving pictures must be cleaned and disinfected," said the Episcopal Committee, launching the Catholic campaign.[46] Although Hays had expected a Catholic declaration of war against the movies, the final reality of the appointment of a committee of bishops to "disinfect" his business was upsetting, to say the least. Catholics may have been only one-fifth of the population, but they were heavily concentrated in cities east of the Mississippi River. Half of Chicago was Catholic, as was Boston. New York, Buffalo, Philadelphia, Pittsburgh, Cleveland, and Detroit had sizable Catholic populations. These cities were important to the movie industry because they were home to huge studio-owned first-run theaters; films were exhibited here before being released in general run. An effective Catholic boycott in a few selected cities could thus seriously hurt the industry.

The Catholic church had national media already in place. Clerical publications included the Paulist *Catholic World;* the Jesuit *America;* Daniel Lord's *Queen's Work,* which penetrated most Catholic schools and youth organizations; Notre Dame's *Sign;* Fordham's *Thought;* the *Ecclesiastical Review,* a journal directed at priests; and for those who wanted their theology in condensed form, *Catholic Digest.* Catholic lay organizations published their own journals: The Knights of Columbus informed its members through its publication *Columbia,* and lay Catholics controlled *Commonweal,* an urbane, sophisticated journal edited by George Schuster.

Most of the 103 American dioceses had a local newspaper, and the church operated a national Catholic news bureau in Washington, D.C., that supplied local papers a Catholic slant to international and domestic news as well as syndicated opinion columns. Father Daniel Lord's weekly column, "Along the Way," was published in most Catholic newspapers. The leading such paper, *Our Sunday Visitor,* was published in Huntington, Indiana, under the direction of Bishop John Noll, and had a national circulation of 650,000. The *Brooklyn Tablet,* the Denver *Register,* the Michigan *Catholic,* Chicago's *New World,* and the Los Angeles *Tidings* were other influential Catholic newspapers. Catholic opinion was also broadcast over the airwaves on "The Catholic Hour," a national radio program. The "radio priest," Father Charles Coughlin, broadcasting from WJR in Detroit, held millions of Americans spellbound with his angry denunciation of Jewish bankers, socialists, communists, and, eventually, New Dealers. Detroit was a hotbed of Legion activity. Would Coughlin add the movies and their Jewish owners to his growing list of conspirators?

Hays feared the Catholics much more than the Protestants (Canon Chase, Rev. Short, and the *Christian Century*) who had been at the forefront of the antimovie campaign. An astute politician, he under-

Figure 8. The Legion of Decency's Bishop John Cantwell. Courtesy Archives of the Los Angeles Archdiocese.

stood that the Catholics – unlike the Protestants, who were split into a multitude of denominations – could mobilize unified Catholic opinion without the help of the secular media. Even more threatening was the prospect of a Protestant–Catholic alliance. Hays was determined to pacify the Catholics. As a first step, in December 1933 – only weeks after the official Catholic announcement of a Legion of Decency campaign – Hays named Joe Breen as chief censor in Hollywood.

It was a shrewd move on Hays's part: He was well aware that Breen had been informing Quigley, Lord, Cantwell, and Dinneen of his every move; but from Hays's perspective, it was better to have Breen as an employee inside the firm, to have some control over him, than to have him totally allied with church forces. Breen's appointment also bought Hays some time. He could privately, as he had done to Quigley, admit that Wingate had failed to enforce the code, but that he, Hays, was committed to firm enforcement and had appointed a Catholic as censor to prove the point. Whether Hays realized the extent to which Breen was conspiring against him and the industry is not clear, but it is doubtful that Hays would have been shocked to discover all the sordid details.

To outsiders the Catholic church in America appeared to be one great monolithic organization that marched forward to a single drum. Mysterious and ritual bound, the church seemingly took orders from Rome. That popular impression, like most stereotypes, was far from the truth: Like any other large organization, the church was beset with internal bickering, political infighting, rivalry among the different orders, petty jealousies, and bitter differences between laity and clergy that often hindered the faithful from uniting behind issues other than the most basic doctrinal theology.

Hays understood this. He closely monitored the internal conflicts within the Legion movement and plotted his strategy carefully. Hays received weekly, and at times daily, reports on the Legion. That the Catholic Legion was badly splintered was apparent from the very inception of the movement.

One group comprised the Episcopal Committee, headed by McNicholas and Cantwell, and their advisers, Martin Quigley and Joe Breen. They advocated a policy of pressuring Hays with threats of boycott and blacklists to force studios to accept Breen's interpretation of the code. They demanded that the Hollywood jury system be abolished but were opposed to national boycotts. Also, they feared that continued publication of blacklisted films would backfire: Human nature, they predicted, would cause Catholics and Protestants alike to see films the church judged sinful. Quigley and Breen developed the strategy adopted by the committee heads: Hays Office self-regulation would remain the cornerstone of movie control; the difference would be, Quigley hoped, that the constant threat of boycott would force Hays and the studios to accept a rigid enforcement of the code by the ever-so-Catholic Breen. This policy, Quigley convinced the bishops, would ensure that films emerged from Hollywood with a moral message. Censorship, blacklists, and boycotts would be unnecessary.

Yet each bishop was a prince unto himself, and although Cardinal George Mundelein had lost the argument in Washington, he had no intention of cooperating with Hays and his policy of self-regulation. Mundelein and his followers – Father Dinneen, Daniel Lord, Cardinal Dougherty of Philadelphia, and Cardinal O'Connell of Boston – launched their own campaign. They announced box-office boycotts, picketed local theaters, published extensive blacklists of immoral films, and encouraged Catholics to write letters of protest to Hays, the studios, and the actors and actresses appearing in the films.

Thus, in 1934 there were two Catholic Legions of Decency jockeying for control. Yet, despite the lack of central control, the Legion of Decency movement spread like a firestorm across the nation. "Purify Hollywood or destroy Hollywood," demanded Bishop Joseph Schrembs of Cleveland. Fifty thousand of his faithful, including Mayor Harry Davis and the papal delegate Cicognani, roared their approval of his declaration of war against Hollywood at a Legion of Decency rally in Cleveland's Municipal Stadium. A torrent of rage against the movies poured from Catholic pulpits and pens across the nation. In Buffalo, a local priest gave his flock a new definition of the word "movies": "M – means moral menace; O – obscenity; V – vulgarity; I – immorality; E – exposure; S – sex."[47] The movies were "a deluge of filth," editorialized the *Brooklyn Tablet*. The Knights of Columbus called the movies "The Scandal of the World." *America* labeled films "unwholesome, crude, sordid and morally objectionable."[48]

Some went so far as to declare movie attendance a sin. *America* warned that movies were a "material sin" that "dishonors God." The Catholic periodical *Extension Magazine* told readers that movies were "an occasion of sin." If Catholics knowingly went to a movie that the church had declared "immoral," they had committed a mortal sin. Catholics divided sins into two groups: venial and mortal. A venial sin was a minor infraction easily forgiven through confession; a mortal sin, on the other hand, was considered a major breech of Catholic dogma and, if not forgiven through confession and serious penance, would result in eternal damnation. Suddenly Catholics faced the prospect of eternal damnation for going to the wrong movie![49]

To ensure that the Catholic faithful would take the church stance against the movies seriously, Bishop McNicholas wrote a Legion of Decency pledge. At masses all across the nation, Catholics were given no choice by their priests but to stand and take the Legion pledge. Movies were "a grave menace to youth, to home life, to country and to religion," the priests intoned, and all Catholics must pledge to God that they would not attend a film judged by the church to be "vile and unwholesome." Supplementing oral pledges during mass, many Catholic churches asked their members to sign a formal document. In a few short weeks Chicago and Boston each reported more than a million converts to the antimovie pledge: Detroit brought in 600,000, Cleveland over 500,000, Providence and Los Angeles each signed up more than 300,000, and Seattle reported 100,000 signatures. By mid-1934 the pledge had been administered to some seven million Catholics. It became a regular ritual in the church, administered in early December, and lasted well into the 1960s.[50]

In May 1934, and with Mundelein's blessing, Lord launched a national protest movement against the industry in his *Queen's Work*. He urged his readers to boycott films cited as "immoral," and began to cite specific examples among that year's productions. He condemned MGM's *Riptide* as "insidious," and denounced Irving Thalberg for making its star and his wife, Norma Shearer, play "a loose and immoral woman"; Lord urged readers to protest directly to Louis B. Mayer. *The Trumpet Blows* (Paramount), *Glamour* (Universal), *Finishing School* (RKO), and *George White's Scandals* (Fox) also were branded as immoral.[51]

Lord poured out four years of frustration in his book *The Movies Betray America*. "I'm sick and tired," he wrote, "of being asked to write articles and make speeches telling how grand the industry is." On the contrary, the movies were, he claimed, a "gigantic travesty" that regularly implants into the minds of boys and girls "crime and lust and passion and murder and horror and vice." Lord cited the Payne Studies as a "terrifying" indictment that proved, in "cold, scientific" fashion, the corruption of values inflicted on America's youth by movies. Breaking ranks from Quigley, Lord joined hands with the Protestant reformers calling for federal block-booking legislation and demanded a box-office boycott by Catholics. He advocated adopting the method Catholics had used for centuries against books: the publication of lists of those deemed acceptable and unacceptable.[52]

In Philadelphia Cardinal Denis Dougherty shunned ambiguity. He condemned all movies as a "menace" to morality and demanded that his parishioners boycott "all motion picture theaters."[53] In Boston Cardinal William O'Connell called Hollywood "a riot of rotten, disgusting" entertainment and challenged Catholics to punish the industry at the box office.[54] Local Legion chapters in Detroit and Chicago published names of "uncooperative" theaters and established "vigilance" committees, which roamed theater districts on the lookout for lax Catholics trying to sneak in to see a condemned film.[55]

Lord's idea of publishing "white lists" of good films and blacklists of bad films caught on. If attending films could be "occasions of sin," then the church had to let Catholic laity know which films were "sinful." Chicago and Detroit took the lead in publishing long lists of films in three categories: approved for family viewing, restricted to adults,

and condemned – that is, forbidden viewing for all Catholics. Individual lists appeared in almost every Catholic diocese across the country as
local priests scurried to the theaters to pass moral judgment on Hollywood fare. The church was unrelenting: Hundreds of movies were
condemned as immoral or indecent in the initial zeal to ban perceived
immorality, including some important works produced by major studios. Early victims (which will be discussed in Chapter 7) on the Catholic hit list included *Dr. Monica,* which dealt with birth control and
abortion; *Laughing Boy,* based on Oliver LaFarge's touching story of
the plight of American Indians in the Southwest; Greta Garbo's *Queen
Christina,* which the priests considered a film about an "immoral"
woman; Warners' *Madame du Barry;* and *The Life of Vergie Winters.*
In their eagerness, some priests banned films that others saw as family
entertainment.

During the first few months there was no coordinated Legion campaign. In Quigley's view the situation was totally out of control and,
unless corrected, would defeat the champions of decency. He quietly
lobbied with McNicholas and the Episcopal Committee to seize control of the movement. Hays would only cooperate, he argued, if blacklists and boycotts were limited to the most flagrant films; the inconsis-
tency of one diocese condemning a film that others found suitable for
adults or children promoted the industry's view that the entire movement was led by narrow-minded church elements out to destroy the
entertainment world. Most of all, Quigley feared that a new Mae West
movie would be released at the height of the decency campaign, be denounced, and, in part because of the campaign, become a smash hit. If
this happened, Quigley feared the opportunity to force the industry to
accept Breen's judgment would be lost. He remained convinced that
only by attacking at the source – the studio during production – could
movies be made acceptable to church reformers.

In Los Angeles Breen fought for control. When Hays announced
him as the replacement for Wingate at the Studio Relations Department in December 1933, Breen was not well known within the industry. He had been working in Los Angeles for Hays for less than two
years, primarily trying to enforce the industry advertising code. In his
new role, Breen had no more power than had Wingate. Despite Hays's
threats to the studios, there was no structural change in the Los Angeles operation: They were still free to take or ignore Breen's advice.
Breen's powers of persuasion were his primary asset. Industry insiders
understood his connections to the church even if these were not yet
fully appreciated. There was little or no comment from the studios on
Breen's appointment, and while some may have suspected he would
try to enforce the code's moral provisions more strictly than had his
predecessor, there was no immediate fear that Breen would be unrea-

sonable. He was, after all, an employee of the Hays Office; his salary, like Hays's, was paid by the MPPDA. Hollywood studios would take a "wait-and-see" attitude toward the association's new censor.

Whatever the studios' expectations, Breen viewed his appointment as a mandate to infuse entertainment films with a strong sense of morality. Deeply committed to the values of the Catholic church, he was determined to force the Hollywood producers to comply. Breen was convinced that it was the Jews in Hollywood who were responsible for the immorality in films.

Breen was a rabid anti-Semite. His views on Jews were well known to the prelates who organized and led the Legion of Decency movement, and must have been known by Hays. Breen made no attempt to keep his view secret. In 1932, after being in Hollywood for only a few months, Breen told Father Wilfrid Parsons that the Jews in Hollywood were "simply a rotten bunch of vile people" among whom "drunkenness and debauchery are commonplace." The code would never work in Hollywood, Breen lamented, because the Jews who controlled the industry were "dirty lice," "the scum of the earth." The entire nation, Breen told Parsons, was being "debauched by the Jews" and their movies.[56] There is no evidence that Parsons objected to this characterization; in fact, the priest-editor staunchly defended Breen over the next several years.

This example of Breen's anti-Semitism was not an isolated one. Breen delighted in informing Martin Quigley that Joseph Scott, at the urging of Bishop Cantwell, had "lashed into the Jews furiously."[57] He told the publisher: "The fact is that these damn Jews are a dirty, filthy lot."[58] Quigley, who wrote hundreds of letters to Breen, did not protest to either Breen, Cantwell, or any other Catholic representative the racial slurs in Breen's correspondence. In a letter to Father Dinneen, Breen again used the "lice" label for Hollywood Jews, who were, he added, a "foul bunch, crazed with sex . . . and ignorant in all matters having to do with sound morals."[59]

It was Breen who formulated the basic plans for the boycott in Philadelphia. In March 1934, he temporarily broke ranks with Quigley. He had been working as censor in Los Angeles for three months and battling tooth and nail with Warner Bros. over *Madame du Barry*. In an attempt to strike back at Warners, he sent a proposal to Philadelphia's Cardinal Dougherty in which he urged the Cardinal to institute a total boycott of films. Breen believed this approach would be especially effective in Philadelphia because it had a large Catholic population and because Warner Bros. controlled its film market, with some three hundred theaters in the area. In his proposal Breen also offered a strategy for dealing effectively with Jews: He urged that the

Figure 9. Hollywood censor Joseph I. Breen. Courtesy the Museum of Modern Art / Film Stills Archive.

Cardinal line up a committee of civic leaders to protest "immoral" movies. "Keep in mind," he wrote, that "Jewish boys" are easily "impressed – and terrified" by public officials. The next step, he advised, was for the committee to pressure the District Manager for Warners, whom Breen described as "a kike Jew of the very lowest type." Tell him – "don't ask him" – to bring Harry Warner to Philadelphia. Warners was especially susceptible to pressure, Breen wrote, because they owned so many theaters in the Philadelphia area.[60] A boycott of this type, Breen wrote, would compel the industry to accept the Catholic plan for enforcement of the code.

His larger point was that it was essential *not* to negotiate with Jews. If you want a Jew to do something, Breen asserted, you don't ask him politely – you just tell him. Breen was convinced that screaming and threatening was the only approach a Jew understood. Although there is no record of a reply from Cardinal Dougherty, he did institute a boycott along the lines suggested by Breen and refused to negotiate with

Warner Bros. representatives during the Legion crisis. Father Dinneen, who received a copy of the Philadelphia Plan from Breen and corresponded regularly with him, made no protest to the letters he received, which labeled Jews "lice" and "kikes."

"The Jews are clannish," Breen told Father Daniel Lord. "They are almost entirely without morality of any kind."[61] He was anxious, he wrote Lord in May 1934 – just weeks before being appointed head of the new Production Code Administration – to work with a national committee to "get after the Jews in this business."[62] The same day he wrote Bishop McNicholas that he was "irritated" at Lord because "when these Jews out here learn that most of his talk is merely talk – our cause is by so much weakened and discredited."[63]

Breen's attitude toward Jews is telling for a number of reasons. It clearly exposes a vicious and hateful racism that dominated his thinking and reappeared in his correspondence over a number of years. It is also obvious that those who received his letters – cardinals, bishops, and priests – made no effort to protest his anti-Semitic outbursts. They may not have shared his exact views, but all apparently saw some merit in placing a man with such views in Hollywood.

Breen's bias against Jews also helps explain his working relationship with the studios throughout his career as censor. He relished, and embellished, his reputation as a short, beefy, pugnacious Irish-Catholic who brought decency to the modern Sodom and Gomorrah. The *Catholic Digest* called him a "No-Man in Yes-Land."[64] "Mr. Breen Confronts the Dragons," headlined a report in Notre Dame's *Sign*.[65] The *Saturday Evening Post* gave an Irish tilt to its article on Breen, "The Back of Me Hand to You," which described Breen as a "Brian Boru at the Battle of Clontarf, with a dash of Mulligan's Guards." He dictated rules to the producers, the *Post* assured its readers.[66] Indeed, Breen was one of the few individuals in Hollywood with the power to curse, scream, and flat out say No to a Jack Warner, Louis B. Mayer, Harry Cohen, David O. Selznick, or Samuel Goldwyn – all of whom were capable of striking terror in the hearts and wallets of the Hollywood community. With a nod they could bestow fame and fortune; a slight gesture indicating displeasure could run through the Hollywood community like brushfire, bringing with it instant destruction. Breen's ability to oppose these titans made him unique in the film community.

Breen treated the moguls and their minions with token respect, but lashed out with verbal fury whenever he believed a studio was attempting to avoid a code stricture. Convinced that the people who made movies were his moral inferiors, he reacted accordingly. He told Father Gerald Donnelly, S.J., that he was the one man "who could cram decent ethics down the throat of the Jews."[67] The "code" enforced over the next several years was to be a curious mixture of the actual Production Code, Breen's own interpretation, his opinions of the Jews, and his social, political, and moral views. The movies were, the Hollywood wags chuckled, "as Breen as possible."[68] Breen simply said, "I am the code!"[69]

It was heady stuff for a 43-year-old ex-journalist who knew nothing about movie production. A series of very unusual circumstances, some of which he had helped orchestrate, had thrust him center stage of the entertainment capital of the world. It was a unique opportunity, and Breen seized it enthusiastically. At first he saw his role as that of a lay missionary for the Catholic church doing God's work among the "pagans," as he came to refer to Hollywood. By 1936, however, he had distanced himself from the Legion of Decency, using it only when it suited him, was barely on speaking terms with his original sponsors, and shunned Martin Quigley. Breen was no puppet for the Legion. If anyone pulled his strings it was Will Hays, not Cardinal Hayes.

When first appointed in December 1933, Breen faced a dilemma: He was paid by the motion picture industry; his job was not to prevent the studios from making films, but to get them passed by local censorship boards with as few cuts as possible. Breen also was keenly aware of the internal split within the Legion movement. His problem was how to satisfy his church, to keep pressure off his boss, Hays, without destroying the basic elements of film entertainment: a dash of sex, a bit of violence, and good-natured ribbing of traditional values.

Could Breen succeed in enforcing the code with enough strictness to satisfy the legions of Catholics without reducing Hollywood's multimillion-dollar fantasy world to pabulum? Would the producers accept the opinions of a journalist–public relations man turned moral reformer? Most important, would the moviegoing public accept their entertainment laced with a strong dose of Catholic morality? While the church attempted to sort out a national policy toward the movie industry, Breen took control of Hays's Hollywood censorship office.

One of Breen's first actions as head of the SRD was to write a new and much stronger definition of "moral compensating values" for the movies. This document is vital in understanding Breen's views; it would be rewritten and refined several times over the next few years, and guided Breen in his attempt to gain control over film content. He went further than even Daniel Lord in advocating film as a vehicle to promote proper social and political behavior. Every film, according to Breen, must now contain "sufficient good" to compensate for any evil that might be depicted. Films that had crime or sin as a major part of the plot must contain "compensating moral value" to justify the subject matter. To Breen this meant these films must have a virtuous character who spoke as a "voice for moral behavior," a character who clearly told the criminal/sinner that he or she was wrong. The behavior of the characters, and the choices they had, must be clearly spelled out. "These were either right or wrong. If they were wrong, they should be labeled as such. It should not be left up to the discretion of an immature mind to decide for himself or herself whether the characters had acted rightly or wrongly," Breen argued.[70] Nor did he believe movies were proper vehicles for moral and ethical debates. There should be no gray areas in moral decisions in the movies. Each film must contain a stern, crystal-clear moral lesson that featured suffering, punishment, and regeneration. He urged that, whenever possible, stars, not stringers, should play the characters personifying good.

Breen had barely settled into his office when Paramount sent to the new censor a script for Mae West's third movie, appropriately titled *It Ain't No Sin*. Moral guardians, Breen included, believed no one was more in need of "compensating moral values" than Miss West. Martin Quigley was embarrassed when his *Motion Picture Herald* declared West one of the box-office champions of 1933. Yet West represented a very difficult problem. She was big box office and brought millions of dollars into a financially strapped industry. Although she offended some, she delighted millions more. Her popularity was as strong in small-town rural America as it was in the so-called sophisticated urban areas. D. W. Fiske, owner-manager of the Fiske Theater in Oak Grove, Louisiana, "Did the best business of the year" with *I'm No Angel*. His experience best summed up the magnetism of Mae West: "Whether they like her or not they all come out to see her. The church people clamor for clean pictures, but they all come out to see Mae West and stay away from the clean, sweet pictures . . . ."[71]

During the spring of 1934, while Quigley and Breen worked toward strengthening the enforcement of the Production Code and the Legion of Decency's boycott movement steamrolled across the nation, Paramount studios was producing their new Mae West vehicle. *It Ain't No Sin* became a test case for Breen, Hays, and the Legion of Decency.

The basic plot was vintage West. Set in the 1890s, West plays Ruby Carter, a St. Louis riverboat queen. Her boyfriend is Tiger Kid, an ex-con and up-and-coming prize fighter. Ruby is hired by New Orleans gambler Ace Lamont as the headline act in his establishment, The Sensation House, and is soon the toast of New Orleans. When one of her many admirers asks her if she is in New Orleans for good, West replies: "I expect to be here, but not for good."[72]

When the first script arrived from Paramount, Breen pulled his entire staff into a day-long conference to pore over the material line by line. Unlike his predecessor, James Wingate, Breen was shocked by the script and told Paramount that he was "compelled to reject in toto" the entire project. His objections were not a matter of cleaning up some bits of dialogue, Breen wrote, because in his view the script was a "vulgar and highly offensive yarn . . . a glorification of prostitution and violent crime without any compensating moral values of any kind." The character West was to play "displays all the habits and practices of a prostitute, aids in the operation of a dishonest gambling house, drugs a prize-fighter, robs her employer, deliberately sets fire to his premises, and, in the end, goes off scot free . . . with her illicit lover who is a self-confessed criminal, a thief, and a murderer." He declared the script in total violation of the code.[73]

Breen's letter sent officials at Paramount, where production had already begun, into panic. They assured Breen that he was "unnecessarily alarmed" over "a harmless comedy." Breen refused to budge and rejected revised scripts submitted in February and March of 1934. Paramount chose to ignore Breen and went forward with production. When the studio submitted a completed film to his office in June, he rejected it. Breen informed Paramount President Adolph Zukor that the "low moral tone" of the film was especially "dangerous when viewed in light of the industry's present position with the public." Privately he wrote to Hays that the studio heads "sneer" and "belittle" industry critics and were determined to produce pictures "without any counsel, guidance or reference" from their New York offices or the Hays Office.[74]

The battle lines were drawn. In Hollywood the studios were determined to make films without interference. In New York the corporate heads were not so sure. The real power in the film industry was in New York, not Hollywood, and the corporate offices allowed studio heads a great deal of freedom as long as box-office revenues produced a steady stream of profits. However, these were trying times, and corporate leaders were uneasy. When Paramount erected huge billboards on Broadway advertising *It Ain't No Sin,* Catholic priests countered with placards announcing "IT IS." The rapidly changing atmosphere was troublesome, and for the first time industry officials in New York sided with Hays and Breen, ordering the studio to tone down publicity on the film to avoid problems with "women's clubs" and "hinterland censors."[75] Hays continued to pressure Zukor, finally convincing him that the studio could have West, but only in a tightly restricted format. New York instructed Hollywood to cooperate with Breen. Mae West would be given an infusion of "compensating moral value."

Given the herculean task of making West moral, Breen demanded that the studio delete all references to Ruby Carter's (West) past as a prostitute, remove all references to her boyfriend Tiger Kid as an ex-con, remove scenes detailing a "five-day affair" between Ruby and Tiger Kid, remove scenes of Ruby stealing jewels from her employer, remove any suggestion that Ruby and her employer were having an affair, and end the film with Ruby and Tiger Kid getting married.[76]

In Breen's version of *It Ain't No Sin*, Ruby is a famous entertainer who is showered with jewels by her admirers, a "woman with a big heart" who spurns every advance by Ace Lamont. When her maid asks her what type of man she should have, Ruby replies uncharacteristically: "A single one." Rather than setting a fire to cover up a murder, Ruby calls the fire department and says (presumably, to the audience), "I've done all I can." Tiger Kid now emerges on the screen as "an ambitious prize-fighter" who is tricked into stealing Ruby's jewels by Ace and accidently kills the villain in a fair fight. He refuses to run away, telling Ruby he must face the police or be forever hounded by them. Ace Lamont, the gambler, now emerges as the villain who plans the robbery, is responsible for burning his own building to escape paying off his bets, and pays for his crimes with his death. In the grand finale Ruby and Tiger accept traditional values by exchanging marriage vows. But even in the marriage scene, Mae got another one-liner: When a member of the wedding party tells her he is the best man, she pauses, looks him over, and deadpans, "Oh no, you're not."

Despite the one-liners, and the obvious impossibility of totally sanitizing West, Breen was confident that his changes infused a sense of compensating moral value into the film. He did not attempt to remove every sexual innuendo from the script, although he insisted that West appear as a "good character," Tiger Kid seem a bit of a dupe, and that all criminal activity center on Ace Lamont. With this accomplished he approved *It Ain't No Sin*.[77] It was a decision he would soon regret.

Another test case in the battle for control of films involved a totally forgettable Hollywood costume drama. In the spring of 1934, Warner Bros. submitted a script for *Madame du Barry*. Very loosely based on the relationship between Louis XV and his last mistress, Jeanne Bécu, Comtesse du Barry, the film purported to be a historical account of events leading up to the French Revolution. In truth, it was nothing more than a bedroom farce with little, if any, historical veracity. An indication of the studio's concern for historical accuracy was reflected in its casting voluptuous Mexican siren Dolores Del Rio as the beautiful French mistress.

When the script arrived at Breen's office, it was immediately held up as an example of the type of film he believed Hollywood should not make. Breen shot back a stinging evaluation of the script to Jack Warner. In his opinion the script for *Madame du Barry* was so "filled with vulgarity, obscenity and blatant adultery" that it was "very dangerous from the standpoint of industry policy" and would "involve the industry in serious controversy with France." The censor informed the studio that it was impossible to approve *Madame du Barry* for production.[78]

Breen's letter infuriated the studio, and Jack Warner demanded a face-to-face confrontation with the new censor. His production boss, Hal Wallis, was determined to challenge Breen's authority. In a meeting with Warner, Wallis, director William Dieterle, and screenwriter Edward Chodorov, Breen remained firm. The sex scenes, he claimed, were too explicit and too numerous. He demanded that all nude scenes – that is, those that even hinted at nudity by flashing a bit of bare back – be removed. He was horrified that Madame du Barry was portrayed as not only a beautiful mistress but also a "pimp" for a king who "was nothing more than an old lech." How could the studio offer the American public a film that showed du Barry redecorating the king's bedroom with ceiling mirrors? Moreover, du Barry was presented in a positive light. The film, Breen concluded, was unacceptable because it would "lower the moral standards of the audience."[79]

Wallis, whom Breen later described as "sneering and argumentative," led the studio charge. He claimed *Madame du Barry* was nothing more than a satirical account of "historical fact" and that anyone who objected had a "dirty mind." Wallis maintained that if Breen was going to demand that the industry not offend anyone, then they might just as well "go into the milk business" because it would be "impossible for the film companies to make pictures" under these restrictions. Wallis refused to accept any of Breen's demands and ordered production to begin. Jack Warner, who deeply resented Breen's interference, took the train to New York to lobby his brothers to fight Hays and Breen.[80]

A little more than a year after the crisis over *Gabriel Over the White House,* the MPPDA Board of Directors was summoned for another emergency meeting to discuss *Madame du Barry.* Louis B. Mayer led a contingent of industry leaders from Hollywood. Breen came to defend his position. Would the industry support Hays and Breen? Or would they decide to support Warner Bros.? The future direction of film was on the line.

After a long and "animated discussion" centering on the "danger to the investment of all the other companies" by the Warner practice of "making films filled with . . . smut," the MPPDA board instructed Will Hays to bring the recalcitrant studio "in line." Warners caved in. Jack Warner called Wallis from New York and ordered him to cooperate fully with Breen. Warner gave his private assurance to Hays that *Madame du Barry* would emerge from the studio as a moral film.[81]

Yet when *Madame du Barry* was screened for the SRD staff, Breen rejected it. Jack Warner was furious. The studio had already invested tens of thousands of dollars by proceeding with production without

Breen's approval; now it faced the prospect of losing the entire investment if Breen refused to approve the film. Warner almost begged Breen to work with his ranking editor to make *Madame du Barry* moral. Breen agreed. He cut the opening scenes of du Barry and the king in bed, eliminated the remaining references to the mirrored ceiling, trimmed all the shots of women in transparent nightgowns and suggestive costumes, and got rid of most of the bedroom scenes. Whatever the studio's original intentions, *Madame du Barry* was no longer a bedroom farce. Breen allowed Warner Bros. to release the movie.[82]

The studio suffered another setback when the New York censorship board rejected the released version as "indecent, obscene and immoral." Ohio threatened to follow suit, and only accepted the film after demanding additional cuts. Hays and Breen faced another crisis: If their agency's standards were not acceptable to the local boards, there would be no reason for the studios to follow their demands. Hays recognized this and lobbied with both Ohio and New York to accept a new and revised edition of *Madame du Barry* – one carrying an important new prologue that would explain to audiences the moral lessons of the debauchery they were to see:

In the reign of King Louis XV of France the Power and Glory of the French courts began to wane – Extravagence and Folly had succeeded at last in arousing in the breasts of the Common People the smouldering embers of Resentment and Revolt. This picture portrays a King unmindful of his People – Selfish, arrogant, unscrupulous – a King who wrecks his Kingdom and bequeaths the ruins to his incompetent grandson. It is a picture to ponder in the light of the succeeding revolution for Freedom, Equality and Human Brotherhood.

New York relented – *Madame du Barry* was now morally safe for the Empire State.[83]

It might have been safe, but with the cuts imposed by Breen, Hays, and the New York and Ohio censorship boards, *Madame du Barry* was completely incomprehensible. *Variety* labeled the film a "travesty" on historical fact.[84] The *New York Times* blasted the film as "blurred" and wondered why it failed to clarify the relationship between du Barry and the king. After suffering through the film, the reviewer hoped he might have the "privilege of wringing Miss Del Rio's lovely neck"; he might have been more satisfied had he wrung the censors' necks instead. While *Madame du Barry* would not have been a great film with or without the interference of the censors, the insistence that the film not deal realistically with the sexual relationship between du Barry and Louis XV made the entire project pointless. Predictably, the film bombed at the box office, a point that did not upset Hays or Breen.

Breen fought similar battles with other studios during the spring of 1934. Despite his victory over *Madame du Barry,* he didn't always win. He refused to pass a Fox musical, *Bottoms Up,* which he judged "vulgar," but a Hollywood jury overruled him.[85] He argued with Warner Bros. over *Merry Wives of Reno,* a comedy-farce about businessmen at a convention, and had "considerable difficulty with Mr. Wallis." While Breen considered taking the film to a jury, he was convinced it was a waste of time. When RKO submitted a script based on Somerset Maugham's *Of Human Bondage,* the story of a crippled medical student who falls hopelessly in love with a prostitute infected with venereal disease, Breen warned that the subject was "highly offensive." RKO insisted on going forward with the project but did accept Breen's suggestion that TB be substituted for VD in the filmed version. At this point in his career, Breen recognized the difference between *Of Human Bondage* and *Merry Wives of Reno.* He told RKO that while he did not like the subject matter, he enjoyed the finished film, which was "a serious attempt" to tell "a very serious story."[86] Privately, he told Hays that all the films were "much worse at the go-off" than when they actually hit the screen, "which proves that our fight must be centered on the script."[87]

"*I have no real authority* to stop the dirty pictures," Breen confided to Archbishop McNicholas. The jury system prevented, in Breen's opinion, any real strengthening of the code.[88] He accused the Hollywood producers of conspiring against him, and it did not appear practical to appeal every case to Hays and the New York Board of Directors. Quigley continued to lobby McNicholas to establish a coordinated program of Catholic action against the industry that would force the studios to accept Breen's decisions as final. He told McNicholas that when a film goes to jury "the system falls down."[89] Unless films were attacked and corrected at the source, the entire movement would fail. McNicholas was pressured from all sides. He refused an offer of alliance from Canon Chase and the Motion Picture Council, telling Chase that he was opposed to "the mania for legislation as the cure-all for our ills." Privately he told Bishop Boyle that he feared association with "professional reformers" who would restrict "complete liberty of action."[90] He deeply resented the conduct of Father Lord, whom he believed had acted without permission from the Episcopal Committee, but was unclear what steps he himself wanted to take. In March 1934 McNicholas finally decided to act, and asked Quigley to use the "greatest liberty in mapping out a program . . . for the Episcopal Committee to follow."[91]

It was the opening toward which Quigley had been working for months. During April and May, Quigley carried on an extensive correspondence with the archbishop and made several trips to Cincinnati. He sketched out his plan of action in some detail. In a surprisingly frank assessment of the problem, Quigley admitted that "our ideas of morality in entertainment differ radically from those held by the vast majority of the public of this country."[92] Nonetheless, like all reformers, Quigley believed it was his duty and that of the church to define what was acceptable moral entertainment and to devise "some method of coercion" to force the industry to accept those standards.[93] Archbishop McNicholas heartily agreed.

Quigley put his ideas in writing, which McNicholas in turn sent to each bishop. The document, a blueprint for the Legion of Decency, is revealing on a number of counts. Quigley once again raised the specter of anti-Semitism by blaming the Jews of Hollywood, "who have no fixed moral convictions," for producing immoral movies. The short-term goal, he recommended, was to pressure the industry by hurting them at the box office. Quigley urged the bishops to do anything they could to achieve this; but he warned that boycotts could not be maintained at "a high pitch indefinitely" because the public "will [soon] resume its old habits." To Quigley, the long-term solution was not boycott, but strict enforcement of the code by Breen. This could be achieved, he argued, by forcing Hays to eliminate the jury system. Quigley also urged that the bishops give up blacklisting in favor of listing films "approved" for Catholic viewing. Finally, he advised the bishops to ignore the anti-block-booking argument that Father Lord and the Protestant reformers advocated: The NRA codes allowed exhibitors to cancel 10 percent of films under contract, which, in Quigley's view, was sufficient to handle "immoral" films. It was not a long-term solution, however, because it did nothing to stop *production* of such films. "Sensational subjects, such as the Mae West pictures, are never cancelled by the exhibitor," he reminded them.[94] Control of production, not cancellation, was the key to success, he stressed.

McNicholas agreed to host a meeting in June to unify Catholic policy behind Quigley's plan. While Quigley, McNicholas, and Cantwell favored cooperation with the industry, the powerful voices of cardinals Mundelein and Dougherty argued for confrontation. They pushed for a policy to punish the industry by continued boycott and blacklisting. The meeting in Cincinnati would determine the direction of the Catholic legions. Invited were the members of the Episcopal Committee, bishops Cantwell, Noll, and Boyle; Father Dinneen, who represented Cardinal Mundelein and the Chicago Legion of Decency; Father John Devlin, head of the Los Angeles Legion; Monsignor Hugh Lamb, who represented Cardinal Dougherty as head of the Philadelphia Legion; Father Edward Robert Moore, head of the Catholic Charities in New York, who represented Cardinal Hayes; and Reverend George Johnson of Catholic University, who represented Catholic schools.

The problem Hays faced was how to prevent an all-out boycott by the Catholic church. His request for an audience with the Legion council was denied. Dinneen had warned McNicholas that Hays was "a foxy boy and will promise anything to stop the campaign. Don't trust him for a minute."[95] "Let Hollywood do real penance" for their sins, Dinneen advised.[96] Mundelein also was "strongly opposed" to any direct negotiations with the industry.[97] Cantwell, acting on Breen's advice, also rejected any direct meeting with Hays, and further demanded that Father Lord be excluded. Cantwell was furious with Lord because Irving Thalberg had protested, in the strongest terms, Lord's charge that he had made his wife, Norma Shearer, play "a harlot." "His unwise and irresponsible statements are doing us harm in Hollywood, and creating much confusion," Cantwell told McNicholas; Lord should be "censured."[98]

Cantwell insisted that Joe Breen be present at the meeting, and Mc-Nicholas invited Martin Quigley; Hays, who had little choice, concurred. In New York, Quigley huddled with Hays and corporate heads to plot strategy during late May and early June. After several meetings Hays gave in. He told Quigley "the Catholic authorities can have anything they want."[99] "Martin Quigley and Joseph Breen were authorized to represent me and to speak for the Association. . . . Their representations as to plans and arrangements were made with our complete knowledge and authority," Hays later admitted.[100]

Quigley's goal was to force studios to submit to Breen's interpretation of the code. He demanded a system that would turn over content decisions to Breen, believing this would guarantee that films would be made without moral violations. Hays agreed.

The solution to the crisis was the creation of a new office of censorship in Hollywood: the famous or infamous Production Code Administration (PCA). Quigley insisted that Joseph Breen be appointed director with expanded powers to enforce both the 1930 Production Code and his newly minted policy of moral compensation. Hays and Quigley hammered out the details. For his part Hays pledged that MPPDA members would not allow studios to begin production until Breen and his staff had approved a final working script. This seemingly minor concession gave the new PCA tremendous leverage over the studios, which depended on tightly coordinated schedules to maximize use of sound stages and productivity from technical and creative personnel. The agreement went further: Once completed, each film had to be resubmitted for final clearance. If it was approved, Breen would issue a PCA seal to the studio. The MPPDA agreed not to distribute or exhibit any film unless it carried the new purity seal.

Hays also agreed to scrap the "producers jury," and assured Quigley that the New York Board of Directors would uphold "any appeal made by Breen's staff in Hollywood."[101] Studios that refused to cooperate with the PCA and Breen would be fined $25,000.[102] As a final gesture to prove their intent, Hays promised that older films already in circulation that were judged by Breen to be offensive, like *A Farewell to Arms* or *She Done Him Wrong,* would be pulled from circulation and recensored. Those films that failed Breen's new moral test would be permanently withdrawn from circulation. (*She Done Him Wrong* did not emerge until the 1960s.)

What did Hays and the industry get in return for these concessions? Quigley promised Hays that the bishops would call off, or tone down, the Legion of Decency campaign. On the eve of the Cincinnati meeting, Quigley took that step when he recommended to McNicholas that the church accept Hays's offer "because the problem would be virtually solved." He added, however, that "the campaign must go on" to keep pressure on the producers; if they do what they promise, "the campaign can be permitted to lapse."[103] Once "effective regulation" was accomplished, the publisher argued, any continuation of a Catholic campaign against the movies "seems to me to be an unreasonable and, perhaps, dangerous policy."[104] Quigley assured Hays that he would personally fight Catholic boycotts and blacklists.

The meeting in Cincinnati in June 1934, while high drama for the press, was pro forma. Everything had been worked out in advance. Breen and Quigley reviewed the situation and summarized for the committee the powers of the new PCA under Breen's direction. Breen discussed his strengthened "voice for morality," which, he assured the priests, would be incorporated into films, and reviewed his increased control over all scripts and final prints. Quigley argued that by controlling the source of production through Breen, further church action was unnecessary.

Only Father Dinneen, Cardinal Mundelein's representative, objected. Dinneen resented Quigley and Breen speaking for the church, argued that neither Hays nor the industry could be trusted, and advocated the continuation of blacklists and boycotts against local theaters as the only effective means of ensuring compliance with Catholic demands. Rather than disbanding, as Quigley wished, Dinneen stressed the need for the church to form a permanent Legion of Decency that would publish national lists of films acceptable to the church. Dinneen, however, was outvoted. The Legion council accepted the compromise proposal from Hays.

To formalize the agreement, both sides issued a press release. From Cincinnati, McNicholas issued a statement, written by Quigley, declaring that the church had no wish to "harm nor destroy" the motion picture business and viewed "with favor" the creation of the PCA, which "will materially and constructively influence the character of screen entertainment." While the statement did not announce the end of the Legion, Hays expected the Catholics to tone down their campaign.[105] The following day, confident that he had the Catholics in tow, Hays released a statement that announced the creation of the PCA with Breen as its director.[106]

While it appeared that the industry and the church had concluded a peace treaty, in Chicago Cardinal Mundelein was fuming. He was "really wild" at being left alone in favor of blacklists and deeply resented "the efforts of B. and Q. to dominate," Dinneen later wrote to Lord. Mundelein thought that Quigley had pulled a fast one on Mc-Nicholas in all but announcing an end to the Legion of Decency, and was determined to keep the Legion active in Chicago. Proving his freedom of action, he ordered Dinneen to continue to publish lists of "immoral" films, and urged Lord to continue his fight without "any hesitation about the Bishops."[107] Chicago was in revolt. Philadelphia continued its boycott, and in Boston, Cardinal O'Connell followed suit. The split within the church was in the open.

Quigley was furious, and Hays screamed foul. The listing of immoral films, which on the surface seemed so easy, proved to be an embarrassment. Catholics faced the problem confronting censors from time immemorial: No one, it seemed, could agree on what was "immoral." While Detroit Catholics were forbidden to see *Murder at the Vanities* or William Powell and Myrna Loy in their smash comedy hit *The Thin Man,* Chicago's Father Dinneen placed both films in a "B" classification: "Objectionable in spots because of their possible suggestiveness of vulgarity or sophistication or lack of modesty. Neither approved nor forbidden but for adults only."[108] In Detroit *Bulldog Drummond Strikes Back* was approved for adults only, while in the Windy City whole families could enjoy the exploits of the popular hero-detective without fear of sin. *Of Human Bondage,* given a purity seal from Breen, was condemned as indecent in Detroit, Pittsburgh, Omaha, and Chicago, but Catholics elsewhere were able to enjoy the filmed version of the classic novel. Pittsburgh condemned the popular madcap comedy of Bert Wheeler and Robert Woolsey in *Cockeyed Cavaliers* as sinful, whereas Catholics of all ages were allowed to see the film in Chicago. Meanwhile, Chicago condemned *Affairs of Cellini, Madame du Barry, Nana, Girl from Missouri, Manhattan Melodrama, Dr. Monica, The Life of Vergie Winters,* the historical dramas *Catherine the Great, The Private Life of Henry VIII,* and *Queen Christina,* and, even before it was released, Mae West's *It Ain't No Sin.* All of these films had passed Breen's office, and most played a full run on the East Coast before encountering the condemnation of the Chicago Legion.

It was a confusing and embarrassing situation. Catholic editors had no idea which list, if any, to print. The lack of consistency on what constituted an immoral film was perplexing. When several areas condemned *Tarzan and His Mate* because some priests thought Maureen O'Sullivan's costumes too brief, Catholics were opened to ridicule. The situation was also compounded by the fact that a film would play in some areas of the country before it reached others. Catholics often innocently went to see comedies like *The Thin Man* or *Cockeyed Cavaliers,* or took the kids to see Johnny Weismuller swing through the trees to rescue Jane, only to discover weeks later, when a film reached Chicago, Detroit, Omaha, or Buffalo, that it was "a situation of sin." Tempers grew short as bishops and priests accused each other of moral failings, and Catholic laity demanded clarification.

Quigley feared "a revolt within the industry" because few people outside the church found these movies indecent or immoral.[109] If Breen's judgments were undermined by church officials, Quigley warned, it would be business as usual in Hollywood. Quigley went public with an appeal for reason. In a signed editorial in *Motion Picture Herald,* directed at calming revolt in the Hollywood community, Quigley attacked the blacklisters and boycotters in the Legion as "over-night experts" who were "floundering helplessly in a morass of confusion and misunderstanding."[110] The motion picture industry was not "an evil thing." It did need "proper regulation of the product at the source of its production" administered through the Hays Office, Quigley stated. This did not mean, as some producers were claiming, that films had to be Pollyanna. The Legion did "not object to red-blooded, virile drama." Neither did it demand "coonskins for dancers." The entire movement, Quigley reassured Hollywood, asked only for enforcement of the 1930 code.

Privately, Quigley pressured McNicholas to silence Father Dinneen and to appeal to cardinals Dougherty and O'Connell to scrap their boycotts. Lord "has gotten quite definitely out of hand," Quigley told McNicholas, and warned that if Chicago continued to give "B" and "C" classifications to movies like *Of Human Bondage* and *Manhattan Melodrama* – a simple murder mystery that Quigley found "a reasonably acceptable picture" – the Catholic cause would be lost.[111] It would be impossible to convince Catholics, let alone the public at large, that these movies were "immoral."

Quigley also appealed directly to Lord and Dinneen for reason. Why, he asked, would they condemn *Of Human Bondage?* When Quigley saw the film he reacted as had Breen. The story was, in his view, "a legitimate dramatic theme" that in no way attempted to glorify sin. The film was not, Quigley stressed, indecent, obscene, or immoral. Nor could he agree with Chicago's evaluation of three historic/

costume dramas: Greta Garbo in *Queen Christina; The Private Life of Henry VIII,* which featured Charles Laughton, Elsa Lanchester, and Merle Oberon; and Alexander Korda's production of *Catherine the Great.* Chicago had given a condemned rating to each, stating that they were "lavish productions exemplifying the lives of men and women of loose morals . . . who . . . indulge in practices that could never be squared with the principles of Catholic morality."[112] "Does that mean," Quigley asked, "that only such characters may be used" as subjects of popular films "whose practices can be squared with principles of Catholic morality"? What about *Dr. Monica* or *The Life of Vergie Winters*? Neither of these films struck him as the type of film over which they had started the campaign.[113]

Lord defended the Chicago rating, and his reply is telling. While Quigley saw moral lessons in the films under question, the priest saw vulgarity. *Of Human Bondage,* Lord wrote, was "a pathological story," "morbid, depressing and unwholesome [although great] in the telling."[114] Lord's opinion had clearly remained unchanged since 1931, when he had told Hays that certain themes were unfit for the movies no matter how delicately Hollywood revealed them. *Of Human Bondage* fit into that category. *The Life of Vergie Winters* and *Dr. Monica* were condemned because they dealt with an "unmarried mother." *Queen Christina* was banned for Catholic audiences because the film, in Lord's view, was a "libel of an odd but eventually heroic and Catholic queen." Nor were these the only films that were troubling: Almost every film produced had "one or more scenes, situations, or bit of dialogue" that made them objectionable for Catholic audiences.[115] The Chicago Legion refused to accept Quigley's plea for reason.

Rebuffed by Chicago, Quigley turned to Boston, where Cardinal O'Connell had appointed a young priest, Father Russell M. Sullivan, S.J., to head the local Legion campaign. In his zeal to purge sin from Boston theaters, Sullivan demanded that no film play in the Boston area until it was censored by a local Legion committee. Failure to meet this demand would result in a total boycott of Boston theaters. If this model were adopted by the Catholics, the industry would face censorship committees in every Catholic diocese across the country. Quigley and Hays were horrified. Quigley, with the blessing of McNicholas and moral support from Hays, dashed to Boston to do battle with another zealot.[116]

Father Sullivan was "domineering and dictatorial" and "vindictive and unreasonable," Quigley later complained. Quigley and McNicholas both pleaded with Cardinal O'Connell to replace Sullivan and allow the industry, "which is striving in good faith to put its house in order," to begin to produce moral films. Very quietly Father Sullivan was transferred to a teaching position at Boston College and, as one local priest told Wilfrid Parsons, "there has not been a word about him or the boycott" since Quigley's visit.[117]

By the end of the summer of 1934 there was still no national policy for Legion activities. Chicago continued to blacklist films and, while the move toward boycott had been stopped in Boston, in Philadelphia Cardinal Dougherty refused to budge. In Los Angeles, Father Devlin reported to Bishop Cantwell that the controversy over lists was harming Legion activities; support was "starting to slip away."[118] In Cincinnati, McNicholas admitted he was "very tired of the motion picture fight."[119] He and Hays made one more effort to reach a compromise. In August the two men again exchanged letters. Hays restated to the archbishop his conviction that self-regulation would clean up the movies, but he complained that the confusion over "Catholic lists" was causing great concern in the industry. Hollywood could not make movies that were limited to children. In his reply McNicholas offered a major concession: He admitted there had to be a clear distinction between movies that could be approved for children and those that could be approved for adults. The Chicago list had not made that distinction: It approved films for "general audiences," but gave "B" (neither approved nor disapproved) or "C" (condemned) to movies with adult themes. The result was a huge number of films falling in the "B" and "C" categories. McNicholas further conceded that "if the emblem [PCA seal] itself could be made a sufficient guarantee" of wholesome entertainment, Catholic lists would be unnecessary.[120] McNicholas wanted out of the film business.

This exchange of letters was very important for Hays. It put in writing, from the official head of the Legion, that films carrying Breen's PCA seal would be accepted as bearing a stamp of approval. Hays realized the difficulty McNicholas faced internally within the church, but he was convinced that if he and Breen could rigidly enforce the 1930 Production Code, the Legion would support rather than attack the movie industry.

Just when it appeared that Hays's problems were finally solved, the New York Board of Censorship dropped two bombs by refusing permits for Mae West's *It Ain't No Sin* and Warners' *Madame du Barry* to play in that city. Breen, Quigley, and Hays were crushed. They knew that if they could not guarantee that PCA-sealed films would be given complete access to domestic markets, especially the massive one in New York, Hays and his PCA were doomed. Paramount and Warners were furious with Hays. Breen was summoned to New York, where he and Hays met privately with New York censors, explaining in detail the changes they had forced on the studios, and stressing that if New York officials rejected the films, all that had been accomplished with the creation of the PCA would be lost. Both films, they emphasized, had begun production before the PCA was established; they were the last of the old breed. Breen told New York censors that he was determined to clean up Hollywood, and Hays pledged his full support. New York relented and gave approval for both films, but insisted that the Mae West film be given a new title. New York approved *Belle of the Nineties* in September, and the film opened on Broadway without interference from local priests.[121]

Temporarily, at least, the Legion crisis was over. Hays had survived unharmed. The concept of self-regulation had not only been confirmed, it had in fact been strengthened by the Catholic movement. Some central questions remained: Had the Legion of Decency been effective in preventing people from going to the movies? Had the Philadelphia boycott really hurt the industry? Had Hays been correct in giving concessions to the Catholics, or should the industry have stood firm, as some producers suggested, and resisted Catholic attempts to impose their own sense of morality on America's most popular form of entertainment?

While working closely with Martin Quigley throughout the Legion crisis, Hays was determined to discover the extent of damage done by the Legion movement. Knowing whether the Legion had been effective would help Hays plot the industry's response. From late July to mid-September 1934, at the height of the Catholic movement, Hays sent one of his employees, Lupton "Lup" A. Wilkinson, who had been a journalist in Atlanta before moving to the MPPDA, on a private tour of twenty American cities. His mission was to interview newspaper editors, movie critics, theater owners, local politicians – in short, the movers and shakers of each community – to assess the impact of the Legion. Did these individuals view the movies as immoral? Did they favor government or religious censorship? On orders from Hays, Wilkinson refused to allow local papers to interview him for publication; he did, however, give them information about the industry's efforts – that is, those of Breen and the PCA – to adhere more closely to the code. Wilkinson's trip gathered revealing evidence of the Legion's impact on American attitudes toward the movies.

When Wilkinson visited Baltimore in early August, *Of Human Bondage* was opening at the Hippodrome Theater. It had been condemned by Chicago's Legion, and delegations of local priests were picketing the theater. The result was that *Of Human Bondage* broke all attendance records at the theater. More than five hundred people had been turned away opening night. The movie critic for the *Baltimore Sun*, Norman Clark, told Wilkinson that because of the Catholic protest against the movies "he had scarcely been able to get into a theater during the past three weeks."122 When the *Sun* editorialized against the Legion, squads of Catholic priests and nuns went door to door urging people to cancel subscriptions to the paper. They failed. In Baltimore, Wilkinson reported, "motion picture attendance had never been better."123

In Chicago, the hotbed of Legion activity, Wilkinson found that the Legion "exercises virtually no audience control." *Of Human Bondage* played to huge crowds at the RKO Palace. After an opening week of sellouts, the film was still going strong after four weeks at the Palace. Nor were Chicago newspapers friendly to the Legion campaign. Wilkinson received assurances from the powerful *Chicago Tribune* "that we have complete faith in the Hays organization" and that the paper would not support the Legion movement. Mae Tinae, movie critic for the *Tribune*, told Wilkinson, "Just clean 'em up a little and this will blow over." The *Chicago Daily News* gave similar assurances.124

"Lup" Wilkinson sent similar reports to Hays from Boston, Buffalo, Cleveland, Detroit, Pittsburgh, and Newark – all urban areas with large Catholic populations that should have been areas of Legion strength. *Of Human Bondage* was "just a few dollars short of the all-time record" at Buffalo Shea's Century Theater, Wilkinson reported. In Detroit "there is no attempt to enforce a local boycott" and business was normal. In Cleveland "the situation is quiet." When Clevelanders heard that *The Life of Vergie Winters,* a story of illicit love, had been condemned, the film "broke box office records." Louis B. Seltzer, editor of the *Cleveland Press,* advised Wilkinson "just forget about the Church row." Harland Fend, movie critic for the rival *Cleveland News,* described the Legion as "a flop" in his city. From Pittsburgh Wilkinson reported "business well above last summer." Kaspar Monahan, movie critic for the *Pittsburgh Press,* knocked many recent movies but "praised *Of Human Bondage* to the skies as a great moral lesson." Outside of a few church people, Pittsburgh cared little for the Legion.125

After a swing through northern cities, Wilkinson turned south to evaluate the effectiveness of the Catholic campaign in the land of Dixie. Richmond, Virginia, reported a surge in movie attendance – up over 20 percent – as people flocked to the theaters to see what all the fuss was about. Vincent Byers, editor of the *Richmond Times-Dispatch,* told Wilkinson the Legion was a dead issue: "We're getting no letters, hearing no kicks" about the movies. In Charleston, South Carolina, Thomas Waring, editor of the *Charleston Evening News,* told Wilkinson "there is no rebellion in Charleston against the movies." In Waring's opinion the main problem was that the industry insisted on "injecting vulgarities" into films. He went out of his way, however, to tell Wilkinson that he did not consider Mae West a vulgarity. *She Done*

Him Wrong "was a classic," and West's "recreation of a certain side of life" was, in Waring's view, "superbly given." Wilkinson also interviewed a local theater owner, who, aware of certain sensitivities within the local community, had always taken pains to play the "really hot stuff" on the "bad side" of town. Wilkinson saw *Born to Be Bad* at the "hot" theater and reported there was a "packed house."[126]

All across the South, Wilkinson found a similar reaction. In Baton Rouge, Louisiana, Miss Ida Blanche Ogden, managing editor of the *Baton Rouge Advocate,* said, "I doubt if people here RESPECT the movies much, but there's certainly no worry about morals." Her publisher, Charles Manship, agreed. After a bit of movie bashing he admitted to Wilkinson that "*She Done Him Wrong* was swell." In Memphis, Tennessee, a local theater owner told Wilkinson he "made more money this summer [1934] than I ever thought was possible." People were flocking to the theaters to see condemned films. In Little Rock, Arkansas, J. W. Hill of the *Arkansas Democrat* reported the paper had not "received a letter knocking pictures in years. I'm not for Father This or Father That, nor for any Baptist or Methodist preachers telling us what to see."[127]

In Jacksonville, Florida, and Birmingham, Alabama, Wilkinson discovered why there was at least some resistance to a Catholic reform movement in the South: Anti-Catholicism was stronger than any fear of the movies. W. N. Perry, general manager of the *Jacksonville Evening Journal,* told Wilkinson what had happened when the Legion crisis hit his city. When the news first broke about a Catholic Legion campaign, two local ministers, both of whom "loved publicity," decided to start a local committee. They invited the local ministers, key members of women's clubs and civic groups, local businessmen, the movers and shakers of Jacksonville society, to strike out against the movies. At the organizational meeting one of the businessmen addressed the group. He was, chuckled Perry, a Ku Kluxer and "foamed at the mouth" about the "Pope of Rome" unhatching a new plot to take over America. The pope, according to the speaker, had been trying for years to take over the American press but had been unsuccessful. The Legion of Decency was a papal plot to take over the movies! Local ministers, the Klansman added, "had been hoodwinked into playing the Catholic game." After the speech, people scurried away as fast as possible, and the antimovie campaign died aborning.[128]

A similar story was recounted in Birmingham by Pete Marzoni, movie critic for the *Birmingham News.* He told Wilkinson that when the Legion uproar reached Birmingham, the local city censor had called a meeting of "all the warhorses of reform." Marzoni had gone to the meeting. The ladies of the club dominated the discussion, and while they all agreed the movies were rotten, "the dear old Ku Klux spirit cropped up – the ladies were afraid lest they might be playing some deep Catholic game." Nothing much came of the Legion in Birmingham. James Mills, editor of the *Birmingham Post,* told Wilkinson "the reformers have pulled a flop here."[129]

Was the Legion a flop? While the church boasted of millions of soldiers in the Legion army, were those recruits really willing to stay away from the movies? The evidence suggests that the Legion was, at least in 1934, a major bluff. Quigley's fears that the church could not sustain an effective boycott were correct.[130] In Portland, Oregon, a city not visited by Wilkinson, a local reporter for the *Portland Oregonian,* Fred Palsey, noted that "the church-inspired Legion of Decency has been packing them in at theaters that had been suffering from slack attendance due to the summer letdown."[131] Palsey surveyed a hundred cities nationally to determine whether Portland's reaction was an aberration. He found support for the Legion in only four cities: Philadelphia, San Francisco, Cincinnati, and St. Louis.

Wilkinson's trip confirmed Palsey's findings. Only in Philadelphia did Wilkinson find evidence that the Catholic campaign had a negative effect on the box office. Everywhere else a natural reaction occurred: People who might not otherwise go to the movies dashed out to their local theaters to see condemned films; regular moviegoers continued to attend as usual. As a result, 1934 was no disaster for Hollywood at the box office: Revenues were up over 1933. The Legion, rather than keeping people away from the movies, had actually stimulated attendance – precisely the reaction many of the bishops had feared.

While the initial outpouring of opinion was favorable to the Legion and against the movies, opinion soon began to swing away from religious censorship. Richard Watts, writing in the *New York Herald-Tribune,* blasted the Legion:

With the Western World showing more than an occasional sign of collapse, and everything from German terrorism to strikes and rumors of war blackening the horizon, you might think that the Legion of Decency could find some more serious matter to fight against than Mae West's terrible influence over the ten-year-old mind.[132]

Even more surprising was the reaction to Breen's new seal of purity. Writer Marc Connelly denounced the Breen label as "idiotic," and claimed it represented "sterilization," not "purity."[133] In Boston, a hotbed of Catholic action, audiences greeted the new PCA seal by "hissing and booing."[134] Nor was this an isolated response. An internal report to Hays noted with some dismay that nationwide there were as "many raspberries" for the "purity seal" as orchids for the new films.[135] Reports of hissing the PCA seal came in from Chicago, Detroit, New York, and Cleveland.

Newspaper editors, no matter how vulgar they found the movies, were leery of supporting the Legion; they recognized censorship when they saw it. Almost unanimously they urged Wilkinson to tell Hays to find some way to restrict children from seeing films with adult themes: *Of Human Bondage* was the example most often cited of a serious film that was unsuitable for children. Few favored government or religious censorship of the movies as a solution.

Despite a flood of articles from religious journals and a constant parade of women's groups and civic organizations to the nation's capital to demand censorship of the movies, there is little evidence that the moviegoing public found the product that entertained them obscene, indecent, or immoral. While many found the movies promoted "bad taste" and, in fact, were often vulgar, few believed that censorship was the answer. What Hays must have found reassuring from Wilkinson's reports was that, in city after city, editors agreed that a slight strengthening of standards in the Hays Office would solve the problem. By September 1934, the Hays Office counted more than two hundred editorials against the Legion of Decency.[136]

Interestingly, Hays did not use the information to attack the Legion movement. He did not launch an anti-Legion campaign in the press. He did not use Wilkinson's reports in any public way. It was in his best interest not to belittle or destroy the Legion: To do so would undercut all the gains he had made in bringing the studios firmly under his control. Hays knew the Catholics were hopelessly split over policy, that the threats of national boycott were bluster, and that Catholics had rejected a common alliance with the Protestants. He worked with Quigley throughout the crisis to control damage to the industry. In fact, Hays was so pleased with Quigley's efforts on behalf of the industry that he paid all of Quigley's expenses associated with Legion activities – and Quigley accepted the money.[137] While the two men disliked and distrusted each other, both their livelihoods depended upon cooperation.

Hays remained silent because his deal with the Catholic church had finally made him a "movie czar." To admit that the Catholics were less powerful than they were would undermine his efforts to rein in Hollywood producers. Hays, and his censor Joe Breen, would continually hold the threat of Legion boycott over the heads of the Hollywood studios. After his experiences of 1930–4, Hays was convinced that the only way to prevent future attacks on the industry and to undercut the arguments for federal legislation was to keep the studios from making controversial films. He agreed with Quigley that control at the source of production was the key to controlling the industry. For Hays, the Legion of Decency was heaven sent. Robert Cochrane, Executive Vice-President of Universal Studios, sensed as much: "The attack on the movies by the various churches is welcomed . . . because it has served to strengthen Hays' hand and tended to make him a czar in fact instead of merely in newspaper headlines."[138]

The key for Hays would be maintaining control. For the remainder of the decade he worked closely with Joe Breen to bring a new morality, sexual and political, to the American screen. It would take another year before the Catholic church would reach agreement on the subject of blacklists, formally set up a National Legion of Decency office in New York, and issue lists of approved films. By that time, the issue of immorality in films had disappeared for all but a few "fanatics," as Joe Breen called them.

Hays and Breen, as keepers of the PCA seal, worked in tandem to sterilize (to use Marc Connelly's word) movies of ideas. Their goal was not to prevent them from being produced, which would have been suicidal; it was to keep movies from becoming vehicles for distribution of controversial moral, social, or political topics. From July 1934 on, Hollywood films took on a decidedly conservative point of view for moral issues: Divorce was a sin, adultery was punished, "modern living" was painted in negative terms, and virtue was rewarded. Politically, films after July 1934 were reluctant to challenge the status quo. Social problems might be raised, but controversial solutions were rarely offered.

The timing of the Legion of Decency and the PCA was perfect. In 1932–3, with the national economy in the throes of the Depression, industry losses had totaled $60 million. When the economy recovered slightly in 1934, Hollywood revenues reflected that change, recording a modest profit of $9 million. Even better was 1935, with an industry-wide profit margin of $30 million. As the economy recovered from its low point in 1932–3, weekly attendance, the barometer of choice in Hollywood, rose to 70 million in 1934 and leveled off at 80 million or so a week for the rest of the decade.

While it seems obvious that the box-office recovery was due to an improving economy, Hays and Breen constantly pointed to the surge in attendance as proof that the public wanted cleaner films. By 1936 few Hollywood corporate officials, studio heads, or producers were willing to argue the point. However, the first two years of the Production Code Administration were filled with challenges to Breen and Hays, as producers fought to make films that challenged the PCA's strictures.

Notes

1 Jack Warner to Irving Berlin and Hal Wallis, *This Is the Army,* Warner Bros. Script Files, USC.

2 The Lord Papers are full of internal correspondence from the Hays Office and the studios. The materials were supplied to Lord to keep him in the Hays camp.

3 Lord to Quigley, May 16, 1933, LP.

4 Hays to Lord, Mar. 18, 1933, LP.

5 Breen to Lord, Mar. 18, 1933, LP.

6 Quigley to Lord, May 17, 1933, LP.

7 Lord to Hays, Mar. 25, 1933, LP.

8 Lord to Breen, May 22, 1933, LP.

9 Lord to Hays, May 26, 1933, LP.

10 Robert Sklar, *Movie Made America*, p. 34.

11 Henry James Forman, *Our Movie Made Children*, pp. 196–213.

12 Arthur Kellogg, "Minds Made by the Movies," *Survey Graphic* 22 (May 1933), p. 248.

13 Ibid.

14 Ibid.

15 Ibid., p. 245.

16 Ibid., p. 250.

17 Fred Eastman, "Your Child and the Movies," *Christian Century* 50 (May 3, 1933), pp. 591–3, and subsequent issues; *New York Times*, May 7, 1933, p. 15; "How Movies Educate," *Nation* 137 (Aug. 9, 1933), pp. 145–6; James Rorty, "How the Movies Harm Children," *Parent's Magazine* 8 (Aug. 1933), pp. 18–19; *School and Society* 39 (Feb. 24, 1934), p. 240.

18 All quoted in MPPDA, "Authoritative Statement Concerning the Screen and Behavior," Dec. 1934, box 47, HP.

19 It would be another five years before the publication of Raymond Moley's *Are We Movie Made?*

20 Regarding the NRA code, see Louis Nizer, *New Courts of Industry*.

21 Quigley to Breen, Aug. 15, 1933, attached to Breen to Lord, Aug. 21, 1933, LP.

22 Cantwell to McNicholas, July 17, 1933, LP. For an excellent account of Cantwell's role in the Legion see Francis J. Weber, "John J. Cantwell and the Legion of Decency."

23 It should be noted that Breen was working for Hays while at the same time plotting with the bishops and Quigley to force the industry to accept more stringent self-censorship.

24 Cantwell to McNicholas, Aug. 14, 1933, National Conference of Catholic Bishops–Episcopal Committee on Motion Pictures (hereafter NCCB-ECMP).

25 Quigley to Breen, Aug. 15, 1933, LP.

26 Ibid.

27 Cantwell to Scott, July 14, 1933, NCCB-ECMP.

28 Cantwell to John J. Burke, National Catholic Welfare Conference, Sept. 20, 1933, NCCB-ECMP.

29 Breen to Quigley, Aug. 4, 1933, LP.

30 Ibid.

31 Ibid.

32 Ibid. Schenck called a private meeting the following day with studio heads and again urged them to fight against this pressure.
33 Ibid.
34 Dinneen to Parsons, Aug. 11, 1933, box 1, PP.
35 Quigley to Breen, Aug. 15, 1933, LP.
36 Ibid., and Parsons to Dinneen, Aug. 14, 1933, PP.
37 *New York Times*, Sept. 13, 1933, p. 26.
38 *Motion Picture Herald*, Aug. 18, 1934, pp. 10–13.
39 *Motion Picture Herald*, Feb. 17, 1934, p. 10.
40 *America* 50 (Dec. 16, 1933), p. 242.
41 Quigley to McNicholas, Oct. 4, 1933, NCCB-ECMP.
42 Cantwell summarized an article that would be published under his name in the February issue of *Ecclesiastical Review,* a publication read by Catholic priests. The article was ghosted by Breen and also contained much of Daniel Lord. See John Cantwell, D.D., "Priests and the Motion Picture Industry." See also Minutes of the Annual Meetings of the Bishops of the United States, 1919–35, NCCB.
43 Cantwell, "Priests and the Motion Picture Industry," pp. 136–46.
44 Ibid., p. 138. This is pure Breen.
45 Minutes of the American Hierarchy, Nov. 15, 1933, NCCB. Cantwell did not want to be chair because he believed he would be subjected to too much pressure from the Hollywood community. McNicholas was a perfect choice – far away from both coasts.
46 Gerard B. Donnelly, S.J., "The Bishops Rise Against Hollywood," *America* 51 (May 26, 1934), cited p. 152.
47 *Buffalo Times*, May 23, 1934 (in box 47, HP).
48 Gerard B. Donnelly, S.J., "Catholic Standards for Motion Pictures," p. 443.
49 *Extension Magazine* 29 (Nov. 1934), p. 27.
50 Donnelly, "The Bishops Rise Against Hollywood," p. 152.
51 "Hollywood Treats Own Code as 'Scrap of Paper' in Great Public Betrayal," *Queen's Work* (June 1934), p. 1–3.
52 Daniel Lord, *The Motion Pictures Betray America* (St. Louis: Queen's Work, 1934).
53 Pastoral letter of Cardinal Denis Dougherty, May 25, 1934, reprinted in John T. McNicholas, "Pastorals and Statements by Members of the American Hierarchy on the Legion of Decency," p. 285.
54 Ibid., p. 284.
55 Ibid.
56 Breen to Parsons, Oct. 10, 1932, box C-9, PP.
57 Breen to Quigley, Aug. 4, 1933, LP. There is no record of a protest from either Quigley or Lord, who regularly received copies of Breen's letters on the movies.
58 Breen to Quigley, May 1, 1932, box 1, QP.
59 Breen to Dinneen, April 1, 1934, box 1, QP.
60 Breen to Dinneen, Mar. 30, 1934, box 1, QP.
61 Breen to Lord, May 23, 1934, LP.
62 Breen to Lord, May 22, 1934, LP.

63 Breen to McNicholas, May 22, 1934, NCCB-ECMP.

64 Timothy Higgins, "No-Man in Yes-Land."

65 Daniel E. Doran, "Mr. Breen Confronts the Dragons."

66 J. P. McEvoy, "The Back of Me Hand to You," *Saturday Evening Post* 211 (Dec. 24, 1941), p. 8.

67 Donnelly to Parsons, Winter 1936, box C-10, PP.

68 Walter Davenport, "Pure as the Driven Show," *Collier's* 94 (Nov. 24, 1934), p. 10.

69 Jack Vizzard, *See No Evil*, p. 103.

70 Ibid., p. 83.

71 Quigley's *Motion Picture Herald* regularly published brief reactions to films from small-town theater owners and managers. The purpose was to let small-town owners know how films drew in markets similar to theirs. While there are complaints about too much sex in films from these owners, they all praised Mae West as good entertainment and even better box office. Reformers who attacked block booking hoped that freeing local owners from this rental practice would solve their problems, but there is no evidence that it would have hurt any Mae West film. It is noteworthy that these evaluations were taken at the height of the Legion of Decency movement and illustrated why Quigley was fearful of an uncensored West film being released during the campaign. See *Motion Picture Herald*, July 29, 1933, p. 55; Jan. 20, 1934, p. 67; Feb. 24, 1934, p. 52; Mar. 17, 1934, p. 56.

72 James Rorty, "*It Ain't No Sin,*" *Nation* 139 (Aug. 1, 1934), pp. 124–7.

73 Breen to Botsford, Feb. 23, 1934; Breen to Files, Mar. 6, 1934; Breen to Botsford, Mar. 7, 1934, *Belle of the Nineties*, PCA.

74 Breen to Hays, June 2, 1934; Breen to John Hammond, June 2, 1934; Breen to Zukor, June 4, 1934, *Belle of the Nineties*, PCA.

75 *Variety*, Oct. 3, 1933, p. 1. Paramount directed that the advertising refer to "come up and see me" as "an invitation to tea."

76 Memo Conference at Paramount, June 6, 1934, *Belle of the Nineties*, PCA.

77 Breen to Hammell, June 6, 1934, *Belle of the Nineties*, PCA.

78 Breen to Jack Warner, Mar. 13, 1934, *Madame du Barry*, PCA.

79 Breen to Files, Mar. 14, 1934; Breen to Warner, Mar. 15, 1934, *Madame du Barry*, PCA.

80 Breen to Files, Mar. 14, 1934.

81 Hays to Albert Warner, Mar. 28, 1934; Hays Memo to Files, April 3, 1934, *Madame du Barry*, PCA.

82 H. J. McCord to Breen, May 5, 1934, *Madame du Barry*, PCA.

83 Albert Howson to Hays, Sept. 25, 1934, *Madame du Barry*, PCA.

84 *New York Times*, Oct. 25, 1934, p. 26; *Variety*, Oct. 30, 1934, p. 16.

85 Breen to Hays, Mar. 8, 1934, *Merry Wives of Reno*, PCA.

86 Breen to Files, Feb. 10, 1934; Breen to Perman, June 7, 1934, *Of Human Bondage*, PCA.

87 Breen to Hays, May 19, 1934, *Of Human Bondage*, PCA.

88 Breen to McNicholas, Mar. 22, 1934, NCCB-ECMP.

89 Quigley to McNicholas, Mar. 20, 1934, box C-76, PP.

90 Canon William Sheafe Chase to McNicholas, Feb. 21, 1934; McNicholas to Chase, Mar. 22, 1934; McNicholas to Boyle, May 11, 1934, NCCB-ECMP.
91 McNicholas to Quigley, Mar. 25, 1934, NCCB-ECMP.
92 Quigley to McNicholas, May 29, 1934, NCCB-ECMP.
93 Ibid.
94 "Notes – The Motion Picture," n.d., Historical Archives of the Chancery, Archdiocese of Cincinnati, Cincinnati, Ohio (hereafter AAC). McNicholas to Breen, May 15, 1934, NCCB-ECMP. In the letter McNicholas writes that the notes sent to the bishops "were prepared by Mr. Quigley."
95 Dinneen to McNicholas, June 2, 1934, NCCB-ECMP.
96 Ibid.
97 Ibid.
98 Cantwell to McNicholas, June 8, 1934, NCCB-ECMP; see also Dinneen to McNicholas, June 9, 1934, NCCB-ECMP. Dinneen warned McNicholas that Hays was "a fixer" who would try to derail the Catholic campaign.
99 Quigley to McNicholas, May 29, 1934, NCCB-ECMP.
100 Hays to McNicholas, Oct. 9, 1934, NCCB-ECMP.
101 Ibid.
102 Quigley to McNicholas, June 12, 1934, NCCB-ECMP.
103 Ibid.
104 Quigley to McNicholas, June 6, 1934, NCCB-ECMP.
105 Press release, June 21, 1934, box 47, HP.
106 Press release, June 22, 1934, box 47, HP.
107 Dinneen to Lord, June 27, 1934, LP.
108 *Harrison's Reports* (July 21, 1934); Quigley to McNicholas, Aug. 20, 1934, NCCB-ECMP.
109 Quigley to Lord, July 31, 1934, QP.
110 Martin Quigley, "The Decency Campaign – Inside and Out," *Motion Picture Herald* (July 21, 1934), pp. 9–11.
111 Quigley to McNicholas, Aug. 20, 1934, NCCB-ECMP.
112 Quigley to Lord, July 31, 1934, QP.
113 Ibid.
114 Lord to Quigley, Aug. 6, 1934, QP.
115 Ibid.
116 Quigley to Cardinal O'Connell, Aug. 1, 1934, QP.
117 Father M. J. Ahern to Parsons, Aug. 18, 1934, WP.
118 Devlin to Cantwell, July 28, 1934, Archdiocese Archives–Los Angeles (hereafter AALA).
119 McNicholas to Boyle, Aug. 12, 1934, NCCB-ECMP.
120 "Decency: The Second Phase," *America* 51 (Aug. 25, 1934), p. 439.
121 Memo to Files, July 13, 1934, *Belle of the Nineties,* PCA. During this controversy Paramount requested, and the PCA agreed, not to release any details of the changes made in the film.
122 Wilkinson to J. J. McCarthy (Hays Office), Aug. 4, 1934, QP.
123 Ibid.
124 Wilkinson to McCarthy, Aug. 14, 1934, box 47, QP.

125 Wilkinson to McCarthy, Aug. 18, Aug. 12, Aug. 17, and Aug. 25, 1934, QP.
126 Wilkinson to McCarthy, Aug. 29 and Sept. 4, 1934, QP.
127 Wilkinson to McCarthy, Sept. 11, Sept. 12, and Sept. 13, 1934, QP.
128 Wilkinson to McCarthy, Sept. 4, 1934, QP. The *Birmingham News* began an anti-Legion editorial campaign soon after Wilkinson's visit. See *Birmingham News,* Sept. 16, 1934 (in box 47, HP).
129 Wilkinson to McCarthy, Sept. 6, 1934, QP.
130 Quigley was given copies of Wilkinson's reports.
131 *Portland Oregonian,* Sept. 16, 1934 (in box 47, HP).
132 *New York Herald-Tribune,* July 15, 1934 (in box 47, HP).
133 *Brooklyn Eagle,* Sept. 20, 1934 (in box 47, HP).
134 *Boston Herald*, Sept. 6, 1934 (in box 47, HP).
135 F. W. Allport to Hays, Sept. 14, 1934, box 110, HP.
136 F. W. Allport to Hays, Sept. 22, 1934, box 110, HP.
137 Quigley to McNicholas, Dec. 31, 1934, NCCB-ECMP. Quigley told McNicholas that Hays paid him for "expenses . . . incurred, directly and indirectly in the interests of the Legion of Decency."
138 *Motion Picture Herald*, Aug. 18, 1934, p. 13.

CHAPTER 7

SEX WITH A DASH OF MORAL COMPENSATION

Imagine the care required to insure that the filming of Tolstoy's novel
conform to the standards set in the Code.　　　　– Raymond Moley

The Production Code Administration headquarters was located in a
four-story building on the corner of Hollywood Boulevard and Western Avenue in Los Angeles. They were, in comparison to the palatial
offices of its adversaries, Spartan. Bare floors and steel desks set the
tone of the office. The censors shared the building with a drugstore on
the first floor and Central Casting on the second. As one of the staff
members later recalled: "It was not unusual to have to struggle across
the foyer through a sullen group of midgets, old maids, bowlegged
cowboys, broken-down boxers, seven foot Russians with bushy
beards, professional looking dandies with pince-nez glasses . . . crip-
ples . . . fanatics and saints" all looking for work.[1] It was, one sup-
poses, a daily reminder that the censors were indeed saving the country from the depravity of the "Sodom of the Twentieth Century."[2]

Breen's PCA staff was enlarged to enable him to review the huge
number of scripts and films the studios submitted. Joining Breen and
Dr. Wingate were Karl Lischka, a linguist who had taught at Georgetown University; Iselin Auster, a screenwriter and journalist; Arthur
Houghton, a New York theatre manager; and Douglas Mackinnon,
who had worked for a number of film companies before coming to
the PCA. Geoffrey Shurlock, who would succeed Breen as director in
1955, joined the organization of censors in 1932.

Despite the enlarged staff and increased authority given Breen, the
battle for control of the studios had just begun, not ended, with the
creation of the PCA. Hays, Quigley, and Breen, with the concurrence
of the MPPDA Board of Directors, had pledged movie "purity" – but
no one in the Hollywood studios had been consulted. What Breen demanded, and Hays accepted, cut to the very heart of the studio power
structure: final script and final print authority. In the studio structure,
authority over the script and final print of a film rested firmly in the

executive offices. It was a jealously guarded power that often determined who really was in power in a particular studio. On the creative
side of the studios, directors, writers, and actors had input into the process but rarely exercised final authority. The films, after all, were a
corporate product, not an individual artistic creation. It was executive
prerogative to determine whether or not a script or film satisfied corporate needs.

Breen achieved entry into privileged sanctuary: the moguls' private
domain. It was no accident that he corresponded directly with studio
heads and executive producers, and only rarely with directors or writers. Every PCA letter to the studios, regardless of which staff member
actually wrote it, went out over Breen's signature – a practice that
firmly established Breen as the voice of authority at the PCA. In film
after film the PCA's first reading of a script brought outright rejection.
Breen's strategy was twofold: First get the studio's attention; then,
from a position of strength, open the negotiations for making the film
acceptable. This initial rejection of a script prevented the studio from
beginning principal photography, and clearly established that it was
Breen and the PCA, not the studio, who determined when a script was
satisfactory. However, Breen did more than simply reject a script: He
went to great lengths to offer suggestions on how an individual scene
or entire scripts could be rewritten to satisfy the code. If the studios
cooperated, Breen was then willing to battle efforts by the Legion or
government censorship boards to impose further restrictions. He became, in time, an ally.

The studios soon learned that cooperation with Breen resulted in
less controversy, larger markets, and less money spent in rewrites and
postproduction editing. The new censor made himself, by force of his
personality and office, an equal with MGM's Louis B. Mayer, Columbia's Harry Cohen, RKO's R. Keith Kahane, Warners' Jack Warner,
and the other studio heads. These were not malleable men, and they
fought Breen until he proved himself beneficial to the production process and to corporate profits. By 1937 making a film "as Breen as possible" became good business policy. While Breen believed he would
bring a stricter morality to movies, during his first year in office elements in the Catholic Legion continued to label the movies as "immoral." Breen was too lenient! His first lesson as a censor was how to
mesh the morality of the code with the entertainment demands of the
industry without driving movie fans away from the theaters.

Although Mae West was an obvious target for the censors, few would
have guessed that an MGM lighthearted comedy starring Jeanette
MacDonald and Maurice Chevalier would cause a major internal crisis in the film industry. Directed by Ernst Lubitsch, a master at por-

traying sex as a frivolous game played by the idle rich, *The Merry Widow* was based on Franz Lehár's frothy 1905 operetta. The setting is the mythical kingdom of Marshovia, where an immensely wealthy widow owns 52 percent of the kingdom. Unable to find a husband, she leaves for Paris. Her departure is an economic crisis for the tiny kingdom, and the king commands Captain Danilo, the kingdom's greatest lover, to woo the widow back to Marshovia. Around this slender plot Lubitsch wound satirical wit, elaborate costumes, dancing, singing, and a heavy dose of bedroom comedy.[3]

When the script arrived at the Production Code Administration, it caused little concern. Breen advised the studio to eliminate all close-up shots of a Paris cancan dance and tone down a few scenes that he deemed a bit risqué. The PCA screened the film in September 1934 and issued its seal of approval.[4]

The Merry Widow was approved by every state censorship board, including New York. In October MGM held a gala premiere at the Astor Theater in New York City. As overhead blue arc lights streamed up and down Broadway, mounted policemen worked to control a huge crowd that had gathered outside the theater to glimpse some of their favorite Hollywood stars. Attending the premiere were two industry men who drew little attention from the thousands of movie fans that October evening. As Will Hays and Martin Quigley settled into their seats, they were unprepared for MGM's version of *The Merry Widow,* which carried Breen's seal of moral purity.

As it unfolds on the screen, the kingdom of Marshovia is preoccupied with sex. The king (George Barbier) is a bumbling fool, and the queen (Una Merkel) spends her leisure time inviting a series of lovers to her bedchamber. When the king accidently discovers Captain Danilo (Maurice Chevalier) in the queen's boudoir, he orders him to Paris to woo the widow Sonia (Jeanette MacDonald) back to Marshovia or be sentenced as a traitor. In Paris, determined to have one last fling before taking up his diplomatic duties, Danilo goes to Maxim's, where he is well known by many of the "ladies" who help customers spend money and drink champagne. Dinner at Maxim's is always served in private chambers, where the "ladies" can entertain the customers.

Unknown to Danilo, Sonia is also at Maxim's, pretending to be one of the ladies of the evening. Naturally, Danilo and Sonia meet, bicker, and then fall in love. Sonia, however, soon discovers that Danilo has been "ordered" to seduce her, and refuses to see him. A failure, Danilo is brought back to Marshovia to stand trial. At his trial all the beautiful women of the kingdom swoon over Danilo and are distraught at the thought of losing their collective lover. Even Sonia returns to testify in his behalf. He did his duty, she tells the court: He lied, he deceived, he cheated. When Danilo professes true love for Sonia, he tells the court he should be hanged when he could have any woman (the men in the courtroom break into wild applause) but is willing to marry just one (the women sigh). In the grand finale, the two lovers are locked in jail overnight. In a royal conspiracy, the king orders a Gypsy orchestra to play romantic music outside the cell while a constant supply of champagne is slipped into the room. The combination works its magic, and before the two lovers can go too far, a minister is rushed into their cell and quickly marries them. Marshovia is saved.

The tiny kingdom may have been saved, but the humorless Quigley was outraged and the Presbyterian elder, Will Hays, was shocked by this flouting of traditional values. How, both wondered, could Breen possibly have approved this film? Quigley cornered Hays in the lobby: Something had to be done to *The Merry Widow* before it was released nationwide. Hays fully agreed.[5]

"The jig is up," Quigley told Breen, if this film was allowed to play without further censorship. If MGM was allowed to produce this type of film "while a campaign is on," Quigley wrote, how could he "assume the attitude, with McNicholas and others, that things are going generally in the right direction?" He viewed the film as an "industry double-cross" and specifically faulted MGM's Irving Thalberg, who "deliberately introduced a lot of filth" into a charming operetta. If no changes were made, Quigley told Breen, he would immediately withdraw his support from the reform movement.[6]

Hays was equally concerned. He contacted MGM corporate officials in New York and expressed his concern over "several suggestive sequences." He telephoned the PCA office, which confirmed that the film had indeed been approved, and then summoned Breen to New York. The long train ride from Los Angeles to New York must have been difficult for Breen. With scenes from *The Merry Widow* playing in his head and the thought of losing his $30,000-a-year job, he admitted to Hays when he arrived in New York that the film as it stands "is not [a] light, gay, frivolous, operetta" but a "typical French farce that is definitely bawdy and offensively – in spots – suggestive." After sternly lecturing Breen, Hays took his censor to the MGM corporate offices in New York, where they previewed the film with Legion of Decency representatives Father Wilfred Parsons, editor of *America,* and Pat Scanlan, editor of the Catholic *Brooklyn Tablet,* along with MGM officials. Hays left, and the group worked until 2:00 A.M. before reaching agreement on cuts that would make *The Merry Widow* worthy of a "purity" seal.[7]

The basic problem was Danilo's preoccupation with sex. The small group of censors decided that Danilo was not "a carefree, happy-go-lucky fellow" but an "immoral person." Changing his temperament "will make him a more attractive character to the mass audiences," who were, in their view, "less sophisticated" than the Broadway audiences that were currently enjoying the film. Thirteen new cuts were proposed to effect this change. Grouped together they centered on removing the "Casanova" image of Danilo, eliminating the sense of Maxim's as a "whore house," and cutting or trimming a scene of Sonia "partially undressed."[8]

The problem now was how to get the cuts into the film, which had already been distributed throughout the country and was ready for general release. Hays called Irving Thalberg, and while there is no record of their conversation, Hays noted that it was "a long one." Given the pressure from New York, Thalberg agreed to the revisions. MGM wired all their distribution offices with instructions to make the required cuts before all play dates. Hays, Breen, and Father Parsons previewed the film once again in New York to ensure that the cuts had indeed been made. On November 1, Will Hays declared *The Merry Widow* fit for American audiences to see.[9]

The experience sobered Breen. He had assumed he knew "immorality" when he saw it, and he failed to see *The Merry Widow* as anything more than a harmless, if sometimes tasteless, bedroom farce. Yet his boss, Hays, his mentor, Quigley, and his supporters, Parsons and Scanlan, saw reckless promiscuity. A chastened Breen returned to Los Angeles, where he began work on three films, Greta Garbo's *Anna Karenina* (MGM) and the Samuel Goldwyn productions *We Live Again* and *Barbary Coast,* which were destined to play important roles in refining what was permissible under Breen's PCA. Each film was censored and issued a "purity" seal by Breen; each, in turn, was condemned by the Chicago Legion of Decency as "indecent" and "immoral."

The Chicago branch of the Legion of Decency exerted influence far beyond the confines of Cardinal Mundelein's diocese. After an initial flurry of ratings by the larger dioceses, Chicago's list was adopted by most ecclesiastical districts. In the fall of 1934 the bishops, at their annual meeting in Washington, D.C., adopted Chicago's ratings as the "official" list for the church. From November 1934 to February 1936, the Chicago Legion functioned as the reviewing board for America's Catholics. Its ratings of films were printed throughout the country by Catholic newspapers, church bulletins, and Catholic lay organizations, and were often read aloud at mass by local priests. It was soon apparent, however, that many people within the church believed the Chicagoans were too strict.

Open disputes arose among local chapters of the Legion when Chicago condemned filmed versions of Zola's *Nana,* Oliver La Farge's *Laughing Boy,* Liam O'Flaherty's *The Informer,* and Tolstoy's *Resurrection* and *Anna Karenina.* These productions were not the cheap, titillating, sex dramas that offended parents and guardians of public morality; they were serious films for adults. Martin Quigley fumed that the Chicago list was "unreliable, inadequate, and incompetent."[10] Fearful that both the public and Hollywood would distance themselves from all reform efforts if serious movies were condemned, Quigley took his complaints to Cardinal Hayes in New York.[11] The cardinal had been a reluctant player in the Legion movement because New York was the major entertainment capital in the nation. Thousands of Catholics made a living in the entertainment industry, and tourists poured into the city to see the latest play or attend one of the flagship theaters. Quigley convinced the cardinal that, in its exuberance, Chicago might well ruin Catholic efforts at reform, and the industry as well. Quigley convinced Cardinal Hayes that he needed to become more involved; he, in turn, urged Archbishop McNicholas to begin "quietly and unostentatiously" to lobby for the Archdiocese of New York to take over Legion duties. Within the year the brouhaha over condemning serious films resulted in the creation of the National Legion of Decency, with offices located in New York under the watchful direction of Cardinal Hayes and Martin Quigley.

It was apparent as of July 1934 that it would be increasingly difficult to screen any material that contained themes of adultery, passion, lust, or greed. Samuel Goldwyn discovered this when he produced Émile Zola's *Nana,* the story of a young woman who gains notoriety on the stage in late nineteenth-century Paris. The heroine takes Paris by storm when she appears as a "nude Venus" in a stage revue. Acquiring celebrity status "despite her inability to act or sing," Nana sleeps her way through Paris society and leaves in her wake a number of ruined men. It was a perfect vehicle for any number of Hollywood actresses.

Instead, Goldwyn sent his agents to Germany, where they signed an unknown Ukrainian actress, Anna Sten, whom the producer pegged as the "next Garbo," to star as Nana. Goldwyn had seen Sten in a German film, *The Murderer Dmitri Karamazov,* and had been smitten by her natural beauty. Determined to have a beautiful, mysterious actress the equal of Garbo and Dietrich, Goldwyn signed Sten to a two-year contract despite the fact that she didn't speak a word of English. When Sten stepped off the boat in New York, a throng of reporters mobbed the "Soviet Cinderella." She delivered her first English line, written for her by Goldwyn's publicity team: "Darling, sweetheart, I lof you."[12] Before the reporters could ask a single question, which would expose her lack of English, Goldwyn's agents whisked the new star off to Hollywood.

In typical Hollywood fashion, Goldwyn pumped out a barrage of publicity on his new star, hired fashion designers to craft her appearance, provided dancing and singing lessons for polish, and kept a dieti-

cian close at hand to control Sten's ballooning figure. Goldwyn hired
a German emigré to teach his star English. After a year of fine-tuning,
and no little investment, Goldwyn was ready to launch Sten's career.
The future Garbo would play the title role of Zola's *Nana*.

While many considered Zola's work a literary classic, it had been
placed on the "forbidden index" by the Catholic church, and a 1932
Hays Office evaluation labeled it little more than a "handbook on har-
lotry and lechery."[13] From the perspective of the Hays Office, there
was "nothing in the story which would serve to deter any girl from following Nana's glamorous and luxurious path."[14] Wingate warned
Hays "it will take a lot of washing up" before *Nana* could be filmed.
The censor worked closely with Goldwyn, trying to make the heroine
a sincere young lady gone wrong. Numerous rewrites produced a
script that Wingate accepted but was "so watered down from the original material" that *New Republic*'s Otis Ferguson called the movie
"an empty creampuff."[15] Changing the nature of Zola's work may
have made it conform to Hollywood's new moral code, but it did not
sit well with his heirs, who were so distraught they charged Goldwyn
with disfiguring the novel "to a point where it is unrecognizable."[16]

The film opened with much ballyhoo in New York in February
1934. "Tek yur monee and ghet hout," Sten told her lover.[17] The
German English teacher Goldwyn had hired left Sten with an almost
incomprehensible accent. Perhaps the only person in the audience
who understood the Ukrainian actress with perfect clarity was Sam
Goldwyn, whose English was notoriously difficult to understand. By
the time Nana commits suicide in the last reel to atone for her sins –
and to satisfy the Hays Office – it was clear that *Nana* was a million-
dollar mistake. Reviewers soon began to refer to Sten as "Goldwyn's
Folly," and Cole Porter immortalized Sten–Goldwyn English with a
lyric in his "Anything Goes":

If Sam Goldwyn can with great conviction
Instruct Anna Sten in diction,
Then Anna shows
Anything goes.

Nana fizzled at the box office on its own merits. Few cared that the
Chicago Legion of Decency branded it as indecent, and even fewer noticed, a year later, when Breen pulled *Nana* from circulation because
it violated the code. He dismissed Zola as little more than "a filthy
Frenchman who grew rich writing pornographic literature."[18]

Goldwyn was not discouraged. Determined to make Sten a star, he
turned to her native Russia for her next screen vehicle. Adapting Tolstoy's *Resurrection* to the screen, however, would prove as difficult as
screening the work of "a pornographic Frenchman." Tolstoy's novel

Figure 10. *Nana,* with Anna Sten and Mae Clarke. Courtesy the Museum of Modern Art / Film Stills Archive.

of a love affair between a prince and a peasant girl had been filmed three times: D. W. Griffith had directed a version in 1909, another with Pauline Frederick in the title role had been made in 1918, and in 1927 Dolores Del Rio and Rod La Rocque had brought yet another interpretation to the screen. While none of these had caused moral outrage, a new version was certain to infuriate Legion Catholics. Goldwyn ignored the purity campaign: "It has not been made until I make it," he told reporters.[19]

Set in the 1870s, Tolstoy's *Resurrection* was a stinging indictment of the rigid caste system that he believed strangled czarist Russia. Tolstoy wound his social commentary around the tragic romance of a handsome Russian Prince, Dmitri Nekhlyudov, and a beautiful young peasant girl, Katusha Maslova. Infatuated by Katusha's beauty, Prince Dmitri, who fancies himself an equalitarian, seduces Katusha but soon drifts back to his comfortable world. Deserted by her prince, the poor girl discovers she is pregnant. Tragedy continues to follow Katusha when her child dies and she is forced into prostitution in order to survive. While Katusha sinks into destitution, Prince Nekhlyudov continues to live the life of the privileged class. He is engaged to a beautiful young girl and his future seems secure.

Prince Dmitri's idyllic world is shattered when he is summoned to serve on the jury in the trial of a young prostitute accused of murdering one of her clients. He immediately recognizes the prostitute as Katusha and, as the trial unfolds, also recognizes her innocence and his own role in causing her downfall. Dmitri's position, however, is not enough to save Katusha, who is sentenced to exile in Siberia. Crushed by the injustice of Russian life and as penance for his sins, Dmitri gives away his property to his serfs, forsakes his fiancée, and follows Katusha into exile.

Goldwyn assembled an all-star cast to produce the film. He hired Rouben Mamoulian, who had directed Garbo in *Queen Christina* and Dietrich in *Song of Songs* to bring the earthy, mystic elements of Sten's personality to the screen. To adapt Tolstoy he hired a crew of writers. First Willard Mack wrote a draft that Mamoulian disliked. Goldwyn then hired playwright Maxwell Anderson to redraft Mack's version, which Goldwyn found wooden. Next he tried Preston Sturges, who brought "snappy nineteenth-century dialogue" to the script but was quickly dismissed.[20] Before Goldwyn was finally satisfied with the script, Leonard Praskins, Paul Green, and Thornton Wilder had all written bits and pieces of dialogue.[21] The combination of cinematographer Gregg Toland, art director Richard Day, and costume designer Omar Kiam added to the Goldwyn touch.

Getting Tolstoy's story of illicit sex, illegitimate birth, prostitution, and corruption approved by Breen and accepted by the Catholic Legion and the state censorship boards would prove formidable. An early PCA evaluation suggested that all reference to illegitimate childbirth had to be struck from the script as a violation of the code.[22] Breen rejected that appeal as too restrictive; it would, he argued, "place our condemnation on some of the finest dramatic compositions of the ages." Instead, Breen opted for built-in denunciation: "If the sin is definitely characterized as sin . . . if it is shown to have been wrong; and if care is taken to see to it that the sin" is not characterized as just or right, then Breen was prepared to allow it in the film. He believed Goldwyn had incorporated enough condemnation into the script, and gave it his approval. While the film had a definite sex theme, Breen found its emphasis on "repentance and retribution" spiritual. "We feel," Breen told Hays, "that his picture could . . . *serve as a model* for the proper treatment of the element of illicit sex in pictures."[23]

The critics agreed. They heaped kudos on *We Live Again* for its production values and accurate reflection of Tolstoy's message. The *New*

York Times called it "the most faithful" of the three film versions and found Sten, whose English had improved dramatically, "stunning."[24] *Harrison's Reports,* which was always quick to carp about immoral films, told readers it was "superb."[25] The *Literary Digest* found the movie mystical and "visually striking."[26]

Yet, where Breen and the critics saw spiritual redemption, the Chicago Legion saw blatant immorality. They condemned *We Live Again.* So did the state censorship boards. Goldwyn complained to Breen that he had "considerable difficulty" obtaining clearance from the public censors, who all snipped bits and pieces out of his film.[27] Breen's model was flawed.

The production history of *We Live Again* was a dress rehearsal for the 1935 production of another Tolstoy novel: David O. Selznick's *Anna Karenina.* Selznick's film was the third screen version of this work. A 1915 adaptation by William Fox had been followed by a 1927 MGM production entitled *Love,* with Greta Garbo as Anna and John Gilbert as her dashing lover, Count Vronsky. The emphasis in 1927 was clearly on love: Garbo and Gilbert steamed up the screen, with one wag noting that Gilbert gave a performance distinguished by "an exhibit of passionate eye-rolling unmatched by anything in his later career."[28] Taking advantage of the chemistry created by Garbo and Gilbert, MGM had released two versions of the film: One in which Anna commits suicide, the other in which the lovers are reunited. Each exhibitor was given a choice of which ending to show. Audiences in 1935 would have no such choice: The Anna of the Breen era would be thoroughly chastised and fatally punished for her sinful transgressions against family, church, and state.

"Imagine," Raymond Moley wrote in his authorized study of the Hays Office, "the care required to insure that the filming of Tolstoy's novel conform to the standards set in the Code."[29] In *Anna Karenina* the heroine deserts her husband and son and lives openly with her lover. She bears an illegitimate child and flouts societal displeasure. In the end, Anna loses her lover and her family and commits suicide. Only with great care, Moley noted, could such a story be filmed. Acceptability of Tolstoy under the newly created PCA would depend on the "atmosphere" of the film. "If the actual adultery is not treated with restraint, if there is much physical contact between the adulterers, if they appear to be enviably happy," Moley wrote, "the film is not acceptable."[30]

The filming of *Anna Karenina* presented Breen with the same problem he faced with *We Live Again.* Breen realized that the industry would look foolish if it banned Tolstoy and other pieces of classic literature simply because they contained sexual themes. Yet any reasonably accurate film of Tolstoy's novel was sure to invoke howls of protest from Legionnaires, especially the Chicago branch: If they condemned *We Live Again,* they were sure to give a "C" to *Anna Karenina.* Breen's problem was to find a way to allow Hollywood to film stories of sexual transgression, yet mute criticism that the movies were promoting immorality.

Selznick, along with everyone else in the industry, was well aware of the internal conflicts within the Legion and of the disagreements between Breen and the Chicago Legion. Selznick noted in his production file that producing *Anna Karenina* would be "complicated by the fact that we undertook the production of the story at a time when the Legion of Decency's outcry was the loudest."[31] Filming the novel was further complicated, Selznick wrote, "by the new code that was drawn up by the producers which had a blanket prohibition against stories dealing with adultery."[32]

Selznick was wrong: There was no "blanket prohibition"; but he was right in his assumption that Breen had instituted new ground rules for portraying cinema sex. Breen held that "sin is not a mistake but a shameful transgression" and must be shown as such. "Wrong is not pleasant but painful, not heroic but cowardly, not profitable but detrimental, not plausible but deserving of condemnation." Breen held that "illicit sex is contrary to divine law." He believed that audiences responded to sexual stimuli, so that vivid movie portrayal "of sex is harmful to individual morality, subversive to the interests of society and a peril to the human race." Seduction, seen by Breen as male initiated, was a subversive activity and "one of the most serious sexual offenses" because it caused distress and dishonor "to the woman and her kin." Special care had to be taken to "eliminate . . . anything that might have a damaging effect upon the hearts and minds of adolescents and children." A world classic such as Tolstoy's *Anna Karenina* could not be "exempted from the test of the code."[33]

Breen's new approach was twofold. He would insist that details of the affairs be kept to an absolute minimum: No lengthy love scenes, no passionate kissing, no hand-holding strolls through the park, no long discussions between the lovers about their relationship unless it emphasized the negative nature of stepping outside societal rules, and no passionate eye rolling as in the past. The physical nature of the relationship would be severely muted. While the audience would know full well what was going on, it would be left to their imagination to conjure up the details.

Even more important, under Breen's PCA films would invoke a cross section of characters representing all strata of society to condemn "illicit" affairs. No longer would one character voice disapproval – as in *A Farewell to Arms,* for example, where Fergie reminds

Catherine and Henry of their mistakes while the rest of society pays little attention. Now the entire film would be used to paint a picture of complete societal condemnation. From the first reel to the last the sinners would suffer. No one walking out of the 1935 version of *Anna Karenina* would have the least doubt that Anna and Count Vronsky had made a tragic mistake in giving in to the temptation of sin.

It was no surprise to MGM officials when they first approached Breen about remaking Garbo's *Love* that he warned it would be "imperative" that the script and film establish Anna and Vronsky's affair as "clearly" and "definitely . . . wrong."[34] To rewrite Tolstoy, Selznick hired dramatist Clemence Dane, author of the play *A Bill of Divorcement*, which Selznick had produced as a film. He wanted Dane because he admired her ability to write forceful roles for women. Selznick envisioned a strong, determined, if tragic, role for Garbo. When he explained the PCA ground rules to Dane, she was "aghast" that Hollywood would permit "much less force a distortion" of Tolstoy's classic morality tale.[35]

It was rare for anyone to comment publicly on Breen's role in the production process. Selznick, however, wrote a contemporary account for his files while negotiating with Breen over the structure his film could take. "Our first blow," Selznick wrote, "was a flat refusal by the Hays office to permit the entire section of the story dealing with Anna's illegitimate child." Breen, who had defended the permissibility of illegitimacy in *We Live Again*, now flatly refused even to consider its inclusion. Selznick was dejected by this decision and contemplated abandoning the project because "we had to eliminate everything that could even remotely be classified as a passionate love scene; and we have to make it perfectly clear that not merely did Anna suffer but that Vronsky suffered."[36]

Dane was disgusted and wanted to quit, but Selznick convinced her to stick with the project. For support in crafting a screenplay, he hired Salka Viertel, who had written dialogue for Garbo's *Queen Christina,* to collaborate with Dane. Selznick instructed his writers to preserve as much as possible from the novel and still remain within the "bounds of good taste and prescribed rules."[37]

Breen saw two versions of the script, one in late December 1934, the other in early January 1935. He read both with "real pleasure" and congratulated MGM on the "fine taste and good judgment" written into them.[38] He assured Hays that MGM's interpretation was "a fine piece of work, quite free from any objection under the Production Code."[39]

Something, however, caused Breen to change his mind: In March 1935, he suddenly withdrew his approval of the script, which he now labeled "extremely dangerous." He told Louis B. Mayer that the script did not punish Vronsky sufficiently. "As we see it he is a seducer, who lives openly with an adulterous woman" and there is "no clear indication that he is condemned or punished for his behavior." Breen demanded that the script include a statement by "an authoritative official" condemning Vronsky and forcing him to resign from the military. Breen was further upset by what he perceived as "intimate physical contact" between Anna and Vronsky. One scene, which took place at the breakfast table, was especially troubling because Breen believed audiences would conclude that they were "living together." Breen was not without sympathy for MGM's problems. "We realize," he admitted, "that the deletion of all scenes showing Vronsky and Anna tender and affectionate and kissing each other may somewhat affect the quality of the story." Nonetheless, Breen demanded revisions.[40]

When Mayer passed on Breen's outburst to Selznick, the producer was irate. Selznick was in the midst of production and Garbo was planning to leave for Europe as soon as her scenes were finished. No one changed Garbo's plans. Your change of mind, Selznick told Breen, will "jeopardize a million dollar investment" and result in our "making a completely vitiated and emasculated adaptation of Tolstoy's famous classic."[41]

In a rare glimpse into the give-and-take of film production under Breen, Selznick wrote a detailed summary of the changes he had agreed to make during the six months it took to develop a script. Selznick reminded Breen that work on the project had begun when, in Breen's words, "the exaggerated and fantastic campaign" was at its height. Everyone, Selznick continued, "was worried sick as to just how far we could go." It was because of that pressure that Selznick agreed to eliminate any suggestion that Anna had an illegitimate child and that, unlike the 1927 version, this version would have no reuniting of the lovers in the last reel. We discussed the adultery theme in some detail, Selznick reminded the censor, and "you agreed that while the story dealt with adultery" the script provided "more than a sufficient punishment under any moral code."[42]

Adultery, after all, Selznick continued, was the theme of the novel. Without it "we have no story left." Selznick defended his breakfast scene as essential, and believed it established Anna and Vronsky's domestic relationship in the most inoffensive way. After all, he reminded Breen, you specifically prohibited us from playing the scene in a bedroom! "I challenge anyone to demonstrate to me how the picture can be made" without reference to intimacy and adultery.[43]

Furthermore, Selznick maintained that the punishment of the two sinners was nonstop throughout the film. Time and time again the script condemned the affair. Vronsky is driven from the army and rebuked by his superiors, "even though it is in violation" of Tolstoy to fabricate that point. Poor Anna is driven to suicide by the realization of what her sins have done. Selznick was exasperated: "I don't know how much further" one could go and still have a movie.[44]

Strangely, Breen wrote back two days later and indicated he had no objections to the script. Selznick completed the film, and when Breen viewed the finished film in late July he told Hays that *Anna Karenina* was "handled very well" and the PCA believed it would be a "noteworthy picture."[45] Why the sudden shift away from agreements Breen had made with Selznick in December and January, and the abrupt moderation of his demands in March?

While there is no positive evidence, it could well be that Breen was using this film to strengthen his own position in Hollywood. He had been under fire from Quigley and the Chicago Legion since his official assumption of duties in July. In December the Chicago Legion struck again when it condemned four new films that Breen had approved: *Limehouse Blues, Men of the Night, The Firebird,* and *Hat, Coat and Glove.* Breen appealed to Bishop Cantwell for a second Catholic opinion. Father John Devlin, Cantwell's Legion representative, concluded after viewing the four films that there was nothing "that would justify their classification as immoral or indecent."[46] Cantwell complained to Archbishop McNicholas that the Chicago ratings were harming Breen's effectiveness in Hollywood.

The internal conflict over what was immoral came to a head in early January 1935, when a delegation of priests, led by Bishop Sheil and Father Dinneen of the Chicago Legion of Decency, descended on Hollywood. These modern crusaders were determined to strike fear in the hearts of the infidels. When the delegation stood outside the gates of Twentieth Century–Fox and demanded entry, the studio caved in. As the priests were shepherded around the Fox lot, they lectured their hosts on the necessity of improved screen morality. Yet the Chicago Legionnaires, perhaps convinced of their own moral righteousness, had violated an unwritten agreement within the Catholic hierarchy: They had invaded a bishop's territory without permission. Cantwell was enraged by this Chicagoan invasion.

Presumably on a fact-finding mission for Cardinal Mundelein, Sheil and Dinneen were in reality trying to have Breen replaced by someone more in tune with their vision of cinema morality. Quigley, although critical of Breen, realized that if Chicago controlled the Legion it could drive the industry away from cooperation. He warned Archbishop McNicholas that the Chicago delegation was "hostile" toward "what we have been trying to do."[47]

In Los Angeles, a chess match began: Bishop countered bishop as Cantwell and Mundelein vied for control of the Legion. The advantage was all Cantwell's. Breen advised Will Hays, who was in Hollywood, not to acknowledge the presence of the Chicago group. Cantwell sent his Legion representative, Father John Devlin, to confer with Mundelein's emissaries. Dinneen "damned the Code, the producers, the pictures," and Breen throughout the meeting, Devlin reported.[48] When Devlin pressed him for specifics, Dinneen had to admit he had seen none of the condemned films except *Of Human Bondage*. He was then forced to admit that a Miss Sally Reilly, secretary with the Chicago Board of Censorship and a parishioner in Dinneen's church, issued the ratings. Devlin was incredulous. Bishop Cantwell summoned Bishop Sheil to his office, where the visiting bishop was "given a call down for coming into the diocese" and ordered to take the evening train to Chicago.[49] Cantwell wrote to all the studios and apologized for the incident; he also requested that in the future no priest be admitted to any lot without his written permission.[50]

After the visit Breen wrote he was "thoroughly disgusted with the Legion of Decency."[51] Yet Breen, Cantwell, and their ally in Cincinnati, McNicholas, emerged the clear winners. Mundelein's vigilantes were vanquished, and Chicago's influence in the Legion began to wane. While the Chicago Legion would continue to rate films for the next year and bestow an occasional "C" rating, McNicholas was determined after the fiasco in Hollywood to remove the reviewing responsibility from Chicago. The studios watched with interest as Breen battled the Chicago Catholics. Watching a discredited bishop literally "run out of town" dispatched a clear message: If the studios cooperated with Breen and Hays, they had little to fear from the Legion.

Fresh from his triumph over Chicago, Breen was ready to take on his other critic: Martin Quigley. When Quigley came to Hollywood in late February, Breen ignored him. Breen, Quigley observed, was "out socially" every night with industry people. With his new house, a butler, three cars, and a chauffeur, Breen had "gone Hollywood," Quigley told Father Parsons.[52] Several weeks passed before the two men got together to discuss the movies, and Quigley noted there was a general atmosphere of "resentment" during their meeting. When Breen bragged he had "single-handedly" conquered Hollywood, Quigley was enraged. Breen then revealed that he had had an offer from Universal Studios that would pay him considerably more than the pittance ($31,000) that Hays was giving him. Quigley protested that the offer was nothing more than a bribe to remove him from the censorship office. Breen quickly ended the meeting.[53] He no longer felt he had to kowtow to Martin Quigley.

Both of these events took place during the production of *Anna Karenina*. Breen may well have been doing nothing more than getting changes he and Selznick had agreed on in the record. He knew the subject matter was controversial and could reasonably predict that the Chicago Legion would condemn the film because of the adultery theme. At any rate, by mid-March 1935 he felt no need to defer to either the Chicago Legion or Quigley.

Anna Karenina, released in September 1935, reeks throughout with moral indignation. Brushing aside all the subplots in Tolstoy's work, the film concentrates on the relationship between Anna and Vronsky. Anna, who lives in St. Petersburg with her husband and devoted son, visits Moscow. She and Count Vronsky (Fredric March) chance to meet at the train station. When Vronsky prepares to help his mother from the train car, a huge puff of smoke belches from the train. He looks up and instead of his mother stepping from the train, a goddess, Garbo, emerges. They are both taken aback and, if not love at first sight, there was an immediate physical attraction between these two beautiful people that the audience immediately sensed.

The affair develops very quickly. Anna and Vronsky both return to St. Petersburg where they keep encountering each other at social functions. Anna tries to resist her feelings, which she knows are wrong. Her husband, Karenina (Basil Rathbone), an important government official, notices her flirtations with the count and delivers a stern rebuke invoking his devotion to the "inviolability" of the marriage ties and her duties and responsibilities as a wife and mother.

This scene is followed immediately by Vronsky's mother warning him that society disapproves of his affair with a married woman. He brushes aside her warning and goes to the stables to prepare for a horse race. At the stables one of his fellow officers delivers a message from the general: "If your name continues to be linked with a certain lady then you will be asked to resign from the regiment." Vronsky blows up. He will resign if necessary.

While the two lovers choose to ignore these "unofficial" warnings, it is clear to everyone in the audience (the intended recipients) that society disapproves. In case anyone slipped out for popcorn during this five-minute sequence, the message is repeated in various forms throughout the remainder of the film.

Despite the best efforts of family and friends to prevent tragedy, Anna and Vronsky continue to see each other. It is all very veiled in the film: no long scenes of romance, no whispering of eternal love – in fact, as Breen had demanded, almost no physical contact at all between the two lovers. Yet there is no question in the mind of the audience that the couple is carrying on a love affair. Their actions in public become more bold, which defines their off-screen actions in private. At a garden party the lovers flirt while playing croquet. Although they believe they are being discreet, everyone at the party is talking about them. When Karenina arrives, he is taken aside and warned by one of the women there that his wife's conduct lacks propriety.

Later Anna and her husband attend the races. Count Vronsky is in the lead when his horse stumbles and falls. For a moment it appears the count has been seriously hurt. Anna is hysterical; she sobs and faints. Everyone knows why. Karenina is humiliated by his wife's emotional display. Karenina and Anna immediately leave.

Karenina and Anna argue on the way home. When they arrive, he summons his wife into his study for a confrontation. He stands stiffly behind his desk, towering over Anna, who stands meekly in front of the desk, her eyes downcast submissively. Karenina begins by telling Anna he knows their marriage had been a mistake. He is stiff, formal, and boring. She is young, vivacious, and beautiful. He continues, "I believe in marriage as a sacrament. I could not consider myself justified in breaking the ties by which we are bound by a higher power." He lectures, rather than talks to, his wife, and insists that "the family cannot be broken up by the whim or caprice or even the sins of one of the partners of marriage." Karenina demands that they continue on with their marriage as if Anna's transgression had never taken place. Suddenly, Anna looks up and says: "But it can't." Karenina retorts: "It must." Anna pleads: "You won't give me a divorce?" Karenina is adamant: "Never! Why should I? To permit you to legalize a sin – to justify your conduct? Never! Our life must continue on." When Anna asks what the alternative is, Karenina threatens to keep her from ever seeing her son again. Anna must choose either her role as mother and wife blessed by God and approved by society, or her role as lover in a union odious to God and disapproved by society.

This whole scene was all very Catholic: Marriage was described as a sacrament, blessed by God, that could never be broken. An unhappy marriage was not a legitimate reason for divorce or sexual transgression. Individual feelings had to be suppressed, and happiness and fulfillment on earth, meaningless as they were, were to be found in traditional roles. Had Anna gone to confession, her priest would have echoed what her husband told her. This scene set the tone for the rest of the movie. Anna, given one last chance at redemption, tossed it aside and would pay with her life for her renunciation.

Instead of taking her husband's advice, Anna and Vronsky run off to Italy. At first they are happy far from the disapproving eyes of Russian society. The canals of Venice are romantic, but life in exile is unexciting. Their love for each other is insufficient to sustain their relationship. (Another clear message to the audience: Passion soon fades; don't be foolish.) Both long to return to Russia: Anna to see her son, Vronsky to resume the carefree life of a handsome military officer. When they do return, they discover their life in exile continues. Anna sneaks into her house to see her son, but is thrown out by Karenina. Vronsky visits his old regiment, but is treated as an outsider. Anna, de-

Figure 11. Greta Garbo and Basil Rathbone in MGM's *Anna Karenina.* Courtesy the Museum of Modern Art / Film Stills Archive.

termined to confront society, demands they go to the opera. Vronsky knows this is a fatal mistake. When Anna insists, he goes along, but fears impending trouble. They are no sooner seated in their box than the whispers and disapproving looks begin. When an inebriated man smiles and bows toward Anna, his wife screams, "How dare you bow to THAT woman."

Shunned by society, the lovers retreat to the country but are soon bored. When Vronsky receives a letter inviting him to join a group of "volunteers" who are enlisting in the Serbian army to fight the Turks, he leaps at the chance. Anna knows this is the end for them, but is helpless to stop him. They quarrel, and Vronsky stomps off in disgust. Anna is crushed. Deserted by her lover, unable to see her son or rejoin society, she goes to the train station seeking to work out a reconciliation with Vronsky before he goes to war. At the station she sees Vronsky from a distance talking to his mother and a beautiful young princess. She knows her life is over. After the train pulls out she waits at the station and throws herself under an oncoming train.

There was not a dry eye in the house when the credits rolled. Garbo was movingly tragic; her husband was an insufferable bore, her lover a shallow cad. Society was callously indifferent as long as its rules were not openly broken. It was Anna who died; Vronsky lived on and, while he confessed he would carry his guilt for Anna's death with him forever, it was a shallow confession. Breen, however, maintained this movie was a model for screen morality: Here, unlike in past films, adultery had been "denounced in speeches and condemned in action" throughout. While Breen admitted that Karenina was cold and uncaring, he found that an "insufficient excuse for Anna's own capital neglect of duty and shameful violation of vows in deserting her husband and son for the arms of her lover." It was clear to Breen that the film established "Anna's guilt" as "plain and inescapable."[54]

Breen was especially pleased over the "strong speeches" delivered by Karenina on the "sanctity and inviolability of marriage as a sacrament," which Breen believed established the husband on the moral side of the conflict. He may have been stiff and formal but he was not, at least in Breen's eyes, a "hypocrite" as Anna charged.[55]

Nor was adultery, Breen stressed to Hays, used to weaken respect for marriage; for the first time in film history, Breen contended, the "matrimonial bond is positively defended – at least in the minds of those who take marriage seriously." The entire mood of the film demonstrated that "there is not a single hour of unalloyed bliss for Anna." Believing that all these factors made *Anna Karenina* safe for audiences, Breen issued seal number 1015 to MGM.[56]

Breen may not have noticed the small, but significant, statements with which Anna defended her actions. It is a fair assumption that most women watching in 1935 felt a strong surge of sympathy for Anna's plight. When Karenina first scolds Anna, he concludes his lecture by telling her that this is for her own good and that, oh, by the way, he loves her. Anna spits back, "You don't love me. You love only position and appearance." In their second confrontation, after Karenina has treated Anna like a child, she looks at him with scorn and says, "Whatever happens, I know this. You'll always be in the right." Karenina cuts her off. Honor must be maintained at all costs, he tells her. Anna defends her actions: "Your honor! Your selfishness, your hypocrisy, your egotism, your social position. All these things must be maintained. You've never considered me as a human being." "AT WHAT COSTS?!" she shouts. "At what costs?" Karenina, cold and uncaring as always: "It is time for my appointment at the ministry." All those women in the audience whose husbands treated them like second-class citizens, who were married to unloving tyrants, who dictated household policy rather than discussed it with them as equals understood what motivated Anna. They might not approve of adultery, but their sympathy was with Garbo, not Rathbone. Even *Harrison's Reports* noted somewhat uneasily that audience sympathy went out to Anna.[57]

Critics were divided on the film's merits. The *Nation* found it "lifeless" and objected to the "purity-sealed" rendition of Tolstoy forced on audiences by the Hays Office. It is "justified only as a museum piece," readers were warned.[58] Garbo "sins, suffers and perishes," wrote *New York Times* reviewer Andre Sennwald. He found the film "dignified and effective."[59] Graham Greene saw only "guilt and misery and passion."[60] It should delight "millions of cinemaddicts who have never heard of Tolstoy," wrote *Time*.[61] Los Angeles critic Rob Wagner found the film's moral preachments outdated. "In the preview audience," he wrote, "witnessing her calvary were many unwed couples living happily together and in no way socially ostracized." When Garbo was cast out of society for deserting home and son to go off with March, society's "behavior seemed very old-fashioned."[62]

Only the Chicago Legion of Decency saw *Anna Karenina* as "indecent," and it condemned the film "for ethical reasons." *Our Sunday Visitor,* the national Catholic weekly that supported the Chicago rankings, demanded that *Anna Karenina* "be boycotted not only in Chicago" but everywhere it is shown.[63] Bishop Sheil, still smarting from his treatment by Cantwell in Los Angeles, wrote a letter to each priest in the Chicago diocese condemning Hollywood and demanding that the film be denounced.[64]

Breen began to receive letters from Chicago Catholics protesting his approval. "All of this emphasizes the rank injustice involved in this Chicago situation," Breen complained to Father Devlin.[65] When MGM and the Exhibitors Association of Chicago complained that the rating was hurting business in Chicago, Breen decided to act. He organized a "jury" of five Los Angeles area priests, headed by Father Devlin, to judge *Anna Karenina*. After viewing the film, the jury concluded it was not "indecent, immoral, and unfit for anyone to see."[66]

Meanwhile, Father Devlin had prepared a long report for Bishop Cantwell on the activities of the PCA under Breen and the impact of the Chicago Legion's ratings on the industry. The PCA, Devlin told his bishop, had rejected sixty-five books and stories out of hand and had forced Hollywood to incorporate "compensating moral values" in countless others. It had also rejected purity seals for films it deemed offensive, such as *Ann Vickers, Song of Songs, Blood Money,* and *Scarface,* all of which had been released before Breen took over. In short, Devlin told Cantwell, Breen and the PCA's enforcement of the code had dramatically improved the moral quality of the movies.[67]

Notwithstanding, he continued, Chicago "has seen fit to condemn" PCA-approved films without offering any reasons for its actions. Devlin charged that Chicago condemned films no priest had seen, and that if this situation were allowed to continue, the church would lose cooperation from Hollywood. "Morality," Devlin wrote, "is a question of Geography." Devlin insisted that PCA-scrubbed "pictures are cleaner," crime "has been stripped of bravado," the studios are more cooperative, "public taste has improved," religion is treated with respect, and "federal censorship has been avoided."[68] If Chicago continued to rate movies, Devlin predicted that Hollywood would revert to a pre-Breen attitude. He strongly recommended that a national office be opened in New York, and that all previewing be undertaken by Mrs. James Looram and her International Federation of Catholic Alumnae (IFCA).[69]

Cantwell's curiosity was piqued. The good bishop, deciding it was time to go to the movies, selected a film condemned by the Chicago priests: *Barbary Coast,* written by Ben Hecht and Charles MacArthur, directed by Howard Hawks, produced by Sam Goldwyn, and adapted from Herbert Asbury's 1933 best-seller, *The Barbary Coast.* The film starred Miriam Hopkins, Edward G. Robinson, and Joel McCrea. It was full of wisecracks, sexual innuendoes, crooked gambling tables, beautiful women, and violence.

From the beginnings of the California gold rush until the earthquake of 1906, San Francisco's Pacific Street between Kearney and Montgomery was the most famous "acre of iniquity" in the world. Real-life characters like Shanghai Kelly, Cowboy Maggie, Calico Jim, and Mother Bronson inhabited the brothels, gambling houses, and dives that dominated the Barbary Coast. Asbury had brought all this to life in vivid detail. While the setting was infamous, one reviewer noted that Asbury "devoted himself with commendable seriousness and even a sort of scholarly piety." However, when Goldwyn announced he was creating a movie version, *Harrison's Reports* warned exhibitors that it was "one of the filthiest, vilest and most degrading books that have ever been chosen for the screen."[70] No matter how much Goldwyn will cleanse the film, the *Reports* predicted, he will give critics the impression that "producers are just waiting for the opportunity to revert to type – that as soon as public pressure is removed, they will go back to wallowing in mud."[71] The Better Motion Picture Council of Cincinnati agreed: They told Breen they protested any film made of this book, "however deodorized" it might be.[72]

Breen and Hays feared that a movie set in the Barbary Coast, which was synonymous with brothels and "red-light" districts, would cause an uproar among moral guardians of all persuasions. Hays was particularly obsessed by the title, which he viewed as "dangerous."[73] He

urged Goldwyn to "abandon" the project, threatened and then pleaded with him to change the title. The producer refused. Everything else,
however, was open for negotiation.[74]

According to Howard Hawks, who directed the film, he, Hecht,
and McArthur worked on the script together:

We would sit in a room and we'd work for two hours and then we'd play
backgammon for an hour. Then we'd start again and one of us would be one
character and one would be another character. We'd read our lines of dialogue and the whole idea was to try and stump the other people.[75]

They did not, however, stump Breen. He did not plead with Goldwyn,
but simply issued a flat rejection of the first draft, which he read in
August 1934. "The whole flavor of the story," Breen told Goldwyn,
"is one of sordidness, and low-tone morality."[76]

Over the next six months Breen and Hays kept close tabs on the
project. Hays met with Goldwyn during his periodic trips to Hollywood, and Breen reviewed drafts of the script, which were increasingly devoid of "illicit" sex but continued to strike the censor as "too
rough and brutal."[77] Slowly the script changed from a story of an area
of San Francisco where men came to find pleasure in drink, prostitutes, and gambling to a typical Hollywood love story that featured a
young couple (Hopkins and McCrea) who fall in love amid unlikely
surroundings. The foil was Edward G. Robinson, who continued his
"tough guy" image as the Barbary Coast gangster. Breen was delighted
with the new direction of the script. He told Hays that it was "definitely not the story which worried us all many months back." It is now a
love story, he told Hays, "between a fine, clean girl" and a sentimental
young man. While the Barbary Coast serves as a background for the
story, there "is no sex, no unpleasant details of prostitution," and,
more important, there is "full, and completely compensating, value
in the picture."[78] Breen told Charles MacArthur that the film was
"the finest and most intelligent motion picture I have seen in many
months." Hecht disagreed. He disliked the film and was disgusted by
the whole process of sanitizing the Barbary Coast: "Miriam Hopkins
came to the Barbary Coast and wandered around like a confused
Goldwyn girl," he later wrote.[79]

When Bishop Cantwell went to see *Barbary Coast* with four priests,
he quite enjoyed the film, and none of the priests found the film immoral. Nor did any of the reviewers. *Time* judged it "painfully unin-
spired."[80] The *New York Times* found the film entertaining but suspected that Hecht and MacArthur were kept "under wraps when they
rescued pure love from the fleshpots."[81] *Scholastic*, a magazine for
American youth, recommended the film "for its authentic background
and characters of the days of gold-discovery."[82] Even *Harrison's Re-*

ports grudgingly admitted that the film would not "demoralize any adult."[83] *Canadian Magazine* reassured Canadians that the movie had "nothing to do with the cheap, tawdry 'coast'" in Asbury's novel.[84] *Newsweek* made the same point for its readers: Goldwyn's version of *Barbary Coast* could not have been made in Argentina, it reported, because the South Americans had just passed a law that movie producers could not "buy a book, throw away the plot and use only the title."[85] From the industry came a more biting comment: *Hollywood Reporter* praised Breen and charged that only "a bigot" or "a fanatic" could find reason to condemn either *Anna Karenina* or *Barbary Coast*.

This statement was aimed directly at Chicago, where the Board of Censorship had followed the Legion's rating and threatened a total ban of the film for the Windy City. Goldwyn was enraged. "At one stage," Breen told Hays, "Goldwyn was in favor of moving into Chicago, hiring a battery of lawyers, and suing the censor board, the Legion of Decency and everybody else within striking distance."[86] Breen, as was normally the case on films he favored, worked closely with the local censors, with Cantwell's endorsement in hand. Trimming a few scenes, Breen opened the Chicago market, enabling Chicagoans – at least, the non-Catholics – to see *Barbary Coast*. Goldwyn was pacified.

By November 1935 it was clear that differences of opinion within the Catholic church threatened the Legion movement. In Hollywood Breen had been effective in forcing a new morality on producers. Hays had backed the new censor and even demanded that he become more strict. Breen had done so, but not to the satisfaction of the Legion in Chicago. When the bishops assembled in Washington, D.C., for their annual meeting, the movies were once again on their agenda.

Archbishop McNicholas opened the discussion. The church had, he told the conclave, improved the content of Hollywood films during the past year. The Production Code Administration, in his opinion, had been a success, but it had become more and more evident that the issue of lists of "white" and "black" films was threatening to divide the Catholic movement. McNicholas urged the bishops to set aside individual differences and agree on a single list of films that would guide all the Catholic faithful. In his view it was essential that such a list continue to list "black" or condemned films. Cantwell agreed, but spoke at length of his displeasure over the number of films his Legion representatives viewed as acceptable, yet had been condemned by Chicago. He told his fellow bishops that he had seen *Barbary Coast* and judged it moral. It was essential, Cantwell emphasized, that the church have unified standards as well as a unified list.[87]

Cardinal Mundelein, who must have been fuming by this time, announced that Chicago would no longer publish a list of movies for the

Legion because they were "not generally appreciated" outside his archdiocese. Bishops Gallagher of Detroit and Curley of Baltimore spoke in defense of the Chicago list and introduced resolutions for Chicago to continue to compile the "official" Legion lists. The resolutions were defeated. McNicholas and Cantwell urged that an official Legion office be opened in New York, and that all Catholic reviewing be done from that office. It was essential, they argued, for New York to perform this function because most movies first played New York City: The films could thus be seen there and their ratings published before they went into general release. After a lengthy discussion, the bishops agreed to establish a National Legion of Decency office in New York under the guidance of Cardinal Hayes; they further agreed that the ratings produced by this new agency would be the "official" list printed in all Catholic publications.[88] As evidence of their continuing commitment to purification of the movies, the bishops approved an appropriation of $35,000 to fund the National Legion office. (The word "National" was specifically used to distinguish it from the Chicago Council of the Legion of Decency.)

McNicholas carefully negotiated a quiet transfer of power from Mundelein to Hayes. Chicago agreed that their final list would be issued on January 31, 1936, with an "appropriate statement" announcing the establishment of a National Legion. The first list issued from New York would be dated February 1936.

Administratively, the National Legion office operated out of the Catholic Charities Office in New York under the direction of Father Edward Robert Moore. Cardinal Hayes appointed Father John Daly, both a priest from St. Gregory's Church in New York and a professor of psychology at the College of St. Vincent, as Executive Secretary. Daly, who knew nothing about the movies, would need all his professional training in psychology to steer a course for the Legion that would satisfy Cardinal Mundelein and his supporters as well as Archbishop McNicholas, Bishop Cantwell, Will Hays, Martin Quigley, Joe Breen, and the movie moguls.

The task of determining the moral values of the movies was given to the Catholic women's organization, the International Federation of Catholic Alumnae. In 1922, under the direction of Mrs. Thomas A. McGoldrick, the IFCA had created a Motion Picture Bureau that adopted the philosophy advocated by Will Hays: "Praise the best and ignore the rest." For twelve years the women had published reviews of good films, which they urged Catholics to support; movies they considered vulgar, tasteless, or immoral were simply ignored. By 1934 more than a hundred women – divided into an East Coast group under the spiritual direction of Rev. Francis X. Talbot, S.J., and a West Coast group under the direction of Rev. John Devlin – worked as film reviewers. Mrs. James Looram compiled the reviewers' comments and published in the *Brooklyn Tablet* a regular column of film reviews that was reprinted in most Catholic publications. These reviews were also broadcast over a twenty-four-station radio network.

When the Legion crisis hit, the women of the IFCA were shunted aside; in typical fashion, the priests took over. The organization was labeled a "puppet of the Hays Office," and its refusal to issue blacklists of condemned films was seen as allowing the industry to continue to produce "immoral" films. By 1936, however, the bishops had come full circle. Father Devlin lobbied Cantwell and McNicholas for IFCA reinstatement as the official reviewing body for the National Legion of Decency, and the bishops voted agreement at the November conclave. The women were back in grace after they agreed to add a condemned category to their reviews.[89]

To avoid the problems caused by the Chicago listings, the National Legion of Decency and the IFCA redefined the rating system to be used in classifying movies. Chicago had had three classifications:

A   "unobjectionable";
B   "considered more or less objectionable in spots because of their possible suggestiveness or vulgarity or sophistication or lack of modesty; neither approved or disapproved"; and
C   "condemned as indecent and immoral and unfit for public entertainment."[90]

The National Legion expanded the categories from three to four, which gave reviewers more latitude in judging films and reserved the controversial "condemned" classification for those few films considered, to use a more modern phrase, "to be without socially redeeming values." The new National Legion rating categories were as follows:

A1 Unobjectionable for general patronage;
A2 Unobjectionable for adults;
B   Objectionable in part;
C   Condemned.[91]

This four-part division was important in several respects: First, it recognized that not all films had to be made for children. By dividing the "approved" category into two parts, general (i.e., including children) and adults, the National Legion could approve films like *Anna Karenina* or *Barbary Coast* for adults without necessarily condoning them for children. Whether or not youngsters could attend "A2" films would be a parental decision. This was significant because the vast majority of films produced by the Hollywood studios and approved by Breen would now fall under these two classifications. The third classification was left purposely vague: "B" films were defined as those that contained one or more scenes, or themes, that some people might find objectionable but that were not, in the opinion of the reviewers, total-ly immoral, obscene, or corrupting. If, in the Legion's view, the over-all mood of the film was positive, it would issue a "B" classification, thus allowing individual Catholics to determine for themselves wheth-er or not it would be sinful for them to attend.[92] The "C" or "con-demned" classification was reserved for those few films considered dangerously "immoral." Martin Quigley had played a major role in the new definitions given to the various classifications.

This dramatic change in Legion criteria, which gave the studios more flexibility in treating adult themes, did not go unnoticed in Hol-lywood. In February 1936, the National Legion of Decency issued its first classification of films. Charlie Chaplin's *Modern Times* was put in the "A" grouping, despite "a few vulgarities"; Marlene Dietrich's *Desire* was approved for adults in spite of "a few long, drawn out kisses and suggestive remarks"; and even Jean Harlow's *Wife Versus Secretary* was approved by the Catholic women. No film was con-demned, but several were placed in the "B" category: *The Walking Dead,* because this Frankenstein spin-off implied that the mad doctor (Boris Karloff) created life in his laboratory; and *Mr. Cohen Takes a Walk,* because a Jewish boy and an Irish girl are married "by a priest and then by a rabbi,"[93] whereas mixed marriages were discouraged by the Catholic church.

The "B" classification was also given to a film that told the story of "a prostitute who, to escape punishment for a murder which she had committed in self-defense, goes to Alaska, becomes a revival leader but later decides to return to San Francisco and stand trial." The re-view noted that the heroine's dialogue was laced with double mean-ings, but judged it all rather "harmless." Catholics were free to see the film if they wished: The Legion did not find *Klondike Annie* "immor-al." This rating invoked rage among many would-be censors, and chuckles from others. Movie fans once again stormed the box office to watch Mae West swivel her hips and to hear her quips.

Paramount anticipated censorship problems with *Klondike Annie,* a satirical view of a prostitute turned religious "do-gooder." In June 1935, long before the studio was prepared to go into production, studio executive John Hammell phoned Will Hays to review the general story line. The setting, Hammell told Hays, was the Alaska gold rush of 1898. The story opens in Shanghai, with West working as a "hostess-croupier" in a gambling house for a wealthy, unscrupulous Chinese mandarin. When he tries to rape West, she defends her "hon-or" and kills him. Forced to flee China, she books passage on a tramp steamer bound for Alaska. Naturally, on the long voyage across the Pacific, the ship's captain falls in love with West, who is forced to fend off his advances. He finds out about her past and threatens to turn her in if she does not "cooperate."

West's bunkmate during the voyage is a young, sour, soul saver, Sister Annie Alden, bound to do good in the gold fields. When this young missionary suddenly dies, West assumes her identity to escape the police. When West arrives in Nome, disguised as the "good Sister," she is a reformed woman. She takes over the mission, raises money, and converts the miners to the straight and narrow. All of this doing good rubs off on West, who renounces her past and falls in love with a handsome, young Canadian Mounted Police officer. Realizing that she will ruin his career if her past is discovered, she returns to San Francisco to stand trial for the murder of the Chinese gambler.[94]

Hays must have been reeling after Hammell finished his description of the plot. West had already caused the Presbyterian elder more than his share of headaches; now she was going to Shanghai to play a concubine to a Chinese gambler whom she kills to "defend her honor"! Who would believe it? Moreover, the thought of West impersonating a missionary horrified Hays. He demanded that Paramount omit any implication of a sexual relationship between the mandarin villain and West, and that she not be allowed to masquerade "as a preacher, revivalist or any other character known and accepted as a minister."[95]

Hammell naturally assured Hays that Paramount would take the greatest care to avoid any reference to a "sex relationship," and that the character of the young missionary would be used to show the contrast between West, the "flippant product of a hard, cruel upbringing," and the "devout mission worker." West will be sincerely converted to good, Hammell stressed. "At no time in the action . . . will religion, religious works, the life and doings of the mission worker, be held up to ridicule in the slightest manner." Hays told Paramount to proceed with a script, then wired Breen and cautioned him that another West script was on its way.[96]

Mae West and her collaborators, Marion Morgan, George B. Dowell, and Frank M. Dazey, pounded out a script during the summer of 1935 and sent it to Breen's office in September with the working title *The Frisco Doll*. The censor took one look at it and rejected it out of hand. Breen told Hammell that West openly and clearly "masquerades as an exponent of religion and as a religious worker" throughout the script. He told Hammell that his pledge to Hays "has not been complied with," and the script would not be approved until Paramount eliminated all references to West as a missionary.[97]

Breen did more than demand changes in the script: He also offered suggestions that would allow Paramount to make the film in compliance with the code. As usual, he demanded that the local dance-halls not be viewed as houses of prostitution. He also worried over a few scenes that seemed excessively violent. However, it was the character of West that most concerned him: He knew that any hint of West's being a religious missionary would invoke howls of protest, and he suggested that the studio change Sister Annie Alder from a missionary to either a settlement worker or a social worker. Along those same lines, he demanded that all gags about West "saving souls" be deleted, and that no Bibles or other religious symbols be seen on the screen. If this were done, Breen believed, the curse of seeming to ridicule religion would be sufficiently reduced to allow him to approve the script.

To change the nature of the character played by West and to convince the audience that she had sincerely converted to good, he urged Paramount to incorporate scenes of "Doll playing games, possibly with rough miners, teaching them Mother Goose rhymes," or playing "charades." "How about Doll as a sort of Carrie Nation, cleaning out the saloon and building up the settlement houses as a rendezvous for the workers." Why not, Breen continued, "have a magic lantern show with Doll singing some old-fashioned songs like 'A Bird in a Gilded Cage' or 'Don't Send My Boy to Prison'"?[98] There is no record of Paramount's or West's reaction; they simply forwarded lyrics for West's musical numbers, "I'm an Occidental Woman in an Oriental Mood for Love," "That May Not Be Love," and "It's Never Too Late to Say No" (during which number Mae gave the opposite impression).

When in mid-October Paramount submitted a revised script, which softened the impression that West was masquerading as a religious missionary, Breen quickly approved the script. He viewed the final print with "pleasure" on the Paramount lot New Year's Eve 1935. *Klondike Annie* would open in New York in February with PCA seal number 1857.[99]

The censorship process made fundamental changes in the *Klondike Annie* that eventually reached the screen. The film opens in San Francisco's "Chinatown," not in Shanghai. West is the fabulous "San Francisco Doll," a famous entertainer working for the infamous Chan Lo (Harold Huber), a Chinese gangster. Chan owns a fancy gambling house frequented by San Francisco's smart set. In the opening scene, two older couples bedecked in tails and evening gowns talk as they prepare for an evening of gambling. "Is the white woman married to Chan Lo?" asks one woman. "I hear he makes every white man keep a respectable distance from her," says another. They snicker.

When Chan Lo appears, the four titter that they desperately want to meet "Doll." The mandarin assures them she will make an appearance and shows them his latest purchase: a rare knife that, he claims, has been used many times in Chinese legend to kill "beautiful ladies unfaithful to their lords." The threat is understood.

Suddenly, huge Chinese gongs sound, announcing that Doll is about to perform on stage. Dressed in elaborate oriental costume, West belts out a rendition of "I'm an Occidental Woman in the Mood for Oriental Love." The audience, naturally, goes wild. Back in her dressing room, Doll and Chan Lo bicker. He sputters his love in clipped Confucian, calling her his "pearl of pearls." Doll retorts, "This pearl of pearls is gettin' unstrung." When Chan demands her loyalty, she complains, "Why do you keep me from having men friends of my own race?" Because, he says, the only good men are dead or unborn. "Which one are you?" she fires back. He slinks away.

These scenes of the film suggest a theme that was forbidden by the code: miscegenation. The dressing-room scene indicates that West no longer cares for Chan Lo, but it appears that they had been lovers. West tells her maid that she has been "caged up for a year." Her maid warns that Chan is a very jealous man, but Doll is determined to escape, and arranges for passage on a ship bound for the gold fields of Nome, Alaska. When Chan discovers her plans, he attempts to kill her; they struggle, and Doll kills the mandarin with his own knife.

Under cover of night Doll sneaks aboard the ship *Java Maid,* bound for Nome. The ship's captain, Bull Brackett (Victor McLaglen), is a tough old salt who immediately turns to mush when Doll boards his ship. He fusses over her endlessly, but she repels his advances until he discovers she is wanted for murder in San Francisco. Doll, above all a practical woman, is now receptive to Brackett's advances.

When the ship stops in Vancouver, another passenger boards: Sister Annie Alder (Helen Jerome Eddy), a plain-Jane settlement worker bound to do good among the sinners in the gold fields. The beautiful, buxom Doll and drab Sister Annie, opposites in every respect, are thrust by circumstances to share a small cabin on the long voyage to Alaska. At first, Doll mocks her new companion. "I decided to make my living by my wits," Doll says. Annie is saddened: "Too many girls follow the line of least resistance." A smiling Doll replies, "A good line is hard to resist."

Sister Annie knows that Doll has seen the underside of life, but she does not condemn her: It must be very hard for a beautiful woman to be good. She offers Doll her favorite book, which has a black cover and is several inches thick. A Bible? No; the camera zooms in on the title, *Settlement Maxims.* Doll takes the book to bed. As they settle in Doll asks, "Do you snore?" "Why, I don't know," Annie replies, "do you?" "Wellllll," Doll answers, "I've never had any complaints."

As they travel together the goodness of Sister Annie smoothes some of Doll's hard edges. Underneath that tough exterior, there is a heart of gold. The film attempts to make the conversion sincere as the two women become good friends. Doll tells Annie she is beginning to look at life differently; Annie is delighted. Suddenly, however, Annie has a heart attack and dies just as the ship arrives in Nome. Before the ship docks, the Nome police board the ship, tipped off that the "San Francisco Doll" is aboard. Brackett tries to keep the coppers out of Doll's room. He is shocked when she opens the door dressed as "Sister Annie" and tells the police that Rose Carlton, alias "San Francisco Doll," has just expired.

In Nome, Doll decides to repay her debt to Sister Annie by helping the settlement house raise money and setting the poor miners on the straight and narrow. Men, of course, are no match for Mae West, no matter how she is dressed. When she rolls her eyes and tells them to be good, they are. The miners give thousands of dollars to the settlement house, and the new Sister Annie is the hit of the town. Even the "dance-hall" girls flock to her side.

A Nome policeman, detective Jack Forrest (Philip Reed), remains suspicious of this beautiful blonde reformer. He follows "Sister Annie" around and, of course, falls totally in love with her, and she with him. Unfortunately, Forrest also discovers her true identity. Before he is forced to break his pledge to uphold the law, Sister Annie changes back to the "San Francisco Doll" and returns to Brackett's ship.

In the final scene, Doll reclines seductively on a couch in Brackett's room. She tells him she wants to return to San Francisco to clear her name. He counters that there is no need to do that because he loves her just as she is. He bends down over her and says, "If I thought I was going to lose ya I'd croak ya." Doll smiles warmly: "Bull, ya ain't an oil painting but you're a fascinating monster." They kiss passionately as the film ends.

Did the two sail off to the South Seas and share a life of happy crime, or did Doll return to San Francisco to clear her name and live happily ever after with her policeman? Everyone in the audience could supply his or her ending.

Another national controversy over Mae West erupted almost as soon as the film was released. The Catholic Legion's "B" classification infuriated many Catholics, including Martin Quigley.[100] In Omaha, Bishop Hugh Ryan, a Mundelein supporter, ignored the Legion rating and issued a ban in his diocese. The Rev. Joseph B. Buckley followed suit in Washington, D.C., urging that all priests support a districtwide boycott. Detroit's Father Joseph A. Luther, S.J., Dean of Men at the University of Detroit, called the National Legion's "B" a "national disgrace."[101] The Catholic *Ave Maria* warned that the Legion's "moral strainer needs to be made considerable finer."[102] In Cincinnati, McNicholas worried that West would cause the smouldering disagreements over blacklists to destroy the fragile Legion unity he had worked so hard to achieve.[103]

When newspaper tycoon William Randolph Hearst bellowed that *Klondike Annie* was "odoriferous," the fracas reached national proportions. Hearstian headlines across the nation screamed that *Klon-dike Annie* was "lewd, immoral and indecent." His chain of papers in nineteen cities condemned the film and refused to accept any ads for it from local theaters. Just why Hearst launched this attack against the film was unclear. Some speculated that West had insulted Hearst's paramour, Marion Davies; others that it was West's snub of movie critic and gossip columnist Louella Parsons, who wrote for the Hearst chain, that had brought down the wrath of Hearst. Another rumor was that Hearst, whose fear of the "yellow peril" had long been a theme in his "yellow press," was enraged by the openness of the mis-cegenation theme in the film.[104]

Whatever prompted it, Hearst's campaign caused a flood of eager customers to storm box offices across the country. When *Klondike Annie* opened at the huge Paramount in New York City, the theater had to extend its hours to accommodate the throngs of fans trying to get in. The first showing was moved up to 8:30 A.M., with the last scheduled show starting at 2:00 A.M.! In upstate Rochester, editorial blasts by Hearst's *Journal American* forced the film to be moved from the 1,900-seat Century to the RKO Palace, which held 3,400! In Boston, the film shattered attendance records: The Metropolitan, which averaged a weekly gross of $22,000, took in $20,000 in two days with *Klondike Annie,* and finished the week's run with a whopping gross of $44,000. In Kansas City, the Newman Theater grossed $6,000 over average with West, and theaters in Buffalo, Denver, Louisville, and San Francisco reported similar increases. In Los Angeles, nine thousand fans had purchased tickets by 1:00 P.M. on opening day. Martin Quigley must have cringed when he read in his *Motion Picture Herald* that the film was averaging a weekly increase of $2,500–$8,500 per theater in national release.[105]

When they left the theater, critics and fans alike were perplexed by all the controversy. Frank Nugent, critic for the *New York Times,* told readers the censors had put West in "a moral straightjacket [*sic*]," resulting in "a tiresome and rather stupid combination of lavender and old japes."[106] Edwin Schallert in the *Los Angeles Times* lamented that "there are all too few of the Westian bon mots" in *Klondike Annie.*[107] Graham Greene was more enthusiastic:

I am completely uncritical of Mae West. . . . I did not find the satire on reli-gious revivalists in bad taste; I thought the whole film fun, more fun than any other of Miss West's since the superb period piece, *She Done Him Wrong,* but then it never occurred to me that Miss West's conversion was intended to be taken seriously.[108]

Harrison's Reports did take it seriously, and judged *Klondike Annie* more "sordid, and even more vulgar" than any of her past films.[109]

Was West legitimate satire? Several female reviewers came to her defense. *Los Angeles Citizen* film critic Elizabeth Yeaman wrote that the film "commits no breach of bad taste," called it "amusing entertainment," and urged her readers to judge for themselves.[110] Eleanor Barnes, writing in the *Illinois Daily News,* called West "a harlot with a heart of gold." Barnes was bemused by this latest rendition, and while she warned that the film was "raw, robust, bawdy humor," it was not offensive. West is West, she told her readers.[111]

The film generated so much publicity and controversy that an unusual number of letters to the editor appeared in local papers. In Los Angeles one woman, her curiosity piqued by Hearst's campaign in the *Los Angeles Examiner,* went to see the film: "I was so mad . . . when I came home I called . . . and cancelled my subscription." *Klondike Annie* was not lewd, she wrote; "on the contrary I thought the picture very mild . . . and I am going to recommend the Mae West film to my friends, and I certainly can see no reason why my children shouldn't see it."[112] Another woman wrote to the *Los Angeles Citizen* that she had attended the movie "much to the disgust" of her neighbor, who condemned the film as immoral. "If there is anything lewd about *Klondike Annie* my sense of morals must be upset," she told the paper. At her urging, the neighbor had then gone to see the film, and enjoyed it so much that she went back to see it twice![113] West even got a fan letter from a Catholic priest: Father Al Dugan from the Holy Cross Church in Los Angeles wrote the sultry star that he found *Klondike Annie* "delightfully humorous."[114]

Everyone, it seems, either loved or hated Mae West. The National Legion had anticipated controversy over *Klondike Annie,* and on three separate occasions Legion reviewers from the IFCA had screened the film. They had also invited Father Philip Furlong of New York's Cathedral College, Dean Ignatius Wilkinson of Fordham Law School, Judge Carroll Hayes, and two prominent lay Catholics, Dr. Paluel Flagg and Dr. Francis Baldwin, all of whom were active in the Legion movement in New York, to offer opinions. While a few argued for a "C" classification, no one judged the film immoral.[115]

When Hearst attacked the film, the Legion held a private conference of priests, lay advisors, and IFCA representatives to discuss strategy: Should the rating be changed from "B" to "C"? From Los Angeles, Father Devlin advised against any change; he had seen the movie with IFCA representatives in Los Angeles and believed the Hearst campaign was "much ado about nothing." Devlin urged Daly to stand firm with the "B" classification.[116]

Martin Quigley argued, however, that the film must be condemned "as unfit" for Catholic consumption.[117] It was his opinion that failure to do so would undermine the Legion's position as moral guardian. Devlin thought differently. He told Daly that "the Industry considers the Legion of Decency as the only group in the country sincere in its efforts for good entertainment. . . . [I]f we get on the Hearst bandwagon then God help the Legion of Decency's influence in the future."[118] Quigley lost the argument, but the Legion did agree to issue a statement, written by him, that condemned West and *Klondike Annie* – without naming them – as "an invasion of public and private morality."[119]

Quigley was not pacified, and remained furious with Daly and the Legion reviewers. He told Archbishop McNicholas that the new head of the Legion was "hopeless" and, in his opinion, had been corrupted by Will Hays. Quigley warned the archbishop that Daly's actions harmed "the elaborate effort which I have long been carrying on to keep Will Hays and his associates impressed with the unconquerable force represented by the Catholic Church's sponsorship of the Legion of Decency." Daly was "putty in the hands of the adroit operators who are Will Hays and his staff," Quigley fumed.[120]

In Los Angeles, Breen carefully watched the events unfold. He was gratified that the Legion, despite tremendous internal and external pressure, had supported his view that *Klondike Annie* was suitable for adult audiences. The state censorship boards confirmed his judgment: Only Pennsylvania made any serious objection to the film. The studios, in turn, could not fail to note that cooperation with Breen had resulted in wider market acceptability. Films censored by Breen sailed through the state boards with little difficulty.

The failure of the Hearst anti-West campaign to generate any public backlash against the movies was telling. On the one hand, the industry was warned that the would-be censors were out there, ready to attack Hollywood on a moment's notice; in that sense, Breen benefited by the Hearst campaign. On the other hand, whatever sense of moral outrage, however limited, there had been in 1934, it had by 1936 dissipated almost entirely. Other than Quigley and Hearst, few perceived *Klondike Annie* – a film that was almost embarrassing in its profession of morality and that had little of the zing and energy of *She Done Him Wrong* and *I'm No Angel* – as a moral threat.

Breen's objective was not to ban West from the screen, but to minimize the criticism he knew would come with any of her films. As long as we have Mae West "we are going to have trouble," he told his staff.[121] When the first script for her next movie, *Go West, Young Man*, hit his desk, he fired back an immediate rejection. Based on the play *Personal Appearances*, West was to play a motion picture star who seduces a handsome, virile young man as she treks cross country on a national tour. Breen protested that "the whole flavor is that of a nymphomaniac." He threatened to have the MPPDA ban the film from theater chains, but producer Emanuel Cohen insisted that he and West could develop an acceptable script. Throughout the summer of 1936 Breen held meetings with Cohen to get the script right. He rejected drafts submitted in May and June, and not until early August did Cohen get a script approved.[122]

After the film's release, Quigley's *Motion Picture Herald* asked whether Mae West enjoyed "an immunity from the operations of the Production Code." While Quigley continued to find West disgusting, and lost no opportunity to tweak Breen, most reviewers agreed with Graham Greene when he wrote that *Go West, Young Man* was "incredibly tedious." He warned his readers that the Westian "wisecracks lack the old impudence."[123] Indeed, they did. The Legion gave West another "B," and state censorship boards passed the film with barely a whimper of dissent. The film was a major box-office disappointment.

West tried again to find a formula that would satisfy both Breen and her fans. In *Every Day's a Holiday,* she played a confidence woman, not a consort. Breen rejected the early script drafts, and Will Hays put West on the agenda of the MPPDA Board in New York. PCA staff poured over the various drafts, went to the studio to examine all costumes for potential offense, and were present on the set during production. The beleaguered Emanuel Cohen raised a white flag of truce. He told Breen "the basic characterization of Miss West . . . is completely different from anything she has ever done before. There are no sex contacts nor sex situations that could possibly arouse the criticism that her pictures previously received."[124]

Breen agreed and gave the film a PCA seal; but West's raw humor had been so bowdlerized that the film not only disappointed fans but even failed to rouse moral guardians. Hays was pleased when the *Indianapolis Star* called *Every Day's a Holiday* "harmless, if rowdy fun."[125] West, no longer allowed to zing men with penetrating wisecracks or tease them with her sexual allure, collapsed at the box office. Unable to survive the new era of morals, West faded from view.

That Breen and his PCA dominated the filmmaking process by 1936 was further illustrated by a David O. Selznick production. Gambling that a love story filmed in Technicolor and starring Marlene Dietrich and Charles Boyer would heat up the screen, Selznick invested over $2 million in a remake of the novel *Garden of Allah,* a turn-of-the century tearjerker written by Robert Hichen.

The novel centers around a young woman, Domini Enfilden, who has been raised in a Catholic convent in Europe. Upon reaching adulthood she has a crisis of religious faith. On the advice of her Mother Superior, Domini leaves Europe, with its pseudo-"civilization," and seeks regeneration in the Garden of Allah, the Saharan desert. Domini travels to Beni-Mora, a walled outpost in North Africa. Here she meets Boris Androvsky who, unknown to Domini, is a runaway Trappist monk. In this romantic setting the two young people fall in love, and Domini soon finds herself pregnant. Boris, overcome by guilt, confesses his past to his lover. Domini, who has rediscovered her religion, convinces Boris to return to the monastery. She, in turn, retires to the Villa Anteoni in the beautiful Garden of Allah, where she lives the remainder of her life.

The book, praised by many critics, was labeled "a reeking monstrosity" by the *Catholic World;* yet despite Catholic condemnation, it was a runaway best-seller, with over two million copies sold.[126] Dramatizations of the novel appeared on Broadway in 1911 and 1918, and a popular filmed version starring Rex Ingram, released in 1927, had been judged "distinguished" by Mrs. Thomas A. McGoldrick of the IFCA.[127]

David O. Selznick had first proposed making a Technicolor version of *Garden of Allah* in 1935. Before proceeding with his idea and investment, however, he had wanted assurances that Catholic opinion would not condemn this project. The story had been filmed before without controversy: Would the Legion now condemn a movie dealing with such sensitive topics? How could the film portray the physical relationship between Domini and Boris? Could Boris return to the monastery after having an affair and a child? Selznick wanted a commitment from Breen that neither his PCA nor the Catholic Legion would object.[128]

Breen already had in his files a very negative reaction regarding this property from Father Daniel Lord, who had told Jason Joy in 1932 that he "strongly advised" against filming *The Garden of Allah* because he thought the material "dangerous."[129] Given Lord's reaction, Breen decided to solicit Catholic opinion. He wrote to Father Wilfrid Parsons of *America;* the Rev. Edward S. Schwegler, head of the Legion in Buffalo; Monsignor Joseph Corrigan, an old friend from Philadelphia and head of the Legion movement in that city; and Father Daly in Los Angeles. Breen asked both of them to read the book and let him know their views on a screen version.

The priests concluded the project was "unwise." Monsignor Corrigan and Devlin were flatly opposed. Parsons thought there was a chance to mesh the book and the code. Schwegler told Breen that the whole idea of "a monk having intimate carnal relations with a woman just grates against the grain." Schwegler also worried about another scene in the book: The monk, who has just left the monastery, finds his way into a cabaret where women dance for the pleasure of men. Sitting in the corner of the club he is spotted by a beautiful dancing girl, who performs her seductive dance for him. If the film were to portray the "barbarically sensual" dancing scene described in the novel, huffed Schwegler, the film would end up on blacklists all over the country.[130]

Breen, however, did not demand that Selznick drop the project. Instead, the censor urged him to make the film into a positive statement for the power of true religion over carnal lust. While the priests believed the subject "unwise," they had all agreed it would be possible for Boris to return to the monastery. Breen encouraged Selznick when he added that "as a Catholic I want to say that I would not be offended."[131]

Selznick was reassured. He told the censor he was prepared to go forward with the project, which would "uphold the church," if Quigley and the British censorship board would give assurances that they had no fundamental objection to the project. Breen reported that neither objected. Convinced that Catholics would not condemn the film out of hand, and that the lucrative British market was open, Selznick went ahead with the project.

He cast Marlene Dietrich as the virgin Domini, who had grown up in the protective environs of a Catholic convent. It was, to say the least, a rather dramatic switch for the German actress. Dietrich, like West, made her living playing women of easy virtue. In *The Blue Angel* (1930) she corrupts an aging university professor, and her role as a seductress-prostitute-cabaret singer was reprised in *Morocco* (1930), *Dishonored* (1931), *Shanghai Express* (1932), *Blonde Venus* (1932), and *The Devil Is a Woman* (1935). One line from *Shanghai Express* perhaps best summarized her screen persona: "It took more than one man to change my name to Shanghai Lily," she tells Clive Brook. Mae West had tried to soften her screen image by playing a bad woman gone good; Selznick cast Dietrich as a woman whose love of her religion (Catholicism) was stronger than her love for her man.

Around Dietrich, Selznick assembled an international cast. Charles Boyer, a promising young French actor, was cast as her monk-lover, Boris. Basil Rathbone, a South African by birth, played Count Anteoni, a European nobleman who finds adventure in the Sahara. A dashing French Legionnaire was played by Australian Alan Marshall. As the exotic Arab dancer who first tempts Boris, Selznick cast Vienna's Tilly Losch. A fatherly priest was played by British star C. Aubrey Smith. To direct this lot Selznick hired Polish-born Richard Boleslawski, who had worked as an actor-director for the Moscow Art Theater and served as a cavalry officer in the Polish army, fighting the Bolsheviks in 1919.

Selznick packed them all up – along with a menagerie of fifteen camels, thirty horses, and a variety of goats, sheep, and donkeys – and sent them to Yuma, Arizona, where the local topography resembled the drifting sands of the Sahara. Construction crews built the "ancient town" of Beni-Mora in less than twenty-four hours. Date palms were trucked in from Los Angeles and phone lines hurriedly strung to keep Selznick, who wisely chose to remain in Culver City, informed. For three weeks the cast lived in a tent city in the desert and battled the heat, sand, scorpions, and rattlesnakes. The thermometer boiled to 148 °F. Makeup melted and tempers erupted. Dietrich fainted twice during shooting. Boyer got nauseated on his first camel ride, and Selznick's three Technicolor cameras had to be stripped and cleaned of damaging sand daily.[132] When the crew returned to Culver City to finish shooting, Selznick trucked eighty tons of Arizona sand back to the studio to ensure authenticity. Why he failed to notice that the actors were cavorting in this sand in heavy British tweed is inexplicable.

The Garden of Allah emerged on the screen a Catholicized movie. The opening scene takes place at the Convent de St. Cecile, located "somewhere in Europe." The first shot of Dietrich has her bathed in candlelight in a small chapel, praying before a statue of the Blessed Virgin. She is observed by the children in the convent (including Dietrich's real-life daughter, Maria), who inquire as to her identity. "Why," a nun replies, "it is Domini Enfilden," who attended this school as a child and has devoted her life to her sickly father, who has just died. In the film Domini has returned to the convent, not out of a crisis of faith, but rather to seek advice from the Mother Superior (Lucille Watson) on what to do with her life. She is rich, beautiful, and confused. The Mother Superior advises Domini to leave Europe and find her future in the desert.

The film cuts to a Trappist monastery in Northern Africa, where "men have sworn eternal vows of chastity, poverty and silence." A French soldier, De Trevignac (Alan Marshall), is about to leave after recovering from battle wounds. He marvels at the monks' devotion, and their ability to live in silence. At his final meal with them he is served a special liqueur made at the monastery by Brother Antoine, the only monk who knows the secret formula. A monk sent to fetch him discovers that Brother Antoine has fled the monastery. As we discover, Brother Antoine is now Boris Androvsky.

Domini and Boris are both bound for the famous walled city of Beni-Mora, and arrive unknowingly on the same train. Domini is the house guest of Father Roubier (C. Aubrey Smith), a wise and kindly priest. Roubier assigns Batouch (Joseph Schildkraut), an English-speaking guide, to show Domini the local sites.

For reasons unknown, Batouch takes Domini to a local den of iniquity: an infamous cabaret where the beautiful Irena (Tilly Losch) performs a seductive dance before hundreds of leering Arabs. Other than the dancers, Domini is the only woman in this seedy establish-

Figure 12. Tilly Losch's dance of temptation for Charles Boyer in David O. Selznick's *The Garden of Allah*. Courtesy the Museum of Modern Art / Film Stills Archive.

ment. It is an atmosphere in which Dietrich would have been comfortable, but where Domini looks horribly out of place.

No matter: When Irena begins to dance, pandemonium ensues. She spots a lonely man sitting in the corner. It is Boris, dressed in a drab suit, clearly nervous and uncomfortable in this environment of sin. Irena rushes to dance for him, twisting and gyrating in front of the poor ex-monk, who is sweating profusely. Domini senses his embarrassment and asks Batouch to do something. Batouch explains that Irena wants money: A coin will send her on her way. When the befuddled Boris finally places a coin on Irena's forehead, she slithers away into the crowd of cheering men.

One could see this scene either as a repeat of the dance of temptation performed in DeMille's *The Sign of the Cross,* or as nothing more than the attempt of a dancer to get her coin. Poor Irena was forced to stay with Boris because the poor clod did not understand the rules. No matter what thoughts might have been running through Boris's mind as Irena danced, the message to the audience was only that she wanted money.

When a fight breaks out, Boris suddenly leaps into action. He dashes across the room and gallantly sweeps Domini to safety. The two, both confused and searching for meaning in life, immediately fall in love. The desert is turned into a romantic playground as the lovers frolic in the sand and take long rides at sunset, Domini strikingly beautiful, Boris properly handsome.

Yet there is something strangely suspicious about him: Whenever the subject of religion comes up, Boris reacts violently. When Father Roubier attempts to talk to him, Boris runs away. When some young women discover his crucifix, he throws it into a pond. When Domini professes interest in this brooding young man, the kindly Father Roubier suddenly erupts into a "voice of morality": "My first duty is to protect you. I warn you most solemnly not to make friends with this man." Domini is taken aback by this sudden outburst: "Forgive me if I disregard your warning, Father." Father Roubier is crushed: "Oh, the paganism of the East. It is the guiding spirit of the land. You have come to a land of fire and I think you are made of fire." Domini rushes off to see Boris.

Nothing can prevent the two lovers from marriage. Father Roubier reluctantly performs the ceremony, and the couple takes a huge caravan deep into the desert for their honeymoon. They wander from oasis to oasis, each setting more beautiful than the last, Domini always in hooded, flowing robes of silk and satin, Boris by day in tailored desert garb and by night in elegant white dinner jacket. They drink champagne and look into each other's eyes. When Boris does not return one evening, Domini climbs a nearby tower and waves a lighted torch for her lover. She is seen, not by Boris, but by a small contingent of French soldiers. "We are a lost patrol," De Trevignac tells Domini as he stumbles to her feet.

The arrival of De Trevignac marks the beginning of the end for Boris and Domini. The French soldier, having been at the monastery, recognizes Boris as the fugitive monk. The gallant Legionnaire refuses Domini's invitation to dinner and storms back into the desert in disgust. Domini is perplexed by this strange behavior. Soon after the departure of De Trevignac, the dashing Count Anteoni (Basil Rathbone), who had befriended Domini in Beni-Mora, rides into camp.

Anteoni has been told by De Trevignac that Boris is a monk, and now has come to expose him. At dinner the count begins to spin an incredible tale of a local monastery famous for its fine liqueur. Alas, he tells his hosts, the liqueur will be made no more because the only man who knew the secret formula has disappeared. This monk died? asks

Domini. No, says Anteoni, he ran away. After taking his final vows? she asks. Sadly, yes, says Anteoni. Domini is outraged. "How horrible! How could he do such a horrible thing?" Poor Boris is distraught: "Why not?" he asks. Boris, says Domini, a "man who has made the most sacred of marriages – a marriage to the church" – cannot forsake that vow. Count Anteoni goes for the kill. "This man who has gone out into the world. What can he expect to find after HIM?" Boris leaps to his defense. "Happiness, joy!" he shouts. Domini stares at Boris. Slowly her face changes to loathing for him as she realizes Boris is the missing monk.

However, this film is about faith and regeneration, not hate. The next day Boris tells Domini his life story. It is clear to both of them that Boris must return to his true calling. They go back to Beni-Mora. In the train station, as they prepare to part forever, Domini consoles Boris: "We are believers, Boris. Surely in that other world – we'll be together forever." Domini begs Boris to forget her. Boris cries out:

No, Domini, no! I will think of you always. Until the end of my life. I was born, perhaps, to serve God but I dare to believe that I was born, too, that I might know your beauty, your tenderness. Since I have been able to pray again, I have begged God, in his mercy, that I have loved you. For in knowing you, I have known him.

They take a carriage to the monastery. After Boris and Domini embrace, Boris marches up the long path to return to his life of chastity, poverty, and silence – and, of course, the production of fine liqueur. In the background a chorus rings out "Gloria, Gloria in Excelsis Deo." Domini breaks into hysterical sobs.

THE END

Breen loved it. He gushed to Selznick that it was "magnificent . . . handled so finely and with such utter delicacy of feeling as to make it a distinguished achievement and enormously creditable to our industry."[133] Dietrich hated it. She later commented that she had almost gagged over her lines. "Imagine," she complained, "having to say, as I did, 'Nobody but God and I know what is in my heart.' The conceit of it! I tell you I nearly died!"[134] She protested to the dialogue director that "this script – you know it – it is twash [trash]."[135] The temperamental star griped so much that Selznick ordered her to stop: "I am getting to the end of the rope of patience with criticism based on assumption that actors know more about scripts than I do," he told Boleslawski.[136]

While Breen and Selznick liked the script, Graham Greene, a Catholic, sided with Dietrich. He found the pontifications on morality overwhelming: "Alas! my poor Church, so picturesque, so noble, so superhumanly pious." Greene was somewhat mollified by the fact that Boris would distill the monastery liqueur. "The thought that this sweet and potent drink will be once again obtainable during licensed hours mitigates for us the agony of the parting."[137]

Other reviewers were split on the film. It was a "four-sided tug of war between God, the World, the Flesh and the Devil" wrote *Rob Wagner's Script*.[138] James Cunningham of the Catholic *Commonweal* praised the film for the "utmost respect and delicateness" of its portrayal of the "daringly unusual theme." The reviewer was upset, however, at the "sensuous dance" by Tilly Losch, which he speculated might make Minsky's "burlesque queens blush with shame." Mr. Cunningham must not have attended many burlesque shows: Tilly Losch performed the dance in a costume that covered her from head to toe. Although she did writhe, the camera centered on her hands; when she twirled, it focused on her legs from the knee down! Minsky's patrons would have tolerated no such modesty.[139]

Quigley sided with *Catholic World*. He was furious when Daly and the women of the IFCA rated *Garden of Allah* "Class A, Unobjectionable for Adults." He thought the film deserved a "C" because of the dance before the monk, which he viewed as one of temptation.

Disagreements within the Legion continued as Catholics debated issues of film morality. Father Daly, who fought with Quigley, was fired by Archbishop McNicholas and replaced as Executive Secretary of the National Legion by the Very Reverend John J. McClafferty in December 1936. However, this move had little impact on either Breen or the production of movies. Breen's battles were with the producers in Hollywood, not the priests in New York. The Papal Encyclical on movies, issued by Pope Pius XI in July 1936, blessed Breen and praised both his efforts and the Legion's for improving movie morality. The pope, under the guiding hand of Martin Quigley, wrote that "crime and vice are portrayed less frequently; sin no longer is so openly approved or acclaimed; false ideals of life no longer are presented in so flagrant a manner to the impressible minds of youth."[140]

Breen could, and did, point with satisfaction to the fact that no PCA-approved film made the Legion's condemned list for the rest of the decade. Only a few foreign and independent films – the most famous being the Czech *Ecstasy,* released in the United States in 1936, which featured a nude Hedy Lamarr – were given a "C" by the Legion. No films made by producers who subscribed to the Hays organization and submitted scripts to Breen were banned from Catholic view. As Breen told Hays, there was "a disposition" on the part of the studios "to accept the opinions and judgments of our office."[141]

In 1936 Breen's office reviewed over 1,200 scripts, had more than 1,400 conferences with producers, directors, and writers, saw 1,459 films (many several times), wrote over 6,000 opinions, and rejected twenty-two scripts from major studios; the latter were all rewritten to conform to PCA guidelines, and released with code approval. Similar figures obtained throughout the remainder of the decade. In 1939, for example, the PCA read 2,873 scripts, held 1,500 conferences with studio officials, wrote 5,184 letters of opinion, reviewed 1,511 films, and rejected early drafts of fifty-three scripts. PCA views prevailed in all cases.[142]

Censorship was simply good business. The studios recognized that when Breen approved a script they had fewer, and less costly, problems with state and local boards and with church groups. Breen took pains to call attention to the fact that box-office receipts began a substantial increase in 1935, for which he claimed responsibility. By 1938 business was booming. U.S. cinema attendance had soared to 83 million a week; worldwide, the weekly average was 220 million! Breen helped guide producers through the morass of international censorship by demanding adherence to his code of morality, and as long as business boomed, the industry was willing to comply. His dominance over screen morality was complete by 1938. The Catholic Legion had few complaints about films bearing the PCA seal.

Breen, however, was also determined to sterilize screen politics. Labeling films with ideas as propaganda, Breen and Hays pressured the studios to preach political conservatism as well as traditional morality.

Notes

1 Jack Vizzard, *See No Evil,* p. 29.
2 Ibid.
3 *Literary Digest* 118 (Oct. 27, 1934), p. 34; Anthony Slide, *Selected Film Criticism, 1931–1940,* p. 151.
4 Breen to Mayer, Mar. 29, 1934; Memo on MGM Conference, Aug. 11, 1934; Breen to Mayer, Sept. 25, 1934, *The Merry Widow,* PCA.
5 Quigley to Breen, Oct. 12, 1934, box D-205, PP; Memo by WWH (i.e., Hays), Nov. 1, 1934, box 47, HP.
6 Quigley to Breen, Oct. 12, 1934, box D-205, PP.
7 Memo by WWH, Nov. 1, 1934, box 47, HP.
8 Breen to Hays, Oct. 22, 1934, *The Merry Widow,* PCA.
9 Thalberg to Hays, Oct. 26, 1934, ibid.; Memo by WHH, Nov. 1, 1934, box 47, HP.
10 Quigley to Cardinal O'Connell, Dec. 19, 1934, QP.
11 Rev. Edward Roberts Moore to McNicholas, Dec. 27, 1934, NCCB-ECMP.
12 A. Scott Berg, *Goldwyn,* p. 235.
13 "Summary of Zola Novel," Mar. 1, 1932, *Nana,* PCA.
14 Ibid.

15 Otis Ferguson, "Stars and Garters," *New Republic* 80 (Oct. 24, 1934), p. 310.
16 Berg, *Goldwyn*, p. 238.
17 "Sam Goldwyn, Anna Sten and *Nana,*" *Harrison's Reports*, Feb. 10, 1934.
18 Breen to Warner, Feb. 2, 1937, *Life of Emile Zola,* PCA.
19 Berg, *Goldwyn,* p. 240.
20 James Curtis, *Between Flops: A Biography of Preston Sturges* (New York: Limelight, 1982), p. 95.
21 Berg, *Goldwyn,* p. 241.
22 Vincent Hart to Breen, Oct. 2, 1934, *We Live Again,* PCA.
23 Breen to Hays, Oct. 8, 1934, ibid.
24 *New York Times,* Nov. 2, 1934, p. 29.
25 *Harrison's Reports,* Oct. 20, 1934.
26 *Literary Digest,* Nov. 17, 1934, p. 35.
27 Wingate to Breen, Oct. 24, 1934, *We Live Again,* PCA.
28 *Time* 26 (Sept. 9, 1935), p. 46.
29 Raymond Moley, *The Hays Office*, p. 101.
30 Ibid.
31 Rudy Behlmer, ed., *Memo from David O. Selznick* (New York: Viking, 1972), p. 78.
32 Ibid.
33 PCA Annual Report 1934, Feb. 15, 1935, PCA.
34 Breen to Mayer, Sept. 25, 1934, *Anna Karenina,* PCA. See also Lea Jacobs, *The Wages of Sin,* pp. 116–31, for an analysis of Breen's role in constructing the film.
35 Behlmer, *Memo from David O. Selznick*, p. 79.
36 Ibid.
37 Ibid.
38 Breen to Mayer, Dec. 21, 1934, and Jan. 3, 1935, *Anna Karenina,* PCA.
39 Breen to Hays, Jan. 3, 1935, *Anna Karenina,* PCA.
40 Breen to Mayer, Mar. 5, 1935, *Anna Karenina,* PCA.
41 Selznick to Breen, Mar. 7, 1935, *Anna Karenina,* PCA.
42 Ibid.
43 Ibid.
44 Ibid.
45 Breen to Mayer, Mar. 12, 1935, and Breen to Hays, July 28, 1935, *Anna Karenina,* PCA.
46 John Devlin to Bishop Cantwell, Dec. 17, 1934, NCCB-ECMP.
47 Quigley to McNicholas, Jan. 5, 1935, NCCB-ECMP.
48 Gerald B. Donnelly to Parsons, n.d., box 1, PP.
49 Ibid.
50 Cantwell to Breen, Jan. 16, 1935; Quigley to McNicholas, Jan. 18, 1935, NCCB-ECMP; Breen to Quigley, Jan. 22, 1935, box 1, PP.
51 Breen to Quigley, Jan. 22, 1935, box 1, PP.
52 Quigley to Parsons, Mar. 3, 1935, box 1, PP.
53 Ibid.
54 Breen to Hays, PCA Annual Report 1935, Mar. 1, 1936, PCA.

55 Ibid.
56 Ibid.
57 *Harrison's Reports* (Sept. 7, 1935), p. 143.
58 *Nation* 141 (Oct. 2, 1935), p. 391.
59 *New York Times*, Aug. 31, 1935, p. 28.
60 John Russell Taylor, *The Pleasure Dome*, p. 26.
61 *Time* 26 (Sept. 9, 1935), p. 47.
62 Slide, *Selected Film Criticism, 1931–1940*, pp. 12–13.
63 *Our Sunday Visitor*, Oct. 11, 1935, p. 7.
64 Ibid.
65 Breen to Devlin, Nov. 15, 1935, box 57, AALA.
66 Breen to J. Miller (Exhibitors Association of Chicago), Nov. 15, 1935, box 57, AALA.
67 John Devlin, "The Motion Picture Industry and the Legion of Decency," Oct. 11, 1935, NCCB-ECMP.
68 Ibid.
69 Ibid.
70 *Harrison's Reports* (Mar. 16, 1935), p. 53.
71 Ibid.
72 Mrs. Ralph E. Oesper (Cincinnati Better Motion Picture Council) to Breen, Mar. 12, 1935, *Barbary Coast*, PCA.
73 Hays to Files, June 20, 1934, *Barbary Coast*, PCA.
74 Breen to Hays, Feb. 5, 1935, *Barbary Coast*, PCA.
75 Jeffrey Brown Martin, *Ben Hecht: Hollywood Screen Writer* (Ann Arbor: University of Michigan Press, 1985), p. 94.
76 Breen to Goldwyn, Aug. 27, 1934, *Barbary Coast*, PCA.
77 Breen to Goldwyn, Feb. 12, 1935, *Barbary Coast*, PCA.
78 Breen to Hays, Aug. 31, 1935, *Barbary Coast*, PCA.
79 William MacAdams, *Ben Hecht: The Man Behind the Legend* (New York: Scribner's, 1988), p. 178.
80 *Time* 26 (Oct. 21, 1935), p. 45.
81 *New York Times*, Oct. 14, 1935, p. 21.
82 *Scholastic* 27 (Nov. 2, 1935), p. 28.
83 *Harrison's Reports* (Oct. 19, 1935), p. 167.
84 *Canadian Magazine* 84 (Oct. 1935), p. 42.
85 *Newsweek* 6 (Oct. 19, 1935), p. 25.
86 Breen to Hays, Oct. 18, 1935, *Barbary Coast*, PCA.
87 Minutes of the Annual Meeting of the Bishops of the United States, 1919–1935, Nov. 13, 1935, pp. 9–14, NCCB-ECMP. These minutes were printed but not published.
88 Ibid.
89 Mary Harden Looram, "National Recognition for Our Motion Picture Bureau," *Quarterly Bulletin of the International Federation of Catholic Alumnae 5* (Mar. 1936), p. 15. See also McNicholas to Cardinal Hayes, Jan. 1, 1936, and McNicholas to Cicognani, Jan. 11, 1936, NCCB-ECMP, for details.
90 "Chicago Council Legion of Decency," no. 1 (Nov. 22, 1935), NCCB-ECMP.

91 Edward Moore to McNicholas, Jan. 18, 1936, NCCB-ECMP.
92 Ibid.
93 "National Legion of Decency," Feb. 1936, NCCB-ECMP.
94 Hays Memo to File, June 25, 1935, *Klondike Annie,* PCA.
95 Ibid.
96 Hays to Hammell, July 2, 1935, *Klondike Annie,* PCA.
97 Breen to Hammell, Sept. 3, 1935, *Klondike Annie,* PCA.
98 Breen to Hammell, Sept. 4, 1935, *Klondike Annie,* PCA.
99 Breen to Hammell, Dec. 31, 1935, *Klondike Annie,* PCA.
100 Los Angeles Examiner, Feb. 29, 1936. For an excellent summary of newspaper reaction see *Motion Picture Herald*, Mar. 7, 1936, p. 20; for Quigley, see Quigley to McNicholas, Mar. 19, 1936, NCCB-ECMP.
101 Mrs. Ernest A. O'Brien to Mrs. James F. Looram, April 7, 1936, NCCB-ECMP. O'Brien and Looram were officials in the IFCA. Luther was a strong supporter of the Chicago Legion of Decency and believed that it was a mistake to transfer the ratings of films to the IFCA in New York.
102 *Ave Maria* 43 (Mar. 28, 1936), p. 408.
103 McNicholas to Quigley, Mar. 12, 1936, NCCB-ECMP.
104 *Los Angeles Citizen,* Mar. 14, 1936 (in Mae West File, Academy of Motion Picture Arts and Sciences; hereafter AMPAS), and *Time* 27 (Mar. 9, 1936), p. 44.
105 *Motion Picture Herald,* Mar. 7, 1936, p. 20.
106 *New York Times,* Mar. 12, 1936, p. 27.
107 *Los Angeles Times,* Feb. 28, 1936, p. 25.
108 Taylor, *Pleasure Dome,* pp. 75–6.
109 *Harrison's Reports,* Mar. 14, 1936, p. 43.
110 *Los Angeles Citizen,* Mar. 14, 1936 (in Mae West File, AMPAS).
111 *Illinois Daily News,* Feb. 28, 1936 (in Mae West File, AMPAS).
112 *Los Angeles Citizen,* Mar. 4, 1936 (in Mae West File, AMPAS).
113 Ibid.
114 Father Al Dugan to West, n.d., QP.
115 Father Edward R. Moore to McNicholas, Mar. 6, 1936, NCCB-ECMP.
116 John Devlin to Daly, Mar. 4, 1936, NCCB-ECMP.
117 Quigley to McNicholas, April 13, 1936, NCCB-ECMP.
118 Devlin to Daly, Mar. 4, 1936, NCCB-ECMP.
119 Ibid.
120 Quigley to McNicholas, April 13, 1936, NCCB-ECMP.
121 Breen to Files, Feb. 10, 1936, *Klondike Annie,* PCA.
122 Breen to Cohen, Aug. 7, 1936, *Go West, Young Man,* PCA.
123 Taylor, *Pleasure Dome,* p. 124.
124 Cohen to Breen, Aug. 31, 1937, *Go West, Young Man,* PCA.
125 *Indianapolis Star,* Jan. 15, 1938 (in Mae West File, AMPAS).
126 *Catholic World* 141 (July 1935), p. 545.
127 See *Garden of Allah,* PCA.
128 Selznick to Breen, Fec. 28, 1935, *Garden of Allah,* PCA.
129 Jason Joy to Lord, Mar. 8, 1932, and Lord to Joy, n.d., *Garden of Allah,* PCA.
130 Edward S. Schwegler to Breen, Feb. 11, 1935, *Garden of Allah,* PCA.

131 Breen to Selznick, Feb. 18, 1935, *Garden of Allah*, PCA.

132 *Newsweek* 8 (Nov. 21, 1936), pp. 20–2.

133 Breen to Selznick, Oct. 9, 1936, *Garden of Allah*, PCA.

134 Quoted in Nash and Ross, *The Motion Picture Guide*, p. 976.

135 Quoted in Bob Thomas, *Selznick* (Garden City, N.Y.: Doubleday), p. 104.

136 Selznick to Boley (i.e., Boleslawski), April 28, 1936, in Behlmer, *Memo from David O. Selznick*, p. 102. See also David Thompson, *Showman: The Life of David O. Selznick* (New York: Knopf, 1992), pp. 206–7, 221–2.

137 Taylor, *Pleasure Dome*, p. 126.

138 In Slide, *Selected Film Criticism, 1930–1940*, p. 80.

139 *Catholic World* 144 (Nov. 27, 1936), p. 134.

140 *New York Times*, July 3, 1936, p. 8.

141 PCA Annual Report 1936, Feb. 15, 1937, PCA.

142 PCA Annual Report 1939, Feb. 15, 1940, PCA.

CHAPTER 8

FILM POLITICS AND INDUSTRY POLICY

Let a movie try to wake people up to their own plight and suggest a
way out, let a movie present a moral, economic or political problem,
and they are advised to hear nothing, say nothing, do nothing.
– Katharine Hepburn, October 28, 1938

Hollywood has traditionally been portrayed as a place that prefers
mindless entertainment over serious movies. The old adage, attributed
to MGM's Louis B. Mayer, that "If you want to send a message – send
a telegram," seemed to summarize Hollywood's attitude toward social and political films. However, movies dealing with social and political issues were common, if not commonplace. Periodically, studios
released movies like *Little Caesar, I Am a Fugitive from a Chain Gang,
Scarface,* or *Gabriel Over the White House,* which combined entertainment and social commentary. These movies made Will Hays and
Joe Breen nervous.

The 1930s offered almost endless subjects for the screen. Newspapers chronicled the cataclysmic events of the Depression: the Wall
Street crash, the millions of unemployed Americans, the resulting
breadlines and soup kitchens. Shanty towns, derisively named "Hoovervilles," dotted the American landscape. Americans followed with
fascination, or apprehension, such controversial figures as Louisiana
Governor Huey Long, with his "Share the Wealth" program; "radio
priest" Father Charles E. Coughlin, whose weekly broadcasts combined theology, politics, anti-Semitism, and economics were religious-
ly heard by millions; California's Francis E. Townsend, who promised
immediate prosperity with his precursor of Social Security; Upton Sinclair, who campaigned for the governorship of California with his
promise to End Poverty in California (EPIC); and William Dudley
Pelly and Gerald Winrod, native fascists from North Carolina and
Kansas, who aped Nazism with rabid preachments of anti-Semitism
and white supremacy. Meanwhile, in Washington, D.C., President
Franklin D. Roosevelt's New Deal tinkered with the economy through

244

a mixture of private enterprise and government intervention unheard of a generation earlier, searching for a formula that would wrench the nation out of its economic doldrums.

On the international scene, a surprising number of Americans admired Mussolini, exhibited a toleration of Hitler's Nazi Germany, and were either repelled by or attracted to Russian communism. The Spanish Civil War, the rise of Hitler in Germany, the domination of East Asia by Japan, and the dramatic events on the home front would appear to be the very stuff that would attract millions of Americans into their neighborhood theaters.

Yet each time a studio submitted a script with social or political implications, the code was invoked to tone down screen preachments. Chain-gang films made Jason Joy fidget. *Gabriel Over the White House* infuriated Will Hays. State and local censors were quick to take offense and label as "propaganda" any film that had an idea in it. Foreign censorship boards were especially sensitive to political commentaries and either snipped them out or banned the film. The overall result was that films with social messages emerged from the studios emasculated. Critics, meanwhile, chided the industry for its timidity in bringing hard-hitting drama to the screen.

This constraint of censorship hung over the studios throughout the decade. It was especially difficult to treat social and political themes with Hays and Breen determined to sanitize film politics. As of July 1934, studios that wished to make films with such content had to run the gauntlet of the emboldened Production Code Administration, which took an increasingly unfavorable view of "message" films.

When Breen assumed full control over the PCA he had two goals. One, as we have seen, was to force the studios to include in films dealing with moral issues a "voice of morality," which would be used to preach proper behavior and illustrate a moral lesson to the audience; every film would then make it clear that evil is wrong and good is right. A second goal was to use the code to force studios to limit social and political commentary. Although moral reformers were less concerned about this type of film, with the exception of gangster movies, Breen and Hays worried that films dealing with controversial topics would lead to increased censorship and a loss of market.

As a parallel to "compensating moral values," Breen coined the term "industry policy" for dealing with those films that, while technically within the moral confines of the code (e.g., *I Am a Fugitive from a Chain Gang* or *Gabriel Over the White House*), were adjudged "dangerous" to the well-being of the industry by Breen or Hays because they dealt with politically sensitive topics.[1]

The PCA, Breen wrote in a memo to his staff shortly after assuming power, would interpret the code as "a full mandate to enforce respect for all *law* and all *lawful* authority" in the movies. Breen reiterated Lord's contention that sympathy must not be directed toward the criminal, then went further: Nothing "subversive of the fundamental law of the land" could be shown in a movie, he wrote. This included portraying high government officials as "untrue to their trust without suffering the proper consequences," or depicting the judiciary or police in any way that might "undermine faith in justice." Anything that might be construed as overt criticism of the government, the free-enterprise system, or the police and courts was, Breen wrote, "Communistic propaganda" and was hereby "banned from the screen."[2]

Films were not vehicles for social and political criticism; rather, in Breen's view, they were opportunities to promote the "social spirit of patriotism." While he saw the movies as entertainment, he clearly recognized their educational potential. Promoting a conservative political agenda, Breen felt he had to protect audiences from Hollywood's "cynical contempt for conventions." He believed that movies must not present real-life situations in vividly realistic terms.[3] They were to adhere to accepted conservative moral standards and were not to challenge, attack, or embarrass the government; they were, in fact, to support the government.

This meant that, in addition to combing each new script for moral transgressions, Breen and his staff kept a sharp eye on the politics in scripts and invoked "industry policy" on those scripts that, in their view, questioned constituted authority, illustrated labor–management conflicts too vividly, or dealt too directly with controversial topics like racism, poverty, or unemployment. Rousing patriotic war films were approved; introspective antiwar films were discouraged. Labeling message films as "propaganda," Breen either urged studios to drop vehicles that fell into these categories, or worked to reconstruct them so they would prove inoffensive. Yet learning to be a censor was a difficult task: Although Breen seemed determined to eliminate political commentary from the movies, during his first year he experienced the same difficulties censoring political issues as he did in censoring moral ones. From the perspective of his critics, Breen was too liberal!

A decade or so after U.S. entry into World War I, millions of Americans were convinced that American participation in the "war to end all wars" had been a tragic blunder. Revisionist historians, journalists, and politicians argued that America had gone to war, not "to make the world safe for democracy," but to secure the repayment of war loans to American bankers and to increase the profits of munitions-makers. In March 1934, *Fortune* published "Arms and Men," an exposé of arms merchants that, once again, accused them of starting and prolonging wars in order to maximize profits.

The public had become so convinced of the truth of the theory –
dubbed "the devil theory of war" by historian Charles Beard – that the
Senate gave approval to Republican Senator Gerald Nye of North
Dakota to conduct a Senate investigation of the American "Merchants
of Death." The Nye Committee, as it was popularly known, opened
its hearings in September 1934. A parade of big businessmen and arms
agents poured into Washington, D.C., to testify. The hearing took on a
circus atmosphere when the three du Pont brothers, Irenee, Lammot,
and Pierre, and their seven lawyers, led by Col. William J. (Wild Bill)
Donovan, descended on Washington to answer questions about their
involvement in international arms. The du Ponts tried to downplay
their role as "arms merchants" but were embarrassed when testimony
disclosed that the company had agreements with European firms to
provide arms in specified areas of the world, had lobbied in Washington and Geneva to derail disarmament movements, paid bribes to Chinese Nationalist authorities to sweeten a du Pont contract, and had
signed a secret contract (later rescinded) to supply Nazi Germany with
arms.[4] Although the hearings produced more sensational headlines
than concrete evidence of international conspiracy, few Americans
disagreed with Senator Nye when he concluded that munition companies were "a discredit to American business" and proposed to nation-
alize arms manufacturing in the United States.[5]

Greedy, fat-cat capitalists conspiring for war were a natural for the
movies. In 1934 producer Walter Wanger, who had explored disarmament as a formula for world peace in *Gabriel,* formed his own production company and signed a contract with Paramount to produce
six films a year. Wanger, who valued his independence from studio
regulations, was, as an independent producer to the studio, free to
choose his own scripts and exercise full authority over their development and production. Fresh from his battles with Hays over *Gabriel,*
and convinced that munitions-makers were responsible for the American entry into World War I, Wanger selected the conspiracy theme of
munition-makers tricking America into war as a sequel to *Gabriel.*
The President Vanishes was a "bitter attack on . . . ruthless munitions
makers who are willing to sacrifice thousands of lives for the sake of
profit," said one critic.[6] The film infuriated Will Hays, and its production served as a stern lesson in the importance of censorship of ideas
for moralist Joe Breen.

Breen read the script for *The President Vanishes,* written by Lynn
Starling, Carey Wilson, and Cedric Worth, in September 1934, while
the Nye hearings were taking place. The script may have appeared to
Breen as truth based on historical fact. The setting for the film is con-
temporary America. In the opening scene President Stanley, played by
Arthur Byron, is informed that war has broken out in Europe. This

president, however, is determined to keep America from repeating the mistake of 1917, and vows to keep America neutral. However, drawing on the theme of the power of the "Merchants of Death," President Stanley is no match for a group of industrialists who are determined to force America into another bloody war for the sake of profit.

The script described the scions of American business who secretly plot against the president as Andrew Cullen (DeWitt Jennings), owner of Federal Steel of America, a man as "cold as the steel he manufactures"; Martin Drew (Walter Kingsford), America's most powerful banker; Roger Grant (Douglas Wood), a newspaper magnate who uses the press to create jingoistic rhetoric for war; and Richard Norton (Charles Grapewin), an oil tycoon admired for building public libraries who secretly plots to overthrow the government by funding a fascist organization of street thugs, the Grey Shirts. Working with these men is Judge Corcoran (Charles Richman), a retired federal judge who, as the most powerful lobbyist in Washington, sells to the highest bidder his ability to bribe congressmen and senators. *Newsweek* later reported the obvious: "Audiences noticed that certain characters resembled Andrew Mellon, John D. Rockefeller, and William Randolph Hearst."[7]

Early in the film the industrialists meet in a Washington hotel room to plot strategy. Cullen opens the meeting:

Munitions is my business. It's up to us to make it America's business. What good are steel and shells and shrapnel if there's nothing to shoot them at? There's a lot of sentimental talk about the last war. Ha! What did it really cost us? Four hundred thousand casualties. Nothing! It gave us the greatest period of prosperity any country ever had. . . .There is another war on in Europe and every minute that we delay getting in costs us millions.

The banker agrees. He has loaned millions to foreign governments: "If we do not get into the war we will never get our money back." Judge Corcoran assures the industrialists that Congress will vote for war despite the president's opposition. The newspaper publisher, Grant, muses. What we really need, he says, is a snappy slogan like "Remember the Maine" or "Make the World Safe for Democracy" that will capture the spirit of the nation and make it impossible for the President to prevent the nation from going to war. They decide the perfect slogan is SAVE AMERICA'S HONOR. In case anyone in the audience missed the point Wanger was trying to make, the scene ends as the men stub out their fat cigars in an ashtray, followed by a quick cut to vultures tearing apart their victims. It is clear that these men have no qualms about using people for cannon fodder if it will increase their profits. Under the guise of patriotism, they lust for another bloodletting.

A montage of newspaper headlines and radio programs that feature the patriotic appeal to honor quickly follow. The gullible public is easy prey for this appeal, and demands American entry into the war. The only opposition comes not from the Republicans or Democrats, but from the American Communist Party. In one of the more amazing scenes in Hollywood history, a young man is shown addressing a street crowd:

Fellow workers it is your blood – my blood – the workers' blood they are after. For what – so the capitalist bloodsuckers [*script calls for the crowd to boo*], yes, yes, so that the capitalist blood-suckers can grow richer. Tomorrow . . . Congress will say we must go to war to protect our honor. Only one thing can stop it – join the Communist party.

The audience is won over by the sincere speech and begins to cheer. As they do the Grey Shirts, led by Lincoln Lee (Edward Ellis) plunge into the crowd and beat the people and the speaker. The police are nowhere in sight.

The film then follows Lincoln Lee, who gives several hysterical Hitleresque speeches demanding that anyone who opposes war be thrown in jail or executed. The legitimate government is helpless to stop Lee's stormtroopers, who silence peace demonstrations. As the people demand war, freedom of speech is the first casualty. Only the American Communist Party urges workers not to be deluded into dying for capitalist profits.

The president views this hysterical demand to enter the war as pure folly, but he too is helpless to stop the national mania for war. As Congress is about to pass a declaration of war, the president, desperate to find a way to prevent it, arranges for his own kidnapping. Suddenly, and inexplicably, national attention is switched away from war to finding the president. During this interlude the conspirators begin bickering among themselves. Given time to come to their senses, the public changes its view, and the president emerges from hiding with this promise: "Not one American boy will be sent to foreign soil to leave his blood there as a security for loans." With the plot uncovered, the conspirators are arrested and democracy is restored.

Wanger envisioned an antiwar film that clearly would take advantage of the publicity generated by the Nye hearings and the general public perception that munition-makers and bankers had tricked Americans into World War I. As an antiwar film, *The President Vanishes* paled in comparison to *All Quiet on the Western Front* (1930). Breen had some concerns over the script, but, surprisingly, in spite of the anti–big business and corruption-in-government theme and the salute to the American Communist Party, he was convinced that, with a few minor changes, the film would conform to the code.[8]

In a series of meetings and letters he warned the producer not to characterize the vice-president as a "drunkard" or a tool of a "gluttonous group of capitalists." He also worried about Wanger's descriptions of the conspirators. From the standpoint of "industry policy," Breen wrote, "I . . . question the advisability of your designating the heavies" as representatives of American industry. "This characterization," Breen advised, "is likely to give the industry no end of trouble because it is certain to be resented quite forcefully." He suggested that Wanger could resolve the problem by making the heavies members of "a combination representing international munitions men with an international viewpoint." In his view, this would "cut down on the criticism." Still, Breen gave Wanger an option: "If you keep the men as they are then indicate they are not characteristic of their respective professions. It should be definitely brought out that the steel people in this country would not have a part in any such nefarious business."[9]

Perhaps Breen believed the conspiracy thesis of America's entry into World War I that was currently being played out in Washington. It certainly makes sense that he would have been influenced to some extent by the Nye hearings. For whatever reason, Breen approved Wanger's script with very few changes and, despite his aversion to Communism, let the "bloodsuckers speech" stand. Breen did, however, ask Hays to see the film. While he believed it did not violate the code, he conceded it might be "questionable" from an "industry policy" position. On his own authority, Breen issued a seal of approval for *The President Vanishes* in November 1934.[10]

When Hays saw the film in New York, several weeks after Breen approved the final cut, he was furious. Just as Wanger had precipitated a crisis with *Gabriel Over the White House,* so too did he with *The President Vanishes.* Once again projectors rolled into MPPDA headquarters. After Hays and his Board of Directors saw the film, Breen was ordered to withdraw the PCA seal of approval. In Hays's view the film was "communist propaganda, subversive in its portrait of American government, contrary to the accepted principles of established law and order, and perhaps treasonable." Hays specifically wanted the impassioned speech of the young communist removed. He ordered Breen to renew negotiations with Wanger and arranged an emergency meeting with the Board of Trustees and Paramount's President Adolph Zukor in New York.[11]

Hays made his position clear to Breen. First he established who was in charge. He told Breen he was to act "as programmed"; that is, he would tell Wanger what had to be done to the film. He was not to negotiate with the producer, but specify the exact nature of the changes required. If the changes were made, Breen was to tell Wanger he would consider reissuing the PCA seal, but that this was not to be considered guaranteed even if all the offending material were removed. Hays wanted Wanger to sweat, and he wanted to deliver another message to Hollywood: It was Hays and Breen who had final-cut authority in Hollywood, not the directors, producers, or studio moguls. To reinforce that message, Hays ordered Adolph Zukor to withdraw the film until the required changes were made.[12] Zukor meekly complied.

The President Vanishes contained no moral issues, but Hays believed it was within the purview of the code to keep "dangerous" films off the screen:

The screen has no right, as a vast popular entertainment medium which must not only reflect correctly our own institutions to our own people but American institutions to the peoples of the world, to present a distorted picture which condemns the banking industry, the oil industry, the steel industry and the newspaper industry per se as warmongers, which presents the Communist Party as the leading protagonist ... and which indicated such banality and corruption in our government and political machinery, that even the Secret Service of the nation cannot be trusted to protect the President of the United States.[13]

Hays, who was often accused of never going to the movies, saw The President Vanishes in his office several times. He thoroughly disliked the film and insisted that no amount of editing could eliminate all of his objections. Yet he was in a difficult position: Breen had given Wanger a seal, and the producer was threatening legal action if the film were to be withdrawn. If Hays feared anything, it was a lawsuit that would expose the system of control the MPPDA enforced. Although Hays and Breen cited "morality" as the driving force behind industry censorship, Wanger could prove that the censors were determined to control more than just that. It would have been most embarrassing, at the height of the Nye hearings, to have the industry explain why it was opposed to a fictional film dealing with corrupt and unethical businessmen seeking to involve the nation in a foreign war. Hays therefore agreed to allow the film to play if the "communist bloodsuckers" speech were removed and if several other cuts were made to tone down the film. When Wanger agreed, Hays conceded the film could be released.

Wanger, however, was determined to challenge the authority of Breen, Hays, and the code. During an interview about the controversy, he told reporters that in his opinion "Hays ought to take over the censorship of the comic strips." The producer secretly plotted to embarrass the movie czar. Instead of making the changes, Wanger released a print of the film to Pennsylvania, which had a reputation as one of the most conservative of the state censorship boards, with the "bloodsuckers" speech intact, hoping that the state would pass it. If it passed in Pennsylvania, Hays would look like a fool for objecting. Wanger's plot backfired when the sensitive political antennas of the Pennsylvania censors locked onto the communist plea. When they demanded the offending scene be removed, the Hays Office discovered the subterfuge. Hays was enraged when the studio admitted the film had been released with "the knowledge" of Paramount officials in Hollywood. Zukor, subjected to another lecture by Hays, gave his personal assurance that only the "approved" prints would be distributed.[14]

Reviews were mixed. *The President Vanishes* "is rather terrifying when one considers how helpless one is against wealthy and brutal forces," said *Harrison's Reports*.[15] The *North American Review* noted the message that big business could manipulate America into war was a "distinctly new departure" for Hollywood, but snickered that the industry solved the crisis by having the president run away.[16] The *New York Times* told readers the film was a "racy and biting melodrama which assaults the war-makers with picturesque violence."[17]

Hays was relieved when the public ignored the film. *The President Vanishes,* with its antiwar, anti–big business theme, represented the type of movie Hays did not want the industry to make. He was determined to be as restrictive with films dealing with social and political issues as he was with those that seemed to challenge traditional moral codes. He made that clear to Breen, who learned a lesson he did not soon forget: It was better to be too strict than too lenient. The studios also were clearly informed that to delve too deeply into issues was to invite costly editorial corrections from the Hays Office. If profits drove Hollywood, it was becoming increasingly clear that it was more profitable to avoid political issues.

The message to avoid sociopolitical themes was delivered even more forcefully to Warner Bros. when they submitted their script *Black Fury,* which dealt with labor problems in the coal industry – an industry that offered ample opportunity for dramatic illustration. The United Mine Workers, led by the controversial John L. Lewis, fought for the basic rights of human dignity in one of the most conservative industries in America. Violence, poverty, and despair were the common denominators of the coal towns of America. While it was recognized that miners worked in almost insufferable conditions, a movie on America's coal industry would have to be placed within the strict constraints set by the PCA.

The script was based on a real incident: the murder of a coal miner by private police in Imperial, Pennsylvania, in 1929. After retiring from the bench, Judge M. A. Musmanno wrote a story about the incident, and Harry R. Irving wrote a play centered around the miserable living conditions of the miners and the murder. Warner Bros. bought both properties and assigned screenwriters Abem Finkel and Carl Erickson to adapt them into *Black Fury*. The studio cast Paul Muni as Joe Radek, a hard-working miner who leads the strikers. Muni, after starring performances in *I Am a Fugitive from a Chain Gang* and *Scarface*, prepared for his role by going to the Pennsylvania coalfields, where he lived and worked with miners for several weeks. Muni's presence in Pennsylvania generated rumors that the film would be a hard-hitting depiction of life in the mines. The National Coal Association was quick to respond: Its spokesman, J. D. Battle, protested to Will Hays that Warners' film had been described to him as "very unfavorable" to coal and "calculated to do a lot of harm if shown." Predictably, Hays assured Battle that the industry would not produce an anticoal film and promised to take up his concerns with Jack Warner. Hays alerted Breen to be prepared when the script came in from the studio.[18]

Breen needed little prodding to be sensitive to the coal-mining industry. Before his involvement with the movies, he had been public relations director for the Illinois Peabody Coal Corporation. In 1929 Peabody's mines had been the scene of violent labor disputes that Breen labeled "a Communist undertaking."[19] "I sure did have my eyes open to the enormity of their [communists] doings," Breen told Father Wilfrid Parsons of *America,* for whom he wrote a series of articles on the subversive nature of communism in America.[20]

When the script arrived at the PCA office in September 1934, Breen and his staff found it disturbing. *Black Fury* contained no moral violations of the code but did raise controversial political issues. As the head of the National Coal Association had feared, the script blamed the miserable working conditions on the mine owner, who kept his workers in a state of modern industrial servitude. The workers finally rebelled with a long and bitter strike. The script then called for a traditional mine-owner response: "Scabs" are hired, and the workers are intimidated by a private police force. The private police rule with terror, beating miners at will, with the approval of the owners. This all made Joe Breen very nervous.

In a long and detailed evaluation of the script, Breen warned studio head Jack Warner of the potential dangers of *Black Fury*. He reminded the producer that there was a great deal of "industrial unrest" in the nation, and urged him to move the blame away from "legitimate labor leaders" and employers and onto the private detectives "who are the crooked agitators." This strategy, according to Breen, would keep the story free from any reasonable criticism.[21]

Rather than simply censor a film, Breen often worked with the studios to eliminate the controversial material while keeping the same general story. Such collaborations prevented the studios from losing money on their investments and allowed Breen and Hays to keep tight control over film content. *Black Fury* was a case in point. Breen told Jack Warner the film could be made if the studio would change the script from a serious critique of working conditions in the coal industry and a depiction of class struggle, to a film that presented a concerned and humane mine owner, working with a legitimate union of well-treated workers, all of whom are tricked into an unwanted and unnecessary strike by outside labor agitators. It was a stroke of creative genius. Warner, who had encountered his own labor problems, was receptive to the image of the kindly owner tricked into a costly strike.[22]

Citing "industry policy," Breen told Warner that although the script did not specifically violate the code, he considered it dangerous to the general well-being of the film industry. Breen requested changes that would make the film a tribute to both management and labor. First, he asked that several lines of dialogue be added to indicate to the audience that conditions in mining, while not perfect, were constantly improving. "The point here," Breen wrote, "is to get a line that may establish the fact that the miners have little to complain about, and that [the labor agitator] is unjust in his criticism of the employing company." Breen also asked Warner to have the head of the legitimate union stress to union members (and the audience) that the recent improvements in working conditions were "reasonable . . . and acceptable to organized labor." Have him state plainly, Breen told Warner, that "if the miners . . . go on strike the company will be justified in invalidating [the contract] and employing other workers to do the work."[23] If this were done, Breen hoped the audience would conclude that the owner was concerned about working conditions and committed to working with the legitimate union to achieve labor harmony.

Breen stressed to Warner how important it was that the president of the company not be presented on the screen as antilabor. It should be made to appear, he told Warner, that the president is forced to hire strikebreakers "very much against his will." The point for Breen was that the owner does not hire "scabs" because he is trying to break the union, but because workers have walked out on a legitimate and binding contract; thus, the owner has no choice.

Restructuring the private police force was a little trickier: They were needed for dramatic purposes and were the "heavies." What Breen wanted was for the film to state clearly that the owner was hiring a private police force to protect his property, not to terrorize his men. As Breen stated: "From a general policy standpoint, it will be a serious mistake, in our judgment, if we definitely show the employing company as countenancing, or approving, the brutal treatment" of the workers. "It should be established," he told Warner, that "this treatment is the responsibility [of] Jenkins and McGee [the industrial detectives] and not the employing company."[24] This was in direct contrast to the original script, but could be accomplished with the simple insertion of a few lines of dialogue suggested by Breen. These would establish for the audience that although the owners hire the special forces, all police violence against the workers is instigated without their approval.

Warners was more than willing to cooperate with Breen. Their experience with *Madame du Barry* had convinced the studio that cooperation was good business. Breen was able to inform Hays that Warners producer Hall Wallis, who had previously battled Breen over every cut, "will follow exactly our recommendations." Breen assured Hays that neither he nor the coal industry need have "the slightest cause for concern." In the revised script, Breen told Hays, "the employing companies and the coal industry . . . are not playing the heavies. They are rather, the victims, as are the men [workers] of the dishonest intrigue of the racketeers." Hays was delighted with the news and congratulated Breen on the rewriting of *Black Fury,* which was done "in exactly the proper way." Hays had also been in contact with Jack Warner, and assured Breen that the studio boss was "in complete sympathy with the purposes."[25] Breen issued seal number 579 to *Black Fury.*

What did American audiences see when they went to the theater in the winter of 1935 to view the explosive *Black Fury,* which starred Paul Muni as the temperamental Joe Radek, Karen Moley as his girlfriend Anna, Barton MacLane as the evil cop McGee, and John Qualen as Radek's pal Mike Shemanski? The Coaltown of the film is a community of neat little homes with picket fences, nice porches, and well-stocked kitchens. The workers and their families, although obviously poor, are well clothed and fed. Their life-style appears to be hard, but pleasant enough. They go off to work each day smiling, joking, and singing.

The mine in which the workers work is no dark, dank, coal-dust-laden mine. It is well lighted, clean, and apparently safe, with shafts at least ten feet high. As the men break for lunch early in the film, all appears calm. These miners are a happy-go-lucky lot, especially Radek, who boasts, "Joe Radek like everybody and everyone like Joe Radek." His work ethic is simple: "Work like a mule" and don't complain. At this point in the film Radek is totally uninterested in the union and is unaware of any problems the workers might have. He has saved enough money to make a down payment on a farm and is about to ask his girl, Anna, to marry him. By implication, any hard-working, thrifty miner could do the same.

As the workers leisurely eat their lunch, a miner named Cronin (J. Carroll Naish) suddenly begins to gripe about working conditions. The conditions here are the worst in the industry, he shouts. But his fellow workers disagree. The union steward, Mike (John Qualen), defends conditions: "That's big talk, Cronin, but things ain't as bad as they used to be and they are getting better all the time." When the two men start to fight, Radek breaks it up – just work and don't worry, is his advice. The audience is soon told that Cronin is not a real miner, but a plant from Industrial Detective Agency, a sleazy organization that feeds off labor unrest. His job is to stir up trouble. It is clear to the audience very early in the film that there are no legitimate complaints in this coal town.

It is Joe Radek who becomes Cronin's unlikely stooge. At a dance on Saturday night, Radek asks Anna to marry him; but Anna, unbeknownst to Joe, hates Coaltown and longs to escape its drudgery. In panic at the prospect of living her life like her mother, she runs off with Slim, a company cop, to Pittsburgh. When Joe discovers that he has been jilted, he gets stinking drunk.

Meanwhile, Cronin has stirred up enough trouble to bring the official union, the Federated Mine Workers, to Coaltown. There is a big meeting of all the miners to decide whether or not the men will go out on strike despite the fact that they are working under a legitimate contract. The union boss, Johnny Farrell (Joe Crehan), makes an appeal to them: The union is in trouble, he says, because some wise guys are stirring things up. Sure, he admits, we have plenty to kick about, but "remember half a loaf is better than none. We think conditions are getting better." He continues with a short history of the struggle the union had in achieving the current contract – the Shalerville Agreement. He reminds the workers they gave the company their word there would be no strike during the terms of the contract. In the event of a strike "they'll throw us out and they will be right 'cause we broke our word." (Breen must have smiled with some satisfaction when the union boss admitted that any strike would be illegal.)

The meeting turns into pure chaos, with the men arguing and fighting among themselves. Cronin shouts Farrell down and claims the union bosses are corrupt. The miners are almost evenly split on whether to work or strike. Suddenly Radek stumbles into the meeting drunk. Cronin manages to push Radek forward as a strike leader, and because he is so popular with the men, the vote for a strike carries the day. Cronin slinks out and reports back to his boss that he has split the union. He hightails it out of town.

When Radek sobers up he finds himself in charge of a strike about which he knows nothing. The miners are shut out of the mine and are soon dispossessed from their homes. The company president, John

Hendricks (Henry O'Neill), says the workers have given him no choice by striking: He must hire replacement workers because of his obligation to the stockholders, and he must protect his property. Reluctantly he hires the private detectives. (This accomplished Breen's goal of deflecting blame for the violence that was about to occur in the film.) When one of them mentions to him that "hunkies" have respect for police on horseback, Hendricks reacts sharply: "Now wait a minute. You are hired to protect my property. You'll be held responsible for any damage." Hendricks adds that he does not want any violence toward the strikers.

Nevertheless, the cops rule the town with terror, beating up strikers at every opportunity. Joe is completely helpless and begins drinking heavily. The men lose their respect for him, and it is clear that the strike is going to fail. His best friend Mike will no longer speak to him. The situation comes to a head when Mike gets into a fight with the cops and is killed. Joe tries to defend him but is beaten senseless and sent to the hospital. Seemingly the movie has no place to go, but suddenly a crestfallen Anna returns to town and inspires Joe to make one last attempt to win the day.

The only thing that Joe can think of is to stage a one-man sit-in. He steals explosives and sneaks into the mine. He wires all the mine shafts and threatens to blow up the entire mine if the company refuses to settle the strike. When the cops try to break in, Joe blows up one of the shafts. This brings national press to Coaltown, and just as suddenly the audience is told that Washington is investigating the cause of the job action. A sudden cut to Washington: The government has uncovered the fact that "criminal parasites" are behind the strike. Joe emerges from the mine a national hero, the detective agency is exposed as the culprit, and the cop who killed Mike is arrested for murder. The strike is over, and life in Coaltown presumably returns to normal. Joe has won, the company has won, the union has won – and, most of all, the PCA has won.

Yet even this bowdlerized version of life in the coalfields was too powerful for state censors in Ohio, New York, and Pennsylvania, all of which banned the film. At the Warner studio Hal Wallis was incredulous: He had cooperated conscientiously with Breen, and the result was a ban by three of the most important states in the domestic market. Hays and Breen also were shocked. Once again, the actions of a state board threatened to undercut their positions with the studios. The Hays Office swung into action to induce the state censorship boards to reverse their decisions.

It was the character of Joe Radek that the states found objectionable. They claimed that the movie had Joe take the law into his own hands by breaking into a company storeroom to steal explosives that he then used to blow up company property. When he emerges from the mine, he is not arrested, but given a hero's welcome. Incredibly, the three censorship boards claimed that this was a clear violation of the Hollywood code because it threw audience sympathy toward a criminal! Breen was being given another lesson in the internal workings of a censor's mind.

Breen assigned Dr. Wingate the task of convincing each of the censorship boards that *Black Fury* was, after his rewriting of the script, a film that supported management and labor. Breen's position was that while, technically, Joe does commit a criminal act, it was "not the act of a criminal." Rather, Joe should be seen as a "stupid fellow gone temporarily mad because of high emotionalism." Breen was convinced that the audience would understand that Joe was not a criminal intent on stealing or destroying property: They would sympathize with him but not with the crime.[26]

Breen was no fool, however. He knew, perhaps better than anyone in Hollywood, the reality of life in the mines. He told Wingate to impress on the censorship boards that there was nothing "immoral, dirty or vulgar" in the film and that the film came nowhere near portraying the reality of a strike in the coalfields. Breen stressed to Wingate that "despite the fact that the . . . miners are evicted from their homes, beaten, and clubbed by the special police," they do not resort to violence. "In ordinary life, there would be a thousand miners doing what Joe does, in order to protect themselves from the brutalizing force of the special police."[27] Breen was furious that the censors would object to such a mild version of a coal strike, and told Wingate to impress upon the local boards the work the PCA was doing in restructuring films to soften their criticism of social and economic conditions during a time of economic crisis.

Wingate hit the road with Breen's message and was successful in opening each state to *Black Fury*. Ohio still demanded that several scenes be clipped, but New York and Pennsylvania passed the film without further cuts. There were no reported revolts in the coalfields of those states by miners inspired by the antics of Paul Muni/Joe Radek. In fact, *Black Fury* was a box-office flop.

Most reviewers panned the film for its failure to deal honestly with the reality of the mining industry. The *Literary Digest* accused Warners of "oversimplification." The *New York Times* branded the film "a handsome defense of the status quo." The *Nation* titled its review "Half a Loaf," and wondered why the studio had to resort to so many "subterfuges" to tell the story. *Theater Arts Monthly* called *Black Fury* "pretty silly, no matter how urgently you believe that miners are badly treated in this unfair world."[28] Film historian Lewis Jacobs objected to the film because it "portrayed [the strike] as a shameless

Figure 13. Paul Muni threatens to blow up the mine in *Black Fury.* Courtesy the Museum of Modern Art / Film Stills Archive.

revolt of workers inspired by outside gangsters. There was little indication of the workers' privations during a strike and the workers' grievances themselves were stated by men obviously supposed to be villains."[29]

Otis Ferguson, writing in the *New Republic,* was more forgiving. He recognized the flaws in the film – that it glossed over the real problems of miners – but still viewed it as "the most powerful strike picture" made in Hollywood. Ferguson praised the film as "great" because the mood of the film illustrated the humiliation of the workers, a life filled with evictions and beatings that created an atmosphere of violence "that shrieks along a man's nerves and settles in his stomach."[30] Ferguson believed that director Michael Curtiz visually illustrated the misery, the dirt, and the desperation of the miners without detailing what happened to them when they were thrown out of their homes or out of work. Perhaps Ferguson saw what UAW president John L. Lewis saw when he praised *Black Fury* for making "a great contribution" to the plight of mine workers.

To Lewis the screen image of dignified, hard-working, honest people who believe in the American dream was the real message of *Black Fury.* All Radek ever wanted was a wife and a farm. In the film the workers of Coaltown were as conservative as the members of the National Coal Association. Yet it is impossible to look at *Black Fury,* even today, without seeing the poverty and desperation of the miners. While the film did not dwell on it, it is clear that the people were living in a company town and in company houses. When they went out on strike, they were dispossessed. Audiences in 1935 did not need long speeches by screen characters to understand what that meant to a family. True, *Black Fury* put a halo on the owner of the mine that most likely was not deserved, but the film also portrayed the miners as honest, God-fearing, hard-working men who wanted nothing more than a fair wage. They were not, as many people viewed union workers, hysterical, bomb-throwing radicals demanding an overthrow of the system. When John L. Lewis saw the miners depicted as honest and hard working, he endorsed the film. When the members of the National Coal Association saw the owner depicted as an honest, sincere man who cared for his men, they endorsed *Black Fury.*

When Joe Breen saw the film he knew that the reality of the coalfields was much worse than that on the screen; to him, *Black Fury* hinted at problems but stated loud and clear that solutions and progress lay within the status quo:

The whole moral of the drama points to the folly of strife, to the desirability of peace, to the interdependence of capital and labor, and to the need of law and order. Intelligent capitalistic management and union labor are fairly presented; communistic agitation is not countenanced; and the government itself has a welcome hand in settling the trouble.[31]

Black Fury was the model for films dealing with controversial issues: business, labor, and government always worked hand in hand for the people.

Creative restructuring had managed to turn *Black Fury* into a confirmation of the status quo. However, when MGM proposed filming Sinclair Lewis's novel *It Can't Happen Here,* which depicted the rise of a fascist dictatorship controlled by a union of government and business that brutalized the people, Hays and Breen knew that it would take more than a few simple changes in dialogue to turn the film into a testimonial for big government.

Lewis began writing *It Can't Happen Here* in May 1935. By December it was in the bookstores and a runaway best-seller. The impetus for the book seems to have come from long political discussions with his wife, Dorothy Thompson, a journalist and political activist whose unflattering remarks about Hitler had gotten her banned from Germany, plus Lewis's own dismay over the political climate in the United States. Lewis, at least in 1935, considered himself a New Deal liberal and was horrified by the national popularity of such demagogues as Huey Long, Father Coughlin, Gerald L. K. Smith, and the undisguised fascism advocated by groups like the Ku Klux Klan. Convinced that America was ripe for a fascist takeover, Lewis wrote *It Can't Happen Here* with the implicit warning that in his opinion it very easily could.

The plot was simple enough. The hero of the story is Doremus Jessup, a liberal small-town Vermont newspaper editor, who watches America degenerate into a fascist state. The villain is Senator Berzelius Windrip, a demagogic politician who wins election to the presidency by appealing to the fears of the populace. Once in office Windrip declares a state of martial law. His private army, the Minute Men, enforce his iron rule through terror. He forms an alliance with big business, the Corpo State, which then puts intellectuals and radicals into concentration camps. Anti-Semitism is adopted as a national policy, and African Americans are returned to a state of servitude. In this climate of repression, big business flourishes. By the end of the book fascism is entrenched in America. Jessup moves to Minnesota, where an incipient counterrevolutionary movement is being organized, but Lewis provides no Hollywood "happy ending"; instead, the novel ends with the Corpo State still in power, and readers are left to draw their own conclusion about the future of American democracy.

Public reaction was stunning. The book sold more than 300,000 copies and, while some critics panned it, most reviews were favorable. Adapted for the stage in October 1936 by Hallie Flanagan, director of the Federal Theater Project, Lewis's message reached an even wider audience. In her efforts to create a national theater, Flanagan coordinated a simultaneous opening of a stage version of *It Can't Happen Here* in thirteen cities across the nation. The play was a smashing success. Touring companies presented hundreds of performances across the nation, and by the end of the run more than 275,000 people, many attending a theatrical production for the first time, had seen the stage version.[32] By the end of the decade Charles and Mary Beard wrote: "In all the years of the depression and turmoil, no novel written in the United States portrayed more dynamically the ideals of democracy pitted against the tyranny of the demagogic dictator."[33]

Any reasonably accurate film based on the book would condemn authoritarian rule and was certain to be banned in Germany, Italy, and Spain. Lewis's portrait of an America dominated by greedy businessmen, governed by corrupt politicians, held hostage by religious frauds, victimized by petty hatreds and eager supporters of a superpatriot, was certain to run afoul of municipal and state censorship boards. The film would be labeled "propaganda" and heavily censored if not banned. Breen and Hays understood this and were determined either to keep *It Can't Happen Here* off the screen, or to so gut its message that it would be a box-office failure.

Had Louis B. Mayer read the book, which he had not, he surely would have found it offensive. But business is business: *It Can't Happen Here* was a hot property, and MGM paid Lewis $50,000 for the rights to the book, announced with some fanfare that Lionel Barrymore would play Doremus Jessup, and assigned Sidney Howard to adapt the screenplay. Hays and Breen shuddered at the thought.

In drafting the script, Howard was careful to expunge material that would obviously raise the Breen's hackles. He eliminated Lewis's references to the homosexuality of the Minute Men, and cut the "illicit sex affair" between Jessup and an advocate of women's liberation, Torinda Pike, which took up much of the book. Yet he kept intact the central image of the book: a dictatorship that maintained its power through violence.

When Breen saw an incomplete draft of the Howard script in December 1935, he immediately informed Hays that although the script contained no direct violations of the code, he was "gravely concerned" over the "likely reaction" by some foreign governments. Should the industry make a film, he asked Hays, that is "hardly more than . . . the Hitlerization" of the United States? Based on the script and his reading of the novel, Breen told Hays that the film, if made, would be banned in Great Britain and France, whereas Germany and Italy would probably ban all MGM productions.[34] Breen then informed Mayer of the potential problems with the script and raised the question of whether or not it was in the best interests of the industry "to sponsor a picture of this nature."[35]

By January Howard had completed a draft and shipped it off to the censors. Breen was appalled by what he read and fired back a nine-page missive to Mayer listing objections to the script. He admitted that all moral problems had been eliminated, but he found the script remained "so inflammatory in nature, and so filled with dangerous material, that only the greatest possible care will save it from being rejected on all sides." If MGM was going to make this film, Breen demanded that the fascist salute of the Minute Men not resemble in any way that of Germany's Brown Shirts. Nor could the film suggest that the American government had abolished the Supreme Court or show an American government killing defenseless people. All scenes showing violence and rioting had to be cut or kept to a minimum. Making this film, Breen warned Mayer, will cause you "enormous difficulty."[36]

Mayer was stunned by the vehemence of Breen's reaction. MGM had cut the sex from the book, and now Breen was gutting it. Quietly the studio asked their foreign representatives for their opinion on whether or not the film could play abroad. It was expected that Germany and Italy would ban the film; the killer blow came when the MGM London representative informed the studio that he would have "extreme difficulty" getting any version of *It Can't Happen Here* past British censors.[37] Mayer informed Lewis on February 16, 1936, that the studio was dropping *It Can't Happen Here* from the production schedule.

The announcement touched off a furor of reaction. In New York Lewis called the suppression of the film "a fantastic exhibition of folly and cowardice." He blamed Hays. "Is the American public," he asked, "to be delivered over to a film industry whose every step must be governed by whether or not the film will please or displease some foreign power?" He added, "I wrote 'It Can't Happen,' but I am beginning to think it certainly can."[38]

MGM remained silent, and Hays glibly countered that "no Association action was taken to prohibit this picture."[39] Quigley's *Motion Picture Herald* cheered the decision to stop production. The *New Republic* told readers that it can't happen here but it can happen in Hollywood.[40] Surprisingly, from St. Louis, Father Lord's *Queen's Work* sided with Lewis: "You feel that you are reading less a fictional prophecy than a ghastly history of things that have happened to America."[41] The *Queen's Work* praised the book and urged Catholics to read it. A filmed version would not have offended Father Lord; but because it would have offended Hitler and Mussolini, and was deemed "dangerous" by the British, Americans never saw a film of *It Can't Happen Here*. The studio made several attempts to resurrect the project throughout the rest of the decade. Sidney Howard wrote three different scripts, but a note in the MGM files stated that "no attempt should be made to revive this without first consulting Mr. Mayer."[42]

Ironically, twenty years later Will Hays used the example of *It Can't Happen Here* in his memoirs to illustrate the freedom of the American screen. "While the Germans were ousting [the novel] *It Can't Happen Here*, and the French were claiming the right to exclude any films they wished on political grounds; ... our people exercised their humor and good sense by welcoming pictures of every sort for whatever they were worth." The people did; it's sad that Will Hays did not.[43]

The history of *It Can't Happen Here* was the exception. Breen was not employed to keep movies off the screen, but to make sure that those that reached the screen fit, both morally and ideologically, within the cozy confines of the code. It was increasingly clear that in Hollywood the process of bringing a property to the screen included making certain that each script was approved by Breen and Hays before any cameras were allowed to roll.

The tight control of ideas in Hollywood was played out time and time again. In the 1930s the United States attracted scores of European artists and intellectuals fleeing the repression of Nazi Germany. Among them was German film director Fritz Lang, whose reputation for filmmaking excellence was established by his futuristic *Metropolis* (1927) and chilling *M* (1931), the tale of a psychotic child-murderer, played by Peter Lorre. As Lang liked to say, he was "the most famous director in Europe."[44] He daringly put some anti-Nazi material in *The Testament of Dr. Mabuse* (*Das Testament des Dr. Mabuse*), which was promptly banned by Hitler. Minister of Propaganda Josef Goebbels summoned Lang to his office to discuss the film and, instead of berating the director, offered him the job of heading the German film industry. Lang was polite, but fled to Paris that evening.

Lang eventually came to Hollywood under a personal contract to David O. Selznick, who was an executive producer at MGM. It was ironic that Lang should come to MGM because Irving Thalberg, although an admirer of *M*, admitted he would not have allowed the film to be produced at the studio.[45] One can only wonder what Breen's reaction would have been!

In a typical display of studio efficiency, Lang's first year on the MGM payroll was spent searching for a project. After surveying the American landscape and, perhaps, reacting to the similarities of mob violence and racial prejudice that he had escaped in Europe, Lang picked the quaint American custom of lynching as the topic for his first American film.

It was a topic very much in the news in the 1930s: Ninety-two lynchings were reported in the United States during the first half of the decade; only ten of the victims were white. American lynchings were committed by white mobs – few of whose members ever stood trial – and the victims were usually black. Lynchings mostly occurred in the South and West but were not exclusive to those regions. The NAACP lobbied Congress to make lynching a federal crime but, although lawmakers introduced some one hundred antilynching bills in the second half of the decade, none was passed. Any film that dealt with lynching was going to be controversial: Could a film honestly portray U.S. race relations? Would such a film find an audience in a nation dedicated to maintaining racial segregation? Could a film honestly portray a Southern mob stringing up a black man accused of raping a white woman? Would such a film find an audience anywhere in America?

In an interview some three decades after the release of *Fury*, Lang said: "If a picture is to be made about lynching, one should have a white woman raped by a colored man, and with this as a basis, still prove that lynching is wrong."[46] However, MGM, specifically Louis B. Mayer, wanted no part of making such a film. Lang learned that

American filmmakers were not arrested or placed in concentration camps for making politically incorrect films; instead, controversial material was simply removed from the script or cut from the film before it ever reached the screen.

Fury, like many of the social films of the decade, was loosely based on real events. In 1933 two men, Thomas Harold Thurmond and John Maurice Holmes, kidnapped and killed Brooke Hart, son of a prominent San Jose family. The two men were captured and jailed. The local sheriff requested additional men from Governor James Rolfe to guard the jail because he feared a mob. Rolfe refused. Several days later the jail was indeed stormed and the two men lynched in a public park. This mob was proud of its work: In order for the crowd of onlookers to get a better view of the bodies, several men got their cars, ringed the two men, and turned on their headlights. Arriving state police found the horrifying sight of the lighted bodies dangling from trees and an angry, hostile mob; they had to fight their way through to remove the bodies with "scores of women, children and men spitting and striking the corpses as they were taken away."[47] When told of the event, Governor Rolfe's only comment was that he "would pardon" any of the good citizens of San Jose charged with murder! No one was ever charged or brought to trial.

From this event screenwriter Norman Krasna wrote a brief, ten-page outline entitled "Mob Rule," which was turned into a screenplay by Barlett Cormack and Lang. *Fury* (1936) would approach lynching through the side door: The victim is a white man, an honest, hardworking American "Everyman," falsely accused of kidnapping. When a hysterical mob storms the jail to lynch him, it burns to the ground; he escapes and is presumed dead. When the real culprits are caught, members of the mob are tried for murder. The film then turns to a study of the mob and the victim's revenge against his attackers. Louis B. Mayer told first-time producer Joseph Mankiewicz that the whole idea "stinks"; still, he allowed Lang and Mankiewicz to forward the script to the PCA.[48]

After reading the script, Breen sided with Mayer and warned the studio that the film must not deal with racial prejudice, criticize law enforcement officials, or be "a travesty of justice" story. Breen did not want another *I Am a Fugitive from a Chain Gang.* He was especially concerned because the original script identified the instigator of the mob as a corrupt U.S. senator. "Why not," Breen suggested, "make him a political boss or some functionary" and not a senator? The studio was also encouraged to keep scenes of violence to an absolute minimum and to ensure that the real culprits were caught and punished. If these elements were incorporated into the script, Breen promised MGM a seal of approval.[49]

Breen's suggestions were incorporated, and the studio cast Spencer Tracy as Joe and Sylvia Sidney as his girlfriend, Katherine. Lang began production but soon discovered that, in Hollywood, the director did not have final control over a film. Not only Breen but also MGM censored his work. "I had various scenes with Negroes in them," he later recalled. "One I remember had Sylvia Sidney looking out a window; she sees a colored girl hanging laundry in the back yard and singing a song – 'when all the darkies are free.'" The scene was cut by MGM as "unnecessary" to the plot. Several other scenes that visually linked blacks as lynching victims were also cut. In one, Lang recalled, the District Attorney is making a case against lynching by citing statistics on the number of people who were so executed; the camera then cuts to a group of blacks who seem to be nodding yes – as if they were in the courtroom. The purpose of the scene was obvious; it ended up on the cutting-room floor.[50] Lang accused MGM boss Louis B. Mayer of ordering the cuts because he wanted blacks limited to shoeshine boys, porters, or mammies in MGM films.[51] For whatever reason, the sequence was deleted.

Joseph Mankiewicz's memory is somewhat different. When *Fury* was given an audience preview, Mankiewicz states, it was laughed off the screen: The German director had included a scene in which Spencer Tracy begins to feel guilty for allowing his murder trial to proceed. Walking down the street, Tracy is followed by Disney-type ghosts; whenever he turns around, the ghosts dash behind trees. The protagonist is going mad, said Mankiewicz, and the audience is howling with laughter. Lang dismissed this American response as infantile and refused to cut the scene. The studio, always in control, did it for him.[52]

Fury, finally released in 1936, featured Spencer Tracy as Joe Wilson, an all-American guy who is driving cross country to pick up his fiancée, Katherine Grant (Sylvia Sidney). As he approaches Strand, a small Southern town, he is mistakenly arrested for kidnapping. The audience knows that this man is innocent, but as soon as he is put in jail the town erupts into a frenzy of hatred. The local sheriff begs the governor for help; but the governor, fearing interference will cost him votes, refuses to send in troops. Meanwhile the citizens begin to act. In the barbershop and hardware store, men talk of taking the law into their own hands. A mob quickly forms and storms the jail, determined to lynch the kidnapper and satisfy its lust for "justice." Ordinary people who are otherwise God fearing and law abiding have, for no apparent reason, have been transformed into blood-thirsty bigots.

Lang constructs the atmosphere of the mob brilliantly. He needs no dialogue for Breen to censor. The camera zooms in on a mother holding up her child for a better view of the attack on the jail; another woman is spotlighted as she prays; a young boy is all eyes as he devours a hot dog. Finally, as the mob storms the jail, Joe and Katherine establish eye contact. They both know he is innocent and is about to die.

In keeping with Breen's demands, the local sheriff heroically fights the mob, but he is easily overcome. In the chaos of the attack on the jail, which is burned to the ground, Joe escapes. Although his body is not found, everyone assumes he was killed in the fire; the only evidence is a charred ring he left behind.

The film now takes a right turn. The local DA finds the real kidnapper (another Breen demand met) and announces that Joe Wilson has been murdered by the mob. At first a study of mob injustice, the film now looks at the destructive nature of revenge and the hypocrisy of the citizens of Strand. Joe is slowly becoming a murderer in his own right as he plots to have the mob convicted of murder. Despite the pleas of his family and his lover, Joe refuses to reveal himself. Meanwhile, the wheels of American justice grind on. The citizens of Strand, including the sheriff, refuse to testify against one another and erect a wall of silence. They smugly believe they will beat the rap. Suddenly the DA brings a newsreel of the attempted lynching into the courtroom. The film is shown, and members of the mob are clearly identified. This evidence convicts the defendants of murder. Finally, just as the judge is about to pass sentence, Joe appears in the courtroom to the collective sigh of relief from the accused. He and Katherine kiss (as demanded by MGM – Lang said, "I hated it") and all is forgiven. Joe and Katherine are all smiles, the judge is all smiles, the mob is all smiles, and Breen and Hays were all smiles. As the *Nation* noted, "nobody's hurt; Joe and his girl are ready to marry and start life over, and the lynchers have had a big scare."[53]

Even with the kiss and requisite happy ending, MGM seemed somewhat embarrassed by *Fury*. Mayer was furious because "it didn't look like a Metro film," and Lang's dictatorial manner on the set nearly caused a mutiny by the crew, who were ready to lynch him.[54] Lang also was bitter. He resented the interference on the set by MGM officials, and accused the studio of attempting to shelve the film. Not until a press preview brought rave reviews did MGM release *Fury*. The press was right: *Fury* became a smash for Lang and MGM, bringing the studio a profit of $250,000.

Frank Nugent in the *New York Times* raved that *Fury* was "the finest original drama the screen has produced this year."[55] Graham Greene said it was "astonishing" and praised Lang for conveying "by sound and image" the terror of the mob. While Greene recognized the ending as "contrived," he labeled the film Lang's "best" work.[56] Some reviewers noticed that potential punches were pulled: The *Nation* called the film "an admirable tract against lynching" but found it less a "social document than it might have been" because the prepro-

duction censorship was "thoroughly effective."[57] *New Republic* critic
Otis Ferguson was more critical; in fact, he was furious over what
might have been. While Ferguson found the first half of the film "powerful," he labeled the second half "a desperate attempt to make love,
lynching and the Hays Office come out even." The movie code was at
work, Ferguson noted, when the movie had the sheriff stand "like
Jesus Christ with a rifle" in front of his jail while the mob pelts him
with stones.[58]

Perhaps all of them were right. *Fury* does stand out from normal
Hollywood fare. Lang was able to convey the feeling of hatred and the
mass hysteria of the mob with few words: the hordes arm in arm, joy-
fully singing as they march to the jail; the horrible taunts of the women in the crowd; the young man who leaps on a bar and shouts
"let's have some fun" – all these brought home the point with chilling
directness. Yet Lang, by his own admission, would have made, and indeed *had* made, a different film. Censorship – in this case, not so much
Breen's as MGM's – had made the film pull some punches.

Lang might have been more comfortable at Warner Bros., a studio
that liked to make films with a spark of gritty reality. Given the success of *Fury,* Warners countered with their own study of hatred and
mob violence: *They Won't Forget* (1937), which Otis Ferguson believed "is just the blood-and-guts sort of thing we've been hollering
for."[59] The film was based on a real event: the sensational 1915
murder–rape trial of Leo Frank, a New York Jew. Frank, who managed a pencil factory in Atlanta, Georgia, was accused of the murder
of a 14-year-old girl, Mary Phagan. Egged on by Tom Watson, a fiery,
rabid racist ("We can lynch a nigger anytime, but when do we get a
chance to hang a Yankee Jew?"), the local prosecutor convicted Frank
despite abundant evidence that he was innocent. The case was so flagrant a miscarriage of justice that Georgia Governor John M. Slaton
commuted Frank's death sentence; but Frank was doomed to die.
A mob, enraged by Slaton's action, seized Frank from the Milledge-
ville prison farm (where an inmate had already slit Frank's throat in
an attempt to kill him), took him some hundred miles by car, and
hanged him near Mary Phagan's birthplace. Slaton and his family were
hounded from Georgia. Ward Greene, a reporter for the Atlanta *Journal,* wrote a vivid exposé, *Death in the Deep South,* which Warners
bought; Robert Rossen and Aben Kandel turned it into a screenplay.[60]

Although the Leo Frank case was a cause célèbre among American
liberals, and many recognized that Frank was innocent yet had been
convicted and then murdered because he was Jewish, Breen insisted
that any film based on this event not be "a perversion of justice" story.

When he read the first script sent from the studio he fired back a long list of objections. "Utterly impossible," he told Jack Warner. Breen was shocked that the script portrayed the police as brutal, the prosecuting attorney as dishonest, the jury as corrupt, the witnesses as perjured, and mob violence resulting in a lynching. All this was bad, but Breen was appalled that no one was punished! "On the contrary," he wrote, "the dishonest DA succeeds in having himself elected to the U.S. Senate, while the honest and conscientious governor is defeated." Breen would not allow a movie in which everyone who cheats is rewarded and everyone who is innocent or honest is punished. "Before we can go forward," Breen concluded, "everyone who commits a crime must be punished by the *process of law.*"[61]

Like Mayer, Warner was stunned. Just a year earlier Breen had told the studio that *Black Legion,* a fictionalized account of the ritualistic Michigan murder of Charles Poole by hooded Americans, was "unacceptable" because it raised the "provocative and inflammatory subjects of racial and religious prejudice."[62] These subjects were verboten, Breen had insisted. Once the script had been changed to straightforward hatred of foreigners, Breen had issued a seal. Despite the censorship, *Black Legion* was a powerful film that the *New York Times* praised as "editorial cinema at its best."[63]

The studio hoped to accomplish the same with *They Won't Forget.* Any hint of Jewishness had been carefully expunged from the script: The man accused is Robert Hale, a northerner who is WASPish to the bone. It was sectional hatred, not religious or racial prejudice, that motivated the local bigots. Breen was not satisfied with this concession, however; the script still offended because it stated directly that American justice was corruptible. Armed with their code, Breen and his assistant, Geoffrey Shurlock, went to Burbank to work out a compromise.

The censors met with director Mervyn Le Roy and the screenwriters. Breen was adamant but agreed the story could be told if it were restructured around a man honestly convicted on circumstantial evidence. As he noted in his file, "instead of indicating there has been a serious perversion of justice, by way of collusion of the DA, the lawyer, and the jury, which results in the conviction for murder of an innocent man, the new version will remove this entirely. This is important."[64] It was indeed important for Breen: While it is impossible to watch *They Won't Forget* and not come away convinced that Hale was the innocent victim of an ambitious and unscrupulous prosecutor, there is no direct dialogue stating in clear and explicit terms that a deal had been struck, money had passed hands, or future elections had been rigged. In fact, the entire film points to a system of justice trying to be fair but overcome by Southern customs that demanded "an eye for an eye." This was enough for Breen. *They Won't Forget* could go into production.

The film is set in the Southern town of Flodden. It is hot, very hot, and the town is preparing to celebrate Southern Memorial Day with a parade of Confederate vets and state and local pols. It is a half-day holiday at Buxton Business College, where a young, handsome college professor, Robert Hale (Edward Norris) teaches. The girls in the class are smitten with Hale, and none more so than Mary Clay, played by 16-year-old beauty Lana Turner. Hale, ignorant of Southern customs, continues to teach his classes until old Mr. Buxton demands that he release them. This incident sets the stage for the role that South versus North would play in the rest of the film. Buxton is irate that Hale does not respect local values, and Hale is humiliated in front of his pupils.

Mary and her friends dash out of the school to enjoy the holiday, but she has forgotten her vanity case and returns to the school. We see Mary in the classroom; she looks to the door, which opens; we return to Mary who, recognizing the person entering, has a startled look on her face. Mary is killed (off camera). The murder sets the sleepy town ablaze. The local prosecutor, Andy Griffin, played brilliantly by Claude Rains, is an ambitious man. He longs to escape Flodden but needs something spectacular to make him a household name in the state. He quickly recognizes that the murder of a beautiful white girl could be his ticket out of obscurity. When the cops tell him they will quickly beat a confession out of the black janitor, Griffin hesitates. "Any fool can convict a colored man of murder," he tells the cop. No, Griffin pledges, "I won't indict until I'm convinced the man is guilty." Ambitious, yes; corrupt, no.

Griffin begins a real, professional investigation trying to find the murderer. He interviews everyone, vigorously questioning the janitor Redwine (Clinton Roseman), Mr. Buxton (E. Alyn Warren), and Mary's beau Joe (Elisha Cook, Jr.). However, he runs into a stone wall: None of them seems to be guilty, or at least there is no real evidence pointing to any one of them. Then the crime reporter for the paper uncovers a hot tip, which he shares with Griffin: It seems Mary Clay had a crush on Robert Hale, and Hale was seen at the school after classes were dismissed. Hale is doomed.

The cops find a suit with blood on it in Hale's apartment and arrest him for murder. He claims his innocence: The blood came from a shave and a haircut at the town barbershop. The barber denies it. The reporters talk to Mrs. Hale (Gloria Dickson), who says that neither of them has been very comfortable living in the South. Then it is discovered that Hale was trying to get a job in Chicago and preparing to leave Flodden. Mary Clay's brothers, clearly a bunch of ignorant rednecks, swear vengeance.

The newspapers, both North and South, begin to play the prejudice angle: The South hates all northerners and Hale is being railroaded, scream northern papers. Southern papers counter that Hale is guilty and that it has nothing to do with his being a "stranger" in the South. The townspeople are convinced that Hale is guilty and tell Griffin he had better bring in this verdict. When Griffin is convinced public opinion is totally on his side, he announces that Hale will be brought to trial for murder. This sets off a frenzy of activity. With national attention centered on Flodden, Griffin and the town are now on center stage – all the more so when a northern paper sends a famous private dick to investigate the charge against Hale. The detective is beaten up and run out of town. The paper then hires a famous defense attorney Gleason (Otto Kruger) to defend Hale.

In order to clarify in the mind of the audience that there is no conspiracy to convict Hale, a scene is inserted just before the trial begins. Local business leaders are concerned that the town is going to erupt in violence and is being held up to ridicule throughout the nation. The men warn Griffin not to make a spectacle of the trial for his own political gain. "Make sure you have the guilty man," they demand. Griffin laughs at them. He accuses the owner of the newspaper of inflaming local opinion against Hale, reminds the banker that he has been quoted in the paper as saying Hale is guilty, and tells another that he vowed to replace Griffin as prosecutor if a guilty verdict is not won. The point here was that the public had already tried and convicted Robert Hale and given Griffin little choice but to proceed.

The trial begins. It is hot, *hot*, HOT. The overhead fans are whirling, and spectators are fanning themselves hoping to keep cool. Andy Griffin approaches the jury. He is sweating, he is crumpled – a mass of wrinkles in a cheap suit. We want a fair trial, he tells the jury. Remember Robert Hale is innocent until proven guilty, but he is guilty and the state will prove it to you beyond a reasonable doubt.

Gleason approaches the jury, impervious to the heat. He wears a double-breasted blazer, starched collar and tie, not a wrinkle in sight. This cool, slick northern lawyer will try to prove that Hale is innocent of murder and a victim of local hatred and prejudice.

The trial centers on two witnesses. The local barber admits to giving Hale a haircut and shave about the time of the murder but very nervously and hesitantly denies cutting him. Incredibly, Gleason does not challenge this testimony. Then Redwine, the janitor, is brought to the stand.

Redwine is really nervous. Black men don't usually testify in southern murder trials. The audience knows that Redwine is about to commit perjury: He has been threatened with lynching unless he testifies that he saw Hale in the school after hours and that Hale was acting very strangely. He so states under sharp questioning from Griffin. Gleason reacts immediately. Under cross-examination Redwine admits he was lying – that he had been asleep all afternoon and did not see Hale. He sobs, "I didn't do it, I didn't do it, I didn't do it."

The jury convicts Hale, despite the lack of clear evidence of his guilt, and he is sentenced to die. Cut to the governor's mansion, where a huge crowd is gathered outside waiting to see if he will commute Hale's death sentence and offer him a new trial. The crowd is angry; the governor talks quietly to his wife. If I intervene, he tells her, it will mean the end of my political career. She smiles at him. Do you believe Hale is guilty? He tells her he has hundreds of letters in Hale's behalf begging for a new trial. There is no evidence of an "unfair" trial; even the Supreme Court could find no reason to overturn the verdict, he tells her. She smiles. Do you believe he is guilty? she asks again. This time the Governor speaks more passionately. The evidence used against Hale is not strong enough for a death sentence, he says. "If ever a man deserved another trial it is Robert Hale." His wife smiles again. "I'm getting tired of public life." The governor announces he is commuting Hale's death sentence.

The Clay brothers are in the crowd. "Let's go," says one. The next scene has the police taking Hale to state prison on a train. Suddenly the train is stopped by the mob, and Hale is tossed to the Clays. As he screams for help, another train comes roaring down the tracks. The camera focuses on an elongated mail sack hanging from a wooden post. The train sweeps the bag away. Robert Hale is dead.

There is one final scene. In Griffin's office the news reporter who helped inflame local opinion against Hale is holding a large election poster: GRIFFIN FOR U.S. SENATE. The two men talk about his chances in the upcoming election; it will be hard but they are confident of a victory. In storms Mrs. Hale. "My husband has been murdered!" Griffin pounds his desk "I'll bring everyone of them to justice." She stares at him incredulously. "You, you both are guilty of murdering my husband," she screams. "The mob at least wanted vengeance – all you two wanted was public attention. I want to kill you just the way they killed Robert but I would rather have you live the rest of your lives with his murder on your conscience." She storms out. Both men are shaken. The reporter turns to Griffin: "Now that it is over, Andy, I wonder if Hale really did it." Griffin watches Mrs. Hale from the window. "I wonder." Fade out.

The reviewers were ecstatic. Le Roy's film was "a courageous, powerful preachment against prejudice," waxed the *Literary Digest*.[65] It was "the most devastating study of mob violence and sectional hatred the screen has yet dared to present" added *Time*.[66] Frank Nugent of the *New York Times* called it "a brilliant sociological

Figure 14. Claude Rains stars in Mervyn Le Roy's courtroom drama *They Won't Forget*. Courtesy the Museum of Modern Art / Film Stills Archive.

drama and a trenchant film editorial against intolerance and hatred."[67] To Otis Ferguson in the *New Republic* the film was "uncompromising."[68] Perhaps the most telling review came from the Atlanta censorship board: The film was banned from Georgia. Mrs. Alonzo Richardson (the woman who had been scandalized by *Possessed* in Chapter 2) told Breen "We will not have the picture in the state. Nobody wants it – not even the most morbidly curious!"[69]

Breen had not stopped Le Roy or Warner Bros. from making the film; but he had insisted that it be structured so that it did not center its criticism of American society on the justice system. Voices throughout the film told the audience that the system was trying to be fair: Griffin pledges not to move until he finds the guilty man, and refuses to allow the police to beat a confession out of the black janitor; a real investigation is conducted; the city fathers express concern over the hysteria the trial is generating; Griffin tells the jury Hale is innocent until proven guilty; and the governor states forcefully that he believes Hale was convicted on slender evidence. However, the system cannot overcome individual prejudice and hatred. It is hatred and public opinion that lynch Hale, not the state. The very title of the movie reinforced that message: *They Won't Forget*.

The film was strong social commentary for the 1930s. While it skirted the racial issue, it was clear that racism, hatred, and prejudice pervaded the atmosphere of Flodden. Strangers were suspect, and Redwine was clearly terrified that he would be lynched because he was black. Le Roy brought all this to the screen without having characters say a word about it. Breen had no objection as long as the film blamed this curious phenomenon on individuals. The Clays were hateful and destructive. The courts might make a mistake, but they were not prejudicial.

Still, Breen and Hays would have liked to see movies like *Fury, Black Legion,* and *They Won't Forget* disappear from the screen. "They seem to grow out of newspaper headlines," he told Hays. However, he assured his boss that the studios were moving away from pictures dealing with "social or sociological questions." Even Shakespeare, Breen added proudly, "seems to be dead on his own doornail."[70] That was little more than wishful thinking on Breen's part. He did do everything in his power to discourage the studios from making controversial films. There is little doubt that Breen's campaign was effective: The studios tired of constantly rewriting scripts to satisfy him; yet they recognized that there were issues – straight out of the headlines, as Breen had said – that were attractive topics for movies. While Breen was not overwhelmed with social movies, such scripts did continue to trickle into PCA headquarters – in some instances, from unexpected sources.

In March 1936, Samuel Goldwyn, his wife Frances, and director William Wyler went to the Belasco Theater in New York to see Sidney Kingsley's smash hit play *Dead End*. The setting is the "dead end" of a New York street that runs into the East River. On one side of the street is the back entrance of the East River Terrace apartment building, home for the rich and powerful of New York. A dock juts out from the building; there, the boats and yachts of the occupants are moored. To these people "depression" is simply a psychological state of mind. A sturdy masonry wall, guarded by a row of spikes on top, separates the wealthy residents of East River Terrace from the squalid tenement buildings that line the other side of the street. For one day – the time period of the play – the privileged class of America is forced to use the back entrance while street repairs are made in the front of its building.

As they leave from their back door, they are suddenly forced to encounter America's poor, for whom depression is a state of being – emotionally, socially, and economically. For the poor, the goal is survival. The streets are littered with garbage, laundry clutters the windows and fire escapes, the noise is deafening, and the scorching heat of summer is suffocating. The East River provides little relief because it is covered by a "swirling scum" caused by city sewers constantly vomiting their guts into it.

Into this environment are thrust the characters whose lives will be, or have been, determined by which side of the wall they live on. The hero of the play is Gimpty, so called because he suffered rickets as a kid growing up on these very streets. He is a product of the local gangs, but managed to finish high school and go on to college. Gimpty graduated with a degree in architecture and yearns to build homes for the poor. Yet the American dream has eluded him: Betrayed by the Depression, which has forced his return to poverty, he spends his days searching for work or daydreaming about tearing down the tenements and replacing them with good, clean public housing. "When I was in school, they used to teach us that evolution made men out of animals. They forgot to tell us it can also make animals out of men."[71]

The two leading female characters are Drina and Kay. Drina lives in the tenements and dreams about escaping. Her parents are dead, and she is struggling to support herself and her younger brother Tommy. It is an almost hopeless task, and Tommy, with little supervision, is getting wilder by the day. Drina, a hard-working girl, is out on strike, desperate for the few dollars more a week that will allow her to escape this neighborhood. While on the picket lines, she and her fellow strikers are beaten by the police.

Drina's counterpart is Kay, whose origins are working class, but who now lives with her rich boyfriend in the East River Terrace. She is smartly dressed and about to leave on a long trip on her lover's yacht. Yet Kay and the would-be architect Gimpty have fallen in love, though it is clear that they will never be able to find happiness together: His hopeless poverty, and her fear of a return to it, prevent them from developing a relationship.

The focal point of the play is a gang of young street kids in training to be criminals: Tommy, the gang leader, "T.B.," so called for the disease he carries, and Dippy, Angel, Spit, and Milty wile away their days by skipping school, swimming in the filth of the river, stealing whatever and whenever they can, playing cards, and getting into fights with rival gangs or one another. They are dirty, rough, foul-mouthed kids, and violence is a natural part of their existence. While they are essentially "harmless" at this stage, several have already tasted reform school, and it is clear that unless something dramatic happens they are destined to live lives of poverty or crime.

On the opposite side of the street is Phillip Griswald, a rich kid who lives in the new apartment building. Griswald, separated from the street kids by the wall, has everything America can offer to its privileged class: a rich father, a French governess, a chauffeur, a swimming pool, and even a doorman who protects him from the street urchins.

The real villain of the play is the environment, but its personification is Baby Face Martin, a wanted killer who has come back to his old neighborhood to visit his mother and see his girl. Martin, a boyhood chum of Gimpty, has undergone plastic surgery to disguise his identity, but he is recognized by Gimpty. Both had been full of promise as kids; Gimpty had gone to college, Martin had turned to crime. Martin laughs at Gimpty's circumstances: Six years of college and what have you got? "You have to take what you want if you want to get ahead in this world," he tells Gimpty. But the pressure of living in the "dead end" is about to turn Martin's homecoming into a nightmare. When he sees his mother, she calls him a killer, a butcher; she curses the day she gave him birth. "I ought to be cut open . . . fer givin' yuh life," she screams. She refuses any of the "blood money" he offers her. Martin's nightmare continues when he finds Francey, the girl of his dreams, has turned into a cheap whore, infected with VD. Life in the tenements has claimed another victim.

Two events illustrate the hopelessness of life on these dead-end streets. Gimpty, who is no physical match for Martin and can see no other way to escape his own personal dead end, rats on the gangster to the FBI for the reward money. In a dramatic gun battle Martin kills an FBI agent before he himself is gunned down. The gang meanwhile has been entertaining themselves by beating up Phillip Griswald. When Griswald's father finds out, he charges out into the street and grabs Tommy, who stabs him in the hand with a knife. Tommy is arrested, and Drina and Gimpty plead with Griswald for compassion. Gimpty tells Griswald:

Martin was a killer, he was bad, he deserved to die, true! But I knew him when we were kids. He had courage. He was a born leader. He even had a sense of fair play. But living in the streets kept making him bad. . . . Then he was sent to reform school. Well, they reformed him all right! They taught him the ropes. He came out tough and hard and mean, with all the tricks of the trade.

Griswald is unmoved. The play ends with the police taking Tommy off to jail and Gimpty promising Drina that he will use his reward money to hire a lawyer for Tommy. The rest of the gang is stoic. As T.B. tells them, "Yuh loin a barrel a good tings at rifawn school." The audience is left to its own conclusion: Tommy might be freed, and Gimpty and Drina could marry and live happily ever after on the reward money; or the system could crush another life, sentencing Tommy to reform school so that he could become the next Baby Face Martin.

Goldwyn was overwhelmed by the play and immediately decided to bring it to the screen. He ordered his agent to pay whatever it cost for the screen rights. (As it turns out, he paid Kingsley $165,000.) With the rights secured, he sailed for Europe.

From the start it seemed like a strange project for Goldwyn, one of Hollywood's most successful independent producers. Goldwyn, like the major studios, had always favored "entertainment" before "message" in his productions. He shunned the "realistic" style adopted by Warner Bros., and had even refused to make gangster films in the early 1930s when they were the rage of the industry because he believed they were a bad influence on children. Instead he had tried to infuse his films with the "Goldwyn touch," a combination of flashy production, stylistic entertainment, and expensive talent. He was "the Ziegfeld of the Pacific," quipped *New York Times* reviewer Frank Nugent.[72] Would that approach to filmmaking work on a project set in the slums with a social message stronger than that of conventional Hollywood entertainment? Given the restraints imposed by the Hays Office, could Hollywood even make a film "of the filth, foul language, cruelty, crime, prostitution, syphilis, and crushing despair bred by tenements" that marked *Dead End*?[73]

Goldwyn assembled an impressive production team and cast for *Dead End.* He hired William Wyler to direct, Lillian Hellman to adapt the play to the screen, designer Richard Day, an Oscar recipient for his set design on *Dodsworth,* to construct the set, and Gregg Toland as cinematographer. Humphrey Bogart was brought over from Warner Bros. to play Baby Face, and Sylvia Sidney came on loan from Walter Wanger for Drina. A Goldwyn contract player, Joel McCrea, was penciled in for the lead role (now renamed Dave), and from New York Goldwyn brought the "Dead End Kids": Leo Gorcey, Huntz Hall, Gabriel Dell, Bernard Punsley, Bobby Jordan, and Billy Halop.

Goldwyn was well aware that there would be censorship problems in bringing the play to the screen. He and Lillian Hellman had successfully taken the lesbian theme out of her play *The Children's Hour* and brought a homogenized version, *These Three,* to the screen. Would the Hays Office and the PCA allow the film to deal with the issue of abject poverty in America? The real message of the play was that there were two classes: the privileged and the oppressed. Where you were born, not how hard you worked, determined your class. It was not a message that Hollywood films had pushed. Anticipating a battle with the censors, Goldwyn announced with typical Hollywood fanfare that "it is about time Hollywood did something of significance to public welfare as well as the usual trivia. This play . . . is one of the greatest social documents ever written."[74] Privately he instructed Lillian Hellman to "clean up the play." She recalled somewhat more vividly that what he meant was "to cut off its balls."[75]

It was obvious to everyone that many of the details of the play – the diseased prostitute, the mistress of a married man, the brutal killing of a policeman, the vulgar language and the criminal activities of the kids – would have to be expunged from the film. Wyler quickly discovered that Goldwyn was fearful of too much realism being injected into the film. While the director wanted to shoot in the slums of New York, to bring to the film a visual starkness contained by the play, Goldwyn insisted that the film be shot on the lot with an elaborate set built by Day. This set cost almost $100,000 to build and was universally praised by the critics, but Wyler branded it "phoney."[76] While the production staff worked hard to litter the set with garbage, Goldwyn cleaned it up. When Wyler protested that slums have dirt, the producer countered with: "Well, this slum cost a lot of money. It should look better than an ordinary slum."[77]

Goldwyn, in addition to being a fussbudget, anticipated the reaction of Breen and the PCA. Breen, when the first script hit his desk, fired back seven pages of "suggestions" to Goldwyn. Do not show, or emphasize, "the presence of filth or smelly garbage cans, or garbage floating in the river," the censor warned. In true Hollywood fashion Goldwyn had fresh fruit trucked in daily to "litter" the set. Breen warned Goldwyn to "be less emphatic, throughout, in the photographing of this script in showing the contrast between conditions of the poor in tenements and those of the rich in apartment houses." He insisted that the language of the kids be cleaned up, the reference to venereal disease be purged, the violence be tamed, and Baby Face not be allowed to kill a policeman. Yet even PCA officials were taken with the play. They called it "magnificently alive" and a "sincere and ruthless document." There was no determination, as there had been with Sinclair Lewis's *It Can't Happen Here,* to keep *Dead End* off the screen.[78]

This fact makes *Dead End* stand out even fifty years after its production. The startling point of the film is not how much of the play was removed from the film, but how much of the social commentary survived both Samuel Goldwyn and Joseph Breen. It is true that some points were softened – the garbage may be sanitized fresh fruit from a Beverly Hills grocer, and the set may not be as realistic as Wyler wanted – but the film still gives an overriding sense of hopelessness. There is no mention of venereal disease, but only the very young and the extremely naive would fail to understand what Francey suffered from and what repelled Baby Face. The kids neither curse nor seem quite as bad in the film as in the play, yet it is clear that they have little education and no skills and are destined to live in the slums; only a miracle will save them from a life of crime. In the film Drina is a stronger character: Not beaten down by her poverty, she is a determined young

Figure 15. Joel McCrea, Huntz Hall, and Humphrey Bogart in Samuel Gold-wyn's *Dead End*. Courtesy the Museum of Modern Art / Film Stills Archive.

woman fighting for a better life; but, despite her best efforts, she fails to keep Tommy out of trouble, and her only hope is Dave's (Gimp-ty's) reward money. Dave – now lacking any hint of childhood rickets – emerges in the film as an all-American movie hero: Tall and hand-some, he is not intimidated by Baby Face; he challenges the criminal's every move and, in the end, kills him in a typical Hollywood gunfight. While this convention seems a bit contrived, it does not alter the fact that Dave is unemployed despite his college education: His dreams of a better world remain dreams. Nor does the film lapse into the sac-charin ending it might have had, with Griswald or the courts forgiving Tommy, and Drina and Dave marrying and moving to the suburbs.

Despite the strong indictment, Breen and the PCA supported and encouraged Goldwyn throughout the production process. They met privately during production to work out agreements on how far *Dead End* could go in its message of poverty and despair in America's urban slums. In exchange for lessening the violence, cleaning up the kids and

Francey, and cutting some of Dave's harangues about social injustice, Breen agreed to lobby women's groups throughout the country in support of the film and to press the British censor to approve the film for the British market. Breen arranged for Goldwyn to make a personal presentation before the New York censorship board and, in a letter to the board, the Hollywood censor stressed that *Dead End* was, in his view, a "strong plea for slum elimination and better housing as . . . crime prevention."[79]

With the agreement in place, Breen issued seal number 3596 to *Dead End* and told Will Hays that, in his opinion, the film was a "distinctive artistic achievement" that carried an "important social and sociological message." The New York board passed the film, as did every other state censorship board. Great Britain accepted *Dead End* without any cuts – which, as one historian noted, was "a far cry from earlier attitudes to the American gangster film."[80] When Austria banned the film, Breen wrote to the censor, Dr. Paul Korets, and told him the film was an "important social document" and had been "widely acclaimed" in the United States; the ban subsequently was lifted. Only in Italy was Breen unsuccessful; there, *Dead End* was branded as "pro-communist" by the Mussolini government.[81]

Strangely, when Paramount tried to bring the Federal Theater Project's powerful stage depiction of America's slums, *One Third of a Nation,* to the screen, Breen reacted quite differently. He was so concerned about the plot that he went directly to Paramount headquarters in New York to stress the need for caution. Breen thought the play, with its "endorsement of government action" in replacing tenements, "anti-capitalistic"; he demanded that all dialogue indicating there was "no need for profit" be stricken, and Paramount officials promised cooperation. Breen was delighted with the revised script, which was now a "love story," with all "references to slum clearance being incidental."[82]

The obvious question is this: Why did Breen and the PCA support *Dead End* when so many other films with social messages, like *Black Legion, Black Fury,* and *Fury,* to name just a few, were much more stringently purged of their social content? Perhaps the reason is that the Catholic church, with its urban base, was sympathetic with the problems described in the play and in the film. Working with kids from depressed families, the Catholic church had seen thousands of Tommys turn into hardened criminals, and had seen the Drinas of this world fight to maintain decency in a world of poverty. In 1936 the *Catholic World,* although advocating stage censorship, praised *Dead End* as a play full of "economic and social significance" that should double "subscriptions this winter to the Boys' Club and the Boy Scouts." Later, the Catholic Legion of Decency strongly recommended the film version to all Catholics. Breen, aware of such support for *Dead End,* cleaned up some of the details, but left the message intact.[83]

The example of *Dead End,* however, illustrates how deeply the PCA cut into the fabric of the Hollywood system. The process of adaptation was tightly controlled by the producer and the PCA, both of which established tight boundaries within which the film must stay. In return for those limitations the PCA bestowed not only a seal, but active support. In lobbying for support from women's organizations and opening foreign markets, the PCA put clear financial rewards behind cooperation. It was less costly for the studios to agree before production on what could stay in the film; also, it was clearly more profitable to have the PCA fighting for you with state and foreign censors, rather than fighting against you.

The case history of Robert Sherwood's *Idiot's Delight,* a film that Breen and Hays believed contained politically dangerous ideas, shows how the PCA used the code to squelch political ideas that deviated from mainstream thinking of the moment. When MGM purged the antiwar theme from the film, Breen fought for expanded markets.

Like thousands of young men of his generation, Robert Sherwood had been caught up in the patriotic fervor of 1917. An undergraduate student at Harvard, he had left college to join the Canadian Expeditionary Force after having been rejected by the U.S. Army. Gassed and wounded in France, he had returned to the United States disillusioned and determined to oppose future wars. Sherwood worked as a journalist and drifted in and out of Hollywood during the late 1920s and early 1930s. In 1935 he captured national attention with his play *The Petrified Forest,* and in 1936 he was awarded the first of four Pulitzer Prizes for his antiwar drama *Idiot's Delight.*

The setting for the play is a small Italian hotel near the Swiss border. This peaceful setting is suddenly disrupted when the Italians close the border and launch a surprise air attack on Paris: The Second World War has begun. The hotel is suddenly full of people desperate to cross into Switzerland: a young English artist on his honeymoon, a French pacifist, a German scientist, an American entertainer traveling with "Les Girls" (a group of six chorus girls), and an American munitions manufacturer traveling with his "Russian" mistress.

The war alters the lives of everyone except the American munitions manufacturer. The English artist decides to return home immediately and join the army. The French pacifist taunts several Italian soldiers who are in the hotel; he is arrested and shot by a firing squad, becoming the first senseless casualty in a senseless war. The German scientist, who was traveling to Switzerland to work on a cure for cancer, is compelled to return to Germany to use his science for war. The American arms merchant is unaffected: He not only expected the war, but conspired to start it and will profit handsomely from it. His treachery continues when he forces the Italians to refuse an exit visa for his "Russian" mistress, Irene, because she knows too much about his role in starting the war.

The American entertainer, Harry Van, is unfazed by the war, for he is apolitical. Van is dead broke and his only concern is how to get to his next engagement so he and his girls can make enough money to get back to the United States. However, Van is fascinated by the beautiful "Russian." She strikes him as someone from his past whom he cannot quite remember. Irene, deserted by her lover, finally admits to Van that they had had a brief, but passionate, love affair in Omaha many years ago. When the Italians open the border, everyone else leaves; only Van and Irene remain at the hotel. While they drink champagne and make plans for the future, the French launch a counterattack against the Italians. The play ends when a stray bomb smashes into the hotel and the two lovers are killed. War is an idiot's delight.

Sherwood's drama was anti-Italian as well as antiwar. Sprinkled throughout the play are numerous references to the incompetence of modern Italy. The hotel was once a sanatorium but "the Fascisti – they don't like to admit that anyone can be sick," says one character. When the Italian air force departs for its sneak attack on Paris, the munitions manufacturer wonders if they will bungle the attack. When seven out of eighteen return, he notes sardonically: "Not bad, for Italians." In case anyone missed the point, Sherwood added a postscript:

The megalomaniac, to live, must inspire excitement, fear and awe. If, instead, he is greeted with calmness, courage and ridicule, he becomes a figure of supreme insignificance. . . . By refusing to imitate the Fascists in their policies of heavily fortified isolation, their hysterical self-worship and psychopathic hatred of others, we may achieve the enjoyment of peaceful life on earth, rather than degraded death in the cellar.[84]

Idiot's Delight opened at the National Theater in Washington, D.C., on March 9, 1936. Its timeliness and controversial content guaranteed considerable attention. The investigation (1934–5) led by Republican Senator Gerald Nye from North Dakota into the role of the munitions industry in World War I (discussed earlier in this chapter) was still fresh in the minds of most Americans. Despite a parade of American arms manufacturers and bankers, including J. P. Morgan and the du Pont brothers, the committee had failed to find direct evidence of a conspiracy; but it did disclose that the war had been tremendously profitable for American business. Millions of Americans agreed with Nye when he declared his investigation proved that we fought "to save the skins of American bankers who had bet too boldly on the outcome of the war and had two billions of dollars of loans to the Allies in jeopardy." Sherwood, for one, believed it.[85]

The Senate investigation results, the popularity of the play, and the rise of Fascism in Europe made *Idiot's Delight* a natural for a Hollywood movie. When Warner Bros. and Pioneer Films expressed an interest in acquiring the property and asked Breen for an evaluation, the PCA censor told both studios he doubted *Idiot's Delight* could be filmed: It "would be banned widely abroad and might cause reprisals against the American company distributing it. The play is fundamentally anti-war propaganda, and contains numerous diatribes against militarism, fascism and the munitions ring."[86]

Breen considered films that were against militarism, fascism, or war "dangerous." In April he alerted the Hays Office that there was renewed interest in *Idiot's Delight,* but assured MPPDA Vice President Frederick Herron that he was "reasonably certain" no studio would make a screen version. "To date, we have discussed it with four of them . . . and all seem to feel that it is too dangerous an undertaking at this time." Interest in Sherwood dwindled until MGM inquired in December 1936 as to the feasibility of bringing the play to the screen. The censor warned MGM that he considered the play dangerous and cited "industry policy" as a reason for not making a motion picture version.[87]

Despite Breen's warning, MGM decided to forge ahead with the project; Breen's role now was to force political correctness on it. From New York came word that the Italian Embassy was bringing considerable pressure against Will Hays to stop the project. Breen was told to inform the studio that if the film was anything like the play, MGM would have "all their pictures banned in Italy and France, and there will be trouble all over the rest of the world." While certain MGM "will clean it up," the Hays Office cautioned Breen "to keep your eyes on the production if and when it occurs because it is full of dynamite."[88]

Throughout the spring of 1937 discussions continued on both coasts about the future of *Idiot's Delight*. The Italian Ambassador continued to threaten Hays that the film, along with all other MGM products, would be banned in Italy. The Ambassador claimed Robert Sherwood was "anathema" to the Italian government, and any project with which he was associated would be "hissed off the screen" in Italy. Hays, determined to keep the Italian market open for American films, ordered Breen to use Mr. R. Caracciolo, Italian consul in Los Angeles, as a "technical" adviser. Given final script approval, the Italian government agreed to cooperate on the production of *Idiot's Delight*.

When Breen informed Metro executives of Caracciolo's role, they raised no objection, pledging that they would not "make the picture" if "there is any likelihood of . . . being denied the Italian market." At this point no one, least of all MGM, raised so much as a question about freedom of expression or showed any concern about altering Sherwood's play to suit the tastes of Il Duce.[89]

Breen began negotiations with the Italian consul. A neophyte in the wiles of international diplomacy, Breen had no idea that he was embarking on a fifteen-month assignment to secure Italian approval. The first round of talks went smoothly: The Italians demanded, and Breen surrendered. Caracciolo issued several ultimatums. His first was that the script must have no connection with the original story and contain nothing offensive to Italy. For obvious reasons the Italians were sensitive to the title, which the diplomat demanded be exorcised from all Italian prints. Moreover, Sherwood's name was not to appear in the credits on any print distributed in Italy.[90]

Breen, eager to pacify the Italians, saw nothing outrageous in Caracciolo's demands. He forwarded the conditions to MGM, confident that a solution was at hand. MGM, however, found his skills as a negotiator in their behalf somewhat lacking. Hunt Stromberg, the film's producer, protested vigorously to Breen that he had already agreed to cut so much material from the original play to "satisfy everyone abroad" that he could not afford also to give up the title: He had paid $125,000 for the rights to the play, whose title, it appeared, was the only marketable part left; and now Breen had bargained that away! Nor would the producer agree to change the script so completely that it would have no connection with the original story. Stromberg insisted that the film retain some antiwar flavor but promised that no Italian character would be depicted in an unfavorable light. He assured Breen that the film would be a love story, not a political statement against Italian fascism. To add to this new emphasis, MGM cast heartthrob Clark Gable as the irresistible Harry Van and Norma Shearer as the beautiful and flirtatious "Russian." The film, Stromberg wrote to the censor, "will not say, as the play did, that Italy started the new war, nor will we hold her Government responsible for hostile or secret intrigue, breaking treaties, or any other such acts." Stromberg assured the PCA chief that MGM held Italy in the "highest respect" and would do nothing to offend that nation.[91]

Breen, now thrust into the role of a middleman, forwarded Stromberg's counterproposal to the Italian diplomat, who graciously accepted MGM's terms. With these preconditions established, the studio brought Robert Sherwood to Hollywood to turn his stormy political tract into a steamy Hollywood love story. Stromberg carefully explained to Sherwood the conditions established by the Italians and accepted by the studio. It was not economically feasible, Stromberg told the writer, to make the film without the foreign market. If Italy refused to accept the film, it was more than likely that Germany, Spain, and Argentina would ban it. In addition, France, Switzerland, and Australia had national censorship laws that severely restricted the political content of films. Stromberg told MGM's Eddie Mannix that Sherwood adopted an "understanding attitude" and was "wildly enthusiastic over our desired treatment."[92]

Perhaps he was more enthusiastic over the additional $135,000 the studio offered him to turn *Idiot's Delight* upside down. Sherwood was both philosophical and practical about censoring his own play. Like so many other writers, Hecht included, Sherwood did not take Hollywood seriously. He was well aware of the censorship system that dominated the industry. In his view, the stage play was the vehicle for political statement; the film was "a pleasant make-believe interlude." By May 1938, Sherwood's new version of *Idiot's Delight* was ready for examination by Breen and the Italians.[93]

When Stromberg sent the script to Breen, he emphasized that Sherwood had "dramatized the preachment against war without having stressed in any way the name or blame on any country." The locale had been switched from Italy to an unnamed Central European location, with the accent now on the building love story between Van and Irene. Esperanto, not Italian, was the "foreign language" of the new script, all uniforms worn by soldiers were specifically designed to be "nondescript," and MGM had taken care to ensure that "no nation is held up to any form of ridicule or criticism."[94]

Breen read the script with "enormous pleasure." He told MGM's Louis B. Mayer that the entire subject matter was "splendidly . . . and . . . cunningly handled," and that while some Central European nations may not like the film, their reaction would "cause no serious worry." Central Europe was not a major industry market.[95]

The only remaining hurdle was to have Caracciolo approve the script so that MGM could begin production. Final approval was to prove more elusive than anyone could have predicted. Consul Caracciolo had returned to Italy for the summer, and the Italian consul in San Francisco, whom Breen contacted, refused to become involved. MGM was furious: Delays in production had already cost thousands of dollars, and the project was still not approved. When Breen offered to hand-carry the script to Italy, MGM was delighted.

In early June 1938, Breen handed Sherwood's love story to Caracciolo at the Grand Hotel in Naples. In a setting befitting a Hollywood movie, the two men discussed the script over apéritifs and agreed to meet at the Excelsior Hotel in Rome in a week. Caracciolo gave his assurances that there would be no problems with the script, but he was about to experience what millions of his countrymen already knew: The Italian bureaucracy was hopelessly inefficient. The opportunity of censoring a Hollywood script merited governmental infighting, and several agencies insisted that each had the final power to approve the script. Delay followed delay until an embarrassed Caracciolo had to admit to Breen that the script was lost in the morass of the Italian bureaucracy; not until June 20 was the beleaguered diplomat able to track it down. Breen was finally told at Lake Como that *Idiot's Delight* had been judged acceptable to Il Duce.[96]

The film finally reached American screens in February 1939, twenty-six months after Stromberg had first contacted Breen. Joining Gable and Shearer were Edward Arnold as the evil munitions-maker and Charles Coburn as the German scientist. Even a cast as powerful as this one, however, could not transform a silly love story set in Central Europe. While some of the antiwar flavor remained in the first reel, the focus of the film was not the folly of war but whether the "Russian" Irene was the same woman with whom Harry Van had had a brief affair in Omaha. Once it was established that she was, the point switched to whether the two lovers would pick up where they had left off. They do, and in the grand finale bombs indeed destroy the quaint little hotel; but, of course, they miraculously miss the lovers. Not only was *Idiot's Delight* shorn of its political punch, it also gave audiences a happy ending.

The critics had a field day with the film. *Newsweek* wondered why Hollywood leaned "over backward" to keep Italy happy. "The Italy of the stage set becomes an Alpine never-never land in celluloid, and its people speak that international language, Esperanto." Otis Ferguson wrote in the *New Republic* that the screen version of *Idiot's Delight* was "no more anti-war than a few squads of well-meaning and offended citizens, pelting a nasty old caterpillar tank with chocolate éclairs." The *North American Review* charged the Hays Office with hypocrisy in turning an antiwar play into "an adventure in obscurantism." Why, the *NAR* asked its readers, was it impossible to have "entertainment, information, or any combination of the two that is clear, sincere, and well told . . . seen on the American screen?" The answer, the *NAR* wrote, was "the Hays Office." Even Sherwood was disappointed. He thought that Shearer was "beautiful" as Irene and Gable "very funny" as Van; but, after seeing the screen version, the writer lamented that "so much was cut from the play it seems confusing."[97]

Harry Martin, film critic for the Memphis *Commercial Appeal,* had predicted in 1938 that MGM would "delete all material [from *Idiot's Delight*] which might offend Il Duce." He believed the film would emerge a tepid love story placed in a war setting:

How much better it would be for us all if Hollywood could make an *Idiot's Delight* that would show to the man and the woman in the audience the dangers of Fascism, something that would bring home to every watcher the manner in which he or she might some day be affected by these dangers if we do not constantly remain on our guard. . . . Hollywood should take its head out of the sands of puppy love and give us a look at the world in which we live.[98]

But Hollywood did not take its head out of the sand. With war only seven months away and the European market drying up rapidly, *Idiot's Delight* did little business in Europe. Despite the efforts of Breen, the film was rejected in Italy and in Spain, France, Switzerland, and Estonia. While the movie was popular in America, it was on the whole a disappointment at the box office.[99]

By the end of the decade Breen had effectively muted political and social commentary from the movies. It was an accomplishment of which he was proud, and he expended considerable effort informing Hays of the degree to which he had been successful in keeping the movies free from comment on the social and political problems of the day. The PCA reports for the period 1935–40 are telling. In 1935 Breen told Will Hays that 122 films, or 23.5 percent of the total Hollywood production, fell into the "social category." By the next year the total had fallen to 104 or 19.4 percent and, as Breen continued to invoke "industry policy," the numbers continued to decline. By 1938, he proudly reported to Hays that only 12.4 percent of industry films dealt with social issues, and in 1939 a mere 9.2 percent, or 54 films, were seen as having any social significance.[100] In 1941 Will Hays contentedly told a Senate investigating committee that less than 5 percent of Hollywood films dealt with social or political topics.[101]

After five years of censorship Breen's power was so entrenched that John Steinbeck's powerful critique of the American economic system, *The Grapes of Wrath,* could be brought to the screen almost without a whimper. Breen was delighted that Steinbeck's biting social critique of America had been written out of the script by the studio long before it had reached him. The censor told Hays that a filmed version would be controversial but could be "defended as legitimate drama." On the screen *The Grapes of Wrath* was, according to Breen, a "story of mother love." It was reduced to one family's struggle in face of "exceptional events" – a modern-day "covered wagon" epic. Breen saw the Joads going west in search of a better life, like the pioneers; and although conditions depicted in the film were "shocking," they were counterbalanced by "good images" and, most important, an "uplifting ending."[102]

Breen did not accomplish this purging alone. There is no doubt that the corporate heads in New York, Will Hays, and the studio heads in Los Angeles were all uneasy with films that broached controversial topics. With or without Breen, Hollywood would not have been a medium for change: It wanted first and foremost to entertain. Yet it is evident that the studios did attempt, no matter how feebly at times, to air important social and political subjects. Whenever they did so, Breen stood firm. It was acceptable to make a *Black Fury* as long as it did not advocate radical change in the status quo. It was permissible to make *Fury* as long as the film did not show an America beset with racism. Films cou.1 hint at problems as long as the solutions offered fell firmly within the confines of the political spectrum. While Breen and Hays would have been happier had the studios simply not bothered to make films that combined entertainment with social issues, they both realized that was impossible. As long as the studios would conform to PCA views, Breen would fight to open markets. His goal, strictly speaking, was not to keep political films off the screen but to prevent them from branching out into unchartered waters by exploring alternative solutions to social, political, and economic problems. As long as the public bought the product, the moguls were willing to accept the shackles of repression for the comfort of profit.

Breen's cozy movie world would soon receive a jolt he could not censor from the American conscience. World War II was not bound by Victorian moral codes. The world would soon be torn apart in an orgy of violence unknown to man before or since. While Breen tried to prevent the studios from making films that labeled the totalitarian dictatorships as a threat to American democracy, he could not prevent events from making the code, and his attempts to apply it in a world at war, appear hopelessly outdated.

Notes

1 Gregory D. Black, "Movies, Politics, and Censorship," *Journal of Policy History*, pp. 110–20.
2 Breen, Memo to Staff, "Compensating Moral Values," June 13, 1934, box 47, HP.
3 Ibid.
4 "Men of Arms," *Time* 24 (Sept. 24, 1934), p. 20.
5 Oswald Garrison Villard, "The International Traffic in Arms," *Nation* 139 (Oct. 3, 1934), p. 371.
6 *Newsweek* 4 (Dec. 15, 1934), p. 18.
7 Ibid; Hays to Zukor, Nov. 23, 1934, *The President Vanishes*, PCA.
8 Breen to Wanger, Sept. 19, 1934, *The President Vanishes*, PCA.
9 Breen to Wanger, Sept. 20, 1934, *The President Vanishes*, PCA.
10 Breen to The General (Hays), Sept. 14, 1934; Breen to Wanger, Sept. 19 and Sept. 20, 1934; and Breen to Hays, Nov. 9, 1934, *The President Vanishes*, PCA.
11 Hays, Memo to Maurice McKenzie, Nov. 21, 1934, and Breen to Wanger, Nov. 21, 1934, *The President Vanishes*, PCA.
12 Hays to McKenzie, Nov. 21, 1934, *The President Vanishes*, PCA.

13 Ibid.
14 *Newsweek* 4 (Dec. 15, 1934), p. 18; Breen to Hays, Jan. 31, 1935, *The President Vanishes*, PCA.
15 *Harrison's Reports*, Dec. 29, 1934.
16 *North American Review* 240 (Feb. 1935), p. 97.
17 *New York Times*, Dec. 8, 1934, p. 18.
18 J. D. Battle to Hays, Aug. 8, 1934, and Hays to J. D. Battle, Sept. 4, 1934, *Black Fury*, PCA.
19 Breen to Parsons, Jan. 4, 1930, PP.
20 Breen wrote for *America* as Eugene Weare, Special Correspondent. For example, see "Applied Culture in Chicago," *America* 39 (May 5, 1928), pp. 85–6, or "Reform in the Coal Fields," ibid. (June 9, 1928), p. 199.
21 Breen to Warner, Sept. 12, 1934, *Black Fury*, PCA.
22 Ibid. Breen was dealing with *The President Vanishes* at the same time that he was working with Warner's on *Black Fury*.
23 Ibid.
24 Ibid.
25 Breen to Hays, Sept. 20, 1934; Hays to Breen, Sept. 24, 1934; Breen to Warner, Oct. 9, 1934, *Black Fury*, PCA.
26 Breen to Hays, Jan. 23, 1935, *Black Fury*, PCA.
27 Breen to Wingate, Mar. 29, 1935, *Black Fury*, PCA.
28 *Literary Digest* 119 (April 27, 1935), p. 34; *New York Times*, April 7, 1935, p. 27; *Nation* 140 (April 24, 1935), p. 491; *Theater Arts Monthly* 19 (June 1935), p. 408.
29 Lewis Jacobs, *The Rise of the American Film*, p. 518.
30 *New Republic* 82 (April 24, 1935), p. 313.
31 PCA Annual Report 1935, Mar. 1, 1936, PCA.
32 Jane DeHart Mathews, *The Federal Theater, 1935–1939: Plays, Relief, and Politics* (Princeton, N.J.: Princeton University Press, 1967), p. 100.
33 Quoted in Sheldon N. Grebstein, *Sinclair Lewis* (New York: Twayne, 1962), p. 143.
34 Breen to Hays, Dec. 18, 1935, *It Can't Happen Here*, PCA. Father Donnelly of *America* was in Breen's office during the PCA staff discussions on the film. According to Donnelly, Breen asked him his opinion of making a film out of the book. Donnelly recommended against it because "of the up-coming election" and because it would result in a loss of the foreign market. Although Donnelly reported that Breen sent a letter "forbidding the filming," there is no such letter in the PCA or MGM files. Just why a Catholic priest would recommend against a film because MGM would lose its Italian and German market is unclear, unless it's a thin disguise for disliking the politics of the book and not wanting to see it on the screen. See Donnelly to Parsons, Winter (early January) 1936, PP.
35 Breen to Mayer, Dec. 18, 1935, *It Can't Happen Here*, PCA.
36 Breen to Mayer, Jan. 31, 1936, *It Can't Happen Here*, PCA.
37 The telegram from London to MGM is signed "1016a." See 1016a to MGM, Feb. 5, 1936, MGM Legal Files, Culver City, California (hereafter MGM-LF).
38 *New York Times*, Feb. 16, 1936, p. 1.

39 For background see Breen Memo to Files, Feb. 17, 1936, *It Can't Happen Here,* PCA.
40 *New Republic* 86 (Feb. 26, 1936), pp. 58–9.
41 "We Agree with Sinclair Lewis," *Queen's Work* (Feb. 1936).
42 Al Block, Memo to File, Dec. 7, 1938, *It Can't Happen Here,* MGM-LF.
43 Hays, *The Memoirs of Will H. Hays,* p. 456.
44 John Russell Taylor, *Strangers in Paradise,* p. 59.
45 Ibid., p. 53.
46 Peter Bogdanovich, *Fritz Lang in America,* p. 32.
47 Nash and Ross, *The Motion Picture Guide,* p. 959.
48 Kenneth L. Geist, *Pictures Will Talk,* p. 76.
49 Breen to Mayer, Jan. 27, 1936, *Fury,* PCA.
50 Bogdanovich, *Fritz Lang in America,* p. 32.
51 Ibid.
52 Geist, *Pictures Will Talk,* p. 80.
53 *Nation* 143 (June 24, 1936), p. 821.
54 Ibid.
55 *New York Times,* June 6, 1936, p. 21.
56 Reprinted in John Russell Taylor, ed., *The Pleasure Dome,* p. 84.
57 "Vatican Over Hollywood," *Nation* 143 (July 11, 1936), p. 33.
58 Breen to Warner, June 18, 1936, *Black Legion,* PCA; Breen to Mayer, Jan. 27, 1936, *Fury,* PCA; *New Republic* 87 (June 10, 1936), p. 130.
59 Otis Ferguson, "New Film in a Dry Month," *New Republic* 91 (July 28, 1937), p. 335. For an excellent discussion of the film see Roddick, *A New Deal in Entertainment,* pp. 152–6, and Roffman and Purdy, *The Hollywood Social Problem Film,* pp. 165–78.
60 *Time* 30 (July 26, 1937), p. 22.
61 Breen to Warner, Jan. 30, 1937, *They Won't Forget,* PCA.
62 Breen to Warner, June 18, 1936, *Black Legion,* PCA.
63 *New York Times,* Jan. 18, 1937, p. 21.
64 Breen to Files, Feb. 2, 1937, *They Won't Forget,* PCA.
65 "Dig at Dixie," *Literary Digest* 123 (June 26, 1937), p. 23.
66 *Time* 30 (July 26, 1937), p. 22.
67 *New York Times,* July 15, 1937, p. 16.
68 Ferguson "New Film in a Dry Month," p. 335.
69 Richardson to Breen, Aug. 31, 1937, *They Won't Forget,* PCA. Breen sent a copy of the letter without comment to Le Roy. The film was banned in Japan but encountered no other censorship problems.
70 Breen to Hays, Feb. 27, 1937, *Black Legion,* PCA.
71 Sidney Kingsley, *Dead End* (New York: Random House, 1936), p. 50.
72 Arthur Marx, *Goldwyn: A Biography of the Man Behind the Myth* (New York: Norton, 1976), p. 203.
73 "*Dead End,*" *Literary Digest* 124 (Sept. 4, 1937), p. 30.
74 *Dead End* Press Book, PCA.
75 A. Scott Berg, *Goldwyn: A Biography,* p. 290.
76 Alex Madsen, *William Wyler,* pp. 155–7.
77 Leonard J. Leff and Jerold L. Simmons, "No Trollops, No Tomcats," *American Film* 14 (Dec. 1989), p. 43.

78 Breen to Goldwyn, April 23, 1937; PCA Review, Oct. 28, 1935; Breen to B. B. Kahane (RKO), Nov. 6, 1935, *Dead End*, PCA.
79 Conference on *Dead End*, April 27, 1937; Wingate to Breen, Aug. 6, 1937, *Dead End*, PCA.
80 James C. Robertson, *The British Board of Film Censors: Film Censorship in Britain, 1896–1950* (London: Croom Helm, 1985), p. 81.
81 Breen to Goldwyn, Dec. 22, 1937, *Dead End*, PCA.
82 F. S. Harmon to Breen, Sept. 18 and Oct. 10, 1939, *One Third of a Nation*, PCA.
83 Euphemia Van Rensselaer Wyatt, "What About Stage Censorship?," *Catholic World* 143 (June 1936), p. 323.
84 Robert E. Sherwood, *Idiot's Delight* (New York: Charles Scribner's Sons, 1936), pp. 54, 102, 190.
85 William E. Leuchtenburg, *Franklin D. Roosevelt and the New Deal, 1932–1940* (New York: Harper & Row, 1963), pp. 218–19.
86 Internal Memo "Idiot's Delight," Mar. 26, 1936, *Idiot's Delight*, PCA.
87 Breen to Warner, April 9, 1936; Breen to Herron, April 11, 1936; Breen, Memo to Files, May 12, 1937, *Idiot's Delight*, PCA.
88 Herron to Breen, Jan. 7, 1937, *Idiot's Delight*, PCA.
89 Herron to Breen, May 7, 1937; Breen to Herron, May 11, 1937, *Idiot's Delight*, PCA.
90 Herron to Fred Beetson, May 7, 1937; Breen, Memo to Files, May 12, 1937; Breen to Herron, May 13 and 21, 1937; Caracciolo to Breen, June 8, 1937, *Idiot's Delight*, PCA.
91 Breen to Herron, May 13, 1937; Hunt Stromberg to Breen, June 23, 1937, *Idiot's Delight*, PCA.
92 Stromberg to Mannix, Aug. 5, 1937, MGM-LF.
93 Stromberg to Breen, May 12, 1938, MGM-LF.
94 Stromberg to Nayfack, Sept 2, 1938, *Idiot's Delight*, MGM-LF.
95 Stromberg to Breen, May 12, 1938; Breen to Mayer, May 13, 1938; Breen to Mayer, Aug. 26, 1938, *Idiot's Delight*, MGM-LF.
96 Caracciolo to Breen, June 20, 1938; Breen to Mayer, Aug. 26, 1938, *Idiot's Delight*, MGM-LF.
97 John Mason Brown, *The Worlds of Robert Sherwood* (New York: Harper & Row, 1965), p. 348; *Newsweek* 9 (Feb. 6, 1939), p. 24; *North American Review* 248 (Sept. 1939), pp. 174–5.
98 Harry Martin, "On the Right Track," *Commercial Appeal*, Oct. 28, 1938, *Idiot's Delight*, PCA.
99 Ibid.
100 PCA Annual Reports 1935–1940, PCA.
101 Koppes and Black, *Hollywood Goes to War*, p. 20.
102 Breen to Hays, Sept. 29, 1939, *The Grapes of Wrath*, PCA. See also John M. Miller, "Frankly my dear I just – don't – care."

CHAPTER 9

CONCLUSION

For several years now, the screen has been held to a dead level of mediocrity and banality fixed in conventional grooves, pinned by a strict set of rules which govern inflexibly the conduct and fate of nearly all of its characters. — *Protestant Digest* (June–July), 1940.

"HAYS PURITY CODER ADAMANT ON RESIGNING," barked the *Variety* headline. In April 1941, 53-year-old Joe Breen, "punch-drunk," he told reporters, from seven years of battling Hollywood producers, resigned as the industry censor. Rumors flew through the movie capital that Breen was headed for a major studio; they were confirmed when RKO's George J. Schaefer announced that Breen had been appointed General Manager of the RKO lot. The purity coder would try his hand at creating entertainment.

There was no little irony in Breen's movement to RKO. For months he had been fighting with Howard Hughes over shots of Jane Russell's cleavage in *The Outlaw* (1943). When Breen rejected a PCA seal for the film he told Hays: "I have never seen anything quite so unacceptable as the shots of the breasts of the character Rio." Hughes disagreed and immediately appealed Breen's ruling. In New York, the Board of Directors watched Hughes's cowboy yarn, ordered a few seconds of overexposure snipped from the film, and told Breen to issue a seal.[1]

Breen was upset with the ruling and complained to Hays that he had "noted a marked tendency on the part of studios to more and more undrape women's breasts."[2] Perhaps Breen was overreacting. He sent a letter to all the studios that demanded all cleavage shots be eliminated and even threatened to reject any film featuring women in tight angora sweaters "in which the breasts are clearly outlined."[3] The sweater industry protested to Hays: Tight angora sweaters were all the rage in 1941, and even the staid *Newsweek* chuckled that industry censors were prowling Hollywood sets "to see that the girls didn't appear in the sweaters that are part of their everyday, off-screen wardrobes."[4]

292

The immediate controversy died when Hughes withdrew *The Out-law,* and Breen moved from the PCA to the RKO lot, where he told employees "too many bad pictures are being released" and vowed to "censor" all RKO products to ensure their purity.[5] Whether Breen's restrictive views would translate into good entertainment was in question.

While Breen's resignation caught many by surprise, insiders were aware that he had been unhappy for some time in his role as the prime guardian of filmdom's morality. During his tenure as PCA censor, Breen had had many tempting offers to leave. He told friends in 1936 that the British had offered him a lucrative contract to take over their national censorship board.[6] There were also several studio offers, all of which Breen had declined. Each time Hays had convinced him that the code would collapse if he left. Breen believed it. He told Father Donnelly that "he was the one man in the country who could cram decent ethics down the throat of the Jews, make them like it, and keep their respect."[7]

The constant pressure, however, wore on Breen. He confided to Pat Scanlan of the *Brooklyn Tablet* that the workload "compels us to work from 14 to 16 hours a day, including 6 or 7 hours' work on Sunday."[8] In 1937 Breen told Martin Quigley his health was shot. "I can hardly sit in a chair for more than a few minutes and my digestion has gone to pot. I frequently vomit without any seeming cause at all."[9] By 1940 Breen was exhausted. He confessed to Father Parsons that he was "getting awfully tired of it all. I have a sort of 'fed up' feeling about it all, which, sometimes, drives me to near insanity. The drive, as you must know, is terrific, and there seems never to be any let-down."[10]

Breen felt "isolated and deserted" as a censor: betrayed by his friends and ridiculed by his enemies. For all his bluster, the No-Man in Yes-Land was very sensitive to criticism. He felt stung by newspaper critics who, Breen said, sneered, laughed, and ridiculed his enforcement of movie decency. Nor was the Legion much help: As early as 1936 Breen complained to Father Donnelly "that the Legion has done absolutely nothing" to support him.[11]

Breen's relationship with the Legion deteriorated further when the Catholic church began to criticize the political content of the movies. An internal Legion report warned the bishops in 1938 that the Hollywood "leftists are losing no opportunity to push and ballyhoo films of [a] social nature."[12] The Legion named names: Their list of leftists included Clifford Odets, John Howard Lawson, William Dieterle, Paul Muni, James Cagney, Jean Muir, Donald Ogden Stewart, Henry Fonda, Edward Arnold, Ernest Hemingway, and Lewis Milestone. The Legion also branded such Hollywood organizations as the Anti-Nazi

League, the Screen Actors' Guild, and the Screen Writers' Guild as communist front organizations.[13]

Especially troubling to Catholics was Walter Wanger's *Blockade* (1938). Written by John Howard Lawson, directed by William Dieterle, and starring Henry Fonda and Madeleine Carroll, *Blockade* entered the troubled waters of the Spanish Civil War, a testing ground for modern arms and ideologies where politics and religion were embroiled in mortal combat. While the Roosevelt administration carefully maintained neutrality, American liberals generally backed the Loyalist government; the right, including the leadership of the Catholic church, supported Franco.[14] The issues of the Spanish conflict were further complicated by huge amounts of arms and men pouring in from Italy and Germany to support Franco, countered by the Soviet Union's support of the Loyalists. Any movie that attempted to deal with Spain was certain to become tangled in controversy.

When Breen first read the script he urged Wanger to avoid taking sides in the conflict, but saw no reason to stop the film. After viewing the final cut, Breen issued a PCA seal to *Blockade,* which opened at New York's Radio City Music Hall in June 1938. While Wanger had been careful to design uniforms that resembled neither faction in the war, and had diluted the political punch by inserting a typical Hollywood love story between freedom fighter Fonda and femme fatale Carroll, the film did illustrate the horrors of modern war. In this case, a port city was blockaded by hostile land troops in the rear and by enemy ships at sea to prevent a food ship from entering the harbor. Slowly the city's people starved. While nothing was said in the film to identify the antagonists, it was clear to the politically informed that the city was being blockaded by Franco's forces. In the final scene Fonda, representing Loyalist forces, turns to the screen audience and delivers a sermon: "It's not war, it's murder. It makes no sense. The world can stop it. Where is the conscience of the world?"[15]

The conscience of the Legion was outraged. They labeled the film "emphatically propagandist in theme, plot, treatment and technique," clearly made by Hollywood leftists. Martin Quigley urged a "C" rating because the film was "associated with communism."[16] He told Breen that Wanger sought "to convey support to the Red cause in Spain."[17] The problem the Legion faced was that the film was not immoral; it was political. Legion officials admitted as much when they informed Archbishop McNicholas that director William Dieterle had recently returned from the Soviet Union and was "very active in . . . causes which are Leftward." Screenwriter Lawson, they pointed out, was associated with the "New Theater League–the Leftist" dramatic group, and producer Wanger, they charged, "has evidenced Leftward leanings."[18] The Legion opted for a special rating, and *Blockade* was "separately classified" as a film containing foreign propaganda.

The church used other organizations to condemn *Blockade*. The Knights of Columbus labeled it "a polemic for the Marxist controlled cause in Spain" and warned Hays that the "well-known sympathies of some of those associated with the picture" were part of a "definite phase of Marxist strategy . . . to acquire a controlling influence over the cinema."[19] The Knights of Columbus picketed the film, and priests urged Catholics to boycott it. Hays admitted to Legion officials that *Blockade* was "a mistake" and ordered a prologue (written by Quigley) added that warned audiences the film contained propaganda.[20] Despite solid reviews, *Blockade* was a bust at the box office because theater chains were afraid of Catholic pickets.

By 1940 Legion officials worried increasingly over what they saw as a trend toward movies with social and political messages. Films such as *Confessions of a Nazi Spy, The Grapes of Wrath, Of Mice and Men,* and Warners' *Juarez* were viewed as little more than propaganda. Martin Quigley and the Legion's Rev. John McClafferty warned Archbishop McNicholas that, in their view, "the move to bring social and realistic messages" to the screen was but a "wedge for the sly introduction of propaganda materials" that "may be more dangerous to the welfare of souls than indecencies and immoralities."[21] As they saw it, communist propaganda was seeping past Breen and into films.

At their annual meeting in 1940, the Legion complained bitterly that the number of "morally objectionable pictures has increased."[22] In a direct rebuke of Breen, the Legion condemned the movie industry for promoting "indecencies" and for allowing a "retrogression toward accepting immoral situations as permissible." The Legion vowed to get tough.

Beginning in 1940 more and more films with adult themes were placed in the "B" classification: "objectionable in part." From a mere twenty such ratings in 1937, the Legion in 1940–1 gave "B" ratings to forty-two films – approximately 11 percent of the features released by the major producers. Universal's 1941 remake of *Back Street* was given a "B" because it dealt with an "adulterous relationship." Breen was furious: He had spent months infusing the film with a voice of morality that condemned the affair throughout the movie.

When the Legion gave a "B" rating to Darryl Zanuck's *Tobacco Road,* Breen challenged Father Lord to find anything suggestive in the filmed version. "We did quite a job on it," he bragged.[23] Reviewers agreed when they panned the film. The *Motion Picture Daily* told readers "the dialog and low-life manners of the people have been deleted, altered or attenuated to the point of dullness."[24] The *New York*

Times said "the process of disinfection" had left the movie "pointless."[25]

From his perspective Breen denied that there had been any "serious letting down of the bars under the Code." He had whitewashed *Tobacco Road* and made *Back Street* a moral tale. He told Father Lord that in over half the cases the Legion had given a "B" rating because one of the characters in the film was either divorced or remarried. "They would have us," he complained, "make only stories of Pollyana and The Rover Boys." They "rant" about the ineffectiveness of the code but know nothing about it. They judge the films "on their own personal likes or dislikes." They have "not always been fair and just."[26] Two weeks after writing the letter to Father Lord, Breen submitted a letter of resignation to Will Hays.

How does one then interpret the movies in this golden era of studio production? Is it important to know who was primarily responsible for the images and messages that were in films? Does it really matter that the films were censored during the production process? Do we need to understand the impact and motives of the Catholic church, the PCA, the state censorship boards, and foreign censorship boards and their relationship to the studio production process to understand American movies?

In a word, yes. This system of self-mutilation was first and foremost a censorship of ideas. The intent of the censors, from the Progressives to the Legion, was to prevent mass entertainment films from challenging the moral, political, and/or economic status quo. Procensorship movements began with moral crusades against Hollywood but quickly became instruments "for suppressing thought."[27]

Jack Vizzard, who worked with Breen at the PCA, told the story (perhaps apocryphal) that, when questioned about specific provisions of the code, Breen had responded, "I am the Code!" This identification is important to remember when trying to place all Hollywood films within the structure of the Production Code. It is not surprising that the personal moral and political values of a censor become the standards for censorship.

The key factor for Breen was how he believed the audience would interpret the character, scene, or film. If Breen was convinced that the audience would sympathize with the criminal or the sinner, he would force the studio to reconstruct the scene or character until he was sure that the audience would leave the theater certain that evil in whatever form was wrong. If Breen was convinced that overall audience reaction would side with his moral and political values, then he was willing to bend the code's provisions; if not, he would cite a specific code provision, or suggest that his friends in the Legion would be offended.

This was usually enough to convince the studios that a rewrite was in order.

The studios understood this aspect of working with the PCA. They negotiated long and hard with Breen, often in private conferences, to convince him that the movie, a character, or a scene was a force for good, not evil. They knew that if they were successful, Breen was willing to battle local censors and even take on the Legion for them.

It is also important to recognize that with or without state censorship boards, the Legion, the Hays Office, or the PCA, Hollywood would not have made a great many social or political films. As Ruth Ingliss observed in her classic study of Hollywood, Breen and the PCA did not encounter an industry "champing at the bit with eagerness to bring challenging ideas and images to the screen."[28] Ben Ray Redman, writing in the *Saturday Review of Literature,* warned readers that while the censorship system "is conspicuously moral; at heart it is purely commercial." The system was "calculated to save the picture-makers time, trouble, and money – above all money."[29] As another perceptive observer of the industry wrote in 1935: "Outside their own temples of temperament, the producers had to consider the bankers, the churches, the prohibitionists, the educators, racial prejudices, touchy foreign governments, exhibitors, and an altogether too capricious public. If they offended in any quarter they were met with reprisals which hit them in their pocketbooks."[30]

In the end, they decided it was easier to eliminate ideas than to try to limit audiences by age groups or make films for specialized, if limited, markets. Yet in so doing they also agreed to censor all discussion of contemporary issues. To Ben Ray Redman, "this censorship, in its largest and most minute manifestations, is nothing but a reflection of [the owner's] greeds and fears." It is this censorship that "makes most Hollywood pictures the emasculated, empty, and meaningless things they are."[31] Almost two decades after Redman wrote his observations, Ben Hecht and David O. Selznick came to the same conclusion.

Even the author of the code, Daniel Lord, found the censorship movement had gone too far in restricting ideas from the screen. When RKO asked for permission to film Liam O'Flaherty's *The Informer,* a study of betrayal and cowardice set in Dublin during the Irish revolution, Breen balked. In his view, the hero of the book was Commandant Dan Gallagher, whom Breen characterized as a "communist . . . devoted to violent revolution." RKO wrote the offending material out of the script, but the Chicago Legion of Decency condemned the film as "nauseating" and demanded that Catholics boycott it. Daniel Lord was "flabbergasted." He wrote to Father Dinneen that *The Informer* had "overwhelmed" him. There was nothing, he told the Chicago priest, "seductive or suggestive or detrimental to morals" in the film.

Why was it put on the condemned list?[32] The answer was that several Irish priests in Chicago took umbrage at the presentation of Ireland. They objected to the scenes of drinking, of poverty, of violence, and most of all found the film "insulting to all the time-honored traditions of Celtic womanhood" because there was a scene of an Irish prostitute in the film.[33] The film was condemned.

That the industry chose to bow to censors, cooperate with the Legion of Decency, and restrict films to the limiting formulas established by the PCA is demonstrated in one last addendum to this story: Breen was a flop at RKO. Just nine months after assuming leadership of the studio, *Variety* reported that another internal shake-up at RKO had sent Breen on an extended vacation.[34] Breen was not out of work for long: Within a few months he was back in his old job as PCA censor.[35]

Why did the industry hire back its old nemesis? One reason was the apprehension the war had created in Hollywood. It was clear by June 1942, the month that Breen resumed his censorship duties, that the federal government was going to use entertainment films to promote the war effort. The Office of War Information (OWI), the government's propaganda agency, established a Hollywood office and began working with studios to infuse movies with propaganda.[36] Bringing Breen back as a potential check on OWI made sense to the moguls.

The other reason was the Legion. Breen was seen as the one person in the industry who could stand up not only to the producers, but to the bishops as well. In November 1941, the Legion struck terror in the hearts of Hollywood producers when it condemned as "immoral" MGM's *Two-Faced Woman,* a lighthearted comedy starring Greta Garbo and Melvyn Douglas, because of its "un-Christian attitude toward marriage."[37] In the film Greta Garbo plays Karin Borg, a ski instructor who is married to Melvyn Douglas, a handsome magazine publisher. When Garbo makes an unannounced visit to New York to see her husband, she discovers him making eyes at a beautiful blonde. To lure her husband from the clutches of the blond trollop, Garbo pretends to be her own twin sister, Katherine Borg, and seduces her own husband. In the original film, Douglas falls in love with Katherine "without a second thought for the blonde, and with merely minor twinges about the nice, outdoorsy wife who is presumably cooling her heels in a distant snowdrift, patiently awaiting his return."[38]

New York's Archbishop Francis Joseph Spellman was outraged. He declared the film an "occasion of sin and dangerous to public morals." Priests in New York denounced the film, and public censorship offices in Boston and Providence promptly banned it. MGM panicked and agreed to make whatever changes the Legion demanded. The film was temporarily withdrawn and new scenes inserted to establish that Douglas was aware his wife was pretending to be his "sister-in-law"; he was going along with her charade for laughs. This took the sting out of the film for the Legion, which gave the revised *Two-Faced Woman* a "B" classification.[39]

In February 1942, when the RKO shuffle left Breen out in the cold, Hollywood producers lobbied Will Hays to bring Breen back to the PCA. Hays was hesitant, and Martin Quigley adamant that Breen not return as censor. The objections centered around Breen's refusal to delegate authority during his reign as censor. However, when representatives from MGM, Paramount, and Warner Bros. insisted that he be reappointed, and when the Legion gave its blessing, Hays offered Breen his old position. He resumed his duties as censor that June.[40]

Breen remained as PCA censor until 1954, by which time both he and the code he tried to enforce had long since become anachronisms. In a post–World War II world that had witnessed some 50 million killed, the Holocaust, and the beginning of the atomic age, Breen wrote new regulations for the movies that attempted to ban abortion, venereal disease, and drug addiction from the screen; but he could not stop the tides of change. A combination of factors – the rise of television with a parallel box-office collapse; the effective deregulation of the industry by the federal government, which opened theaters to foreign and independent production; a series of Supreme Court decisions extending First Amendment protections to movies; determination by a new breed of independent producers to challenge his authority; and lung cancer – finally drove Breen into retirement in 1954.

He had grown to hate Hollywood, which he called a "sink of iniquity." The new breed of writers, directors, and producers who increasingly challenged him in his last years were "pagans."[41] He stepped out of the PCA a bitter man. One wonders what crossed his mind when the Academy of Motion Picture Arts and Sciences in 1954 awarded him a special Oscar for service to the industry.

Will Hays, meanwhile, had retired from the MPPDA in 1945 and lived quietly for nearly a decade in his hometown of Sullivan, Indiana. He died in 1954. A year later Father Daniel Lord, who had paid little attention to the movies after 1935, died in St. Louis. Martin Quigley remained an active critic of the movies until his death in 1964.

Joe Breen died in a Hollywood convalescent home at the age of 75 in 1965. A year later the industry scrapped the code and instituted a ratings system that warned patrons about potentially offensive content. An era had passed.

Censorship prevented Hollywood from interpreting the morals and manners, the economics and politics, and the social and ethical issues facing American society in direct and honest terms. The industry chose instead to interpret all social and political themes through the restrictive lens of the code. The industry censors set the boundaries. Rather than becoming a barometer, or even a mirror, movies in the golden age of studio production were held hostage by the box office. As long as the industry was determined to reach the largest possible market, it was susceptible to economic blackmail, whether from religious organizations, special interest groups, or foreign governments. The moguls worshiped revenue more than they respected honesty. One can only speculate what might have been if those few producers, directors, writers, and actors who were interested in producing films dealing with important issues had been allowed to say what they wanted. We will never know how many films might have been made that were not, and how different those films that were made might have looked. At least some Hollywood films might have approached the moral, social, and economic issues of the day in a more honest and forthright manner. This is not to say that the movies would have been a great champion for the social issues of the day; but they might indeed have defined a truly "golden era."

Notes

1 Leff and Simmons, *The Dame in the Kimono*, p. 111.
2 Ibid.
3 *Newsweek* 17 (April 21, 1941), p. 52.
4 Ibid. (May 12, 1941), p. 61.
5 *Variety*, June 25, 1941, p. 4.
6 Donnelly to Parsons, Winter 1936, box C-10, PP. It seems unlikely that the British would have offered this job to an American; more likely Breen was using this type of ploy for a pay raise.
7 Ibid.
8 Breen to Scanlan, April 24, 1935, box B-10, PP.
9 Breen to Quigley, Sept. 25, 1937, box 1, QP.
10 Breen to Parsons, Jan. 16, 1940, box 1, ibid.
11 Donnelly to Parsons, Winter 1936, box C-10, PP.
12 Rev. Michael J. Ready to Amleto Giovanni Cicognani, April 19, 1938, NCCB Archives, Washington, D.C.
13 Ibid. Breen and Martin Quigley were regularly sent internal Legion of Decency reports; see QP.
14 Koppes and Black, *Hollywood Goes to War*, p. 24.
15 Ibid., p. 25.
16 Rev. John J. McClafferty to McNicholas, June 3, 1938, NCCB-ECMP.
17 Quigley to Breen, April 24, 1939, box 1, QP.
18 McClafferty to McNicholas, June 3, 1938, NCCB-ECMP.
19 Joseph F. Lamb, New York Knights of Columbus, to Hays, June 16, 1938, NCCB-ECMP.

20 McClafferty to McNicholas, June 11, 1938, NCCB-ECMP.
21 McClafferty to McNicholas, June 5, 1939, NCCB-ECMP.
22 McClafferty to McNicholas, Oct. 22, 1940, NCCB-ECMP.
23 Breen to Lord, Mar. 1, 1941, LP.
24 *Motion Picture Daily*, Feb. 21, 1941, p. 24.
25 *New York Times*, Feb. 21, 1941, p. 16.
26 Ibid.
27 Robert Forsythe, "Who Speaks for Us?" *New Theater* 56 (Aug. 3, 1936), p. 6.
28 Ruth Inglis, *Freedom of the Movies*, p. 183.
29 Ben Ray Redman, "Pictures and Censorship," p. 3.
30 *Harper's* 170 (Mar. 1935), p. 480.
31 Redman, "Pictures and Censorship," p. 3.
32 Lord to Dinneen, May 21, 1935, LP.
33 Dinneen to Lord, May 22, 1935, LP; Rev. E. Oliver Boyle to Editor, *Commonweal* 23 (Mar. 6, 1936), p. 526.
34 *Variety*, Mar. 25, 1942, p. 7.
35 Martin Quigley was opposed to Breen's return to the PCA. He argued that Breen kept the PCA a "one man" operation. Quigley favored appointing a new director and strengthening the PCA staff. See McClafferty to McNicholas, Mar. 28, 1941, NCCB-ECMP.
36 See Koppes and Black, *Hollywood Goes to War,* for an account of the relationship between the PCA and OWI.
37 McClafferty to McNicholas, Nov. 21, 1941, NCCB-ECMP.
38 *Newsweek* 18 (Dec. 8, 1941), p. 69.
39 Ibid., p. 60. See also D. W. Kelly, MGM Production Department, to McClafferty, Dec. 2, 1941, for details of MGM's changes, and McClafferty to J. Robert Rubin (MGM), Dec. 5, 1941, NCCB-ECMP, on the Legion's reaction to them.
40 For details see "Memorandum for the Archbishop," Feb. 2, 1942; McClafferty to McNicholas, April 1 and May 1, 1942, NCCB-ECMP.
41 Breen to Lord, Aug. 9, 1950, LP.

APPENDIX A

WORKING DRAFT OF THE LORD-QUIGLEY CODE PROPOSAL

Reasons Supporting a Code
TO GOVERN THE MAKING OF MOTION AND TALKING PICTURES

Formulated by
Association of Motion Picture Producers, Inc., and The Motion Picture
Producers and Distributors of America, Inc.

REASONS SUPPORTING PREAMBLE OF CODE

I. Theatrical motion pictures, that is, pictures intended for the theatre as distinct from pictures intended for churches, schools, lecture halls, educational movements, social reform movements, etc., are primarily to be regarded as ENTERTAINMENT.

Mankind has always recognized the *importance* of entertainment and its value in rebuilding the bodies and souls of human beings.

But it has always recognized that entertainment can be of a character either HELPFUL or HARMFUL to the human race, and in consequence has clearly distinguished between:

a. *Entertainment which tends to improve* the race, or at least to recreate and rebuild human beings exhausted with the realities of life; and

b. *Entertainment which tends to degrade* human beings, or to lower their standards of life and living.

Hence the MORAL IMPORTANCE of entertainment is something which has been universally recognized. It enters intimately into the lives of men and women and affects them closely; it occupies their minds and affections during leisure hours, and ultimately touches the whole of their lives. A man may be judged by his standard of entertainment as easily as by the standard of his work.

So *correct entertainment* raises the whole standard of a nation.

Wrong entertainment lowers the whole living conditions and moral ideals of a race.

Note, for example, the healthy reactions to healthful, moral sports, like baseball, golf; the unhealthful reactions to sports like cockfighting, bullfighting, bear baiting, etc.

Note, too the effect on ancient nations of gladiatorial combats, the obscene plays of Roman times, etc.

II. Motion pictures are very important as ART.

Through a new art, possibly a combination art, it has the same object as the other arts, the presentation of human thought, emotion, and experience, in terms of an appeal to the soul through the senses.

Here, as in entertainment:

Art *enters intimately* into the lives of human beings.

Art can be *morally good,* lifting men to higher levels. This has been done through good music, great painting, authentic fiction, poetry, drama.

Art can be *morally evil* in its effects. This is the case clearly enough with unclean art, indecent books, suggestive drama. The effect on the lives of men and women is obvious.

Note: It has often been argued that art in itself is unmoral, neither good nor bad. This is perhaps true of the THING which is music, painting, poetry, etc. But the thing is the PRODUCT of some person's mind, and the intention of that mind was either good or bad morally when it produced the thing. Besides, the thing has its EFFECT upon those who come into contact with it. In both these ways, that is, as a product of a mind and as the cause of definite effects, it has a deep moral significance and an unmistakable moral quality.

Hence: The motion pictures, which are the most popular of modern arts for the masses, have their moral quality from the intention of the minds which produce them and from their effects on the moral lives and reactions of their audiences. This gives them a most important morality.

1. They *reproduce* the morality of the men who use the pictures as a medium for the expression of their ideas and ideals.
2. They *affect* the moral standards of those who through the screen take in these ideas and ideals.

In the case of the motion pictures, this effect may be particularly emphasized because no art has so quick and so widespread an appeal to the masses. It has become in an incredibly short period *the art of the multitudes.*

III. The motion picture, because of its importance as an entertainment and because of the trust placed in it by the peoples of the world, has special MORAL OBLIGATIONS:

A. Most arts appeal to the mature. This art appeals at once *to every class,* mature, immature, developed, undeveloped, law abiding, criminal. Music has its grades for different classes; so has literature and drama. This art of the motion picture, combining as it does the two fundamental appeals of *looking at a picture* and *listening to a story,* at once reaches every class of society.

B. By reason of the mobility of a film and the ease of picture distribution, and because of the possibility of duplicating positives in large quantities, this art *reaches places* unpenetrated by other forms of art.

C. Because of these two facts, it is difficult to produce films intended for only certain classes of people. The exhibitor's theatres are built for the masses, for the cultivated and the rude, the mature and the immature, the self-respecting and the criminal. Films, unlike books and music, can with difficulty be confined to certain selected groups.

D. The latitude given to film material cannot, in consequence, be as wide as the latitude given to *book material.* In addition:
   a. A book describes; a film vividly presents. One presents on a cold page; the other by apparently living people.
   b. A book reaches the mind through words merely; a film reaches the eyes and ears through the reproduction of actual events.
   c. The reaction of a reader to a book depends largely on the keenness of the reader's imagination; the reaction to a film depends on the vividness of presentation.

   Hence many things which might be described or suggested in a book could not possibly be presented in a film.

E. This is also true when comparing the film with the newspaper.
   a. Newspapers present by description, films by actual presentation.
   b. Newspapers are after the fact and present things as having taken place; the film gives the events in the process of enactment and with the apparent reality of life.

F. Everything possible in a *play* is not possible in a film.
   a. Because of the *larger audience of the film,* and its consequential mixed character, psychologically, the larger the audience, the lower the moral mass resistance to suggestion.
   b. Because through light, enlargement of character, presentation, scenic emphasis, etc., the screen story is *brought closer* to the audience than the play.
   c. The enthusiasm for and interest in the film *actors* and *actresses,* developed beyond anything of the sort in history, makes the audience largely sympathetic toward the characters they portray and the stories in which they figure. Hence the audience is more ready to confuse actor and actress and the characters they portray, and it is most receptive of the emotions and ideals presented by their favorite stars.

G. *Small communities*, remote from sophistication and from the hardening process which often takes place in the ethical and moral standards of groups in larger cities, are easily and readily reached by any sort of film.

H. The grandeur of mass settings, large action, spectacular features, etc., affects and arouses more intensely the emotional side of the audience.

   In general, the mobility, popularity, accessibility, emotional appeal, vividness, straightforward presentation of fact in the film makes for more intimate contact with a larger audience and for greater emotional appeal.

   Hence the larger moral responsibilities of the motion pictures.

REASONS SUPPORTING THE GENERAL PRINCIPLES

I. No picture shall be produced which will lower the moral standards of those who see it. Hence the sympathy of the audience should never be thrown to the side of crime, wrong-doing, evil or sin.

This is done:

1. When *evil* is made to appear *attractive* or *alluring* and good is made to appear *unattractive*.

2. When the *sympathy* of the audience is thrown on the side of crime, wrong-doing, evil, sin. The same thing is true of a film that would throw sympathy against goodness, honor, innocence, purity or honesty.

Note: Sympathy with a person who sins is not the same as sympathy with the sin or crime of which he is guilty. We may feel sorry for the plight of the murderer or even understand the circumstances which led him to his crime. We may not feel sympathy with the wrong which he has done. The presentation of evil is often essential for art or fiction or drama. This in itself is not wrong provided:

a. That evil is *not presented alluringly*. Even if later in the film the evil is condemned or punished, it must not be allowed to appear so attractive that the audience's emotions are drawn to desire or approve as strongly that later the condemnation is forgotten and only the apparent joy of the sin remembered.

b. That throughout, the audience feels sure that *evil is wrong* and *good is right*.

II. Correct standards of life shall, as far as possible, be presented.

A *wide knowledge of life and of living* is made possible through the film. When right standards are consistently presented, the motion picture exercises the most powerful influence. It builds character, develops right ideals, inculcates correct principles, and all this in the attractive story form.

If motion pictures consistently *hold up for admiration high types of characters* and present stories that will affect lives for the better, they can become the most powerful natural force for the improvement of mankind.

III. Law, natural or human, shall not be ridiculed, nor shall sympathy be created for its violation. By *natural law* is understood the law which is written in the hearts of all mankind, the great underlying principles of right and justice dictated by conscience.

By *human law* is understood the law written by civilized nations.

1. The *presentation of crimes* against the law is *often necessary* for the carrying out of the plot. But the presentation must not throw sympathy with the crime as against the law nor with the criminal as against those who punish him.

2. The *courts of the land* should not be presented as unjust. This does not mean that a single court may not be represented as unjust, much less that a single court official must not be presented this way. But the court system of the country must not suffer as a result of this presentation.

REASONS UNDERLYING PARTICULAR APPLICATIONS
Preliminary:

I.   *Sin and evil* enter into the story of human beings and hence in them-
     selves are *dramatic material*.
II. In the use of this material, it must be distinguished between sin which
     repels by its very nature, and *sins which often attract*.
     a. In the first class come murder, most theft, many legal crimes, lying,
        hypocrisy, cruelty, etc.
     b. In the second class come sex sins, sins and crimes of apparent hero-
        ism, such as banditry, daring thefts, leadership in evil, organized
        crime, revenge, etc.
     The first class needs far less care in treatment, as sins and crimes of
     this class are naturally unattractive. The audience instinctively con-
     demns and is repelled.
     Hence the important objective must be to avoid the hardening of the
     audience, especially of those who are young and impressionable, to the
     thought and fact of crime. People can become accustomed even to
     murder, cruelty, brutality, and repellent crimes, if these are sufficiently
     repeated.
     The second class needs real care in handling, as the response of hu-
     man natures to their appeal is obvious. This is treated more fully below.
III. A careful distinction can be made between films intended for *general
     distribution*, and films intended for use in theatres restricted to a *limited
     audience*. Themes and plots quite appropriate for the latter would be
     altogether out of place and dangerous in the former.
     Note: In general this practice of using a general theatre and limiting
     its patronage during the showing of a certain film to "Adults Only" is
     not completely satisfactory and is only partially effective.
     However, maturer minds may easily understand and accept without
     harm subject matter in plots which do younger people positive harm.
     Hence: If there should be created a special type of theatre, catering
     exclusively to an adult audience, for plays of this character (plays with
     problem themes, difficult discussions and maturer treatment) it would
     seem to afford an outlet, which does not now exist, for pictures unsuit-
     able for general distribution but permissible for exhibition to a restrict-
     ed audience.

I.   CRIMES AGAINST THE LAW
     The *treatment of crimes* against the law must not:
     1. *Teach methods of* crime.
     2. *Inspire potential criminals* with a desire for imitation.
     3. *Make criminals seem heroic* and justified.
     Revenge in modern times shall not be justified. In lands and ages of
     less developed civilization and moral principles, revenge may some-
     times be presented. This would be the case especially in places where
     no law exists to cover the crime because of which revenge is commit-
     ted.

Because of its evil consequences, the *drug traffic* should not be presented in any form. The existence of the trade should not be brought to the attention of audiences.

The use of liquor should never be excessively presented even in picturing countries where its use is illegal. In scenes from American life, the necessities of plot and proper characterization alone justify its use. And in this case, it should be shown with moderation.

II.   SEX

Out of regard for the sanctity of marriage and the home, the triangle, that is, love of a third party by one already married, needs careful handling. The treatment should not throw sympathy against marriage as an institution.

Scenes of passion must be treated with an honest acknowledgment of human nature and its normal reactions. Many scenes cannot be presented without arousing dangerous emotions on the part of the immature, the young, the criminal classes.

Even within the limits of *pure love*, certain facts have been universally regarded by lawmakers as outside the limits of safe presentation.

In the case of *impure love*, the love which society has always regarded as wrong and which has been banned by divine law, the following are important:

1. Impure love must *not* be presented as *attractive and beautiful*.
2. It must *not* be the subject of *comedy or farce*, or treated as material for laughter.
3. It must *not* be presented in such a way as to *arouse passion* or morbid curiosity on the part of the audience.
4. It must not be made to seem *right and permissible*.
5. In general, it must *not* be *detailed* in methods and manner.

III.   VULGARITY; IV. OBSCENITY; V. PROFANITY; hardly need further explanation than is contained in the Code.

VI.   COSTUME

General Principles:

1. The effect of nudity or semi-nudity upon the normal man or woman and much more upon the young and immature person, has been honestly recognized by all lawmakers and moralists.
2. Hence the fact that the nude or semi-nude body may be beautiful does not make its use in the films moral. For, in addition to its beauty, the effect of the nude or semi-nude body on the normal individual must be taken into consideration.
3. Nudity or semi-nudity used simply to put a 'punch' into a picture comes under the head of immoral actions. It is immoral in its effect on the average audience.
4. Nudity can never be permitted as being *necessary for the plot*. Semi-nudity must not result in undue or indecent exposures.

5. Transparent or translucent materials and silhouette are frequently more suggestive than actual exposure.

VII. DANCES
Dancing in general is recognized as an *Art* and as a *beautiful* form of expressing human emotions.

But dances which suggest or represent sexual actions, whether performed solo or with two or more, dances intended to excite the emotional reaction of an audience, dances with movement of the breasts, excessive body movements while the feet are stationary, violate decency and are wrong.

VIII. RELIGION
The reason why ministers of religion may not be comic characters or villains is simply because the attitude taken toward them may easily become the attitude taken toward religion in general. Religion is lowered in the minds of the audience because of the lowering of the audience's respect for a minister.

IX. LOCATIONS
Certain places are so closely and thoroughly associated with sexual life or with sexual sin that their use must be carefully limited.

X. NATIONAL FEELINGS
The just rights, history, and feelings of any nation are entitled to consideration and respectful treatment.

XI. TITLES
As the title of a picture is the brand on that particular type of goods, it must conform to the ethical practices of all such titling.

XII. REPELLENT SUBJECTS
Such subjects are occasionally necessary for the plot. Their treatment must never offend good taste nor injure the sensibilities of an audience.

APPENDIX B

FILMS CONDEMNED BY THE LEGION OF DECENCY

Chicago Legion of Decency, 1934

Affairs of a Gentleman
Affairs of Cellini
Ariane
Back Street
Catherine the Great
Design for Living
Don Juan
Dr. Monica
Enlighten Thy Daughter
Fighting Lady, The
Finishing School
Firebird, The
Fog Over Frisco
Gay Bride, The
Girl from Missouri
Girls for Sale
Glamour
Good Dame
Hat, Coat and Glove
He Was Her Man
I Have Lived
It Ain't No Sin (a/k/a
   Belle of the Nineties)
Jimmy the Gent

Kiss and Make Up
Laughing Boy
Lazy River
Life of Vergie Winters,
   The
Limehouse Blues
Little Man What Now?
Madame du Barry
Manhattan Melodrama
Men in White
Men of the Night
Merry Wives of Reno
Modern Hero, A
Morals for Women
Nana
Narcotic
Notorious but Nice
Of Human Bondage
One More River
Picture Brides
Playthings of Desire
Private Life of Henry
   VIII, The
Registered Nurse

Riptide
Road to Ruin
Sadie McKee
Scarlet Empress
Scarlet Letter, The
She Had to Choose
Side Streets
Sisters Under the Skin
Smarty
Springtime for Henry
Straight from the Heart
Such Women Are
   Dangerous
Tomorrow's Children
Trouble in Paradise
Trumpet Blows, The
Uncertain Lady
Unknown Blonde
Upperworld
Wharf Angels
Wild Gold
Women in His Life
Youth of Russia, The

Chicago Legion of Decency, 1935

All of Me
Anna Karenina
Barbary Coast
Cynara
Devil Is a Woman, The

Ecstasy
Flirtation
Gambling with Souls
Gay Bride, The
George White's Scandals

Guilty Parents
High School Girl
Informer, The
It Ain't No Sin (a/k/a
   Belle of the Nineties)

309

Java Head   *Mysterious Mr. Wong,*   *Protect Your Daughter*
Merry Wives of Reno   *The*   *Queen Christina*
Modern Motherhood   *No More Ladies*   *Scoundrel, The*

National Legion of Decency, New York, 1936

Guilty Parents   *High School Girl*   *Java Head*

National Legion of Decency, New York, 1937

Damaged Goods

Condemned by Lord, 1934

Born to Be Bad   *Kiss and Make Up*   *Smarty*

SELECTED BIBLIOGRAPHY

The bulk of research done for this book was in the archives listed below. The debate over the issue of film content and censorship generated thousands of articles in contemporary journals and magazines during the 1930s; it is impractical to list even a small fraction of the articles written and published on this subject. Those used substantively are cited in the chapter notes; this bibliography lists only the pieces of a more general nature that interested readers might want to consult.

Archives

Archives of the Archdiocese of Cincinnati, Cincinnati, Ohio. [AAC]
The Archive Center, Archdiocese Archives–Los Angeles, Mission Hills, Calif. [AALA]
Cecil B. DeMille Papers, Harold B. Lee Library, Brigham Young University, Provo, Utah. [DM]
Will Hays Papers, Indiana State Historical Society, Indianapolis, Ind. [HP]
Daniel Lord Papers, Jesuit Missouri Province Archives, St. Louis, Mo. [LP]
Wilfrid Parsons Papers, Georgetown University, Washington, D.C. [PP]
Production Code Administration Files, Margaret Herrick Library, Academy of Motion Picture Arts and Sciences (AMPAS), Beverly Hills, Calif. [PCA]
Martin Quigley Papers, Georgetown University, Washington, D.C. [QP]
United States Catholic Conference [Bishops] Archives, Washington, D.C. [NCCB-EMPC]
Warner Bros., MGM, and 20th Century–Fox Production Files, University of Southern California, Los Angeles, Calif. [USC]

Books

Addams, Jane. *The Spirit of Youth and the City Streets* (New York: Macmillan, 1909).
Adler, Mortimer. *Art and Prudence* (New York: Longmans, Green & Co., 1937).
Balio, Tino. *Grand Design: Hollywood as a Modern Business Enterprise, 1930–1939* (New York: Charles Scribner's Sons, 1993).

Beman, Lamar T. *Censorship of the Theater and Moving Pictures* (New York: H. W. Wilson, 1931).

Berg, A. Scott. *Goldwyn: A Biography* (New York: Knopf, 1989).

Bergman, Andrew. *We're in the Money: Depression America and Its Films* (New York: NYU Press, 1971).

Bogdanovich, Peter. *Fritz Lang in America* (New York: Praeger, 1969).

Bordwell, David, Janet Staiger, and Kristin Thompson. *The Classical Hollywood Cinema: Film Style and Mode of Production to 1960* (New York: Columbia University Press, 1985).

Bowser, Eileen. *The Transformation of Cinema, 1907–1915* (New York: Charles Scribner's Sons, 1990)

Boyer, Paul S. *Purity in Print: The Vice Society Movement and Book Censorship in America* (New York: Charles Scribner's Sons, 1968).
    Urban Masses and Moral Order in America, 1820–1920 (Cambridge, Mass.: Harvard University Press, 1978).

Brownlow, Kevin. *Behind the Mask of Innocence* (New York: Knopf, 1990).

Carmen, Ira H. *Movies, Censorship and the Law* (Ann Arbor: University of Michigan Press, 1966).

Ceplair, Larry, and Steven Englund. *The Inquisition in Hollywood: Politics in the Film Community, 1930–1960* (Garden City, N.Y.: Anchor Press/ Doubleday, 1980).

Chase, William L. *Catechism on Motion Pictures in Interstate Commerce* (New York: New York Civic League, 1921).

Christensen, Terry. *Reel Politics: American Political Movies from* Birth of a Nation *to* Platoon (New York: Blackwell, 1987).

deGrazia, Edward, and Roger Newman. *Banned Films: Movies, Censors and the First Amendment* (New York: R. R. Bowker, 1982).

Dooley, Roger. *From Scarface to Scarlett: American Films in the 1930s* (New York: Harcourt Brace Jovanovich, 1979).

Ernst, Morris, and Pare Lorentz. *Censored: The Private Life of the Movie* (New York: Jonathan Cape & Harrison Smith, 1930; reprint New York: Jerome S. Ozer, 1971).

Facey, Paul W., S.J. *The Legion of Decency: A Sociological Analysis of the Emergence and Development of a Social Pressure Group* (New York: Arno Press, 1974).

Feldman, Charles. *The National Board of Censorship of Motion Pictures, 1909–22* (New York: Arno Press, 1975).

Fernett, Gene. *American Film Studios: An Historical Encyclopedia* (Jefferson, N.C.: McFarland, 1988).

Fine, Richard. *Hollywood and the Profession of Authorship, 1928–1940* (Ann Arbor: UMI Research Press, 1979).

Finler, Joel. *The Hollywood Story* (New York: Crown, 1988).

Fisher, James Terence. *The Catholic Counterculture in America, 1933–1962* (Chapel Hill, N.C.: University of North Carolina Press, 1989).

Forman, Henry James. *Our Movie Made Children* (New York: Macmillan, 1933).

Gabler, Neal. *An Empire of Their Own: How the Jews Invented Hollywood.* (New York: Crown, 1988).

Gardiner, Gerald. *The Censorship Papers: Movie Censorship Letters from the Hays Office, 1934–68* (New York: Dodd, Mead, 1987).

Gardiner, Harold C., S.J. *Catholic Viewpoint on Censorship* (Garden City, N.Y.: Hanover House, 1958).

Geduld, Harry. *The Birth of the Talkies: From Edison to Jolson* (Bloomington: University of Indiana Press, 1975).

Geist, Kenneth. *Pictures Will Talk: The Life and Films of Joseph L. Mankiewicz* (New York: Charles Scribner's Sons, 1978).

Gomery, Douglas. *The Hollywood Studio System* (New York: St. Martin's Press, 1986).

Halsey, William. *The Survival of American Innocence: Catholicism in an Era of Disillusionment, 1920–1940* (Notre Dame: University of Notre Dame Press, 1980).

Hamilton, Ian. *Writers in Hollywood, 1915–1951* (New York: Harper & Row, 1990).

Hampton, Benjamin B. *History of the American Film Industry from Its Beginnings to 1931* (New York: Covici, Friede, 1931).

Hanson, Miriam. *Babel and Babylon: Spectatorship in American Silent Film* (Cambridge, Mass.: Harvard University Press, 1991).

Harris, Marlys J. *The Zanucks of Hollywood: The Dark Legacy of an American Dynasty* (New York: Crown, 1989).

Haskell, Molly. *From Reverence to Rape: The Treatment of Women in the Movies* (New York: Holt, Rinehart & Winston, 1974).

Hays, Will. *The Memoirs of Will H. Hays* (Garden City, N.Y.: Doubleday, 1955).

Hemingway, Ernest. *A Farewell to Arms* (New York: Charles Scribner & Sons, 1929).

Higham, Charles, and Joel Greenberg. *Hollywood in the Forties* (New York: A. S. Barnes, 1968).

Huettig, Mae D. *Economic Control of the Motion Picture Industry* (Philadelphia: University of Pennsylvania Press, 1944).

Humphries, Reynold. *Fritz Lang, Genre and Representation in His American Films* (Baltimore: Johns Hopkins Press, 1989).

Inglis, Ruth. *Freedom of the Movies: A Report on Self-Regulation* (Chicago: University of Chicago Press, 1947).

Izod, John. *Hollywood and the Box Office, 1895–1986* (New York: Columbia University Press, 1988).

Jacobs, Lea. *The Wages of Sin: Censorship and the Fallen Woman Film, 1928–1942* (Madison: University of Wisconsin Press, 1991).

Jacobs, Lewis. *The Rise of the American Film* (New York: Teacher's College Press, 1939).

Jarvie, Ian. *Hollywood's Overseas Campaign: The North Atlantic Movie Trade, 1920–1950* (New York: Cambridge University Press, 1992).

Jowett, Garth. *Film: The Democratic Art* (Boston: Little, Brown, 1976).

Kanin, Garson. *Hollywood: Stars and Starlets, Tycoons and Flesh-Peddlers, Moviemakers and Moneymakers, Frauds and Geniuses, Hopefuls and Has-Beens, Great Lovers and Sex Symbols* (New York: Viking, 1967).

Kauffmann, Stanley, and Bruce Henstell, eds. *American Film Criticism: From the Beginnings to Citizen Kane* (New York: Liveright, 1972).

Kindem, Gorham. *The American Movie Industry: The Business of Motion Pictures* (Carbondale: Southern Illinois University Press, 1982).

Knight, Arthur. *The Liveliest Art* (New York: Macmillan, 1959).

Koppes, Clayton, and Gregory D. Black. *Hollywood Goes to War: How Politics, Profits and Propaganda Shaped World War II Movies* (New York: The Free Press, 1987).

Koszarski, Richard. *An Evening's Entertainment: The Age of the Silent Feature Picture, 1915–1928* (New York: Charles Scribner's Sons, 1990).

Kuhn, Annette. *Cinema, Censorship, and Sexuality, 1909–1925* (New York: Routledge, 1988).

Lane, Tamar. *What's Wrong with the Movies?* (Los Angeles: Waverly, 1923).

Lawrence, Frank M. *Hemingway and the Movies* (Jackson: University of Mississippi Press, 1981).

Leff, Leonard J., and Jerold L. Simmons. *The Dame in the Kimono: Hollywood, Censorship, and the Production Code from the 1920s to the 1960s* (New York: Grove Weidenfeld, 1990).

Le Roy, Mervyn. *Take One* (New York: Hawthorn Books, 1974).

Lord, Daniel A., S.J. *Played By Ear* (Chicago: Loyola University Press, 1955).

Lorentz, Pare. *Lorentz on Film: Movies 1927 to 1941* (New York: Hopkinson & Blake, 1975).

McGilligan, Pat, ed. *Backstory I: Interviews with Screenwriters of Hollywood's Golden Age* (Berkeley: University of California Press, 1986).

Madsen, Axel. *William Wyler: The Authorized Biography* (New York: Crowell, 1973).

Maltby, Richard. *Harmless Entertainment: Hollywood and the Ideology of Consensus* (Metuchen, N.J.: Scarecrow Press, 1983).

Marion, Frances. *Off With Their Heads: A Serio-Comic Tale of Hollywood* (New York: Macmillan, 1972).

Martin, Olga. *Hollywood's Movie Commandments* (New York: Arno Press, 1937).

Marx, Samuel. *Mayer and Thalberg: The Make-Believe Saints* (New York: Random House, 1975).

Mast, Gerald. *A Short History of the Movies* (New York: Pegasus, 1971).

May, Lary. *Screening Out the Past: The Birth of Mass Culture and the Motion Picture Industry* (New York: Oxford University Press, 1980).

Millichap, Joseph R. *Steinbeck and Film* (New York: Ungar, 1983).

Moley, Raymond. *Are We Movie Made?* (New York: Macy-Masius, 1938).

The Hays Office (New York: Bobbs-Merrill, 1945).

Mordden, Ethan. *The Hollywood Studios: House Style in the Golden Age of the Movies* (New York: Knopf, 1988).

Muser, Charles. *The Emergence of the American Cinema to 1907* (New York: Charles Scribner's Sons, 1990).

Nash, Jay R., and Stanley R. Ross, eds. *The Motion Picture Guide* (Chicago: Cinebooks, 1985–7).

National Conference on Motion Pictures. *The Community and Motion Pictures* (New York: MPDA, 1929).

Nizer, Louis. *New Courts of Industry: Self-Regulation Under the Motion Picture Code* (New York: J. S. Ozer, 1971).

Oberholtzer, Ellis P. *The Morals of the Movie* (Philadelphia: Penn Publishing, 1922).

O'Brien, David. *American Catholics and Social Reform* (New York: Oxford University Press, 1968).

O'Connor, John E., intro to Howard J. Green, *I Am A Fugitive from a Chain Gang* (Madison: University of Wisconsin Press, 1981).

Peary, Gerald, ed. *Little Caesar* (Madison: University of Wisconsin Press, 1981).

Perlman, William, ed. *Movies on Trial* (New York: Macmillan, 1936).

Phillips, Gene D. *Fiction, Film, and Faulkner: The Art of Adaptation.* (Knoxville: University of Tennessee Press, 1988).

Powdermaker, Hortense. *Hollywood, the Dream Factory: An Anthropologist Looks at the Movies* (Boston: Little, Brown, 1950).

Prindle, David F. *The Politics of Glamour, Ideology and Democracy in the Screen Actors Guild* (Madison: University of Wisconsin Press, 1988).

Quigley, Martin. *Decency in Motion Pictures* (New York: Macmillan, 1937).

Ramsaye, Terry. *A Million and One Nights: A History of the Motion Pictures Through 1925* (New York: Simon & Schuster, 1926; reprint ed, 1964).

Randall, Richard S. *Censorship of the Movies* (Madison: University of Wisconsin Press, 1968).

Roddick, Nick. *A New Deal in Entertainment: Warner Brothers in the 1930's* (London: British Film Institute, 1983).

Roffman, Peter, and Jim Purdy. *The Hollywood Social Problem Film: Madness, Despair, and Politics from the Depression to the Fifties* (Bloomington: Indiana University Press, 1981).

Rosen, Marjorie. *Popcorn Venus: Women, Movies and the American Dream* (New York: Coward, McCann & Geohegan, 1973).

Rossow, Eugene. *Born to Lose: The Gangster Film in America* (New York: Oxford University Press, 1978).

Rosten, Leo. *Hollywood: The Movie Colony and the Movie Makers* (New York: Harcourt, Brace & Co., 1941).

Schatz, Thomas. *The Genius of the System: Hollywood Filmmaking in the Studio Era* (New York: Pantheon, 1988).

Schumach, Murray. *The Face on the Cutting Room Floor: The Story of Movie and Television Censorship* (New York: William Morrow, 1964).

Shadoian, Jack. *Dreams and Dead Ends: The American Gangster/Crime Film* (Cambridge, Mass.: MIT Press, 1977).

Sklar, Robert. *Movie Made America: A Cultural History of American Movies* (New York: Vintage Books, 1975).

Slide, Anthony. *Selected Film Criticism, 1931–1940* (Metuchen, N.J.: Scarecrow Press, 1982).

Solan, Kay. *The Loud Silents: Origins of the Social Problem Film* (Chicago: University of Illinois Press, 1988).

Taylor, John Russell, ed. *The Pleasure Dome: The Collected Film Criticism of Graham Greene, 1935–1940* (London: Secker & Warburg, 1972).
Strangers in Paradise: The Hollywood Emigrés, 1933–1950 (London: Faber & Faber, 1983).
Thomas, Bob. *Thalberg: Life and Legend* (Garden City, N.Y.: Doubleday, 1969).
Thomas, Tony. *Howard Hughes in Hollywood* (Secaucus, N.J.: Citadel Press, 1985).
Thompson, Kristin. *Exporting Entertainment: America in the World Film Market, 1907–1934* (London: British Film Institute Press, 1985).
Thorp, Margaret. *America at the Movies* (New Haven, Conn.: Yale University Press, 1939).
Vizzard, Jack. *See No Evil: Life Inside a Hollywood Censor* (New York: Simon & Schuster, 1970).
Wilson, Robert, ed. *The Film Criticism of Otis Ferguson* (Philadelphia: Temple University Press, 1971).

Articles

Allen, Robert C. "Motion Picture Exhibition in Manhattan, 1906–1912," *Cinema Journal* 8 (Spring 1979), 2–15; reprinted in John Fell, *Film Before Griffith* (Berkeley: University of California Press, 1983), pp. 162–75.
Ames, Richard S. "The Screen Enters Politics," *Harper's* 171 (Mar. 1935), 473–82.
Barrows, Edward M. "Motion Pictures: Success Through Self-Regulation," *Reviews of Reviews* 85 (Mar. 1932), 32–5, 60–3.
Berchtold, William. "The Hollywood Purge," *North American Review* 238 (Dec. 1934), 503–12.
Black, Gregory D. "Hollywood Censored: The Production Code Administration and the Hollywood Film Industry 1930–1940," *Film History* 3 (1989), 167–89.
"Movies, Politics, and Censorship: The Production Code Administration and Political Censorship of Film Content," *Journal of Policy History* 3 (1991), 95–129.
Boyle, Hugh C. "The Legion of Decency: A Permanent Campaign," *Ecclesiastical Review* 90 (1934), 367–70.
Burnham, John C. "The Progressive Era Revolution in American Attitudes Toward Sex," *Journal of American History* 59 (1973), 885–908.
Campbell, Russell. "*I Am a Fugitive from a Chain Gang,*" *Velvet Light Trap* 1 (1971), 17–20.
Cantwell, John J., D.D. "Priests and the Motion Picture Industry," *Ecclesiastical Review* 90 (Feb. 1934), 136–46.
Collier, John. "Censorship and the National Board," *Survey* 34 (Oct. 2, 1915), 9, 73.
"The Learned Judges and the Films," *Survey* 34 (Sept. 4, 1915), 513–15.
Corey, Herbert. "How Hays Made the Sun Shine," *Nation's Business* 17 (Oct. 1929), 45–6, 174–6.

Corliss, Richard. "The Legion of Decency," *Film Comment* 4 (Summer 1969), 24–61.

Couvarnes, Francis G. "Hollywood, Censorship, and American Culture," *American Quarterly* 44 (Dec. 1992), 509–53.

"Hollywood, Main Street, and the Church: Trying to Censor Movies Before the Production Code," *American Quarterly* 44 (Dec. 1992), 584–682.

Curry, Romona. "Mae West as Censored Commodity: The Case of *Klondike Annie*," *Cinema Journal* 31 (1991), 57–84.

Degenfelder, E. Pauline. "The Four Faces of Temple Drake: Faulkner's *Sanctuary*, *Requiem for a Nun*, and the Two Film Adaptations," *American Quarterly* 28 (Winter 1976), 544–60.

Donnelly, Gerald B., S.J. "Catholic Standards for Motion Pictures," *America* 51 (Aug. 18, 1934), 443–5.

Doran, Daniel E. "Mr. Breen Confronts the Dragons," *Sign* 21 (Jan. 1942), 327–30.

Eastman, Fred. "The Menace of the Movies," *Christian Century* 47 (Jan. 15, 1930), 75–8.

Ferguson, Otis. "The Legion Rides Again," *New Republic* 105 (Dec. 22, 1941), 861.

Fisher, Robert. "Film Censorship and Progressive Reform: The National Board of Censorship of Motion Pictures, 1909–1922," *Journal of Popular Film* 4 (1975), 143–56.

Forsythe, Robert. "Who Speaks for Us?," *New Theatre* 56 (Aug. 3, 1936), 6–9.

Furnas, J. C. "Moral War in Hollywood," *Fortnightly* 143 (Jan.–June 1935), 75.

Garesché, Edward. "The Parish Priest and Moving-Pictures," *Ecclesiastical Review* 83 (May 1927), 465–78.

Gilman, Catheryne Cooke. "Government Regulations for the Movies," *Christian Century* 48 (Aug. 26, 1931), 1066–8.

Gomery, Douglas. "Hollywood, the National Recovery Administration, and the Question of Monopoly Power," *Journal of the University Film Association* 31 (Spring 1979), 47–52.

Haralovich, Mary Beth. "Mandates of Good Taste: The Self-Regulation of Film Advertising in the Thirties," *Wide Angle* 6 (1984), 50–7.

Higgins, Timothy. "No-Man in Yes-Land," *Catholic Digest* 4 (May 1944), 92–6.

Israel, Edward L. "Morals and the Movies," *Forum* 92 (Oct. 1934), 200–3.

Jowett, Garth. "A Capacity for Evil: The 1915 Supreme Court Mutual Decision," *Historical Journal of Film, Radio and Television* 9 (1989), 59–78.

"Moral Responsibility and Commercial Entertainment: Social Control in the United States Film Industry 1907–1968," *Historical Journal of Film, Radio and Television* 10 (1990), 3–31.

Kelly, Gerald, S.J., and John Ford, S.J. "The Legion of Decency," *Theological Studies* 18 (1957), 387–433.

Langley, Tom. "Will Hays: Puppet Dictator," *New Theatre* 55 (Feb. 2, 1935), 11–12.

Leff, Leonard J. "The Breening of America," *Pacific Modern Language Association* 106 (May 1991), 432–45.

Levenson, Joseph. "Censorship of the Movies," *Forum* 69 (April 1923), 1404–14.

McConell, Robert L. "The Genesis and Ideology of *Gabriel Over the White House*," *Cinema Journal* 5 (Spring 1976), 7–26.

McNicholas, John T. "The Episcopal Committee and the Problem of Evil Motion Pictures," *Ecclesiastical Review* 90 (1934), 113–19.

"Pastorals and Statements by Members of the American Hierarchy on the Legion of Decency," *Catholic Mind* 32 (Sept. 8, 1934), 321–7.

Maltby, Richard. "'To Prevent the Prevalent Type of Book': Censorship and Adaptation in Hollywood 1924–1934," *American Quarterly* 44 (Dec. 1992), 554–616.

Miller, John M. "Frankly my dear I just – don't – care: Val Lewton and Censorship at Selznick International Pictures," *Library Chronicle of the University of Texas at Austin* 36 (1986), 10–31.

Noll, John F. "Can Catholics Really Reform the Movies?" *Ecclesiastical Review* 90 (1934), 366–72.

Peet, Creighton. "Our Lady Censors," *Outlook and Independent* 153 (Dec. 25, 1929), 645–7.

Phillips, Charles. "The Movies and Catholic Taste," *Ave Maria* 35 (Mar. 5, 1932), 303–7.

Phillips, Gene. "Faulkner and the Film: The Two Versions of *Sanctuary*," *Literature/Film Quarterly* 1 (1973), 263–73.

Raeburn, John. "History and Fate in *I Am a Fugitive from a Chain Gang*," *South Atlantic Quarterly* 85 (Autumn 1986), 329–38.

Redman, Ben Ray. "Pictures and Censorship," *Saturday Review of Literature* 19 (Dec. 31, 1938), 3–4, 13–14.

Rosenbloom, Nancy J. "Between Reform and Regulation: The Struggle over Film Censorship in Progressive America, 1909–1922," *Film History* 1 (1987), 307–25.

Seldes, Gilbert. "The Movies in Peril," *Scribner's* 97 (Feb. 1935), 81–6.

Shaw, Albert. "Will Hays: A Ten Year Record," *Review of Reviews* 85 (Mar. 1932), 30–1.

Stallbaumer, Virgil. "Making the Motion Picture a Factor for Good," *Homiletic and Pastoral Review* 37 (Feb. 1937), 467–75.

Taylor, Winchell. "Secret Movie Censors," *Nation* 147 (July 9, 1938), 38–40.

Trumbo, Dalton. "Frankenstein in Hollywood," *Forum* 87 (Mar. 1932), 142–6.

"Vatican over Hollywood," *Nation* 143 (July 11, 1936), 33.

Weber, Francis J. "John J. Cantwell and the Legion of Decency," *American Ecclesiastical Review* 151 (Oct. 1964), 237–47.

Whelan, Russell. "The Legion of Decency," *American Mercury* 60 (June 1945), 655–63.

Yeaman, Elizabeth. "The Catholic Movie Censorship," *New Republic* 96 (Oct. 5, 1938), 233–5.

Dissertations

Bernstein, Matthew H. "Defiant Cooperation: Walter Wanger and Independent Production in Hollywood 1934–1949," Ph.D. dissertation, Communication Arts, University of Wisconsin–Madison, 1987.

Linden, Kathryn Bertha. "The Film Censorship Struggle in the United States from 1926 to 1957, and the Social Values Involved," Ph.D. dissertation, School of Education, New York University, 1972.

Litzky, Leo. "Censorship of Motion Pictures in the United States: A History of Motion Picture Censorship and an Analysis of Its Most Important Aspects," Ph.D. dissertation, School of Education, New York University, 1947.

McLaughlin, Mary L. "A Study of the National Catholic Office for Motion Pictures," Ph.D. dissertation, Communication Arts, University of Wisconsin–Madison, 1974.

Martin, Robert Francis, III. "Celluloid Morality: Will Hays' Rhetoric in Defense of the Movies 1922–1930," Ph.D. dissertation, Speech, Indiana University, 1974.

Phelen, John Martin, S.J. "The National Catholic Office for Motion Pictures: An Investigation of the Policy and Practice of Film Classifications," Ph.D. dissertation, Journalism, New York University, 1968.

Sargent, John A. "Self-Regulation: The Motion Picture Production Code 1930–1961," Ph.D. dissertation, Speech/Theater, University of Michigan, 1963.

FILMOGRAPHY

Affairs of Cellini, dir. Gregory La Cava (United Artists, 1934)

Alibi, The, dir. Roland West (United Artists, 1929)

All Quiet on the Western Front, dir. Lewis Milestone, prod. Carl Laemmle, Jr. (Universal, 1930)

Ann Vickers, dir. John Cromwell (RKO, 1933)

Anna Karenina, dir. J. Gordon Edwards (Fox, 1915)

Anna Karenina, dir. Clarence Brown, prod. David O. Selznick (MGM, 1935)

Baby Face, dir. Alfred E. Green (Warner Bros., 1933)

Bachelor Apartments, dir. Lowell Sherman (RKO, 1931)

Back Street, dir. Robert Stevenson (Universal, 1941)

Barbary Coast, dir. Howard Hawks (Goldwyn, 1935)

Belle of the Nineties (orig. *It Ain't No Sin*), dir. Leo McCarey (Paramount, 1934)

Big House, The, dir. George Hill (MGM, 1930)

Bill of Divorcement, A, dir. George Cukor, prod. David O. Selznick (RKO, 1932)

Billy the Kid, dir. King Vidor (MGM, 1930)

Birth of a Nation, dir. D. W. Griffith, prod. D. W. Griffith & Harry E. Aitken (Epoch, 1915)

Black Fury, dir. Michael Curtiz (Warner Bros., 1935)

Black Legion, dir. Archie Mayo (Warner Bros., 1936)

Blind Husbands, dir. Erich von Stroheim (Universal, 1919)

Blockade, dir. William Dieterle, prod. Walter Wanger (United Artists, 1938)

Blonde Venus, dir. Josef von Sternberg (Paramount, 1932)

Blondie Johnson, dir. Ray Enright (Warner Bros., 1933)

Blood and Sand, dir. Fred Niblo (Paramount, 1922)

Blood Money, dir. Rowland Brown (20th Century, 1930)

Blue Angel, The (*Der blaue Engel*), dir. Josef von Sternberg (UFA, Germany, 1930)

Bombshell (a/k/a *Blonde Bombshell*), dir. Victor Fleming (MGM, 1933)

Born to Be Bad, dir. Lowell Sherman (20th Century, 1934)

Born to Love, dir. Paul Stein (RKO–Pathé, 1931)

Bottoms Up, dir. David Butler (Fox, 1934)

Bulldog Drummond Strikes Back, dir. Roy Del Ruth (United Artists/20th Century, 1934)

Call Her Savage, dir. John Francis Dillon (Paramount, 1932)

Camille, dir. Fred Niblo (MGM, 1927) (Norma Talmadge version)

Capital versus Labor, dir. Van Dyke Brooks (Vitagraph, 1910)

Catherine the Great, dir. Paul Czinner, prod. Alexander Korda (LMP/United Artists, Great Britain, 1934)

Citizen Kane, dir. Orson Welles (RKO, 1941)

City Streets, dir. Rouben Mamoulian (Paramount, 1931)

Cocaine Traffic, The (a/k/a *The Drug Terror* or *The Underworld Exposed*), uncredited dir. (Lubin, 1914)

Cockeyed Cavaliers, dir. Mark Sandrich (RKO, 1934)

Confessions of a Nazi Spy, dir. Anatole Litvak (Warner Bros., 1939)

Criminal Code, The, dir. Howard Hawks (Columbia, 1931)

Dancing Lady, dir. Robert Z. Leonard (MGM, 1933)

Dawn Patrol, The, dir. Howard Hawks (Warner Bros., 1930)

Dead End, dir. William Wyler (Goldwyn, 1937)

Design for Living, dir. Ernst Lubitsch (Paramount, 1933)

Desire, dir. Frank Borzage, prod. Ernst Lubitsch (Paramount, 1936)

Devil Is a Woman, The, dir. Josef von Sternberg (Paramount, 1935)

Dishonored, dir. Josef von Sternberg (Paramount, 1931)

Dodsworth, dir. William Wyler (Goldwyn, 1936)

Don't Change Your Husband, dir. Cecil B. DeMille (Famous Players–Lasky, 1919)

Doorway to Hell, dir. Archie Mayo (Warner Bros., 1930)

Dr. Jekyll and Mr. Hyde, dir. Rouben Mamoulian (Paramount, 1932)

Dr. Monica, dir. William Keighley (Warner Bros., 1934)

Dracula, dir. Tod Browning (Universal, 1931)

Drug Traffic, The, dir. Stanley Walpole (Eclair, 1914)

Duck Soup, dir. Leo McCarey (Paramount, 1933)

Ecstasy (Extase), dir. Gustav Machaty (Electra/Jewel, Czechoslovakia, 1932)

Every Day's a Holiday, dir. Edward Sutherland (Paramount, 1937)

Faithless, dir. Harry Beaumont (MGM, 1932)

Farewell to Arms, A, dir. Frank Borzage (Paramount, 1932)

Finger Points, The, dir. John Francis Dillon (First National, 1931)

Finishing School, dir. George Nicholls, Jr. (RKO, 1934)

Firebird, The, dir. William Dieterle (Warner Bros., 1934)

Foolish Wives, dir. Erich von Stroheim (Universal, 1921)

Forbidden Paradise, dir. Ernst Lubitsch (Paramount, 1924)

Four Horsemen of the Apocalypse, The, dir. Rex Ingram (Metro, 1921)

Frankenstein, dir. James Whale (Universal, 1931)

Front Page, The, dir. Lewis Milestone (Howard Hughes, 1931)

Fury, dir. Fritz Lang (MGM, 1936)

Gabriel Over the White House, dir. Gregory La Cava, prod. Walter Wanger (Cosmopolitan/MGM, 1933)

Garden of Allah, The, dir. Richard Boleslawski (Selznick International Pictures/United Artists, 1936)

George White's Scandals, dir. George White, Thornton Freeman, and Harry Lachman (Fox, 1934)

Girl from Missouri, dir. Jack Conway (MGM, 1934)

Glamour, dir. William Wyler (Universal, 1934)

Go West, Young Man, dir. Henry Hathaway (Paramount, 1936)

Gone with the Wind, dir. Victor Fleming [George Cukor et al., uncredited], prod. David O. Selznick (MGM, 1939)

Governor's Boss, The, dir. Charles E. Davenport (Governor's Boss Photoplay, 1915)

Grapes of Wrath, The, dir. John Ford (USA, 1940)

Hat, Coat and Glove, dir. Worthington Miner (RKO, 1934)

Hell's Highway, dir. Rowland Brown, prod. David O. Selznick (RKO, 1932)

I Am a Fugitive from a Chain Gang, dir. Mervyn Le Roy, prod. Hal B. Wallis (Warner Bros., 1932)

Idiot's Delight, dir. Clarence Brown (MGM, 1939)

I'm No Angel, dir. Wesley Ruggles (Paramount, 1933)

Informer, The, dir. John Ford (RKO, 1935)

Iron Man, dir. Tod Browning (Universal, 1931)

It Can't Happen Here (MGM, unproduced)

James Boys in Missouri, The, dir. unknown (Essanay, 1908)

Jazz Singer, The, dir. Alan Crosland (Warner Bros., 1927)

Juarez, dir. William Dieterle (Warner Bros., 1939)

King Kong, dir. Merian C. Cooper and Ernest B. Schoedsack (RKO, 1933)

King of Kings, The, dir. Cecil B. DeMille (Pathé, 1927)

Kiss Me Again, dir. Ernst Lubitsch (Warner Bros., 1925)

Klondike Annie, dir. Raoul Walsh (Paramount, 1936)

Ladies of the Big House, dir. Marion Gering (Paramount, 1931)

Last Mile, The, dir. Sam Bischoff (World Wide, 1932)

Last Parade, The, dir. Erle C. Kenton (Columbia, 1931)

Laughing Boy, dir. W. S. Van Dyke (MGM, 1934)

Life of Emile Zola, The, dir. William Dieterle (Warner Bros., 1937)

Life of Vergie Winters, The, dir. Alfred Santell (RKO, 1934)

Limehouse Blues, dir. Alexander Hall (Paramount, 1934)

Little American, The, dir. Cecil B. DeMille (Mary Pickford Film/Artcraft, 1917)

Little Caesar, dir. Mervyn Le Roy (Warner Bros., 1930)

Love, dir. Edmund Goulding (MGM, 1927); based on Tolstoy's *Anna Karenina*

Love Affair, dir. Thornton Freeland (Columbia, 1932)

M (M, Mörder unter Uns), dir. Fritz Lang (Nero Films, Germany, 1931)

Macbeth, dir. J. Stewart Blackton (Vitagraph, 1908)

Madame du Barry, dir. William Dieterle (Warner Bros., 1934)

Madame Satan, dir. Cecil B. DeMille (MGM, 1930)

Male and Female, dir. Cecil B. DeMille (Famous Players–Lasky, 1919); based on Barrie's *The Admirable Crichton*

Manhattan Melodrama, dir. W. S. Van Dyke (MGM, 1934)

Manslaughter, dir. Cecil B. DeMille (Famous Players–Lasky, 1922)

Mark of Zorro, The, dir. Fred Niblo (Fairbanks/United Artists, 1920)

Marriage Circle, The, dir. Ernst Lubitsch (Warner Bros., 1924)

Men Call It Love, dir. Edgar Selwyn (MGM, 1931)

Men of the Night, dir. Lambert Hillyer (Columbia, 1934)

Merry Widow, The (a/k/a *The Lady Dances*), dir. Ernst Lubitsch (MGM, 1934)

Merry Wives of Reno, dir. H. Bruce Humberstone (Warner Bros., 1934)

Metropolis, dir. Fritz Lang (UFA, Germany, 1926)

Modern Times, dir. Charles Chaplin (Chaplin/United Artists, 1936)

Molly Maguires, The, or Labor Wars in the Coal Mines, dir. unknown (Kalem, 1908)

Monsieur Beaucaire, dir. Sidney Olcott (Paramount, 1924)

Morocco, dir. Josef von Sternberg (Paramount, 1930)

Mr. Cohen Takes a Walk, dir. William Beaudine (Warner Bros., 1935)

Murder at the Vanities, dir. Mitchell Leisen (Paramount, 1934)

Murderer Dmitri Karamazov, The (a/k/a *Karamazov; Der morder Dmitri Karamasoff*), dir. Fyodor Ozep (Terra/Tobis, Germany, 1931)

My Four Years in Germany, dir. William Nigh (Warner Bros., 1918)

Mysterious Dr. Fu Manchu, The, dir. Rowland V. Lee (Paramount, 1929)

Nana (a/k/a *Lady of the Boulevards*), dir. Dorothy Arzner (Goldwyn, 1934)

Night After Night, dir. Archie Mayo (Paramount, 1932)

Night Riders, dir. Alexander Butler (Samuelson Film, 1920[?])

No Man of Her Own, dir. Wesley Ruggles (Paramount, 1932)

Of Human Bondage, dir. John Cromwell (RKO, 1934)

Of Mice and Men, dir. Lewis Milestone (United Artists, 1939)

Old Wives for New, dir. Cecil B. DeMille (Famous Players–Lasky, 1918)

One Third of a Nation, dir. Dudley Murphy (Paramount, 1939)

Outlaw, The, dir. Howard Hughes (RKO, 1943)

Painted Veil, The, dir. Richard Boleslawski (finished by W. S. Van Dyke) (MGM, 1934)

Phantom of the Opera, dir. Rupert Julian (Universal, 1925)

Plow That Broke the Plains, The, dir. Pare Lorentz (U.S. Resettlement Agency, 1936)

Possessed, dir. Clarence Brown (MGM, 1931); based on Selwyn's *The Mirage*

President Vanishes, The, dir. William A. Wellman, prod. Walter Wanger (Paramount, 1934)

Private Life of Henry VIII, The, dir. & prod. Alexander Korda (London Films, Great Britain, 1933)

Private Lives, dir. Sidney Franklin (MGM, 1931)

Public Enemy, The, dir. William A. Wellman, prod. Darryl Zanuck (Warner Bros., 1931)

Queen Christina, dir. Rouben Mamoulian (MGM, 1934)

Queen of Sheba, dir. J. Gordon Edward (Fox, 1921)

Quick Millions, dir. Rowland Brown (Fox, 1931)

Red Dust, dir. Victor Fleming (MGM, 1932)

Red Kimono, The, dir. Walter Lang (Vital, 1926)

Reform Candidate, The, dir. Frank Lloyd (Pallas Pictures, 1915)

Riptide, dir. Edmund Goulding (MGM, 1934)

River, The, dir. Pare Lorentz (U.S. Farm Security Administration, 1937)

Robin Hood, dir. Allan Dwan (Fairbanks/United Artists, 1922)

Safe in Hell, dir. William A. Wellman (Warner Bros., 1931)

Scarface: Shame of the Nation, dir. Howard Hawks, prod. Howard Hughes (United Artists, 1932)

Secret Six, The, dir. George Hill (MGM, 1931)

Shanghai Express, dir. Josef von Sternberg (Paramount, 1932)

She Done Him Wrong, dir. Lowell Sherman (Paramount, 1933); based on Mae West's play *Diamond Lil*

Sheik, The, dir. George Melford (Famous Players–Lasky, 1922)

Shopworn, dir. Nick Grinde (Columbia, 1931)

Sign of the Cross, The, dir. Cecil B. DeMille (Paramount, 1932; rereleased with additional footage, 1944)

Sin of Madelon Claudet, The, dir. Edgar Selwyn (MGM, 1931)

Sinner's Holiday, dir. John G. Adolfi (Warner Bros., 1930)

Son of the Sheik, dir. George Fitzmaurice (Paramount, 1926)

Song of Songs, dir. Rouben Mamoulian (Paramount, 1933)

Star Witness, dir. William A. Wellman (Warner Bros., 1931)

Story of Temple Drake, The, dir. Stephen Roberts (Paramount, 1933); based on Faulkner's *Sanctuary*

Suffragettes' Revenge, dir. unknown (Gaumont, 1913)

Tarzan, the Ape Man, dir. W. S. Van Dyke (MGM, 1932)

Tarzan and His Mate, dir. Cedric Gibbons and Jack Conway (MGM, 1934)

Ten Commandments, The, dir. Cecil B. DeMille (Paramount/Famous Players–Lasky, 1923)

Testament of Dr. Mabuse, The (Das Testament des Dr. Mabuse), dir. Fritz Lang (Nero Films, Germany, 1933)

These Three, dir. William Wyler (Goldwyn, 1936); based on Hellmann's *The Children's Hour*

They Won't Forget, dir. Mervyn Le Roy (Warner Bros., 1937); based on Ward Greene's *Death in the Deep South*

Thief of Baghdad, The, dir. Raoul Walsh (Fairbanks/United Artists, 1924)

Thin Man, The, dir. W. S. Van Dyke (MGM, 1934)

This Is the Army, dir. Michael Curtiz, prod. Jack L. Warner & Hal B. Wallis (Warner Bros., 1943)

Three Girls Lost, dir. Sidney Lanfield (Fox, 1931)

Tobacco Road, dir. John Ford (20th C.–Fox, 1941)

Trial of Mary Dugan, The, dir. Bayard Veiller (MGM, 1929)

Trumpet Blows, The, dir. Stephen Roberts (Paramount, 1934)

Two-Faced Woman, dir. George Cukor (MGM, 1941)

Underworld (a/k/a *Paying the Penalty*), dir. Joseph von Sternberg (Paramount, 1927)

Unfaithful, dir. John Cromwell (Paramount, 1931)

Union Depot, dir. Alfred E. Green (Warner Bros., 1932)

Very Idea, The, dir. William LeBaron (RKO, 1929)

Vice Squad, The, dir. John Cromwell (Paramount, 1931)

Votes for Women, dir. Hal Reid (Reliance, 1912)

Walking Dead, The, dir. Michael Curtiz (Warner Bros., 1936)

We Live Again, dir. Rouben Mamoulian (Goldwyn, 1934); based on Tolstoy's *Resurrection*

Why Change Your Wife?, dir. Cecil B. DeMille (Famous Players–Lasky, 1920)

Wife Versus Secretary, dir. Clarence Brown (MGM, 1936)

INDEX

Numbers in italics indicate illustrations.

327